CW00572525

The Sochi Project

An Atlas of War and Tourism in the Caucasus

Rob Hornstra
Arnold van Bruggen

An Atlas of War and Tourism in the Caucasus

aperture

The 2014 Winter Olympics are being staged in a subtropical conflict zone.

The Sochi Project

A year after the Winter Olympics opened in February 2014, Russia has descended into a bloody conflict with Ukraine, experienced a ruble crisis, and achieved near-pariah status in the diplomatic world. It was not the scenario that President Vladimir Putin and the International Olympic Committee (IOC) envisaged when Sochi was awarded the Games in 2007. Between 2009 and 2013, photographer Rob Hornstra and I, writer Arnold van Bruggen, traveled extensively throughout the region. *The Sochi Project: An Atlas of War and Tourism in the Caucasus* is our account of the construction of the Games and the events that played out around it.

It is incredible how long ago the Olympic episode already seems. Readers will, however, note one constant: the Russia that built the most expensive Olympics ever, from scratch, in a subtropical resort surrounded by conflict zones, is the Russia that believes in fairy tales; fairy tales without a happy ending for the countless victims of the megalomania and political cynicism that have gripped the country for years. "This is the new face of Russia, our Russia," exulted Dmitry Chernyshenko, head of the Sochi organizing committee, during the closing ceremony. He was right in every respect.

In January 2007, Rob and I find ourselves on the beach of the small, unknown country of Abkhazia. Miami Beach, as the locals call this part of town. Behind us is the capital, Sukhum, once a beautiful city bustling with Soviet tourists. In 2007 Sukhum's palm trees have lost their luster and the buildings are in ruins. For fifteen years the country has been almost completely isolated. The war between this rebellious province and the Georgian motherland has left its mark. At the time, no country in the world recognized Abkhazia. Only Russia has opened its border for trade and hands out Russian passports to anyone who requests one. We drive along crumbling roads and past bombed-out houses. We see the remnants of beautiful hotels and sanatoria. But we are struck most by the lack of people. More than half the population has fled, leaving behind a deserted paradise.

The next day we drink vodka from Russian bullet cartridges with Danish and English UN soldiers tasked with monitoring the ceasefire between Abkhazia and Georgia. In Land Cruisers with large antennas they drive across the demarcation line, an old, tumbledown bridge over the Inguri River. There is a pervasive air of desolation and hopelessness.

Two months later we see Putin on television speaking in English about Sochi, his dream candidate for the 2014 Winter Olympics. "Sochi is a unique place. On the seashore you can enjoy a fine spring day, but up in the mountains it's winter," he says of the subtropical Russian city. "Sochi is going to become a new world-class resort for the new Russia and the whole world. And we shall be happy, happy to see you in Russia and in Sochi as our guests. The Olympic family is going to feel at home in Sochi."

Sochi is located near the border of Abkhazia. This surprising news surfaces at the same moment that we are publishing stories about that broken, discordant little country. What a controversial choice: the Winter Olympics in a subtropical coastal city. Ice skating under the palm trees, between the tea plantations and summer hotels, at a seaside resort.

Two years after Sochi is awarded the Games, we visit the city for the first time. We have launched the Sochi Project, in which we have translated our amazement at Sochi winning the Olympic bid into a five-year slow journalism project. The decision to hold the Winter Games in a subtropical resort town is daring to say the least, but to do so on the border of a conflict zone is even bolder. Moreover, on the other side of the mountains is the North Caucasus, where a war between separatist groups and pro-Russian security forces has been raging for years. In fact, reviewing the history of this region, one quickly recognizes that the roots of the current conflicts can be traced back generations to power struggles between the Persian, Russian, and Ottoman empires.

If the Games are successful, one anticipated byproduct is that they would help reclaim Russia's place on the world stage and make the so-called "humiliation of the 1990s," when the Soviet Union collapsed and Russia lost its status as a global power, a thing of the past. But the story of modern, prosperous Russia is set against a backdrop of contrasts: poverty, refugees, violence, and human rights violations. There are countless stories to be told. Five years is barely enough to do justice to the enormous complexity and texture of this region.

Sochi in March 2009 is a world away from Sochi 2014. The airport is like a bus stop, the kind more common in the hinterland of the former Soviet Union than in an international travel destination. One narrow road clings to the endless coast heading northwest. Another winds up into the mountains and is so treacherous that it claims countless victims every year. Sochi is a coastal city without a commercial port. All goods are transported along this single, busy coastal road, which is not designed to handle the traffic. The result is daily gridlock and endless traffic jams. For the Games, all the infrastructure and facilities have to be built from scratch.

When we first visit in 2009, twelve and a half miles (twenty kilometers) south of downtown Sochi, blue fences are being erected around the perimeter of an old state farm. The inhabitants of the surrounding villages have been told that within a few years, stadiums, hotels, media centers, and an Olympic village will replace their houses, gardens, and estates. All the new facilities will be within walking distance of one another in the Imeretinskaya lowlands on the coast, because, as the Olympic officials make clear, these will be the most compact and efficient Games ever.

In old Sochi meanwhile, some inhabitants are becoming nervous. According to the Olympic bid book, the city's major monuments will be spruced up and the old sanatoria—Lenin's palaces for the proletariat—will be transformed into modern four- and five-star hotels. We decide to put the city's famed offerings to the test and book a two-week stay at Metallurg, the sanatorium for metal workers. While we revel in the clay massages, herbal tea, and daily senior-citizen discos, we meet a depressed manager who complains, "the Soviet mentality and rudeness that prevail scares people away." But, he promises, "if the staff can't adapt, they'll be fired. Before 2014, we'll have changed this town beyond recognition."

We return to Sochi year after year, working our way through the incredible mountain of meaty, grilled *shashlik*, through the pumping and pervasive Russian chanson music, and through the stench of sweat and sun cream that characterizes the city. Tourists are referred to locally as *bzdykhs*: the overweight bodies perspiring beer and spirits, the bare torsos in sandals, the noisy eaters surrounded by drunken bluster and tacky music. Once established as a grand spa town, Sochi has declined considerably. The Games are no match for the hordes of returning Russian tourists who besiege the cheap sanatoria, apartments, and hotels every summer: they are happy the way things are.

As time marches on, however, we begin to catch a glimpse of Putin's dream for Sochi around the various Olympic building projects. Every time we visit we book a tour of the Olympic facilities and see the stadiums, roads, airport, tunnels, new train tracks, ski slopes, and villages appearing out of nothing. Members of the organizing committee's communications staff look like they come from another planet. Fresh and modern, they represent millennial Muscovite Russia: dressed in designer clothes and glued to their iPhones, they vacation abroad, speak decent English, and enthusiastically promote the Russian project of the century. It is a world away from the Sochi of yore, where English and an international outlook have never been necessary: Russian tourists have been filling Sochi to capacity for more than a century. This we find to be in striking contrast to the other side of the mountains. In Arabic the Caucasus Mountains are called *Jabal Al-Alsun*, the mountains of languages. The area covered by the Sochi Project is home to more than thirty nationalities with almost as many languages.

The mountains are spectacular. From the perspective of natural beauty, it is no hardship to work in the Caucasus. Our few trips into the mountains take us to thundering waterfalls, clear springs, or picnic spots in stunning valleys. An invitation to someone's home invariably ends with a lavish meal of pan-Caucasian delicacies. If we make it that far, that is.

The first time we go into the mountains in the North Caucasus, we are arrested by Chechen soldiers and interrogated in a bunker belonging to the FSB (Russia's Security Service). We had come to behold the Chechen Switzerland, a promise made by the local mayor several years earlier. He has failed. The FSB officer tells us that he still hauls terrorists—extremist separatists from the Caucasian Emirate with ambitions for an independent Islamic North Caucasus—from the woods on a weekly basis. We are released with a warning, but when two prototypical insurgents (battered from their years outside "polite society"—lame or one-eyed, with long, unkempt beards, and bearing Kalashnikovs under their arms) sit down next to us in the local café, we decide the mountains can wait another day.

The war against the separatists is being fought up in the mountains, but the cause of the violence can be found on the plains below them. The North Caucasus is the poorest region in the Russian Federation. In the struggle against the various independence groups that have emerged since the fall of the Soviet Union, an incredible amount of damage has been inflicted here, in countless, often nameless conflicts and wars. Hundreds of thousands of refugees have fled the small area for neighboring republics, other regions of Russia, or abroad. The smoke of the last major conflict—the Second Chechen War between 1999 and 2006—may have cleared, but the Kremlin-appointed local regimes remain, riddled with corruption, bloated by billions of stability subsidies, and utterly powerless to tackle the crippling unemployment and poverty in their own backyards. The YouTube videos showing local rulers dancing at extravagant weddings and handing out dollar bills or gold bars are infamous.

The violence has not diminished in recent years. The major attacks in Moscow, including those on the subway in 2010 and at the airport in 2011, have attracted international attention. Far more often, however, terrorism is carried out in the Caucasus itself, on its own people—police stations, checkpoints, officials, and civilians. The government response is ruthless and frequently indiscriminate. Suspects regularly disappear behind bars without due process or are forced to confess under torture. Some disappear entirely, to be discovered later in shallow graves or never to be heard from again. Human rights activists, journalists, and lawyers are also frequent targets. Anna Politkovskaya and Natalya Estemirova are the best known but by no means the only victims.

In response to the government brutality and corruption, both violent separatism and orthodox Islamic Salafism are gaining in popularity. The violence is spiraling out of control and is certainly not decreasing. And, it is said, but almost impossible to prove, local politicians, police, security forces, separatists, and insurgents are all involved in a messy mix-up of economic, political, and power struggles. "Islamists?" said several people who had seen the insurgents up close. "Don't make me laugh; they're mafia."

Working in the North Caucasus is not easy. There are countless laws, rules, and above all, bureaucrats and security forces that make a journalist's job all but impossible. However, the obstacles we faced only strengthened our resolve to tell our stories. Over the years we were detained regularly, questioned about peculiar violations, and then fined for something completely unrelated. It is frustrating, but the individual stories we recorded in the region put everything into perspective. The inhabitants often lead poor, uncertain lives. You do not have to be Islamist, or otherwise disagree with the pro-Russian governments, to disappear, either into a prison camp or an unmarked grave. An unshaved head, suspicious website, insinuation by a neighbor or dubious friends and relatives can be enough to put your life on the line. All this lay within four hundred miles of Olympic Sochi. You could drive from one side of the area to the other in a matter of hours. The region is like an active volcano, and every day is a waiting game to see where and when violence will erupt. It is little wonder then that Russia, in cooperation with foreign security forces, including those from the UK and the U.S. (particularly following the April 2013 bombing of the Boston Marathon and the realization that the suspects hailed from Dagestan, one of the many conflict regions nearby), earmarked an enormous sum of money to secure the Games.

Little more than a stone's throw from the stadiums on the coast, another conflict zone, Abkhazia, is even closer to Sochi. Stray off piste from the Olympic ski resort of Rosa Khutor and you will likely cross into this country, where the UN once decreed that Georgia had the right to exercise territorial integrity.

Since the so-called August War between Georgia and Russia in 2008, everything has changed. Russia began recognizing Abkhazia as an independent country. In Russia's wake, Venezuela, Nicaragua, Nauru, and Tuvalu also declared the rebellious province independent. The UN was expelled and Russian troops took over guarding the newly defined border between Abkhazia and Georgia. The border with the conflict zone moved one hundred twenty-five miles to the southeast and the hundreds of thousands of refugees in Georgia have lost all hope of returning home.

Russia's support filled Abkhazia with self-confidence. With the Games on its doorstep, the new country felt the promise of global fame and perhaps even diplomatic recognition. In any event, Abkhazia appeared to be nearing the end of its isolation as well as receiving salvation for its stagnant economy. The government focused on fixing up a number of roads and schools while private investors—often Russians—bought up dozens of restaurants and hotels. Several branches of IKEA, or more accurately, rip-offs of the Swedish giant that import furniture from the outlet in South Russia, opened on Sukhum's main thoroughfare. These were accompanied by Japanese and Chinese restaurants, an Australian hamburger chain, and an Oilily clothing store: the world had finally arrived in Abkhazia, it seemed.

The euphoria was short lived. On a visit in 2013, Abkhazia seemed to have sunk back into lethargy. The Games had done little for the country. The Japanese restaurant had closed. Pebbles from the Kodori River were being dredged for Olympic building projects in Sochi, but this was hardly the windfall anticipated. Like every other year, the mandarin orange harvest in the fall is the enterprise that generates the most money. That's it.

Meanwhile, we kept returning to Sochi. It is a city that, if you are not a fan of mass tourism, you should not visit too often or stay in too long. Compare it to an English seaside town: a few days of fish and chips are more than enough. But Sochi changed over the years. The profits from the huge contracts handed out for the Games slowly trickled into the city. Trendy coffee bars, restaurants with French chefs, and expensive hotels with Swiss managers appeared. We saw Sochi being transformed from a small, impoverished, faded spa town into a mini "Moscow-on-the-Sea." If you knew where to look, that is.

A final price tag of more than fifty billion dollars must have seemed worth it—after all, Russia has oil and gas to spare. Local entrepreneurs, as well as former prime minister and prominent opposition politician Boris Nemtsov (slain in February 2015), estimate that roughly half of that money disappeared into the pockets of the many contractors and sub-contractors. These may have been not only the most expensive but also the most corrupt Games ever.

Demonstrations against environmental damage, destruction of the coastal lowlands, and demolition of houses were largely restricted to a small group of amateurs and first-time activists. In 2009 there had been a glimmer of hope when Nemtsov announced his candidacy for mayor of Sochi. The foreign press flocked to the city and for a moment there seemed to be momentum. But democracy in Russia remains illusive, virtual. In the face of unscrupulous and hasty Olympic builders and the big bucks and power of the Kremlin, Nemtsov and the activists didn't have a chance. Local opposition to the Games was not as widespread as had been anticipated. Many residents complained about the inconvenience, but nonetheless hoped to benefit from higher tourist revenues during and after 2014.

In the Games' coastal and mountain clusters, the Olympic structures look like UFOs. In late 2012 and early 2013, these UFOs were being tested, surrounded by muddy building sites where construction still continued around the clock. The organizing committee and international sports federations were nervous: would it be ready in time? But the Games have always been ready on time. The question is at what price.

International, opaquely political decisions, such as the selection of Sochi as Olympic host, have far-reaching implications for a region. Sochi was turned upside down for an enormous sum of money. In the North Caucasus, the security and human rights situation worsened again as the Games approached. Security forces and Russia's local despots were given free rein to pacify the region by 2014. They were unsuccessful. Billions of dollars in relief funds were being pumped into the region to kick-start the economy and job market. But the money disappeared or was invested in ski resorts in areas so unstable that tourists stayed away.

In fact the IOC, and the many representatives of the various countries and sports federations within it, made a gross miscalculation when they selected Sochi in 2007. One cannot view the Games as a single, isolated event. It is impossible to ignore the lack of infrastructure in a country where inequality is rife, and to overlook the violence and human rights violations in the surrounding areas. The IOC claims to be attentive to the legacy of events like these. It will be interesting in the coming years to see which way the scales tip. At the beginning of 2015, environmental activist Evgeny Vitishko was still languishing in a Siberian penal colony for voicing ecological concerns about the construction of the Games. During 2014, several championships, competitions, and a Formula 1 race were organized in Sochi, but the global G8 summit due to take place there in June was cancelled. And now Sochi's position as host of the 2018 FIFA World Cup is looking increasingly uncertain. For a brief moment, Sochi was a deafening sporting and political triumph. After the first successful ski run and the first circuit of the new ice rink, critics were silenced and sports commentators were gushing in their enthusiasm. Putin feted several heads of state. Russia had its moment in the spotlight and Putin celebrated his fifteen-year reign in spectacular style. But after Putin's greatest fear was realized—a democratic revolution in a neighboring country that could spill across the border—he effectively negated any political gains he may have made. Russia, for now, seems all played out.

Rob and I planned to continue following the people we have portrayed and described in this and our other books. Olympics aside, this is a region that deserves slow, thoughtful description. That might have been a positive side effect of Sochi 2014: that the region—rich in history, culture, and natural beauty—gets the attention it deserves. But in fall 2013, around the same time that the first edition of this book was published, the Ministry of Foreign Affairs in Moscow made it clear that we were no longer welcome in Russia: for an undefined period and for undefined reasons. A Russian diplomat confirmed that our work in the North Caucasus and our numerous encounters with the security forces almost certainly played a role. We keep trying to go back, and hope that numerous other journalists and photographers are doing the same. There are still hundreds of stories to tell in the small, embattled Caucasus and in large, troubled, but endlessly fascinating Russia. Unfortunately, the denial of our visas is symptomatic of Russia's current state. Our hearts go out to all those who, in spite of everything, try to make the best of their situation.

—Arnold van Bruggen, February 2015, The Netherlands

Table of Contents

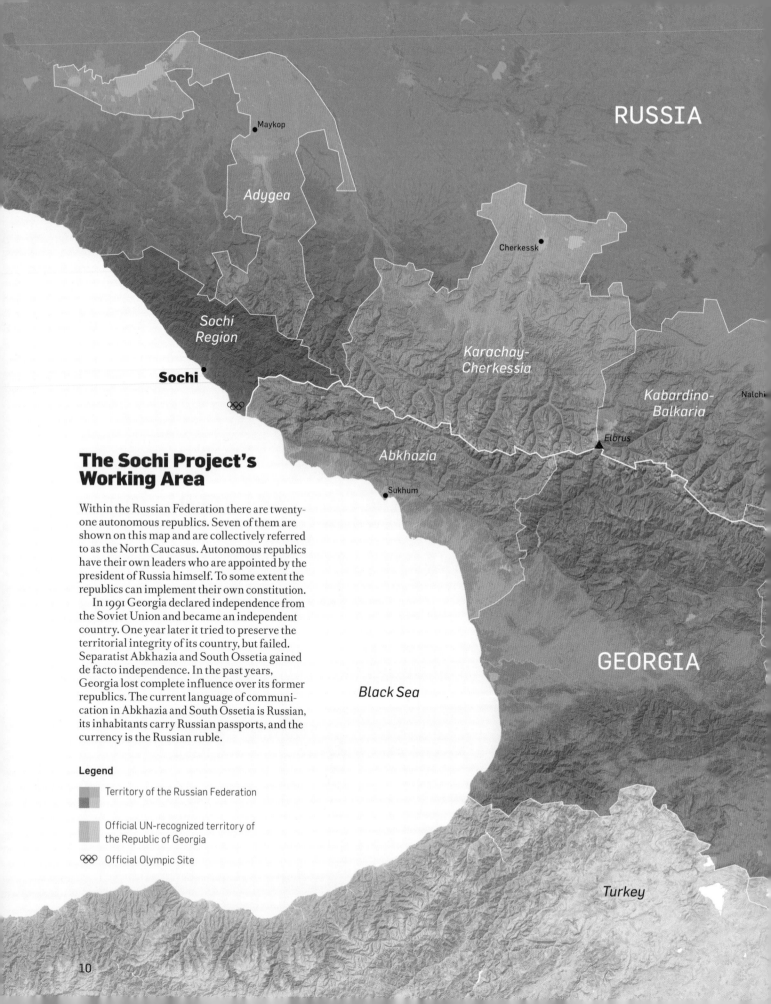

RUSSIA

Maykop

Adygea

Cherkessk

Sochi Region

Sochi

ⓞⓞⓞ

Karachay-Cherkessia

Kabardino-Balkaria

Nalchi

Elbrus

Abkhazia

Sukhum

The Sochi Project's Working Area

Within the Russian Federation there are twenty-one autonomous republics. Seven of them are shown on this map and are collectively referred to as the North Caucasus. Autonomous republics have their own leaders who are appointed by the president of Russia himself. To some extent the republics can implement their own constitution.

In 1991 Georgia declared independence from the Soviet Union and became an independent country. One year later it tried to preserve the territorial integrity of its country, but failed. Separatist Abkhazia and South Ossetia gained de facto independence. In the past years, Georgia lost complete influence over its former republics. The current language of communication in Abkhazia and South Ossetia is Russian, its inhabitants carry Russian passports, and the currency is the Russian ruble.

GEORGIA

Black Sea

Legend

▨ Territory of the Russian Federation

▨ Official UN-recognized territory of the Republic of Georgia

ⓞⓞⓞ Official Olympic Site

Turkey

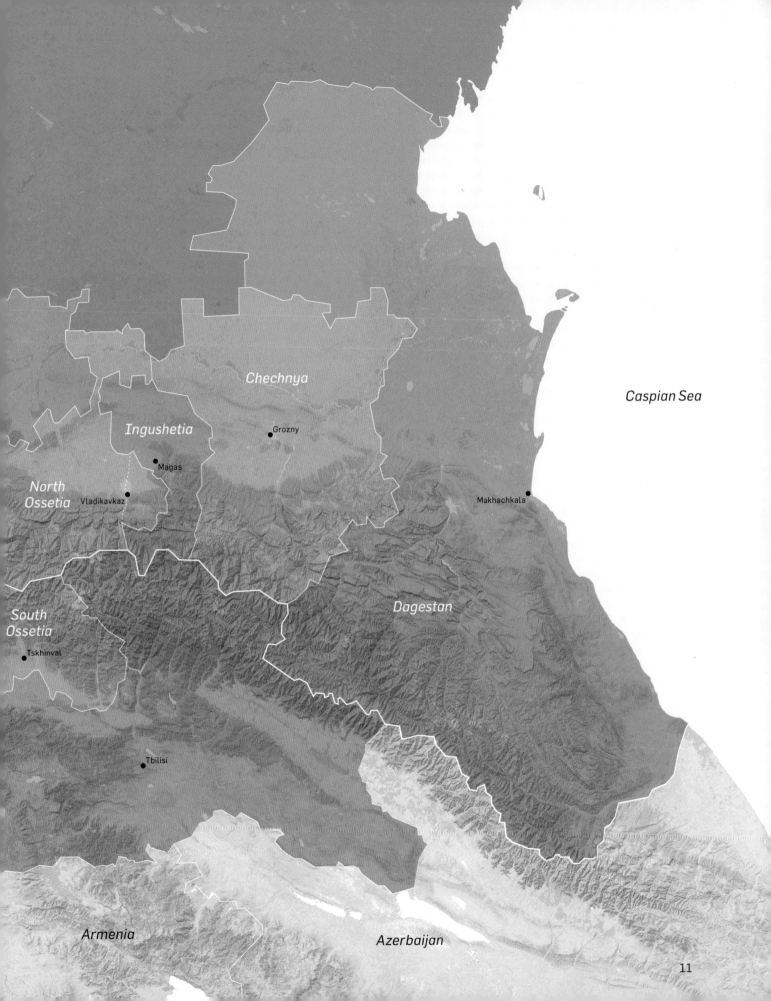

Chechnya

Ingushetia

Grozny

Magas

North
Ossetia

Vladikavkaz

Makhachkala

Caspian Sea

South
Ossetia

Dagestan

Tskhinval

Tbilisi

Armenia

Azerbaijan

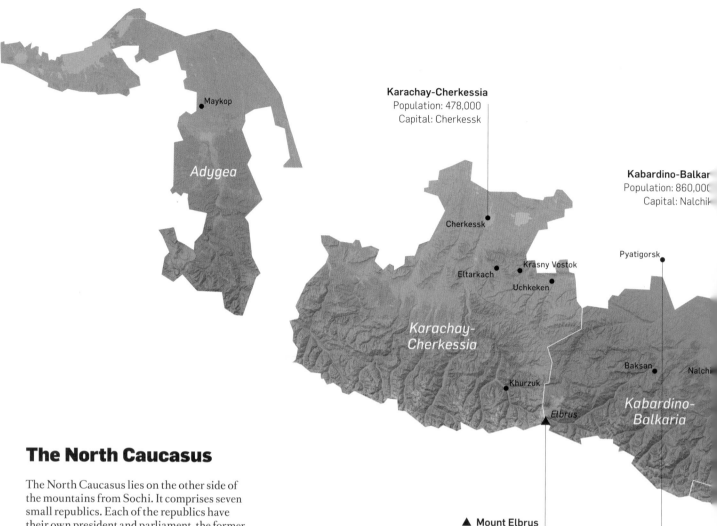

Karachay-Cherkessia
Population: 478,000
Capital: Cherkessk

Kabardino-Balkar
Population: 860,00(
Capital: Nalchik

Adygea

Maykop

Cherkessk

Pyatigorsk

Karachay-Cherkessia

Eltarkach

Krasny Vostok

Uchkeken

Baksan

Nalchi

Khurzuk

Elbrus

Kabardino-Balkaria

▲ **Mount Elbrus**
At 5,621 meters, Mount Elbrus
is Europe's highest peak.

The North Caucasus

The North Caucasus lies on the other side of
the mountains from Sochi. It comprises seven
small republics. Each of the republics have
their own president and parliament, the former
of which is appointed directly by the Russian
president. From east to west, the region is
barely 375 miles wide—you can drive from one
side of it to the other in half a day. It is home
to more than thirty peoples, each with their
own language and culture, including
Russians and Cossacks who conquered the
area in the nineteenth century. The North
Caucasus is Russia's poorest and most violent
region. Resistance to Soviet and Russian
domination has simmered here for hundreds
of years. Almost all of the terrorist attacks
carried out in Russia in recent decades
originated in the North Caucasus.

Pyatigorsk
Pyatigorsk, along with nearby
Yessentuki, Kislovodsk, and Mineralnye
Vody, is the Caucasian outpost in
Southern Russia. Famous for its spas,
the area also has a long military
tradition as a base for the North
Caucasus. It was here, too, that
writers such as Lermontov, Tolstoy, and
Pushkin developed their wild, fearless,
romanticized images of the Caucasus.

Legend

Republics of the North Caucasus,
part of the Russian Federation

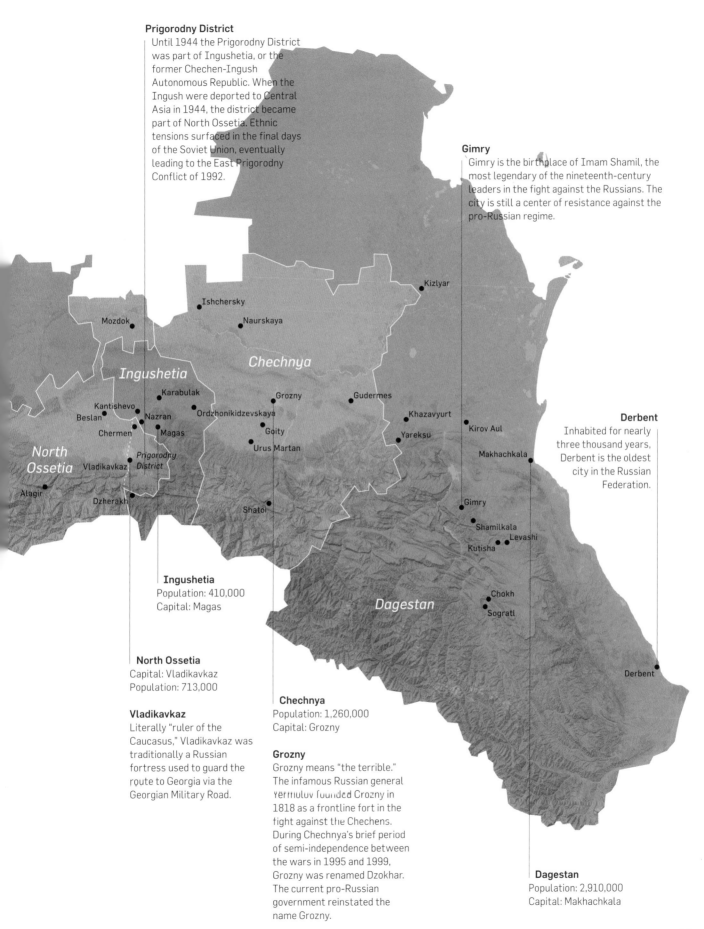

Prigorodny District

Until 1944 the Prigorodny District was part of Ingushetia, or the former Chechen-Ingush Autonomous Republic. When the Ingush were deported to Central Asia in 1944, the district became part of North Ossetia. Ethnic tensions surfaced in the final days of the Soviet Union, eventually leading to the East Prigorodny Conflict of 1992.

Gimry

Gimry is the birthplace of Imam Shamil, the most legendary of the nineteenth-century leaders in the fight against the Russians. The city is still a center of resistance against the pro-Russian regime.

Derbent

Inhabited for nearly three thousand years, Derbent is the oldest city in the Russian Federation.

Chechnya

Ingushetia

North Ossetia

Prigorodny District

Dagestan

Kizlyar

Ishchersky

Naurskaya

Mozdok

Karabulak

Kantishevo

Beslan

Nazran

Ordzhonikidzevskaya

Grozny

Gudermes

Khazavyurt

Yareksu

Kirov Aul

Chermen

Magas

Goity

Urus Martan

Makhachkala

Alagir

Vladikavkaz

Dzherakh

Shatoi

Gimry

Shamilkala

Levashi

Kutisha

Chokh

Sogratl

Derbent

Ingushetia
Population: 410,000
Capital: Magas

North Ossetia
Capital: Vladikavkaz
Population: 713,000

Vladikavkaz
Literally "ruler of the Caucasus," Vladikavkaz was traditionally a Russian fortress used to guard the route to Georgia via the Georgian Military Road.

Chechnya
Population: 1,260,000
Capital: Grozny

Grozny
Grozny means "the terrible." The infamous Russian general Yermolov founded Grozny in 1818 as a frontline fort in the fight against the Chechens. During Chechnya's brief period of semi-independence between the wars in 1995 and 1999, Grozny was renamed Dzokhar. The current pro-Russian government reinstated the name Grozny.

Dagestan
Population: 2,910,000
Capital: Makhachkala

Republic of Georgia, Including Abkhazia and South Ossetia

Georgia and Abkhazia lie in the south of the Caucasus. Abhkazia borders Sochi, while Georgia only shares borders with the republics in the North Caucasus. Historically, Abkhazia and South Ossetia were part of Georgia more often than not. Following the collapse of the Soviet Union and emerging radical Georgian nationalism around 1990, however, fighting broke out between the districts. Since 2008 Abkhazia and South Ossetia appear to have achieved definitive independence, although this status is only recognized by powerful neighbor Russia, as well as Nauru, Nicaragua, Tuvalu, and Venezuela.

Legend

State of Georgia

Former autonomous and now independent republics Abkhazia and South Ossetia

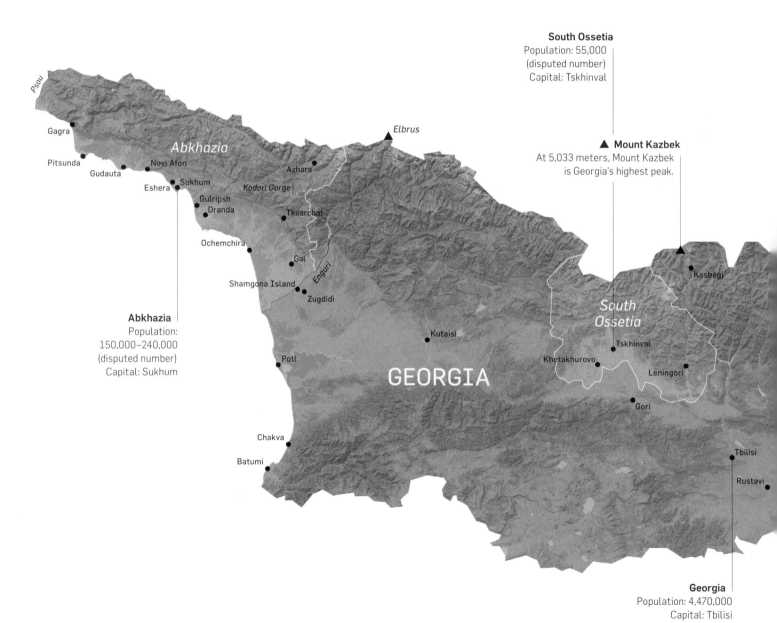

South Ossetia
Population: 55,000
(disputed number)
Capital: Tskhinval

▲ **Mount Kazbek**
At 5,033 meters, Mount Kazbek is Georgia's highest peak.

Abkhazia
Population:
150,000–240,000
(disputed number)
Capital: Sukhum

Psou

Gagra

Pitsunda

Gudauta

Novi Afon

Eshera

Sukhum

Gulripsh

Dranda

Ochemchira

Gal

Shamgona Island

Zugdidi

Abkhazia

Azhara

Kodori Gorge

Tkuarchat

Enguri

▲ Elbrus

Kutaisi

Potl

GEORGIA

Kasbegi

South Ossetia

Tskhinval

Khetakhurovo

Leningori

Gori

Chakva

Batumi

Tbilisi

Rustavi

Georgia
Population: 4,470,000
Capital: Tbilisi

Sochi Region

With a coastline of more than eighty miles and varying climates (subtropical on the coast, alpine in the towering Caucasus Mountains), Sochi is a major tourist attraction for Russians. The coast is crowded with hotels and sanatoria —the spa resorts that made the city famous. In the twenty-first century, Sochi is garnering increasing international attention thanks to the summits organized here by President Vladimir Putin. The town's crowning achievement was winning the bid to host the 2014 Winter Olympics, followed by a Formula 1 race, and the 2018 FIFA World Cup. Sochi has become Russia's new summer capital.

Sochi Region
Population: 343,000
Capital: Sochi

Sochi
Sochi is home to the oldest sanatoria, such as Ordzhonikidze, Metallurg, and the place where the wholesome recreation all began: Riviera Park, now an amusement park. Stalin spent as many months of the year as he could in Sochi, from where he then ruled the Soviet Union.

Krasnaya Polyana
Krasnaya Polyana and Estosadok are situated in the mountains above Sochi. The two farming villages have changed beyond recognition since the construction of new hotels, media centers, and athlete villages built for the Games.

⚭ Mountain Cluster
Spread over five sites—all built specifically for the Games—this is where the skiing events will take place.

▲ Mount Rosa
At 2,320 meters, Mount Rosa is the Winter Olympics' highest peak.

Adler
The airport is located in Adler, and the hotels and facilities here are newer than in Sochi. The town expanded rapidly in the 1970s and 1980s, a trend that is being repeated today with the construction of a new airport, train station, and highways.

⚭ Coastal Cluster
Seven stadiums, a media center, an Olympic village, and numerous hotels will be built around a large square on the Black Sea. A train will connect the coastal cluster to the mountain cluster at Krasnaya Polyana.

Orlyonok
Magri
Makopse
Ashe
Lazarevskoe
Volkonka
Golovinka
Vardane
Loo
Uchdere
Plastunka
Dagomys
Sochi
Bytkha
Matsesta
Khosta
Kudepsta
Adler
Veseloe
Krasnaya Polyana
Estosadok
Psou

Pankisi Gorge
Telavi

"Sochi is nice, but you need a lot of money."

Ibragimpasha Sadekov
Makhachkala, Dagestan, 2012

Ground Zero

In five years this will be Sochi 2014, the event millions of people will talk about for years to come. The residents of Sochi compare the arrival of the Games to an enormous spaceship that has descended on the plains of *Sovkhoz Rossiya*, so alien is it to them. For decades the Russian summer capital, Sochi will become the Olympic winter capital, a transformation from black to white, a complete revolution. When we took this photograph in 2009, the sovkhoz's (state-owned farm) land had just been expropriated. Refugees from impoverished Abkhazia, a few kilometers away, were temporarily allowed to take over the wasteland behind the blue fences. They grew corn and grain and lived in this extended trailer.

This is the least touristy part of Sochi, with fewer sanatoria but more family hotels, small businesses, and farms. The new ice skating rinks will soon be built on this land. From here a road, built at a tremendous cost, will ascend into the mountains and the ski slopes around the village of Krasnaya Polyana.

Nearby, plans are underway for transport harbors, a new airport, a high-speed rail link, five-star hotels, a media village, an athletes' village, and more. Work has yet to begin, but President Putin has promised that everything will be ready on time. Originally estimated to cost $12.5 billion, the Sochi Games will be the most expensive Olympics ever.

Do you want to know how it ends? Take a look at pages 340–41. The spaceships will land, eventually.

Adler, Sochi region, Russia, 2009

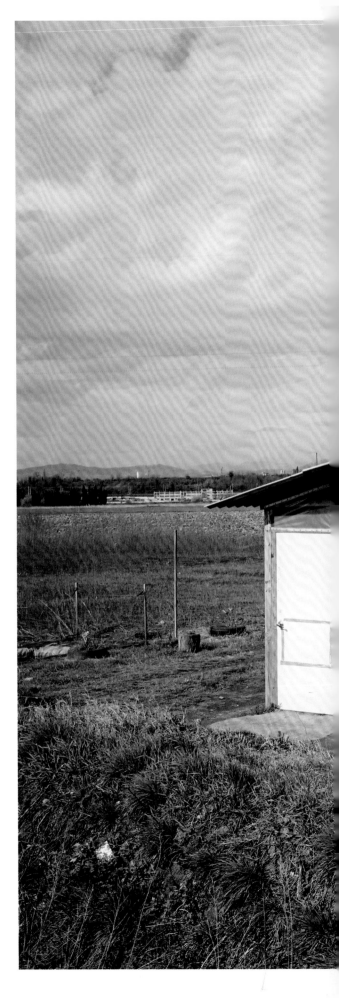

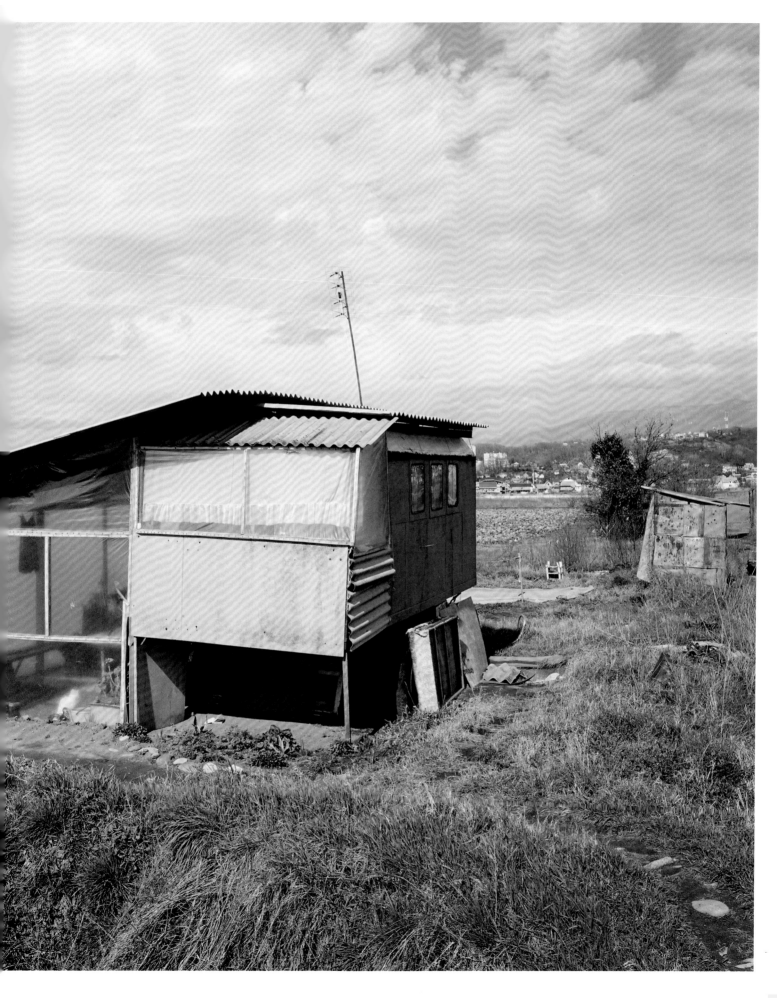

Empty Land

From the ice skating rinks in the next bend of the Black Sea coast, the small country of Abkhazia is plainly visible. When Russia was awarded the Games in 2007, Abkhazia was still a conflict zone where United Nations troops and a Russian peacekeeping force oversaw a ceasefire between Georgia and its breakaway province. Less than eighteen months later, after the war between Georgia and Russia in August 2008, Russia recognized Abkhazia and another autonomous province, South Ossetia. Abkhazia was no longer a conflict zone, but a full-fledged country—although only Nauru, Nicaragua, Tuvalu, Vanuatu, and Venezuela agreed. No other nations have recognized Abkhazia.

Following the civil war between Georgians and Abkhazians in 1993, Abkhazia fell into deep isolation. Informal contact with Russia and Georgia was scarce, difficult, and illegal. The region was largely empty as more than half of the prewar inhabitants had fled. They left behind abandoned houses, ruined buildings, and an economy geared toward tourism without any tourists.

This is how we find Abkhazia, more than fifteen years after the civil war, when we visit a dilapidated seaside resort where the apartments between the pine trees are on the verge of collapse. "Not for long," the mayor of the town Pitsunda assures us. Sochi 2014 will put Abkhazia on the tourist map.

Novi Afon, Abkhazia, 2013

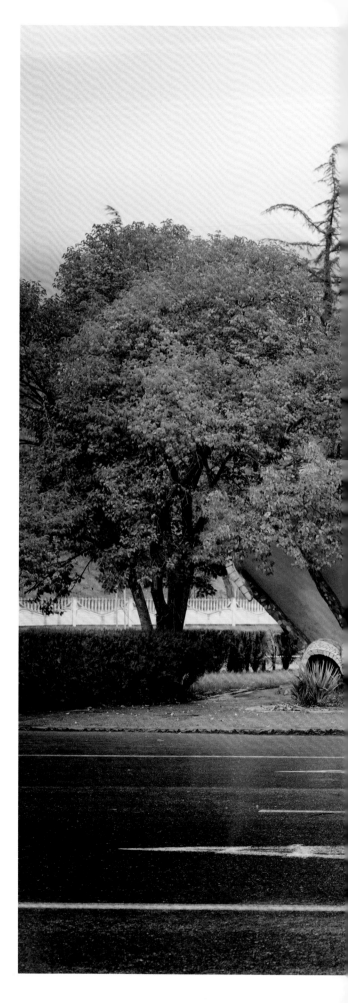

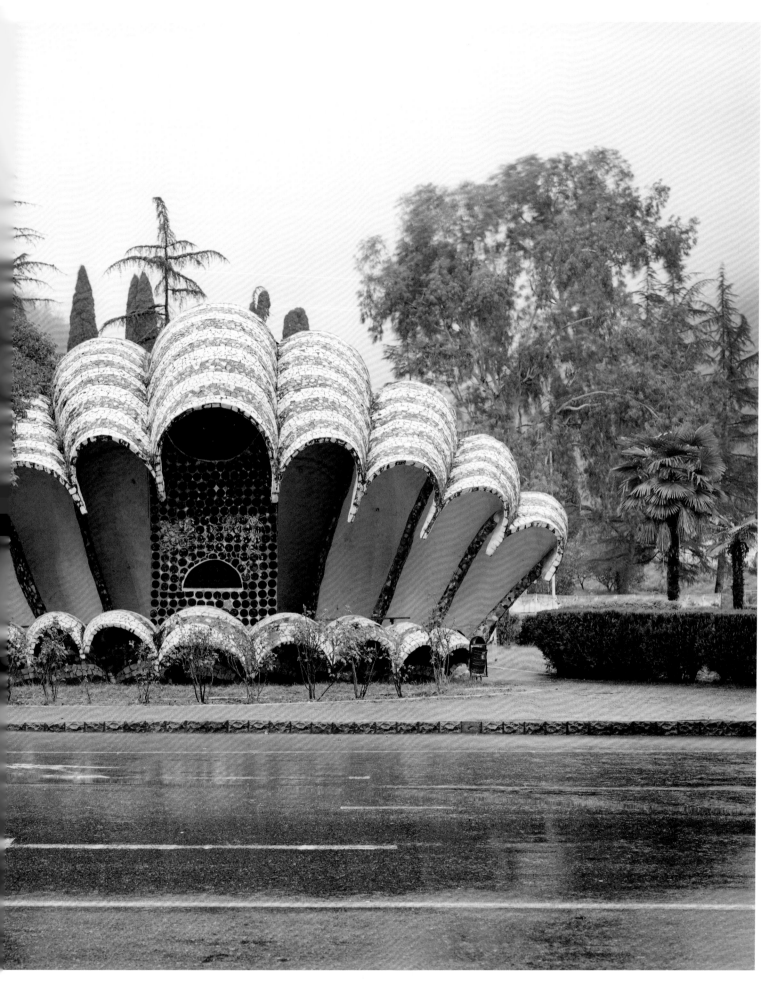

On the Other Side of the Mountains

On the other side of the mountains from the Olympic ski slopes, you have to climb several more peaks and navigate a number of treacherous passes to reach the North Caucasus, the poorest region in Russia. The poverty is the first thing that anyone who actually makes this journey will notice. Villages are still without running water or gas. People live self-sufficiently because jobs are scarce. Factories have closed down and the land once belonging to the collective and state farms has been carved up or lies fallow.

Russia has fought for the North Caucasus for centuries. The North Caucasus has fought back for just as long. Violence, terrorism, and counter-terrorism are the region's most pressing problems. Poverty often causes people to resort to desperate alternatives, which are sometimes offered by radical, ideologically driven groups, such as the separatists in the mountains. The North Caucasus was seen as a problem that Putin had to solve in the years prior to the Games. Yet even in 2011 the head of the FSB, Russia's security service, said that his greatest fear was a North Caucasian terrorist attack in Sochi.

Kutisha, Dagestan, 2012

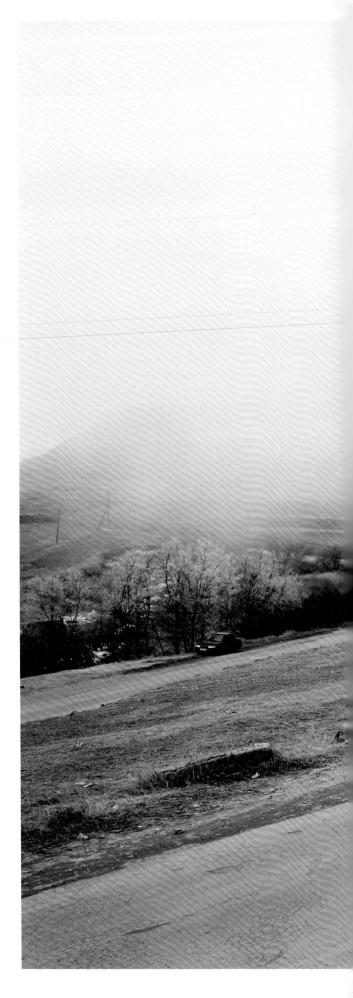

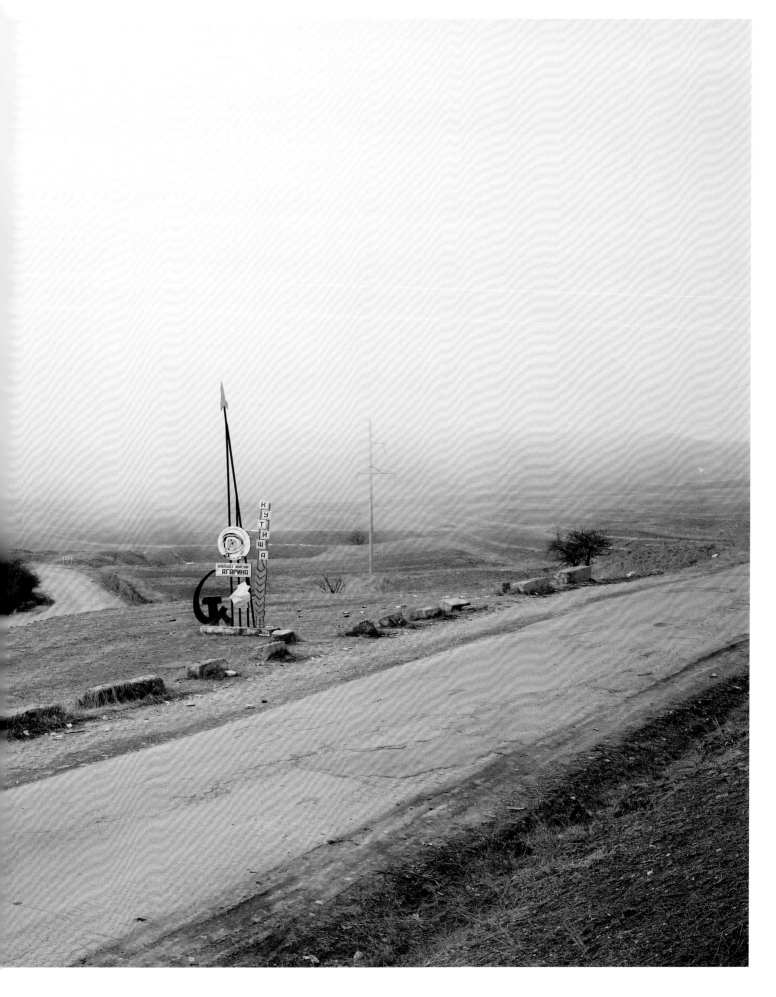

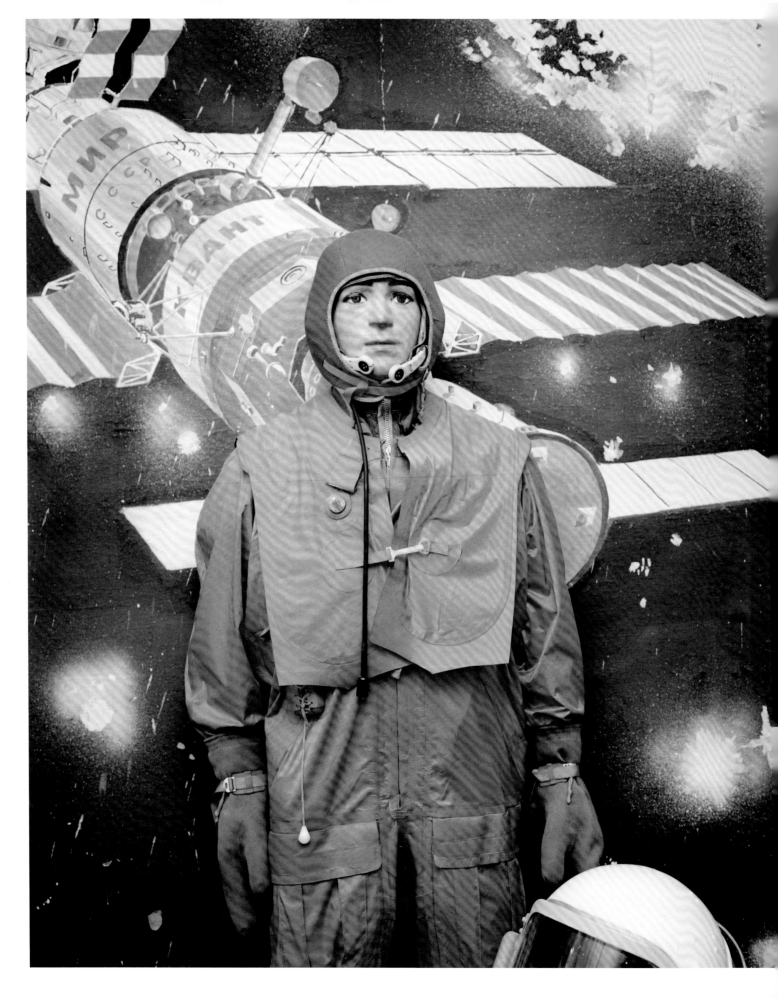

The People's Elite

Orlyonok is a vast children's camp for the pioneers of the Soviet Komsomol youth organization. Here the children of acclaimed veterans, officers, Soviet heroes, Stakhanovites, *nomenklatura*, artists, and writers were at an advantage. Yet this place, with its own well-equipped space museum, was also hit hard by the fall of the Soviet Union during the impoverished, chaotic nineties. Then oil and gas prices went up and President Putin dropped by.

"I weep when I see what has become of our heritage," Putin said during a visit to the camp in 2003. Today, everything is freshly painted and the grounds are once again filled with boys and girls in smart uniforms. As Stalin called his writers the "engineers of the soul," the library here is called the "pharmacy of the soul." The name does not dampen the enthusiasm of librarian/pharmacist Jadrevskaya Bronislava, who has been encouraging children to read since 1964. When we enter, a group of eighteen-year-olds, the oldest of the so-called "professional camp," is obediently reading Shakespeare's *Macbeth* aloud. None of these future elite speaks English to us, which is rather surprising.

Orlyonok symbolizes the partial restoration of the Soviet Union under Putin, whose goal is to erase the shame of the nineties and the collapse of Russian power. To this end, Orlyonok is being restored, Sochi will be the most grandiose Winter Olympics ever, and Stalin has reappeared in the history books as if Khrushchev's secret speech in 1956 never happened.

Orlyonok, Sochi region, Russia, 2011

Hotel Zhemchuzhina

Built in 1978, Zhemchuzhina (meaning "pearl") is a sprawling Soviet hotel on Sochi's beachfront. It is its own world. In addition to 956 rooms, the complex encompasses eight restaurants, fourteen bars, two nightclubs, shops, a swimming pool, a theater, and a billiards room. The waiters in the American Diner can still remember how foreigners were catered to in the eighties, when they were made to feel at home in their restaurant with hamburgers and the option to pay in dollars.

Once checked in it is unnecessary to leave the hotel. You can spend all day swimming laps in the enormous saltwater pool, lying on the beach, dining in the numerous restaurants on the promenade, or lounging on an artificial peninsula in the center of the complex.

Zhemchuzhina has become increasingly expensive. Floor after floor has been refurbished. Profitable oddities have gradually disappeared; rooms with breakfast included used to cost one-and-a-half times the amount of a similar room with breakfast paid for separately.

Dozens of hotels such as Zhemchuzhina line Sochi's crowded coast. Built in the Soviet Union's heyday and neglected in the murky eighties and nineties, the hotel owners believe that the Games are their saving grace. All the major hotels are being overhauled to bring Sochi up to international standards.

Sochi, Russia, 2011

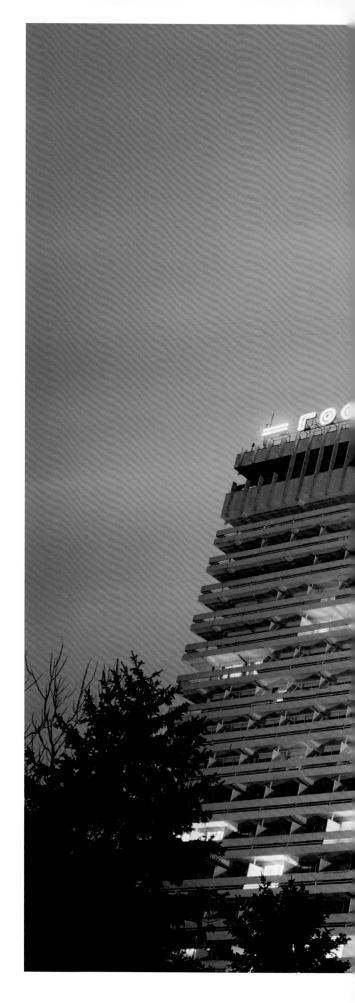

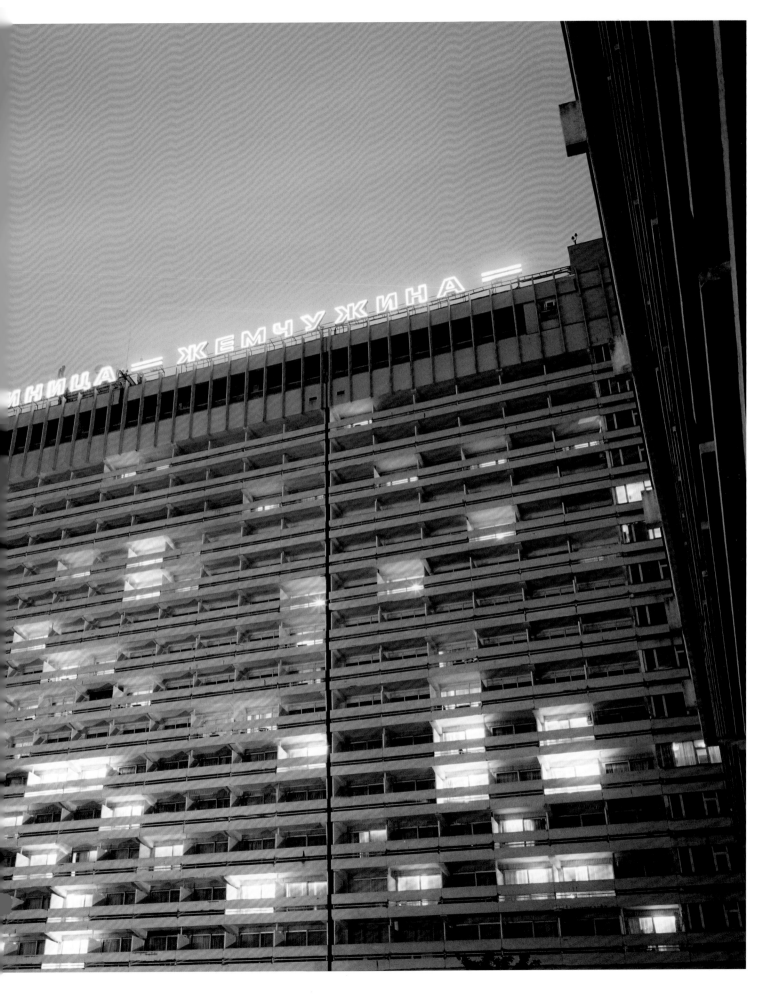

Natalya Shorogova, Our Floor Lady

Each level in Hotel Zhemchuzhina has its own floor lady, who oversees the correct use of the rooms, monitors which guests come and go, and takes laundry home to supplement her income. Natalya was our favorite, not only because of her eye-catching appearance but also because she had turned her floor into a second living room, with warm words on arrival and motherly advice on departure.

One evening we decide to go to the twenty-four-hour restaurant. A middle-aged Russian chansonnier sings chansons until 11:30 p.m., when seven striptease dancers take over. It surprises us that the women in the audience (there are many married couples) are not at all offended. The dancers writhe like snakes against the visitors, making no distinction between men and women.

When we return, Natalya is waiting for us. She sees that we have been drinking and nods modestly and amiably to us. "Good night," we call exuberantly as we stagger into our brown, wood-paneled rooms.

Sochi, Russia, 2011

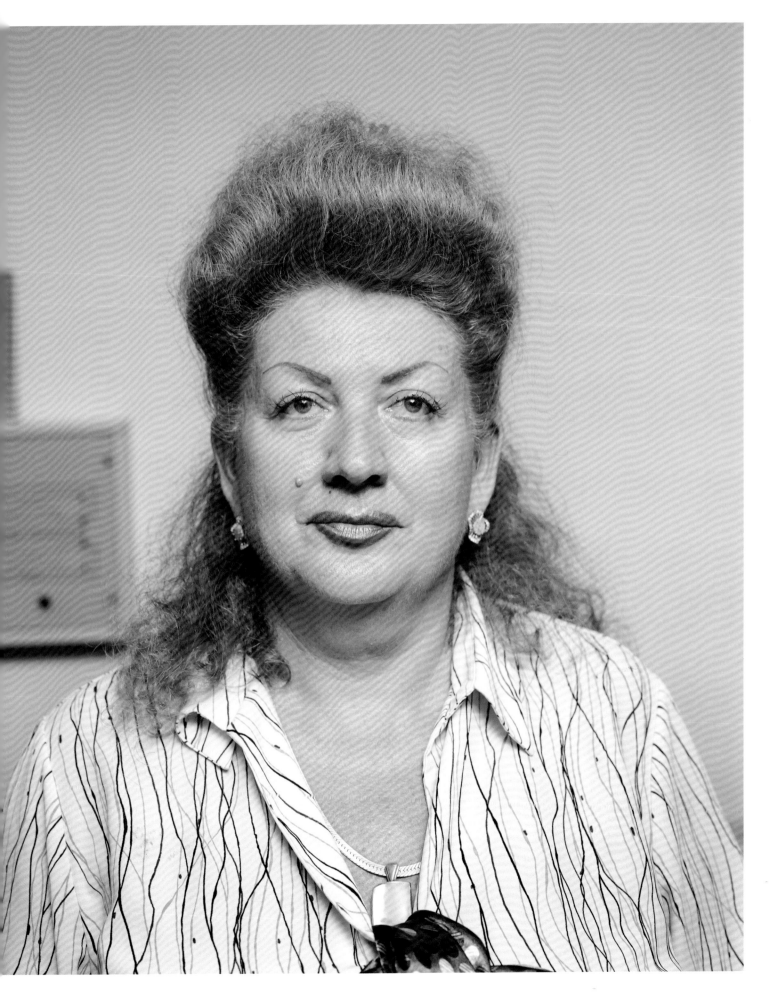

Cabaret Club

Occasionally during the low season,
Zhemchuzhina is filled with visitors to the
nearby convention centers: bankers from
Moscow, businessmen from across Siberia,
and the odd international guest from the
film festival. At these times Zhemchuzhina's
three nightclubs are arguably busier than in
the summer. Cabaret Club cashes in on its
front-row seats, plies patrons with Crimean
champagne, and puts on almost old-fashioned
entertainment: a singer, a piano, and dancers.

Sochi, Russia, 2011

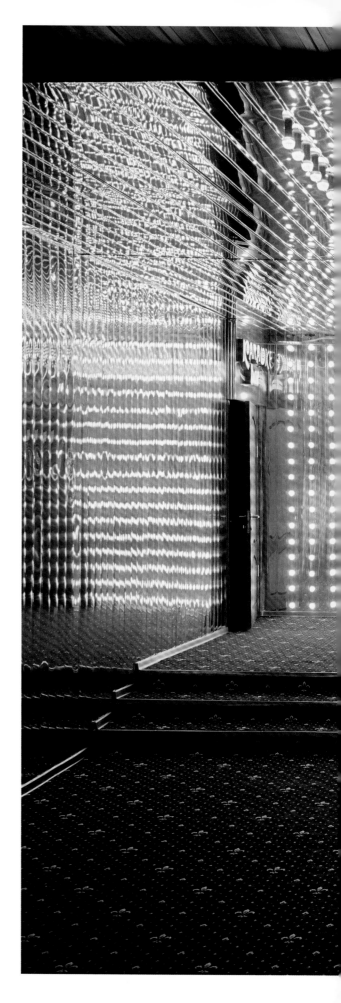

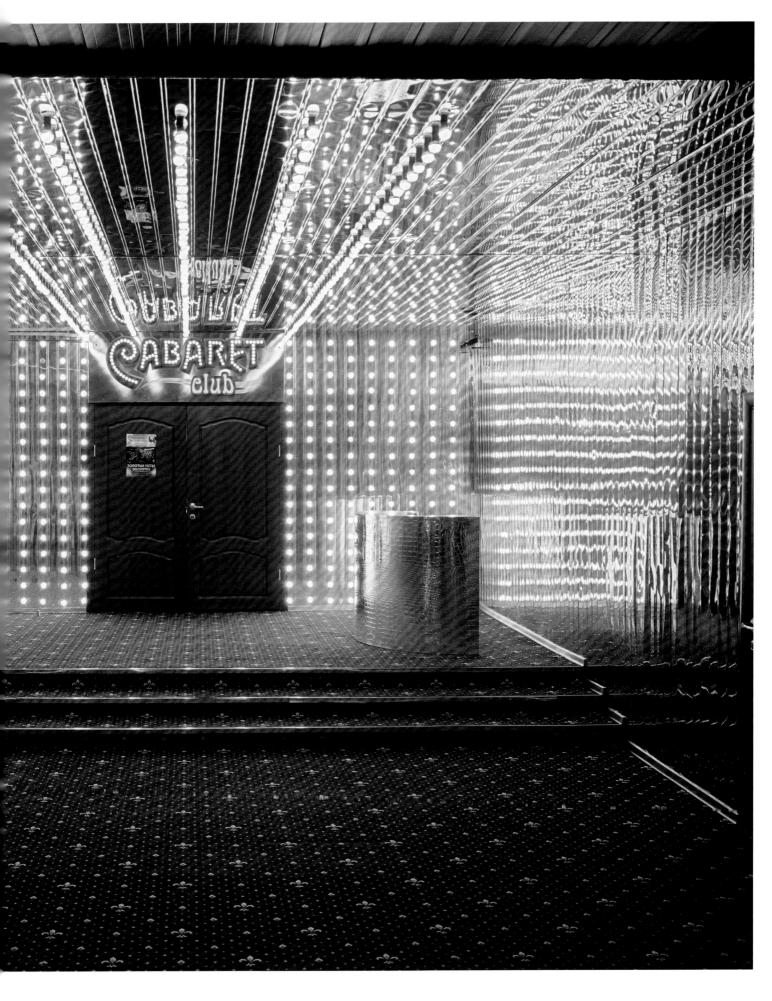

Aliona

Aliona dances in Lubava restaurant, on an upper floor of Hotel Zhemchuzhina. On stage, a man sings and cracks jokes with the audience, made up of a family, a couple, and two tables of leering men. One by one the dancers make their appearance. They spin around a pole and then visit each table in turn, for as long as it takes to relieve the occupants of as much money as possible.

Sochi, Russia, 2011

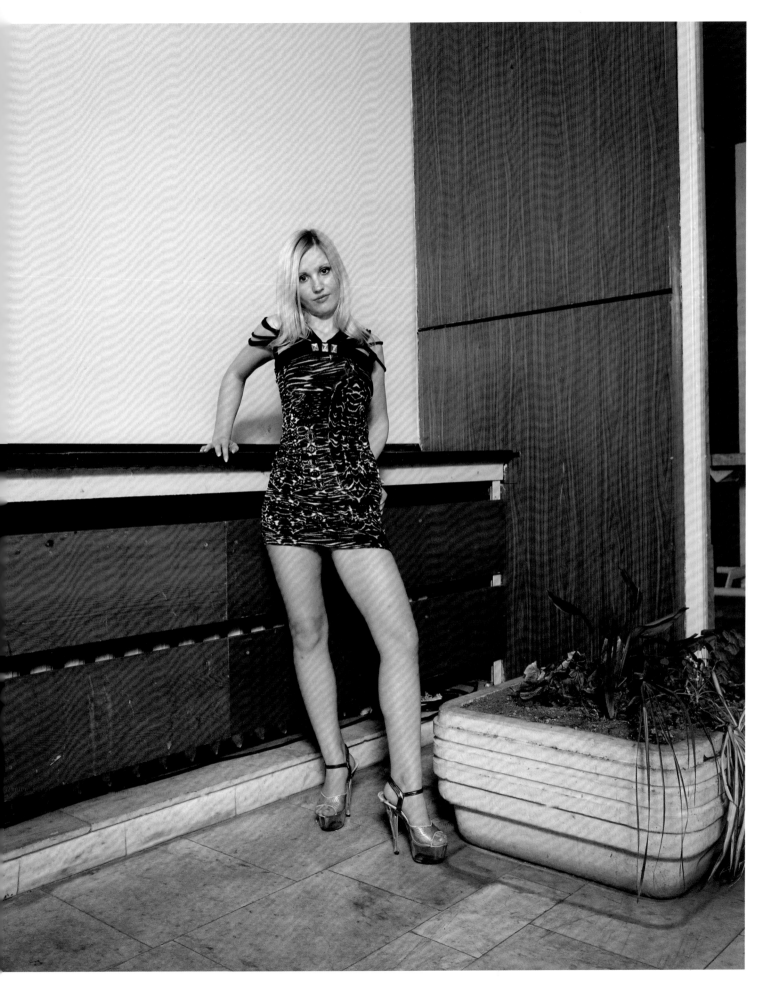

New Developments

New apartments are going up next to the pompous entrance of Sanatorium Metallurg. Every square inch of undeveloped land in Sochi is subject to speculation. The closer the Games get, the faster the pace of construction and the flashier the commercials touting the expensive properties. The relatively small sanatoria surrounded by extensive parks are no longer viable. Lenin's palaces for the proletariat are slowly losing ground to the new palaces of speculators and oligarchs.

Sochi, Russia, 2009

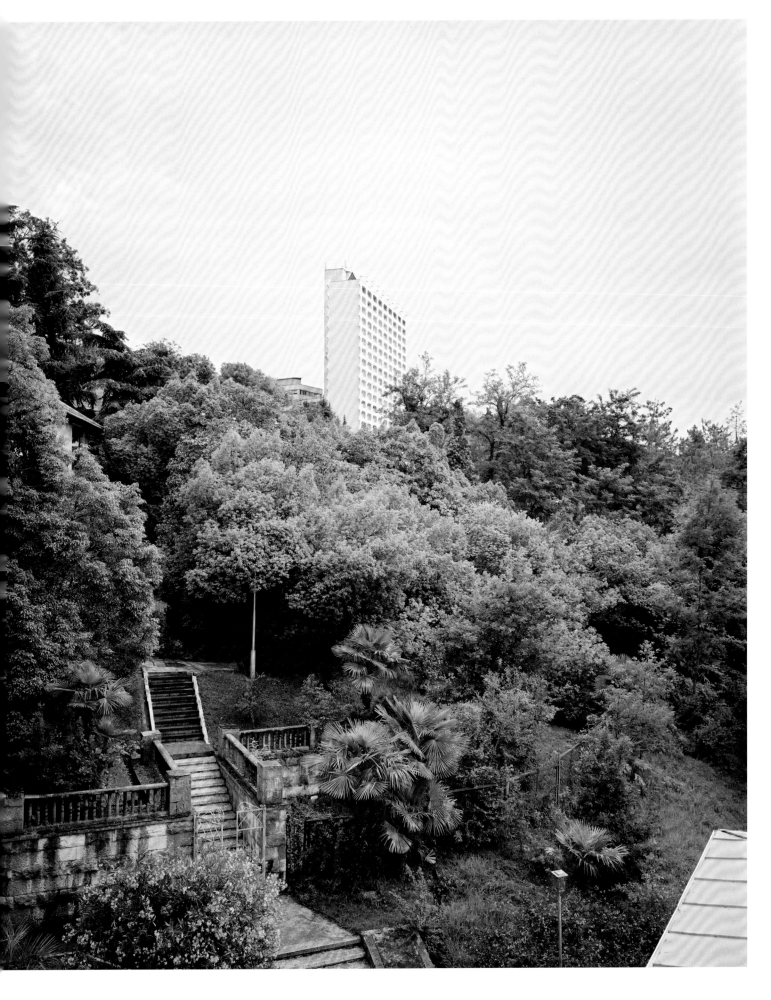

Dima Burned His Legs

Matsesta, a village a few hundred meters inland from Sochi, is renowned for its magical sulfur baths. Its name appropriately means "fire water." The sulfurous water is employed throughout the village. There is a treatment for every ailment. Lung patients hang over devices attached to what look like gas masks. Busloads of visitors arrive each day from Sochi to improve their health. Outside the sanatorium an entire industry has developed of old ladies flogging their honey, herbal teas, and painted birch-bark vignettes.

Little Dima burned his legs at a wild barbecue party thrown by his parents. His doctor prescribed a visit to Matsesta. He now sleeps in one of the sanatorium's small rooms, and for six minutes three times a day he sits with his burned legs under running sulfurous water. Any longer and the remedial effects of the powerful water would be worse than the complaint, says the attending nurse.

Matsesta, Sochi region, Russia, 2009

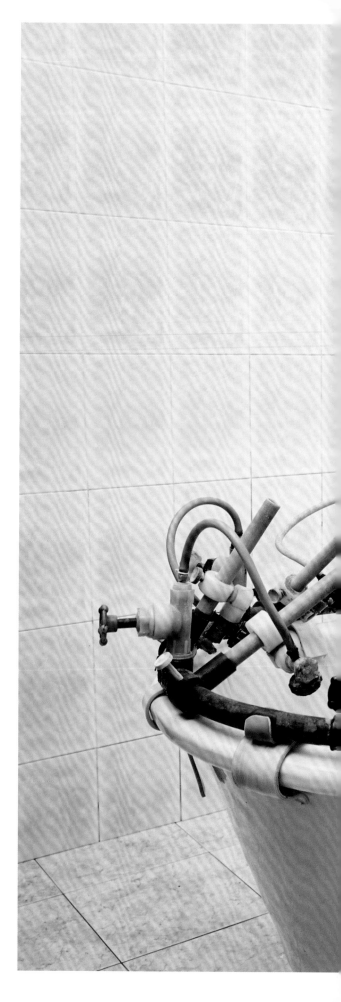

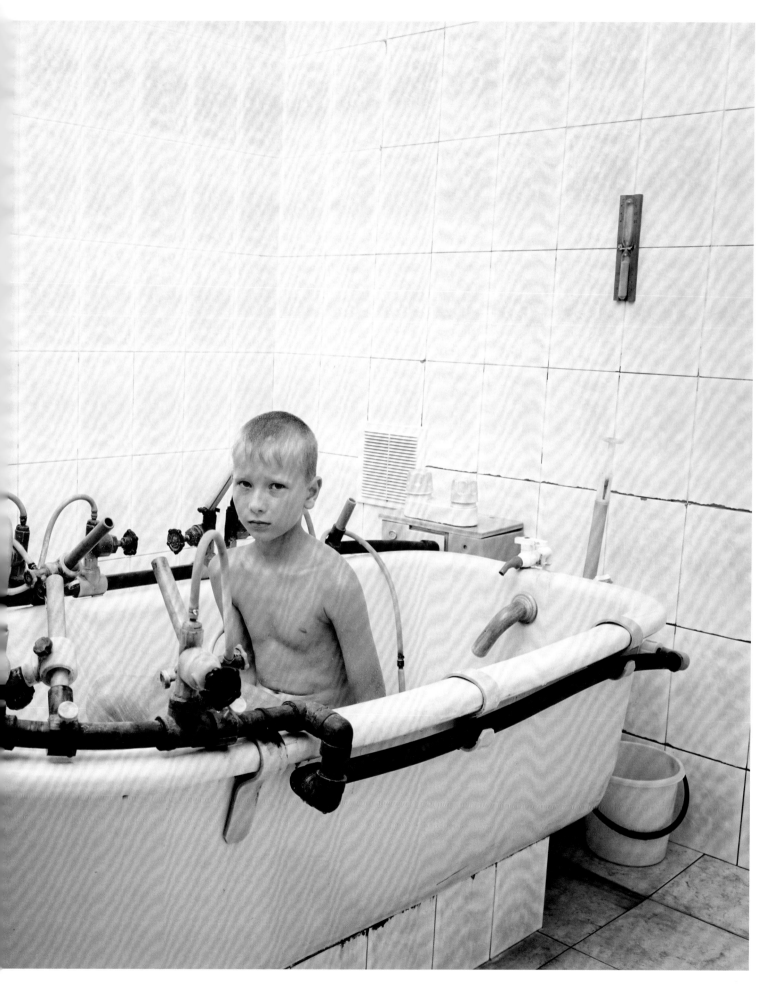

All Possible Cures

Using radiography, infrared- and electro-
magnetically charged sulfurous clay, the
doctors and nurses at Sanatorium Metallurg
do everything in their power to cure their
patients. At an allotted time, guests plod to
the treatment rooms, change, and wait obediently on a bed or chair.

Sanatorium Metallurg, Sochi, Russia, 2009

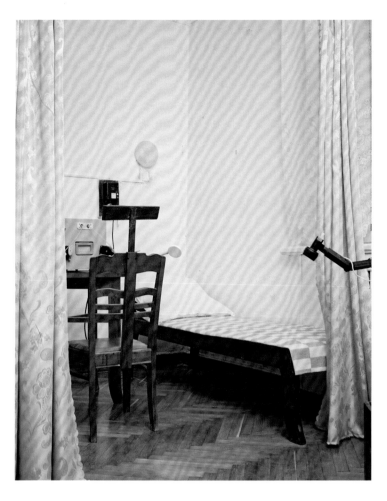
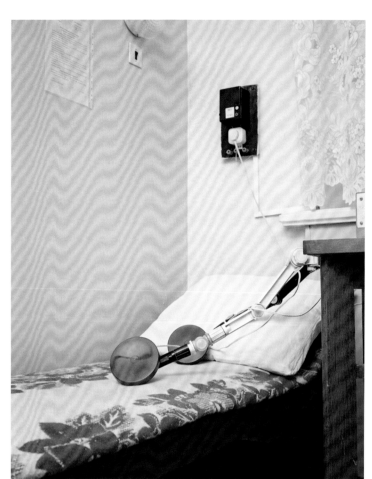
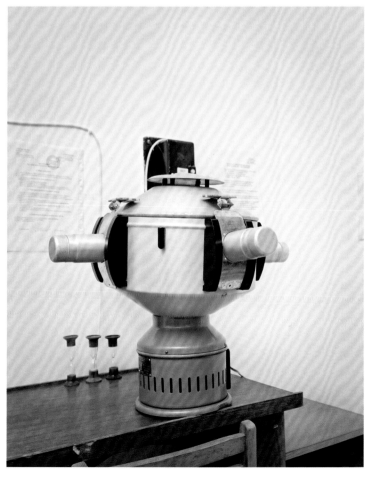
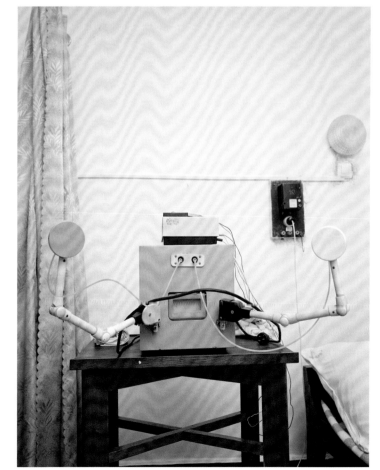

Sanatorium Metallurg

Metallurg, on Kurortny Prospekt, is one of
Sochi's most famous sanatoria. Built to
accommodate metalworkers, it is located next
to the enormous Red Army sanatorium and
Ordzhonikidze, the sanatorium for miners.

Postcard of Sochi, Russia, 1980s

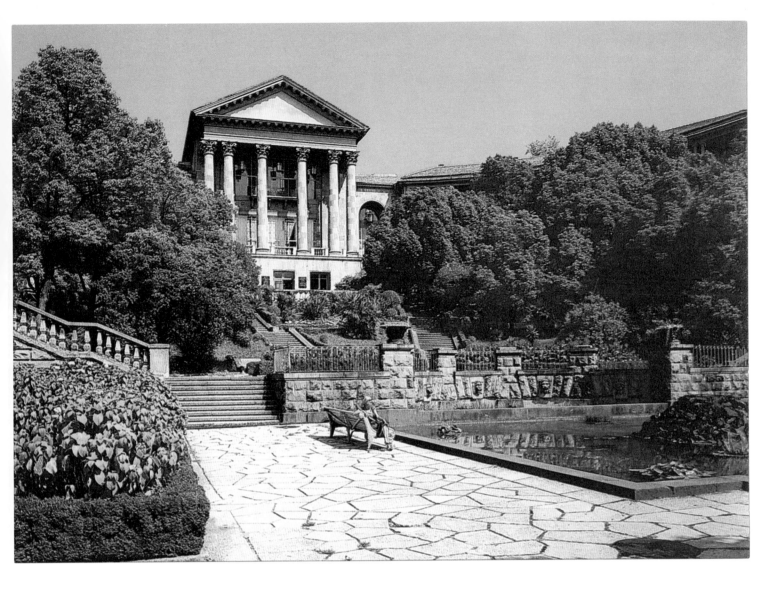

"The Soviet mentality and rudeness that still prevail here scare people away. If the staff can't adapt, they'll be fired."

Siraj Sartakati
Sochi, Russia, 2009

Friendly, Service Oriented, and One Hundred Percent Relaxing

This is old Sochi, the only subtropical city in present-day Russia; a spa town where the sun, the mountains, the ocean, and the medicinal spring water are worshipped. On the long coastal road from Tuapse in the north, past Sochi and Adler, and south into Abkhazia and Georgia toward the Turkish border, endless rows of sanatoria fill the landscape. They are palaces for the proletariat, as Lenin once decreed.

When the October Revolution caught Russia by surprise, in 1917, Sochi still had relatively little to recommend it. The city had just outgrown its status as the last stronghold against the Caucasians and Turks and was situated in the middle of a swamp where malaria was rife. Yet the warm climate and strategic location quickly led to great activity on the narrow coastal strip at the foot of the mighty Caucasus Mountains. Inspired by German spas such as those at Baden-Baden, where famous Russian writers, including Turgenev, Tolstoy, and Chekhov, conversed with the European elite, tsarist Russia began building its own retreats on the shores of the Black Sea.

It was only under the Soviet Union that Sochi grew into the extensive spa town it is today. All the ministries, army units, unions, and factories erected holiday accommodations and remedial resorts for their employees. Small, young Sochi became a grand dame. Its palm trees, flowers, and tepid waters were immortalized in hundreds of songs. A trip to Sochi as a reward for hard work or to recuperate from an injury or illness was the best thing that could happen to a Russian at the time.

Sochi also became a refuge for Soviet leaders, acclaimed cosmonauts, actors, and other members of the jet set. It was said that the indefatigable Leonid Brezhnev could never have stayed in power for so long had he not immersed himself in Matsesta's medicinal baths for several weeks every year.

The collapse of the Soviet Union also heralded the decline of the sanatoria. Under capitalism, the palaces for the proletariat were no longer profitable. Today, valiant attempts are being made to preserve the sanatoria in their original state. They remain fully booked year-round. Workers arrive in the summer; retired and infirm employees fill up the rest of the seasons. It is a hopeless cause, however. The often poorly constructed buildings are too large to be maintained with the paltry income generated by the guests. While the patrons lament the visible decay, the managers bemoan the fact that their palaces are not yet five-star facilities.

We wanted to pull the same trick as old Brezhnev had. In 2009 we chose Metallurg, the neoclassical sanatorium for metalworkers, as the place to cure our feigned heart and back problems. We picked Metallurg not only because it was such a beautiful sanatorium but also because it had been selected as an Olympic "object" and was due to undergo rapid renovation leading up to 2014.

The all-inclusive holiday could have been invented in Sochi. The vouchers, *putyovkas*, handed out by companies, unions, and government bodies offer employees a package that includes meals, movie screenings, treatments, and accommodation. According to the nursing staff a treatment in Sochi is only beneficial after at least two weeks' rest, an unheard of luxury. The scheme still attracts thousands of civil servants, laborers, invalids, and those in search of tranquility from across Russia.

"Don't you find it terribly boring here, with all those old people and outdated treatments?" Siray Sartakati, the twenty-eight-year-old marketing manager of Metallurg, asks us. "Look at this beautiful building. Shouldn't there be clubs, bars, and terraces?" On the contrary, we have been in the monumental sanatorium for a week and are having a wonderful time among Russia's elderly and infirm. Every day we are massaged, drink mineral water and revolting tea, and bathe for twenty minutes in a radon bath. Three times a day a gigantic buffet of delicious meatballs, rice, porridge, and mountains of cakes is laid out for us. Whether the treatment has any health benefits remains to be seen; it certainly does not benefit your weight. In the evening the sanatorium organizes a disco and karaoke. Then all hell breaks loose, as the elderly guests throw themselves around the dance floor as if possessed. It is an entertaining spectacle.

Siray has very different plans for Metallurg. "Everything has to be luxuriously finished, made from real European materials. The atmosphere has to remain the same, but the quality has to be significantly improved." He taps the window frames, walls, and bronze doorknobs. The owner, the Association of Unions, has appointed him to overhaul the institution. "It all has to be finished by 2014, in time for the Winter Olympics. We'll then no longer be a sanatorium but a five-star hotel." Siray is sitting on a gold mine. Metallurg is a miniature Versailles, where one can descend through extensive gardens, down endless steps past fountains and ponds to the private beach. The canteen is a stately ballroom. It is still a palace for the proletariat, as it was once intended, but not for much longer if Siray has his way. He has the enthusiasm to pull off the ambitious transformation, but it remains to be seen whether his bimonthly trips to the local IKEA in Krasnodar are enough to give the hotel the facelift he envisions.

Now that new managers are trying to save the buildings and parks and to tap additional sources of tourism, the old proletariat may well miss out. If the transition continues, Russia's growing middle class and elite will vacation here in the future. The neighboring sanatorium, called Sanitorium USSR, is already making a brave attempt, and has retranslated the acronym for the Union of Soviet Socialist Republics to instead stand for the Russian equivalent of Friendly, Service Oriented, and One Hundred Percent Relaxing. "The Soviet mentality and rudeness that still prevail here scare people away," says Siray. "If the staff can't adapt, they'll be fired. But for 2014 we've changed this town beyond recognition."

Cooking for Three Hundred Guests

Mealtimes at Sanatorium Metallurg are fixed. Every day at 8 a.m., 1 p.m., and 6 p.m., the door of the majestic dining room opens. This is only the start of the chefs' work, however. At high speed, they roll the next batch of meatballs, fill bowls of kefir (a yogurt drink) and *smetana* (sour cream), and prepare liters of tea and lemonade.

In the morning, cabbage is served with porridge, meatballs, sausages, and mashed potatoes. Dessert is coffee and a few sweet snacks. Lunch is cabbage, broth, mashed potatoes, and cutlets. Sometimes there are sausages, too. Dessert is coffee and sweet rolls. Supper usually features mashed potatoes, often with cabbage, cutlets, and soup. Yogurt and salad also occasionally appear.

Sanatorium Metallurg, Sochi, Russia, 2009

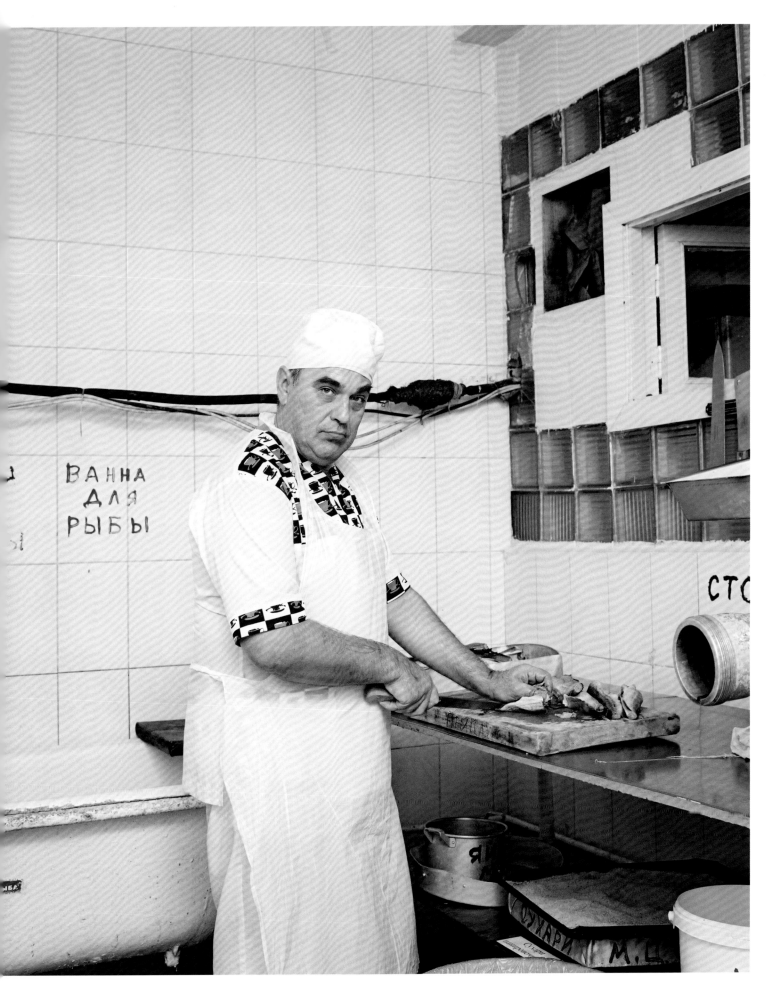

The Beach

The railway line from Sochi to Sukhum in Abkhazia hugs the coast. Behind it rise the sanatoria of Adler, just south of Sochi's large, famous Stalinist sanatoria. Hotel rooms in Adler are marginally cheaper, which is immediately apparent on the beach. The permanent residents disdainfully call these tourists *bzdykhs*, a word unknown outside Sochi. But anyone who has been to a beach resort will understand what it means: the overweight bodies sweating beer and spirits, the bare torsos and toes in sandals, the noisy eaters surrounded by drunken bluster and tacky music.

The locals have little choice but to put up with them. Well-heeled Russians take refuge in Sochi's fancier hotels or more often opt for Italy, Turkey, or Thailand. The Games may bring a level of quality that would discourage the *bzdykhs*. It is more likely, however, that the city will become more expensive, chaotic, and crowded, keeping away more than just the *bzdykhs*.

Adler, Sochi region, Russia, 2011

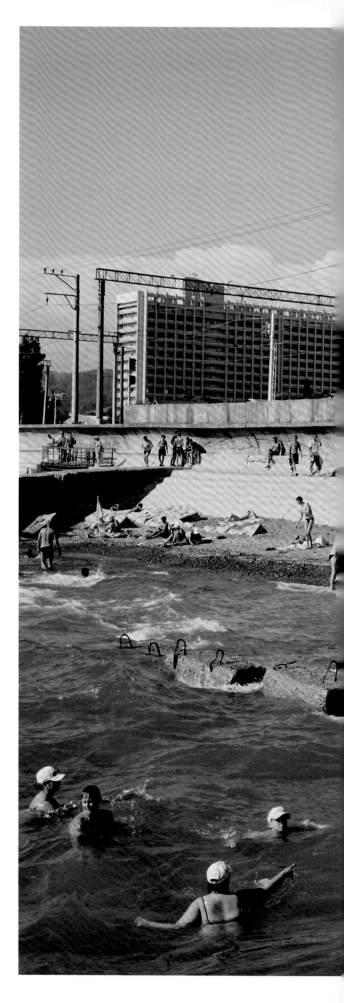

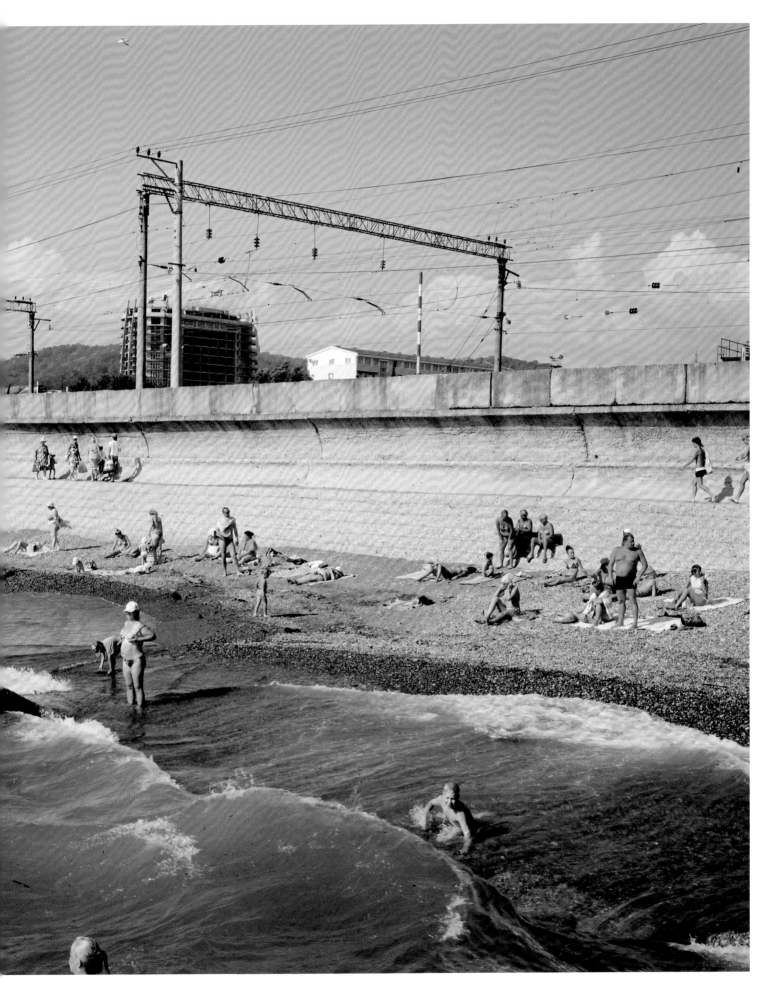

Miners and Sailors

Every year, Mikhail Pavelivich Karabelnikov, seventy-seven, travels eighteen hundred miles from Novokuznetsk to take his vacation in Sochi. He was a miner for thirty-seven years and gradually worked his way up to foreman, in charge of some 150 miners. His promising career came to an abrupt end when he refused to become a member of the Communist party, he says proudly.

Karabelnikov goes to the beach as often as he can during his stays at Sanatorium Metallurg. He is one of a small group of old-timers who gravitate toward one another in the dining room. In the evenings they sit together in the gardens drinking vodka. During the day they hang out on the beach terrace with a chessboard, beer, and packs of cigarettes within easy reach.

Sanatorium Metallurg, Sochi, Russia, 2009

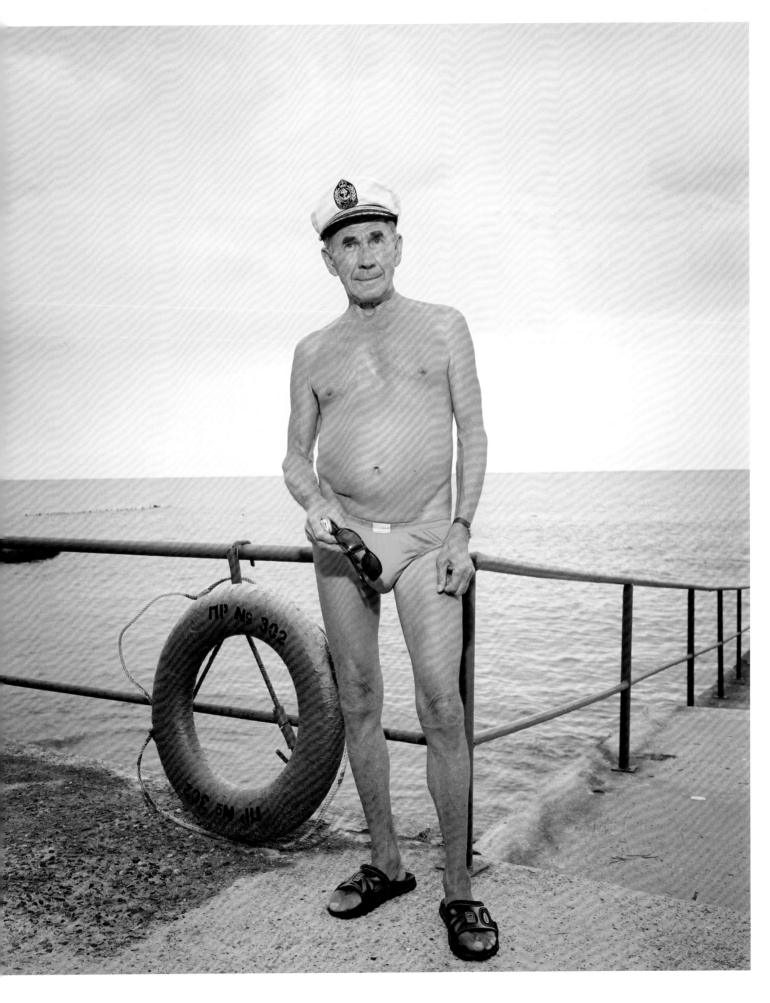

"Putin looked and looked, and then he found it: the only place in Russia without any snow, to organize the Winter Games."

Katya Primakova
Sochi, Russia, 2009

Sweaty Parties until 11 p.m.

The nights in the sanatorium are wild.
Chess players gather on the terraces. Some
have brought hip flasks of vodka with them.
A man plays the accordion and the onlookers
sing along to the melancholy notes. Upstairs
in the ballroom the lights are turned on,
reflecting in the ponds in front of the palace.
DJ Lydia hits the music and the guests flock
in. After each song, the dancers retreat to the
chairs around the edge of the room to catch
their breath. The brave among them immediately return to the dance floor. Sweaty revelers
crowd the narrow balconies for a quick smoke.
At 11 p.m. the music stops: no cure without
a good night's sleep. Metallurg dances again
the following evening and the evening after
that, year in, year out, while it still can.

Sanatorium Metallurg, Sochi, Russia, 2009

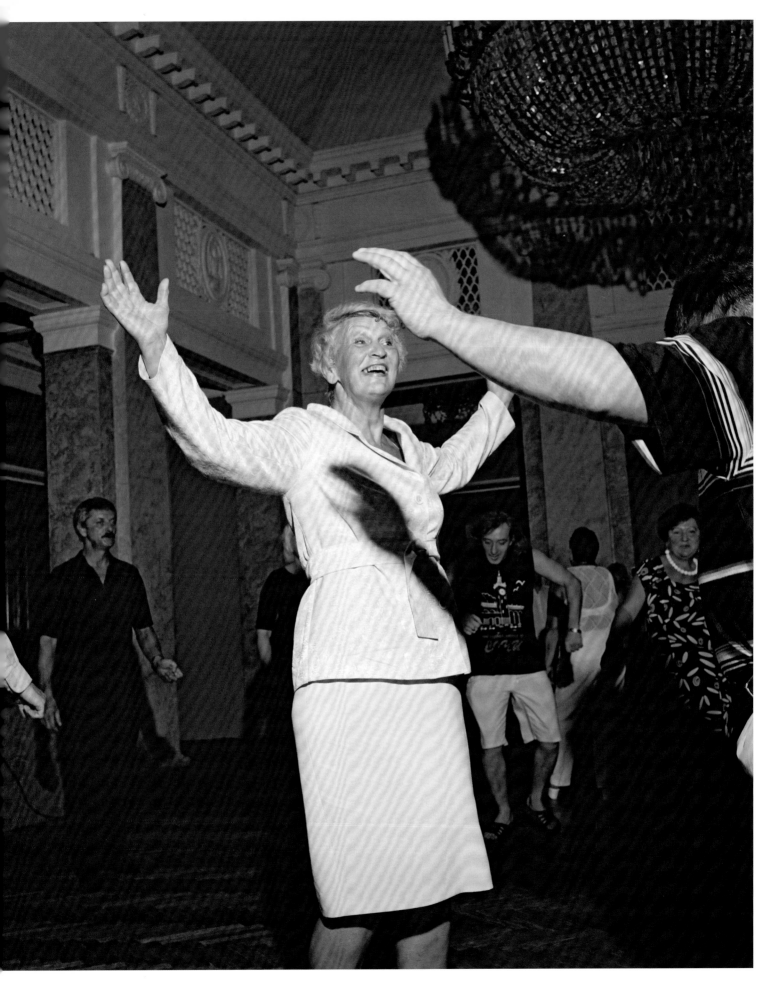

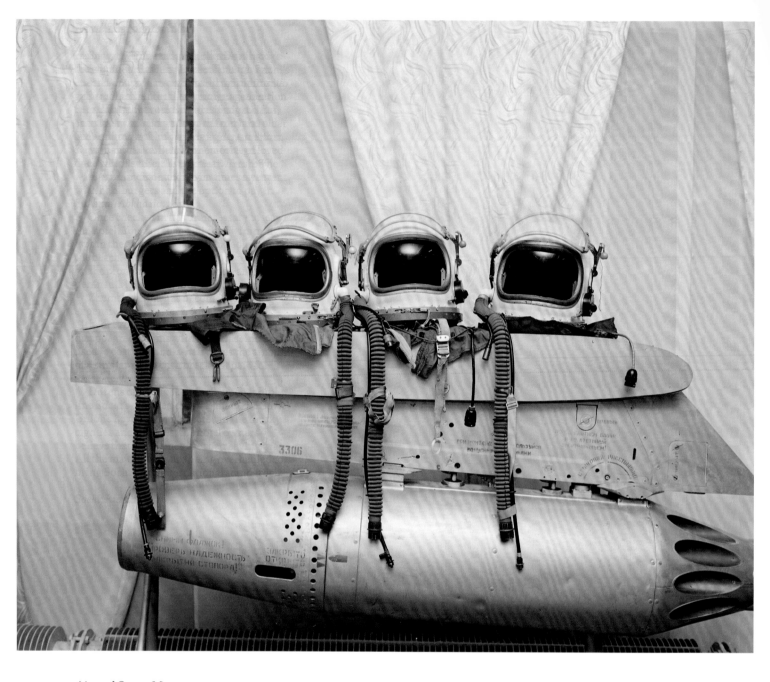

Air and Space Museum

One of the Soviet Union's greatest achievements was arguably its space program, advances in which sparked intense competition with the United States. These accomplishments are grandly commemorated at Orlyonok Children's Center, which displays original objects from cosmonaut Yuri Gagarin's heyday and the years thereafter.

Orlyonok, Sochi region, Russia, 2011

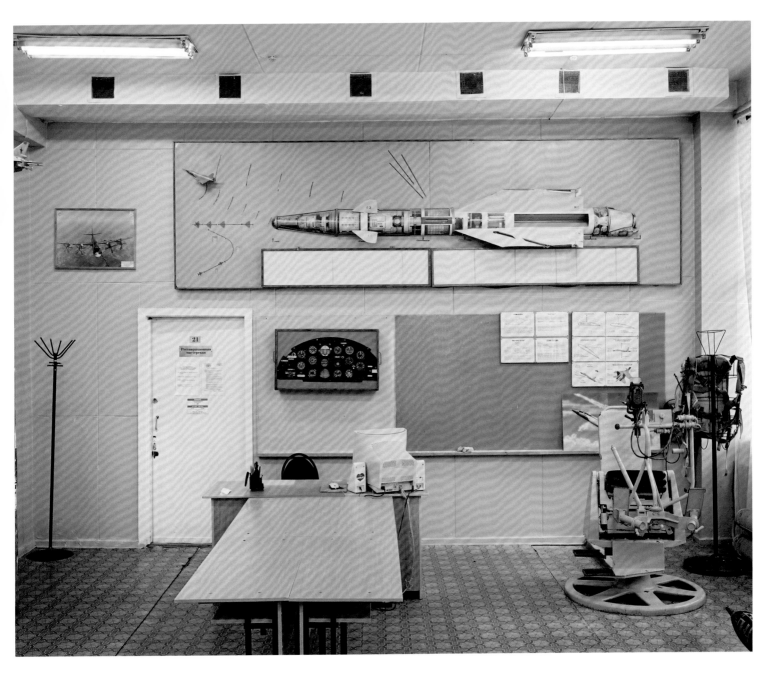

Nightlife

The region's promenades extend for dozens of kilometers, from Adler in the south to Dzhubga in the north. The promenades in the various resorts are almost indistinguishable from each other: packed with identical wooden souvenir stands and a long row of restaurants, almost all of which serve the same food and play similar music. Before and after dinner, the predictable life of a tourist plays out: strolling, playing, singing, drinking, chasing away stray dogs, and stealing a kiss in a dark corner of the beach.

Loo, Sochi region, Russia, 2011

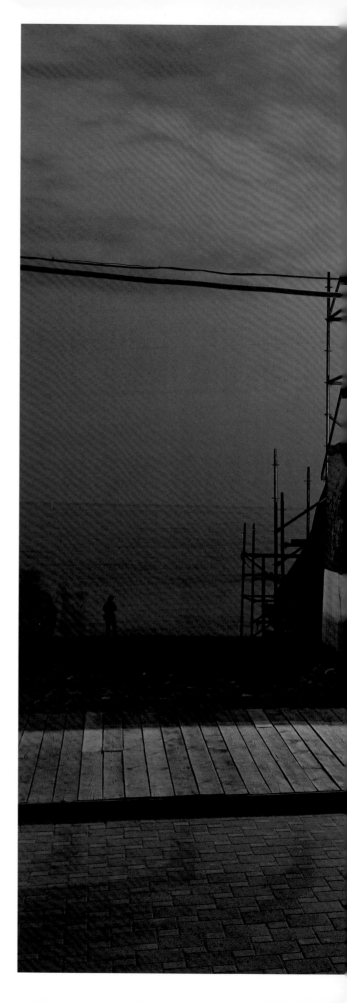

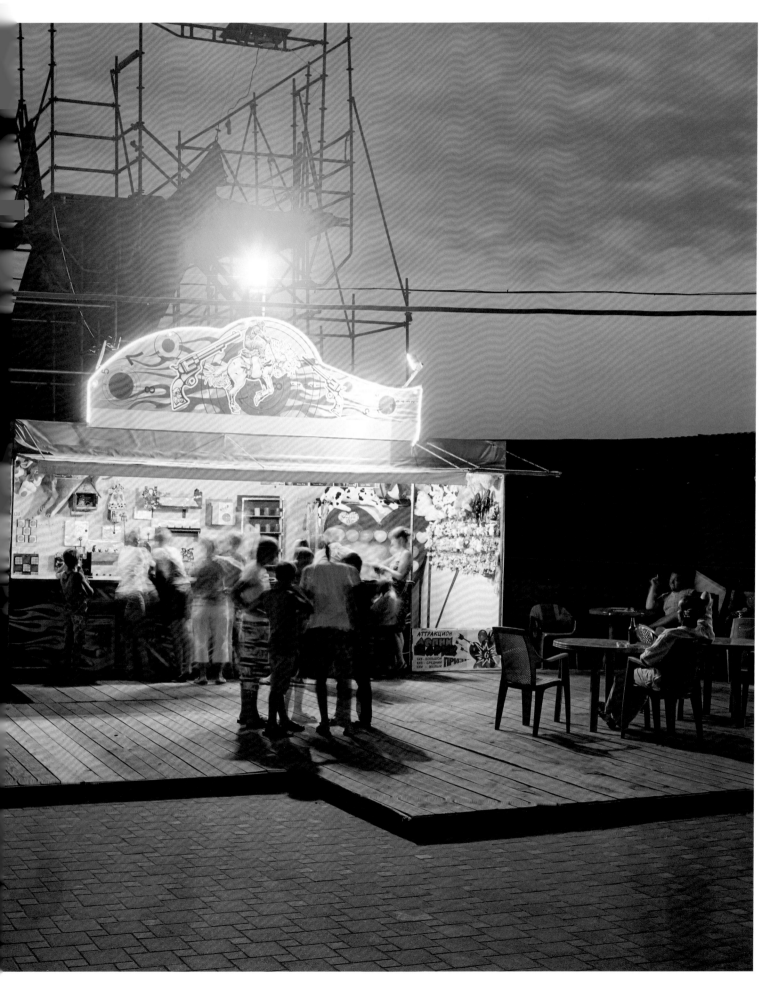

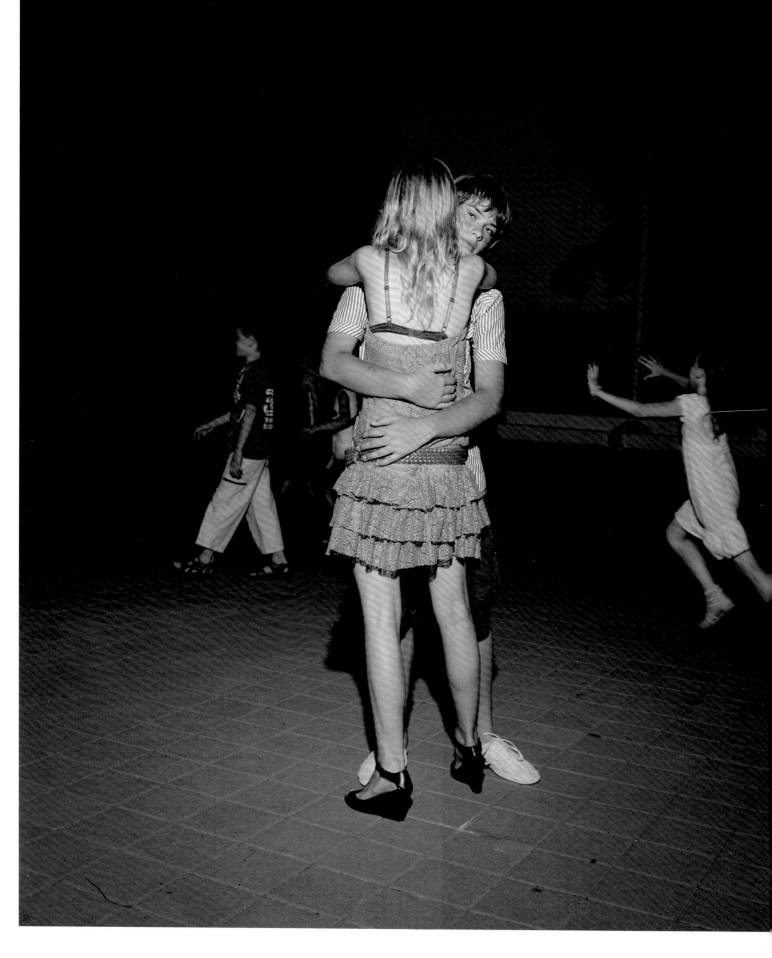

Saying Good-Bye

Saying good-bye to a summer love is never easy. In Russia's vast interior, you might live thousands of miles apart. You might never see each other again. But here, on the dance floor of the children's camp, you can believe for a moment that it will last forever.

Orlyonok, Sochi region, Russia, 2011

Paradise

Pitsunda is the calling card of Abkhazia, the
tiny country on Sochi's southern border.
Seven apartment blocks stand in a row, half
obscured by the pine trees that skirt the beach
on this narrow peninsula.

Postcard of Pitsunda, Abkhazia, 1980s

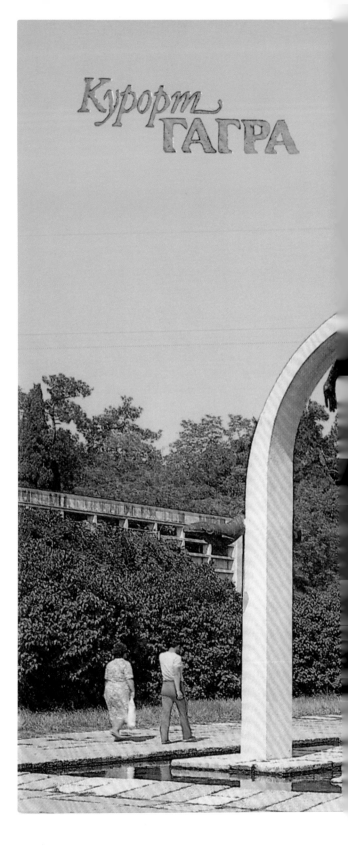

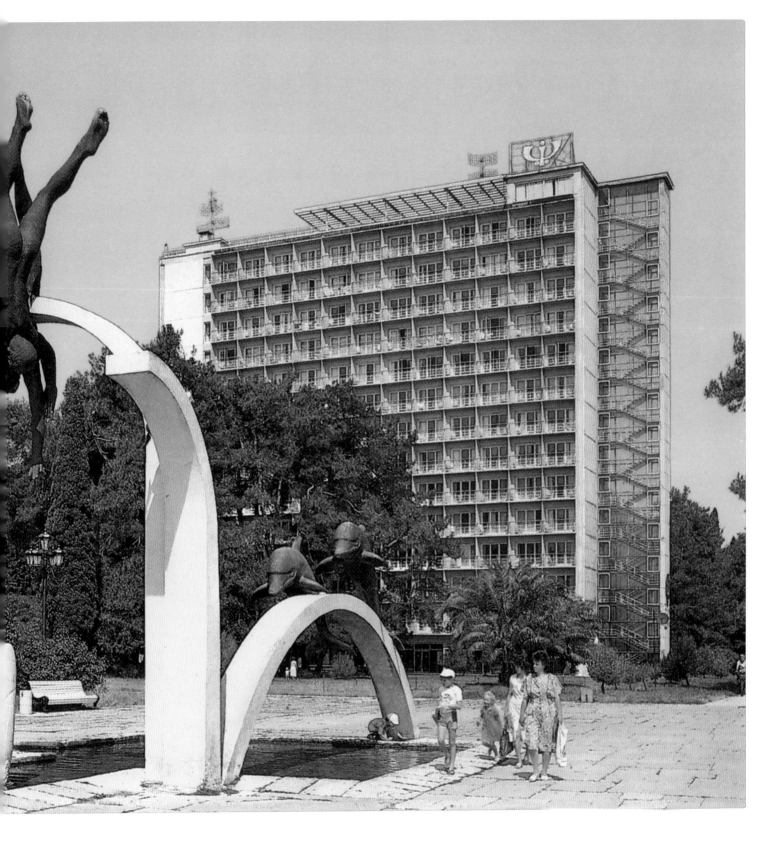

"We need the courage to move forward, not to look back so much."

Milana Vozba
Sukhum, Abkhazia, 2013

New Abkhazians

"Just imagine if it were modern and stylish...." sighs Milana Vozba, twenty-two. We are standing outside one of Pitsunda's high-rise hotels. In the background the surf breaks on the pebble beach, producing a pleasant soundscape. A handful of Russian tourists enjoy the spring sun. In early March it is already 71°F (22°C). "These buildings damage our country's reputation. Imagine, we have snow in the mountains and at the same time we have the sea. And can you smell the flowers?" Milana is as nationalistic as the other two hundred thousand inhabitants of this tiny country on the Black Sea, but she is also aware of the slow rate of change. "It's because our country is so isolated," she says, "and corrupt, and lazy. Our climate is too temperate and our soil too fertile. But there are advantages as well. Our long isolation means that we've had time to reflect on who we are and what we want. Everyone knows that nature is our calling card. While Sochi is being ruined, we've remained a paradise."

Milana belongs to the generation of Abkhazians—between ages twenty and forty—that looks outward. They have lived through the hard times at home, while abroad they have tasted open societies and education. "We respect everyone who fought in the 1992–93 war of independence against Georgia and we respect our elders—that's part of our culture. Georgia still won't officially say that it will never use violence against us again, but we need the courage to move forward, not to look back so much."

Angela Pataraya, twenty-five, calls herself "the last war generation." "The generations behind me didn't experience the war," she says. "They are concerned mainly with the latest fashions and phones. My generation doesn't care about that." She studied international relations and spent a year in California as part of an exchange program. She is now trying to find work with a peacekeeping NGO and frequently travels to Turkey to meet the Abkhazian diaspora, which has lived in Turkey for 150 years but might consider returning. She would, that's how much she loves her country.

Angela never misses an opportunity to point out how beautiful our surroundings are and how much potential they create for the country. As part of the same exchange program she also went to Tbilisi, Georgia. "Georgians are power hungry and arrogant," she says of the experience. She doesn't believe in any conciliation. "But hopefully we can be normal neighbors. They can come here on holiday if they want." She was young during the war. The thing she remembers most is macaroni with sugar. "It came from some emergency rations that were distributed in Gudauta [Abkhazia]." A Russian army base was located in Gudauta, so the city was spared heavy fighting, but Angela knows people who died.

In the garden of a sanatorium is a small statue of a man with a video camera. "That's my uncle," Angela tells us, "He was shot by a Georgian sniper. We now have our independence, but it came at a price. And we—the younger generation and those after us—must always remember that." She and her peers are reinventing their country. "The Soviet Union destroyed so much. I want to think, do, and dream Abkhazian. But I often think and dream in Russian and many of our traditions have been lost."

Some evenings we have dinner with Angela in Sukhum's Japanese restaurant, one of the symbols of this recovering country. It is an unlikely place, with DJs, wealthy Abkhazians, and reasonable food and drink.

"I hope that one day we'll be like Japan," Angela fantasizes. "Very modern, but also loyal to our own traditions." Her phone rings. She is called every ten minutes by men—brothers, we assume, but they could be nephews. "Security," Angela calls them. They check whether she is all right, where she is, and what she is doing. "Abkhazia is sometimes oppressive, but that's the way it should be. I absolutely want to marry an Abkhazian man and stay here."

A few days later we are sitting in our rented apartment in the center of Sukhum. We call Angela to go over the schedule and complain that the pizza delivery service has failed for the fourth time. Once again we eat yogurt and sausages from the late-night shop across the street. Half an hour later Angela calls us back. "Is this your house?" We hear honking. She and her security are outside. They pull a steaming pizza box from the back seat. "I told you it works," she says proudly.

Paradise Lost

The waves break on the pebble beach. The fountain has run dry. The state-owned hotels have been undergoing refurbishment for years, but no one can say when they will be finished. The smell of fresh shashlik and *khachapuri* cheese bread drifts from the village in the forest. Pitsunda is slowly recovering from the years of war and isolation, but no one seems in a hurry to prepare for the Games.

Pitsunda, Abkhazia, 2013

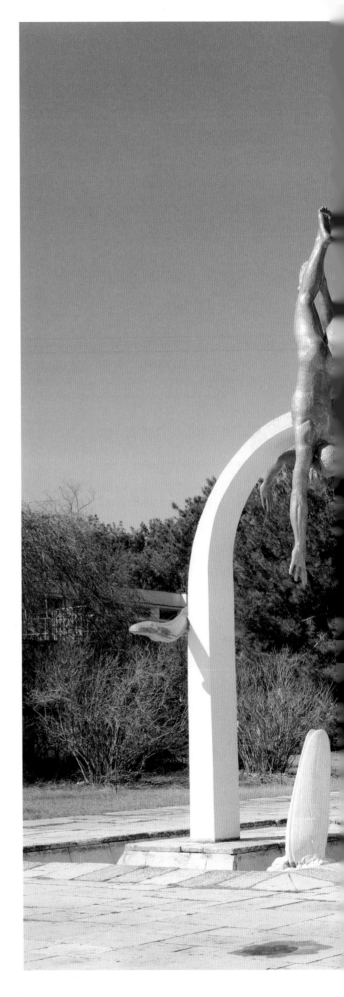

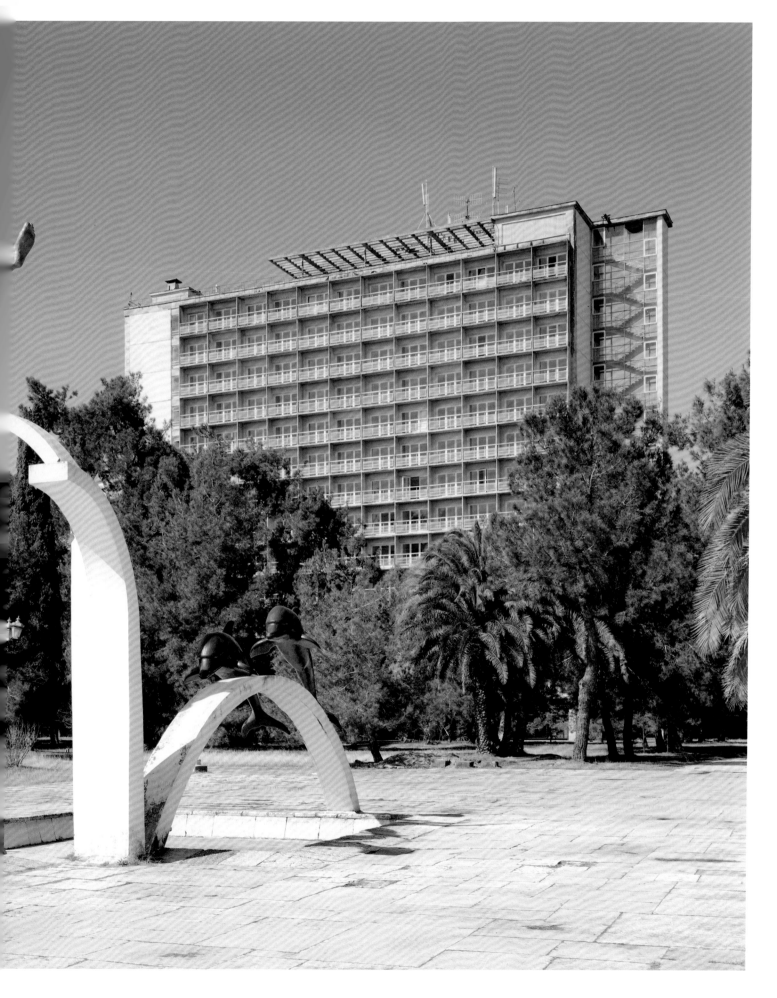

Akhra and Angela

Traveling through Abkhazia, we pass the
Kodori River. Akhra and Angela get out of
the car and show us the only place where the
Games have had an impact. A small factory
has been built in the river. Diggers scoop up
pebbles from the riverbed and deposit them
in waiting trucks. Once full, the trucks turn
onto the highway and head north to Sochi.
Akhra and Angela have mixed feelings about
the factory. It generates money, but at the same
time it destroys Abkhazia's most important
feature, its nature.

Kodori River, Abkhazia, 2013

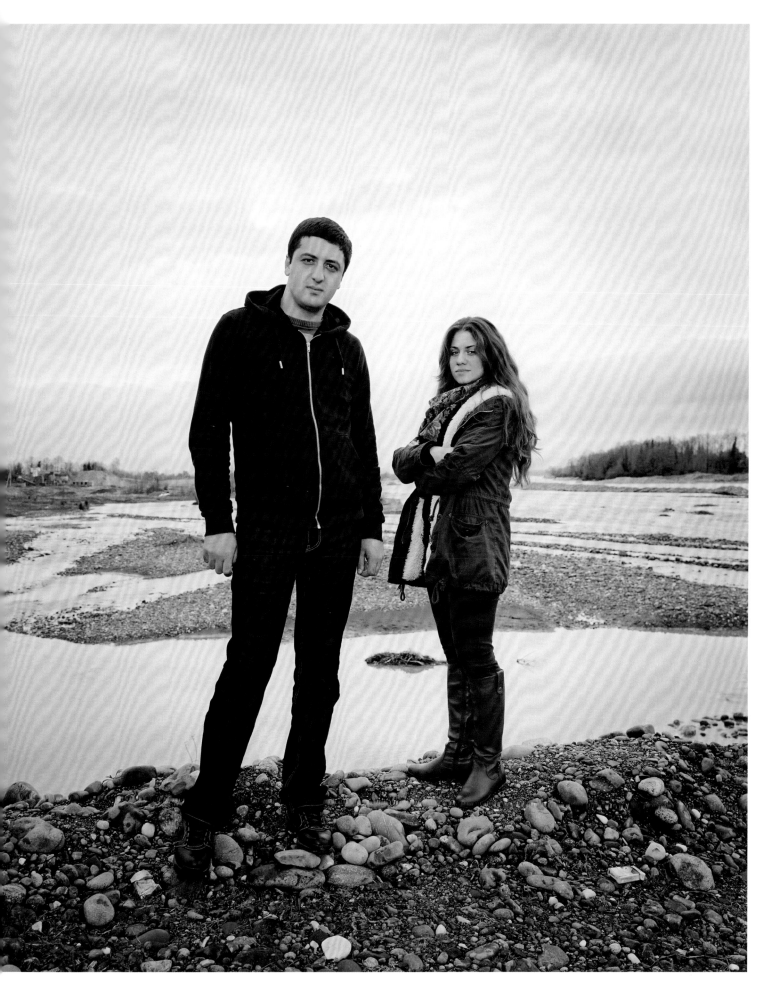

A Redundant Pier

The ferry terminal in the center of Sukhum is gradually being spruced up, and restaurants are appearing on the different decks of the concrete structure. When we took this photograph, regular ferry services were not yet running. Before the August War, which took place between Georgia and Russia in 2008, Georgian forces occasionally carried out patrols to intercept Abkhazian boats, making ferry travel treacherous. Abkhazians could risk getting to Sochi on a twice-daily ferry service from Gagra, a city north of Sukhum. Life in Abkhazia is slowly returning to normal. At the far end of the pier, two hundred meters into the sea, Café Apra is one of the signs that things in Sukhum are improving.

Sukhum, Abkhazia, 2010

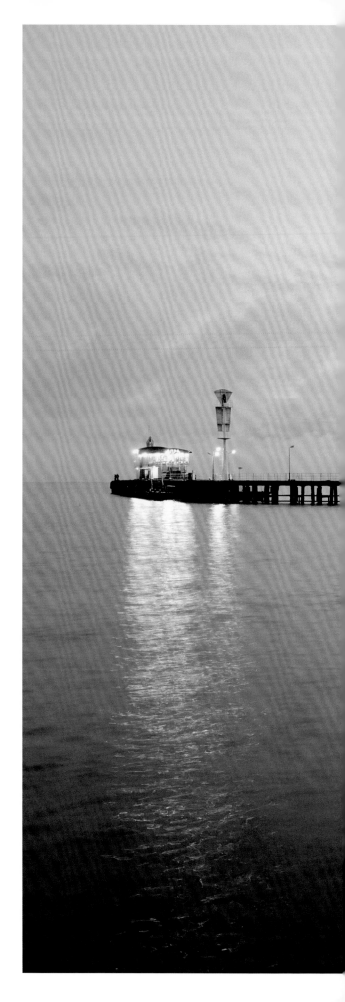

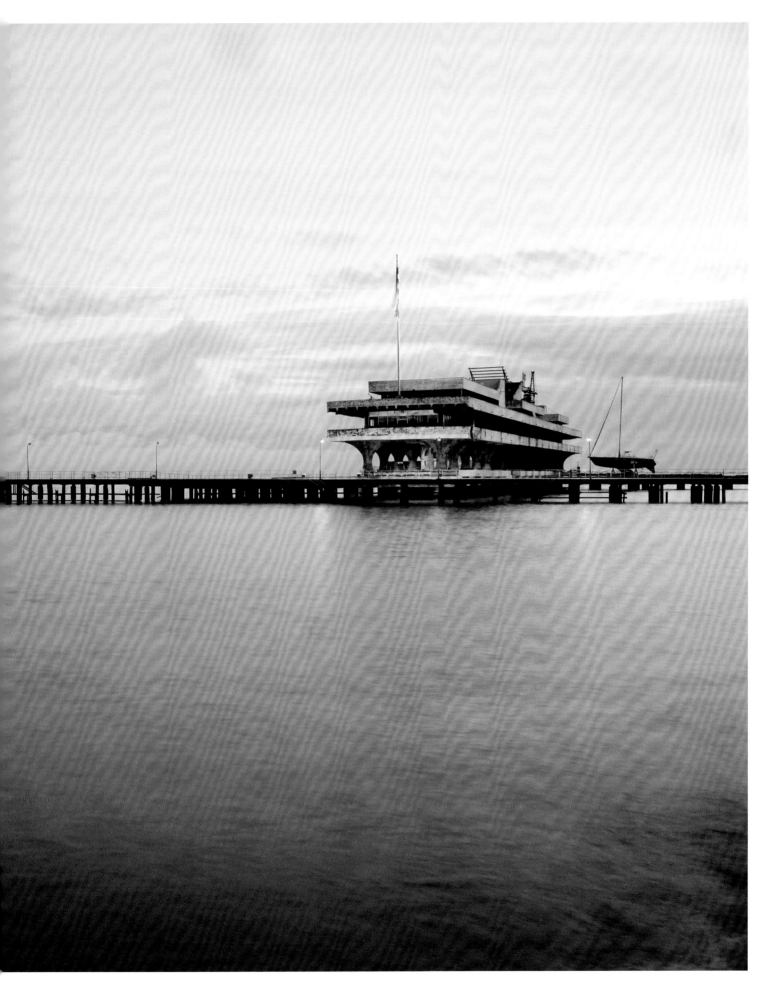

The Postmaster

The stately nineteenth-century post office lies on Prospektor Mira, the main street of the capital, Sukhum. As we walk in, two ladies look up with a startled air; they are not used to clients coming in. We want to send a postcard to Europe, we tell them. They shrug indifferently. They pull a bunch of stamps out of the cash register and give us the price in rubles. Can we use Abkhazian stamps? The women glare at us almost viciously through the window. Could we see the postmaster instead? We would like to learn the story behind this and are grateful for our journalists' alibi. A few minutes later we are led to the main office, past rooms with brown paneling, typewriters, the occasional computer, and a lot of indistinct green plants in large pots.

Eduard Konstantinovich Piliya, seventy-two, is the director of the Abkhazian Post Office. He receives us in his large office at the end of the hall. He apologizes for the fact that the tea lady has left, but grins broadly as he pulls a few glasses out of the cupboard. He screws the antenna off a cell phone that is lying on his desk and fills up our glasses with vodka. Cheers!

Eduard is way beyond retirement age, but his job has been kind of improvised for the last fifteen years. "Before the war I had more work," he admits frankly. "But since then I have published more than two hundred Abkhazian stamps!" He takes albums out of his wooden filing cabinet and leafs through them one by one. "These are true collector's items." He has stamps with animals, stamps with landscapes, stamps with Abkhazian heroes, and even a stamp with John Lennon on it. But he is most proud of the stamp that shows Abkhazia in the eighth century. "That's when we were at our greatest," he says proudly. These days he is just muddling along. He and his staff continue to collect mail, but people do not really send each other letters in Abkhazia. "They tend to visit each other instead," he says. "The country isn't that big."

Sukhum, Abkhazia, 2009

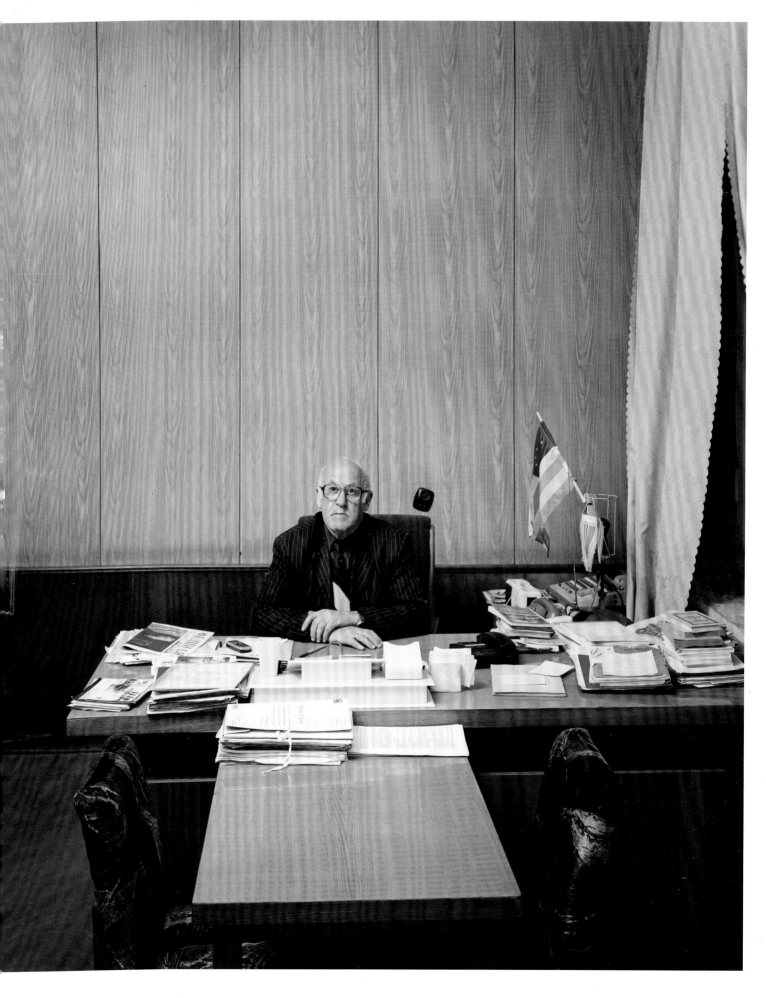

The Countryside

"I'll show you what our countryside looks like," Valentina says, having just met us in the cultural center in Gulripsh, a village to the south of Sukhum. "Life may not be as luxurious as it is in the city, but we have everything we need and we know how to celebrate that."

After a bumpy ride over Vladimirovka's sandy roads, we arrive at the home of eighty-five-year-old widower Mikhail Dzadzumiya, Valentina's great-uncle, and his bewildered family. We soon experience, in its deadliest form, how rural boredom combined with Abkhazian hospitality can get out of hand. While we are given a tour by Mikhail—a veteran of the Katyusha weapons factories near Moscow—we see a suspicious amount of activity in the kitchen. Less than fifteen minutes later we are drinking *chacha*, the grape drink so potent it disinfects the stomach, allowing us all to eat with our hands. At least, that's what we're told. There is always a reason to drink. Things deteriorate completely. Mikhail's granddaughter is excused from drinking; she is the youngest and serves us. The oldest—the widower—is the *tamada*, the toastmaster. He makes toasts to everything imaginable. His daughter and daughter-in-law maintain the pace by pointing sternly at our glasses if we don't drain them. The granddaughter, dressed in a red tracksuit, refills the glasses in a split second, with a satanically charming laugh. The *tamada* and Valentina start singing the Soviet song "Heart," from the film *Jolly Fellows*, which was shot in Abkhazia. Everyone joins in. We prepare to leave, but the drinking continues outside. More people arrive and join the carousing. We are toasted extensively. We start to find it embarrassing. In a moment of sobriety I try to calculate how many liters of *chacha*, champagne, cognac, and wine have already been consumed this afternoon. At least several salaries and pensions' worth. It is still light. "So this is the countryside," Valentina calls euphorically. The family gets upset when we admit defeat. "You have to stay," orders the girl in the red tracksuit, pouring us more red wine. Only when Mikhail, with a grandchild on his shoulder, keels over against a tree does something snap. The party momentarily comes to an end—long enough for us to say good-bye. We have survived. The following day we are utterly useless.

Vladimirovka, Abkhazia, 2009

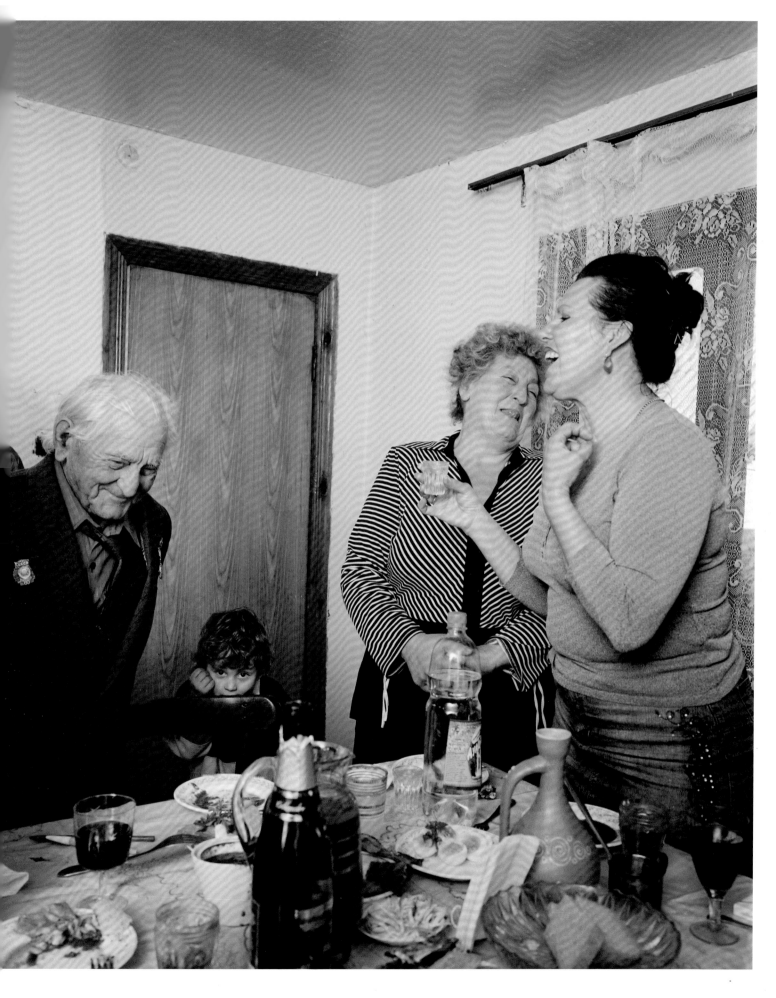

Abkhazia University

On the green hills above Sukhum lies
Abkhazia's university. Bit by bit it's being
renovated. In its worn down gymnasium
students train to become a sports teacher or
professional sportsman. Wistfully, in the
middle of the hall, the Olympic Rings hang.
For now, no sportsman will be able to represent Abkhazia in official international
contests.

Sukhum, Abkhazia, 2010

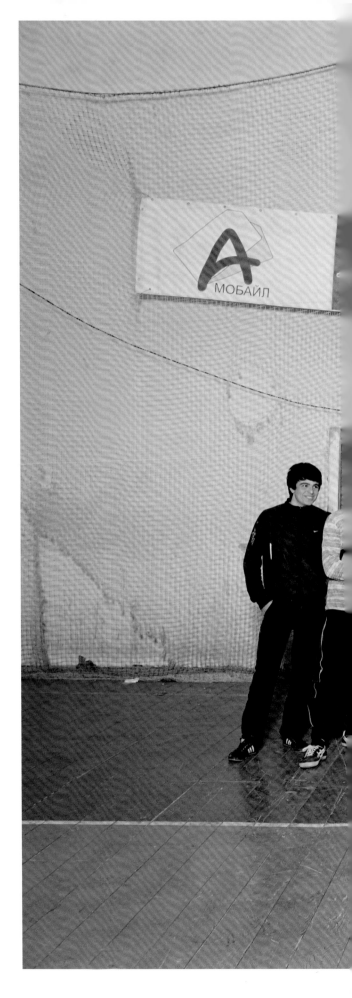

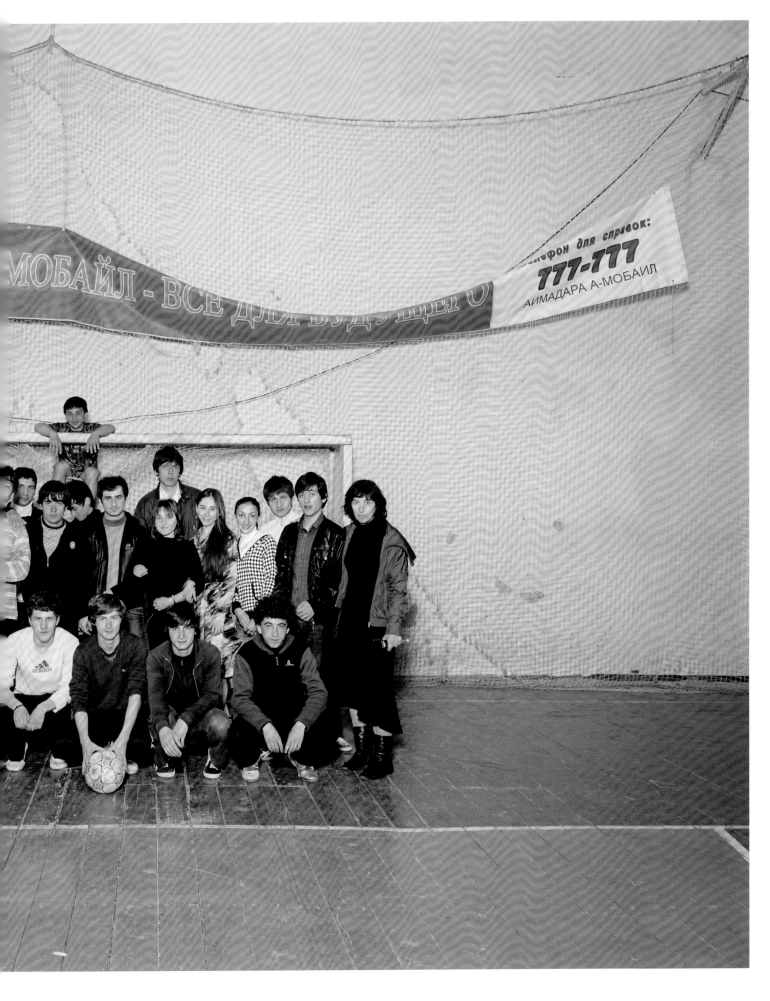

Abkhazia's Greatest Achievement

In the hills above Sukhum is a monkey laboratory, possibly the most popular tourist attraction in Abkhazia. It is a depressing place. Visitors are received by a small army of monkeys, who sit huddled in a dirty cage, carefully grooming one another. Others sit shivering on poles in separate enclosures. The buildings of the research institute loom in the background. Women in white nurses' uniforms carry troughs, mops, and brooms through the green streets. Cages protrude here and there from the buildings, and an occasional monkey hesitantly peers out at passersby.

Vladimir Spironovich is one of the researchers at the institute. He immediately discredits a story that has been circulating: in the Soviet era, monkeys were crossbred with people to create a super species with the intelligence of humans and the brute strength and dexterity of monkeys. It is a fantastical story, Spironovich admits, but he cannot emphasize enough: It. Is. Nonsense. "What we have done," he says proudly, "is help confirm important breakthroughs in global cancer research."

Somewhere behind one of the buildings is a rotting wooden platform. This is a historical site. In this installation, monkeys from the laboratory were subjected to extensive shaking and g-forces to prepare them for space travel. "We sent eight monkeys into space," Spironovich says with pride.

The institute is now reaching for a new frontier: using a Russian spacecraft to put the first monkey on Mars. "Humans can't yet handle the radiation on the journey," he says. Filled with compassion, we leave the monkeys behind us.

Sukhum, Abkhazia, 2010

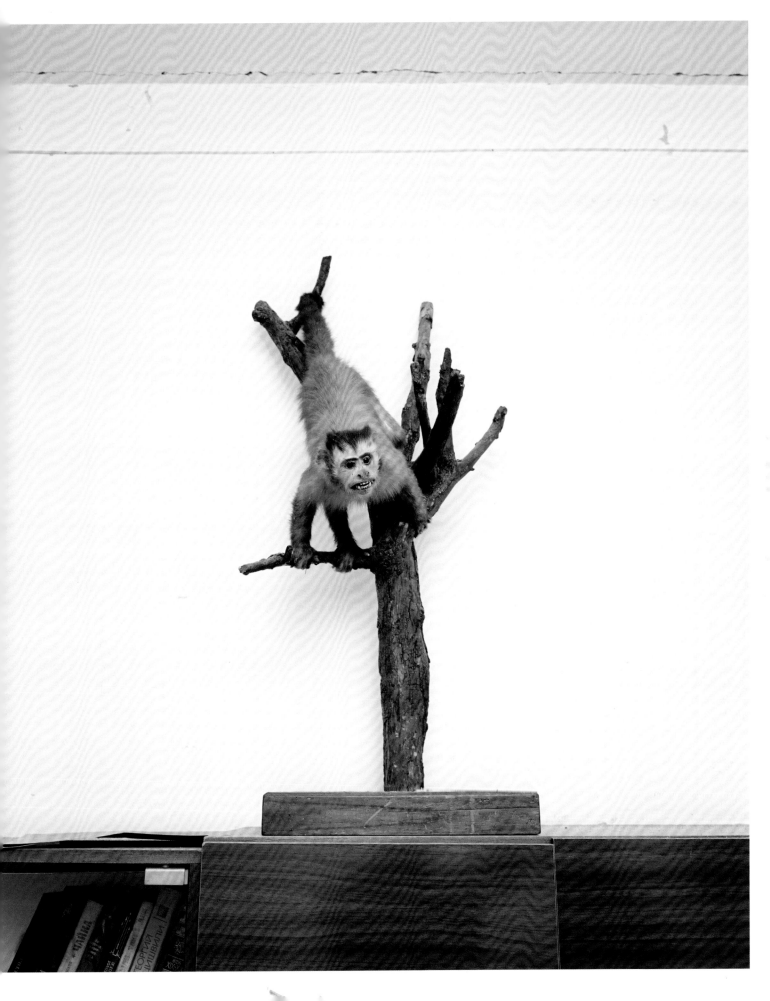

All Is Lost

Tatyana Petrovna, head of the Pathology and Physiology Department, sits in her office at the primate center.

Sukhum, Abkhazia, 2010

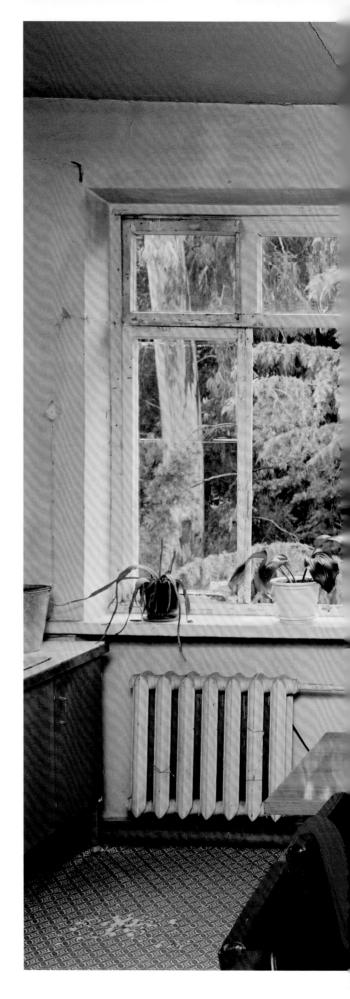

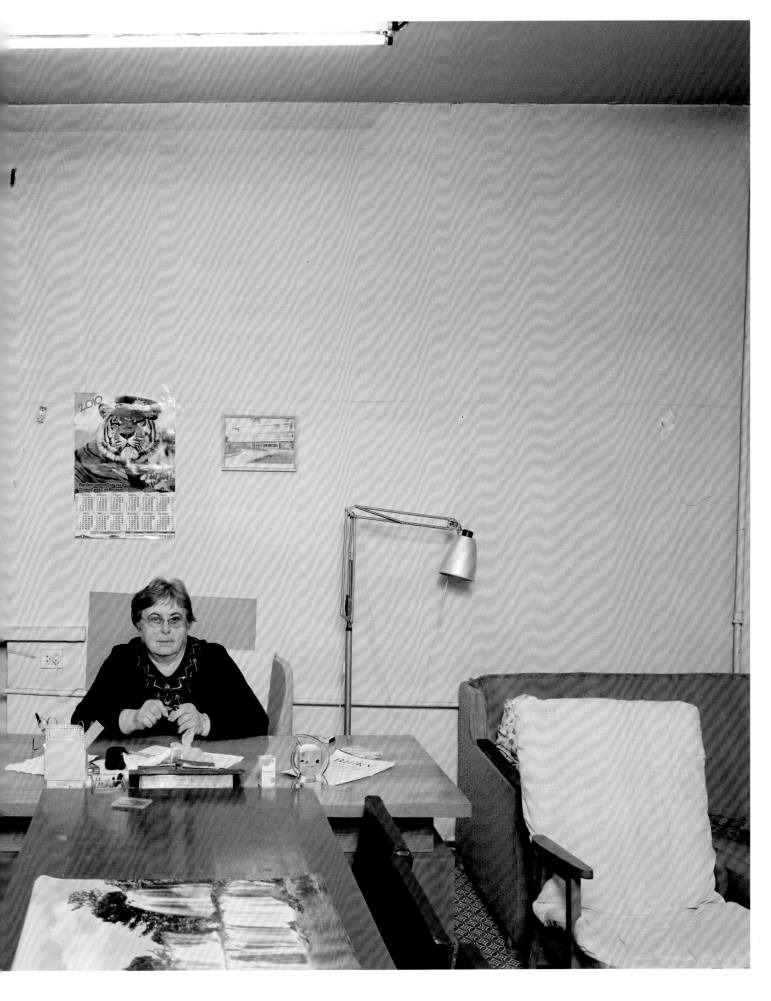

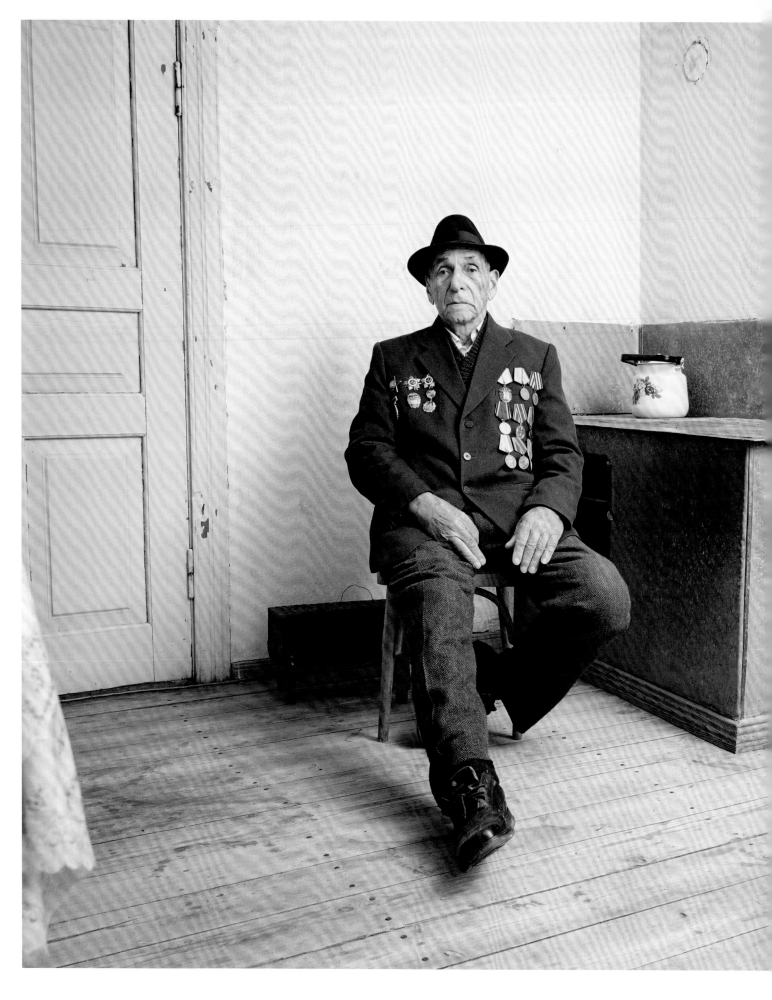

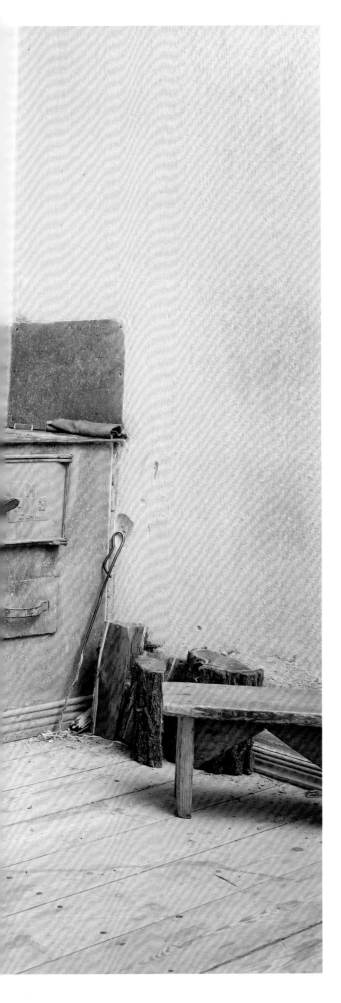

Nikolay Has Had Enough

Nikolay Yefremovich Zetunyan, eighty-eight, sits in his living room with a magnificent view of the Black Sea. Despite the subtropical climate and stunning location, most of the houses in Eshera are empty. During the war with Georgia in 1993, the ethnic Georgians were driven out of the village and the young men and women were killed in the fighting. Only a quarter of the population remains. There are simply not enough people to keep the village going, leaving it to fall into further disrepair. Nikolay is unconcerned. He believes that his time has come and he is making his own coffin.

Nizhny Eshera, Abkhazia, 2009

Peace at Last

Nikolay finally died in 2012, after struggling
with ill health for a year. His simple grave is
in Eshera's hilltop cemetery, overlooking
Sukhum. His house has been locked up and
abandoned. His wife lives with one of their
daughters some distance away. Once a year
someone comes to pick the mandarins in the
garden.

Nizhny Eshera, Abkhazia, 2010

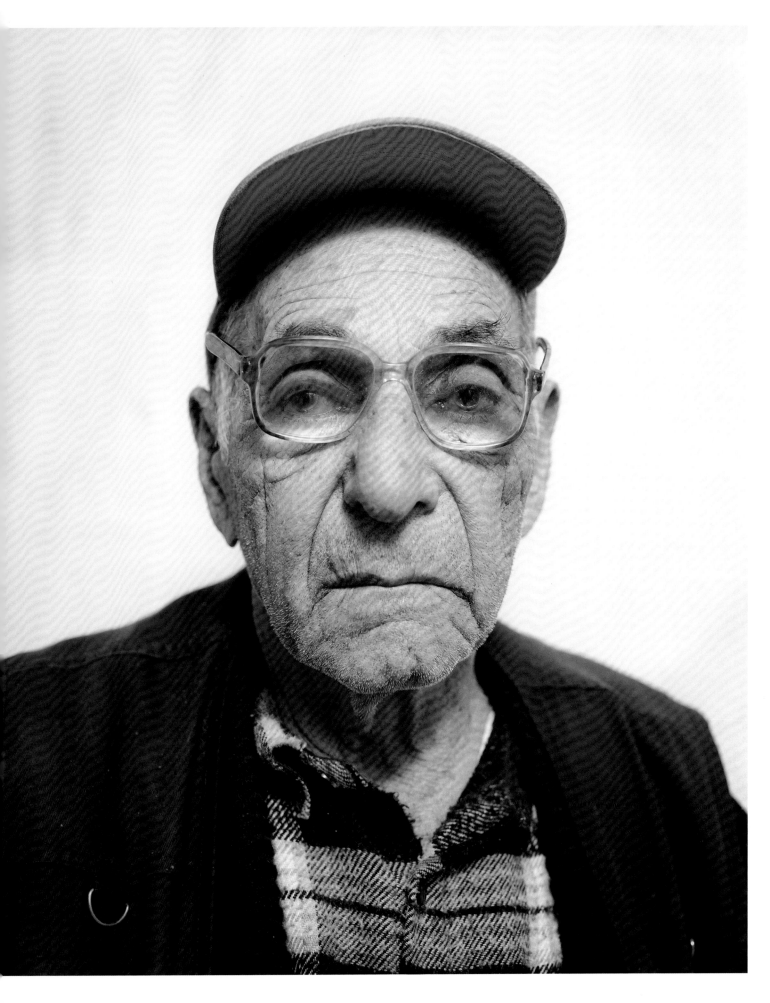

Diaspora

Nesdet Askin's ancestors fled Abkhazia
during the colonial wars that Russia waged
in the nineteenth century. His family has
since lived in Turkey for four generations,
but Nesdet remains strongly attached to his
Abkhazian roots. This picture shows Nesdet
and his siblings.

Kayseri, Turkey, 2010

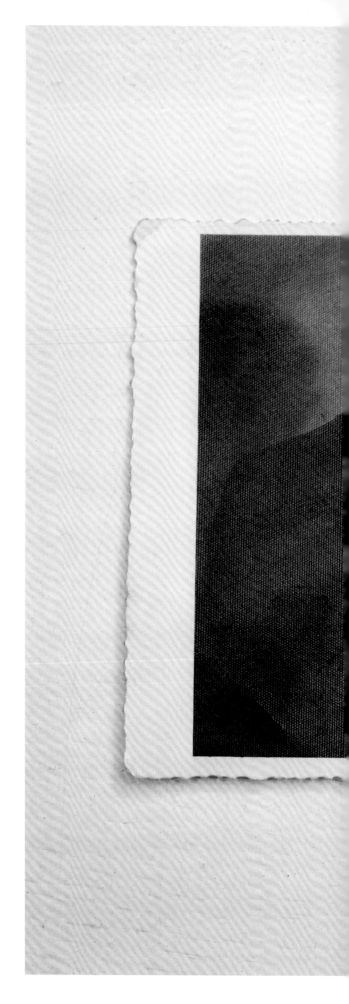

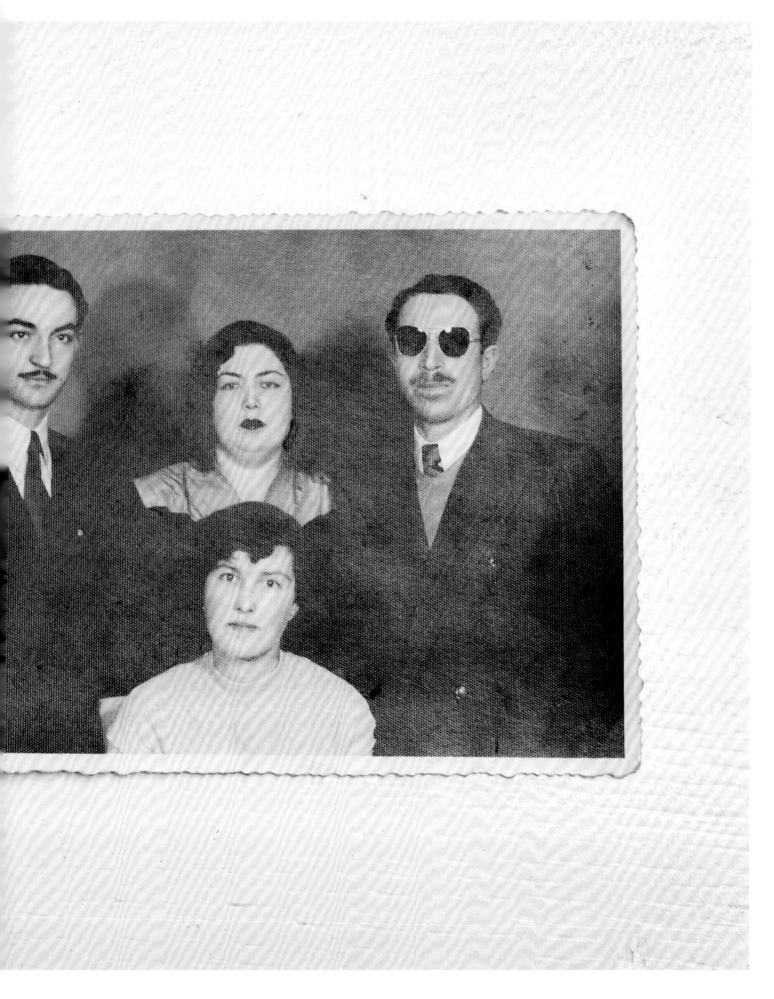

"There are two million people in the Abkhazian diaspora. If only a fraction of them come back, our future will be bright," the Abkhazian foreign minister said to us in 2007. We listened with disbelief. Yet on a subsequent trip through Turkey, we encounter Abkhazians everywhere: in Istanbul, Ankara, and the village of Kayseri on the arid plains of Uzunyayla. The villagers talk with ease about the Caucasus, about the problems in Abkhazia; they tell us their family histories, but they seem Turkish to the core. We can detect no trace of the Caucasus. That is until they take us to their cultural centers: we see green Circassian flags and banners showing the Abkhazian hand, as well as traditional dance dresses, mountain costumes, and all the accompanying accessories. Old photographs were used to reproduce daggers and swords, revolvers and patterns in an effort to maintain some kind of link with the motherland. Turkish Abkhazians romanticize their tiny country; how it stood up to the much larger Georgia—the Turks themselves contributed weapons and manpower. They romanticize the fighting spirit, the dances, and the music. It appears at first glance to be homesickness, but it is more often self-affirmation, similar to how immigrant groups in the United States have cultivated their roots. How many Irish Americans ever returned permanently to Ireland?

If these Abkhazians did return, the empty country would quickly become densely populated. All the abandoned homes of the displaced Georgians would be insufficient to accommodate the influx. But the chance of that happening, which Abkhazia so longs for, seems small. "Our graves and the graves of our recent ancestors are here," says the Turkish Abkhazian Ayyund. "We've worked hard for these houses. This is our motherland now."

Kayseri, Turkey, 2010

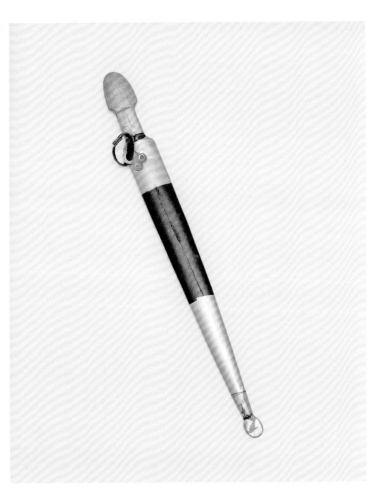
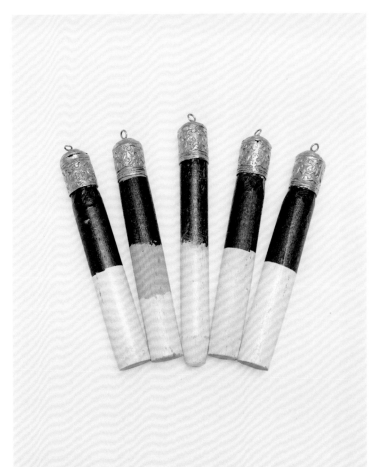
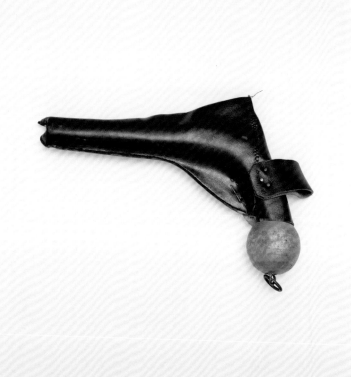
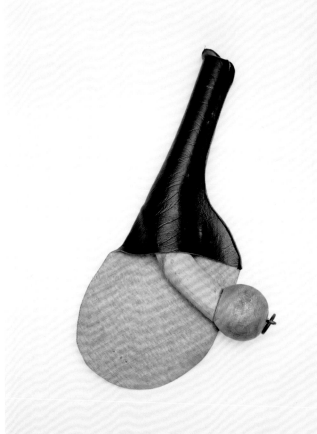

TB in Abkhazia

Vladislav Vladimirovich Demyanov, sixty-three, is a true *Homo Sovieticus*. He was born in Western Ukraine and raised in Omsk. His parents were war veterans and celebrated musicians in a Red Army orchestra. "As a child I traveled all over the place," he says. When he started high school he moved in with relatives, but by the age of thirteen he had already seen the inside of a juvenile prison, for what he claims was a minor offense. "It was the first of thirty-eight years I would spend in prison," he laughs. It was there and in the labor camps that he learned the tricks of the crook's trade. He had tattoos of Lenin and Stalin inked on his chest. "In Russia you have Putin and the state, and then you have the thieves. They have their own laws and their own state. If people have problems, we can solve them—for a ten-percent commission. The police can't do that."

Demyanov first contracted tuberculosis in a prison camp in 1977. In 1988, in yet another camp, he caught his current strain of the disease, multidrug-resistant TB, for which he is being treated in a hospital through a program run by Médecins Sans Frontières. Treatment for MDR-TB can take more than three years and offers no guarantee of a cure. Demyanov loves Abkhazia, where he has lived since the war. He is now looking forward to being discharged, and he hopes to elope with a young, ideally seventeen-year-old, girl.

Gulripsh, Abkhazia, 2009

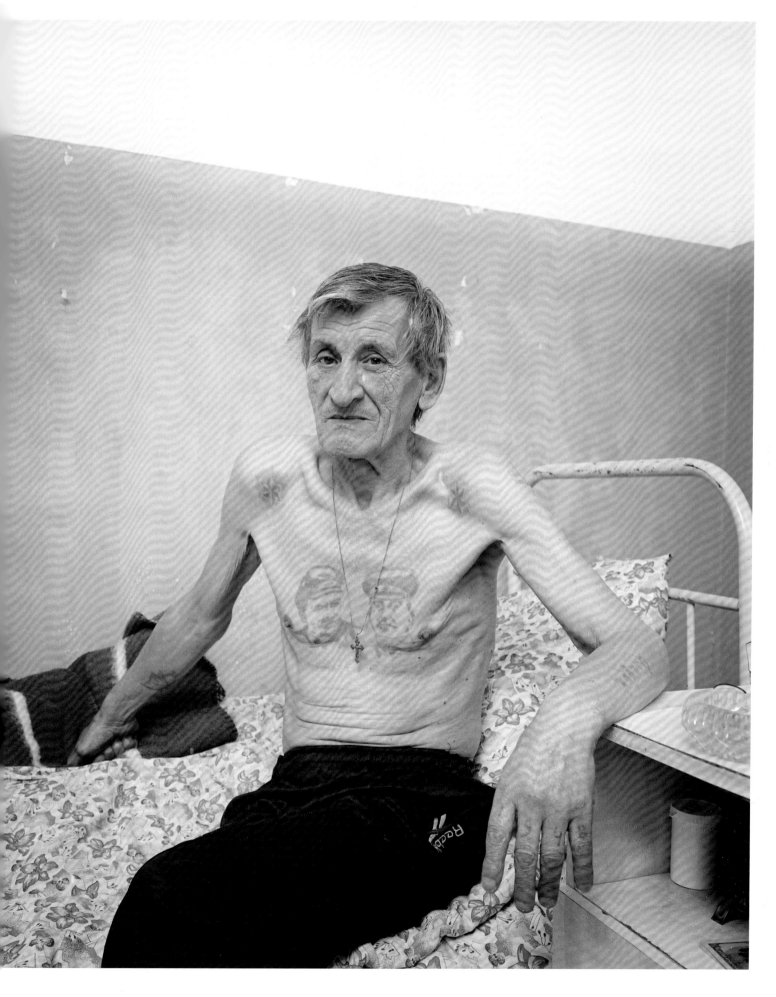

"Georgia can't give up Abkhazia, just like you can't give up your liver."

Gogo Khaindrava
Tbilisi, Georgia, 2007

The Train Has Stopped Running

Ochamchira was one of the many stops on the long train ride from Moscow to Baku, Azerbaijan. The train crossed the mountains at Krasnodar, headed toward Sochi. From there, it continued to Sukhum, then on to Ochamchira, Zugdidi, and across the mountains again toward Tbilisi. That route no longer exists. Ochamchira is now the last stop before no-man's-land, the demilitarized zone patrolled by United Nations troops until the war in 2008. The railroad tracks are overgrown or broken. The bridge over the river to Georgia, across which tens of thousands of refugees once fled in the space of a few days, has been destroyed and is now used only by smugglers.

In the pretty, light-blue train station—which appears to have been built sometime in the 1950s—the ceiling has collapsed. A Russian freight train is bringing building materials: Russia wants to repair the track to serve its nearby army base.

Ochamchira, Abkhazia, 2010

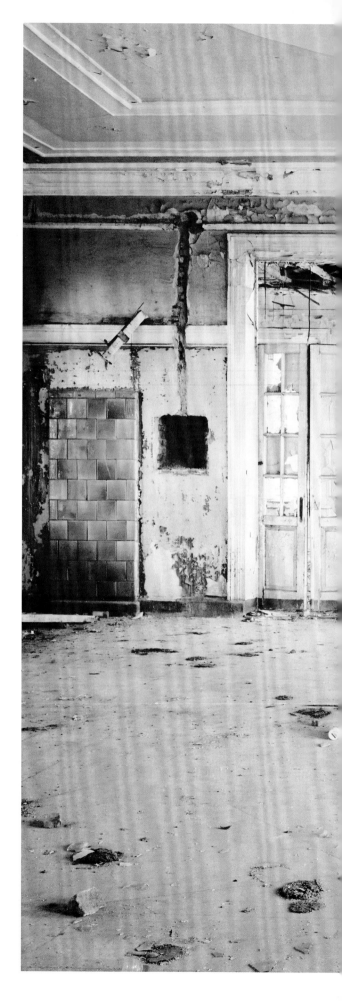

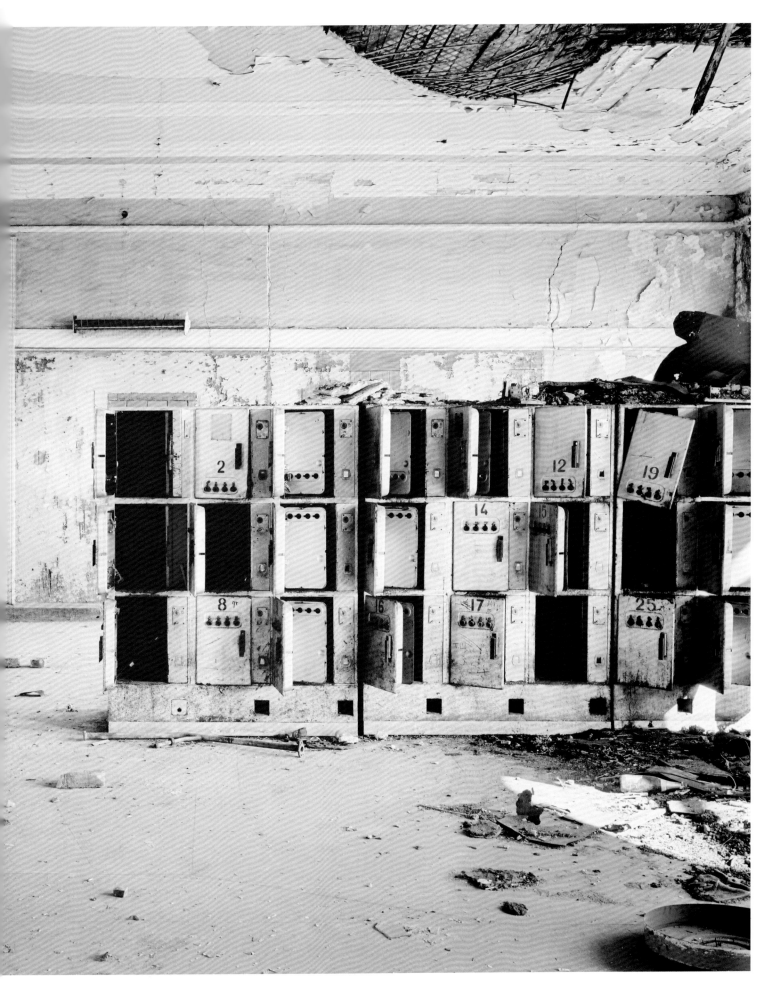

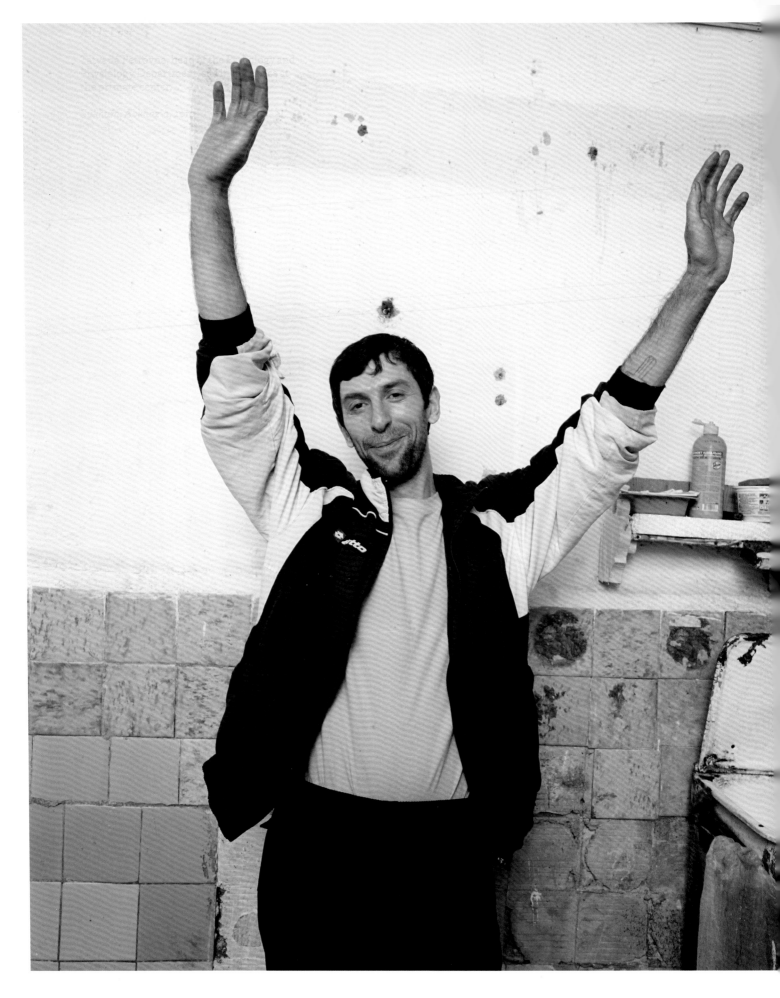

The Only Prison

Roman the cook is the only prisoner we are allowed to photograph in Abkhazia's only prison, Dranda. The other inmates are locked up in cells of which we are given a brief glimpse. We see large rooms with beds, mattresses, and a small heater. Dozens of men lie around, sit on the beds, and stare at us rather wildly. It is the kind of prison you would imagine in a place like this. Only the orthodox chapel is new. "The prisoners sing here every Sunday," says the guard who shows us around. The majority of the cells are empty, as they have yet to be renovated. "Most of the prisoners are in here for theft, murder, or drugs," he says. One of the most notorious cases is a man who stoned a Russian couple to death. The perpetrator is incarcerated here, as are all Abkhazian prisoners—265 at the time of our visit in 2010. "We can accommodate eight hundred," says the director, "but fortunately the crime rate in our country is falling."

Roman is delighted with the unusual visit from foreigners. Outside the prison gates is a row of stalls, where visitors can buy fresh ingredients for their friends or relatives inside. This is how the kitchen accesses good meat and herbs such as parsley. Roman gives the contents of one of the shiny new cauldrons another stir with his ladle and dishes up plates of fresh *plov*. "Life here isn't so bad," he says. "We cook three times a day, and the guards don't beat us."

Dranda, Abkhazia, 2010

Plov, Uzbek-Style

Roman uses parsley in the *plov*, an Uzbek
rice dish that he cooks every day for his
fellow prisoners. "Coriander would be
better," he says, "but try getting hold of that
in here."

Dranda, Abkhazia, 2010

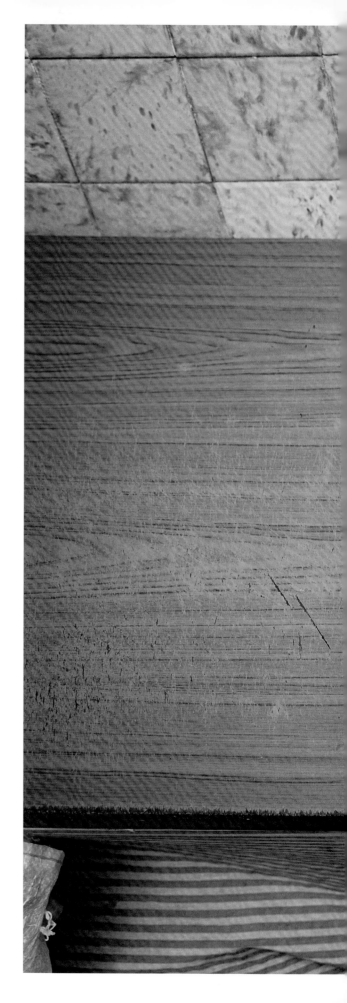

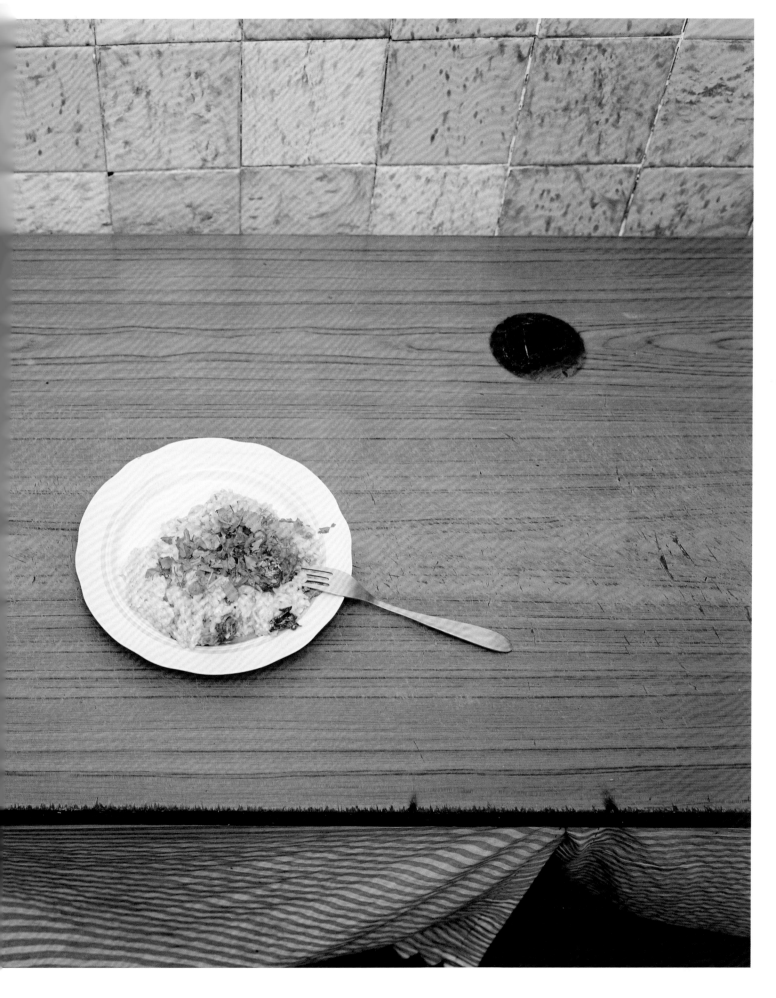

Novi Raion

The last addition to Sukhum before the war was Novi Raion ("new neighborhood"), a spacious suburb of relatively luxurious apartments. It was a popular place to live until fighting broke out and it was caught between the Abkhazian and Georgian fronts. It has been largely neglected in the twenty years since the conflict. Those who could moved away; those who stayed often live without water and gas, surrounded by burned-out or abandoned buildings.

Sukhum, Abkhazia, 2009

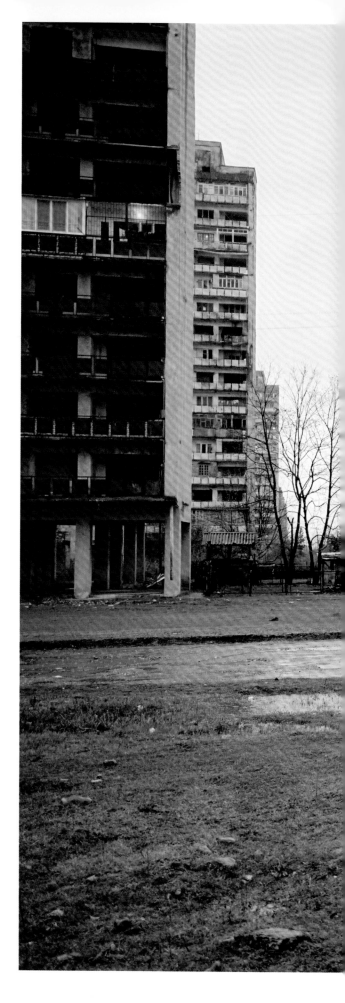

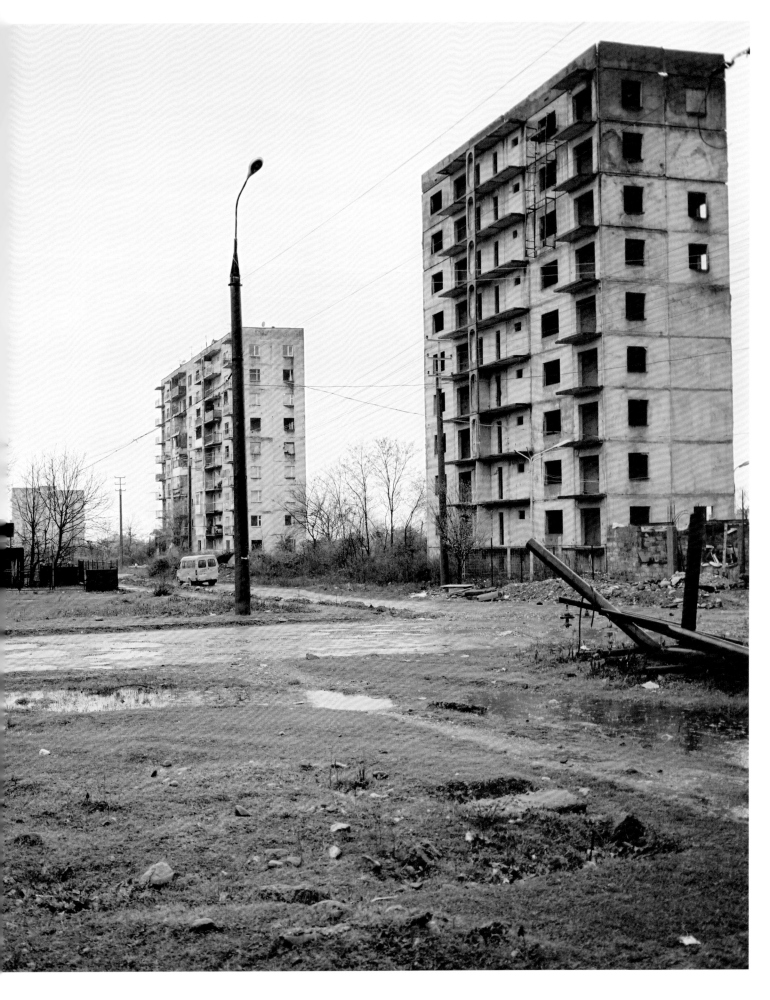

New Novi Raion

During our fourth and last visit to Abkhazia, renovations in Novi Raion are underway—slowly but unmistakenly. Small restaurants appear, newly built private houses, and one of the large, flat buildings—distinctive for this area of town—has even been rebuilt.

Sukhum, Abkhazia, 2013

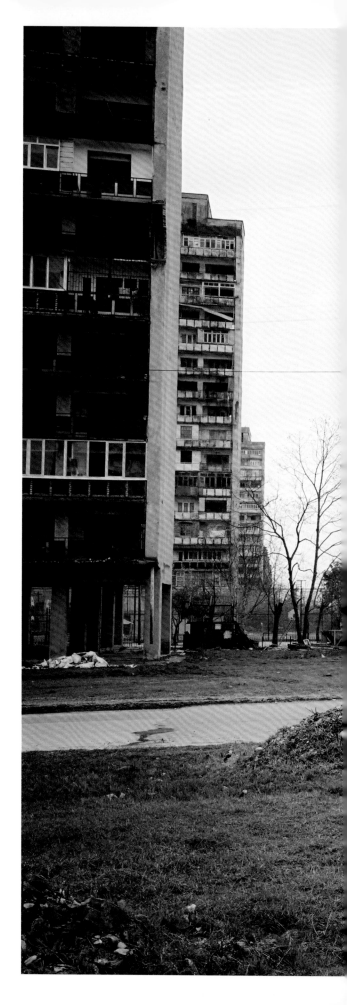

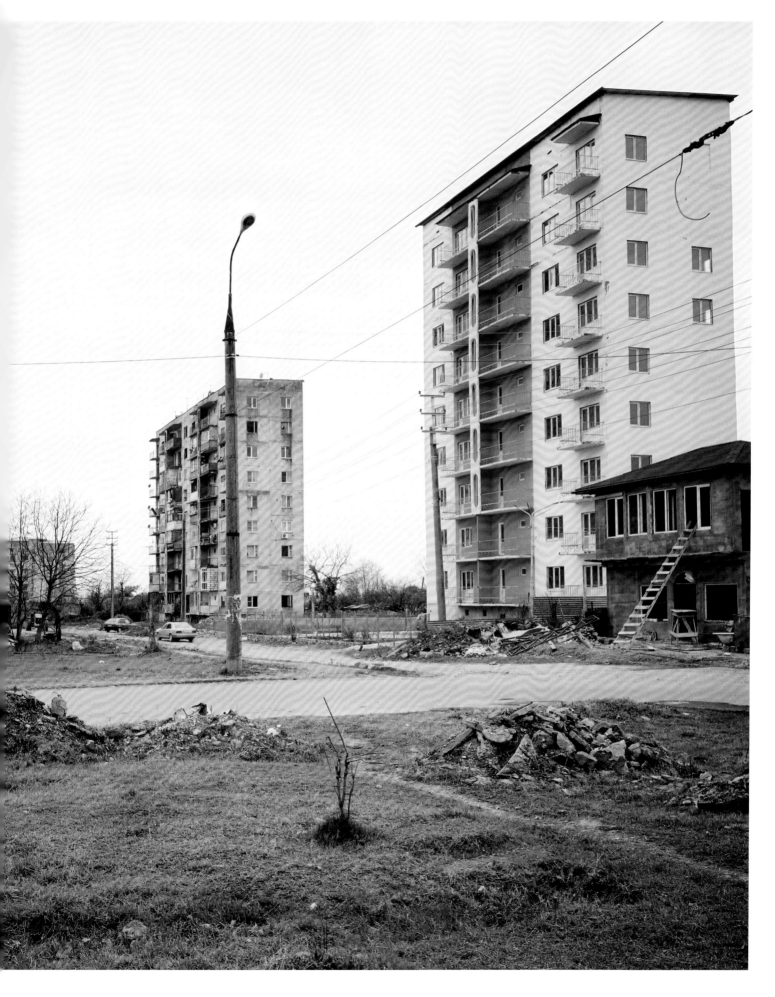

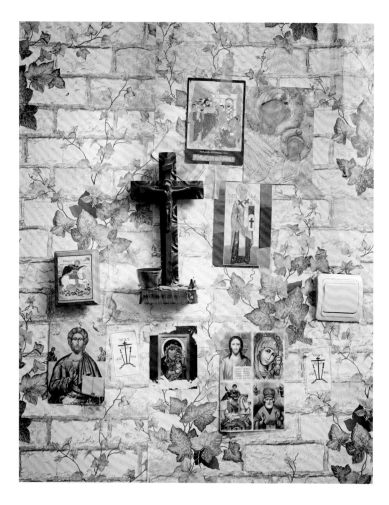
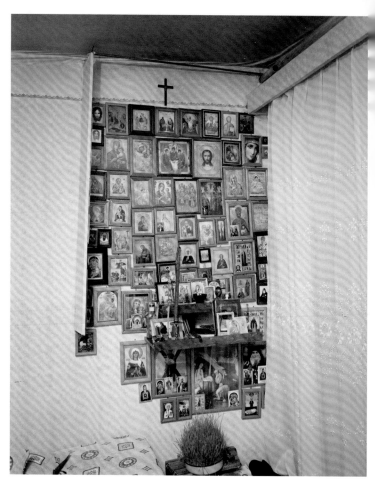
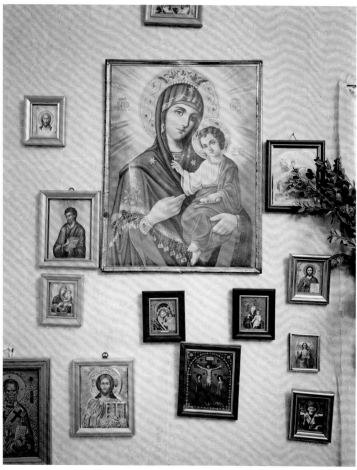
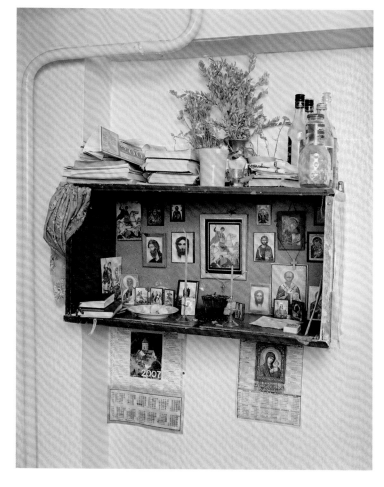

Praying for a Lost Paradise

Small altars adorn the rooms of Abkhazian refugees.

Tbilisi, Georgia, 2007–10

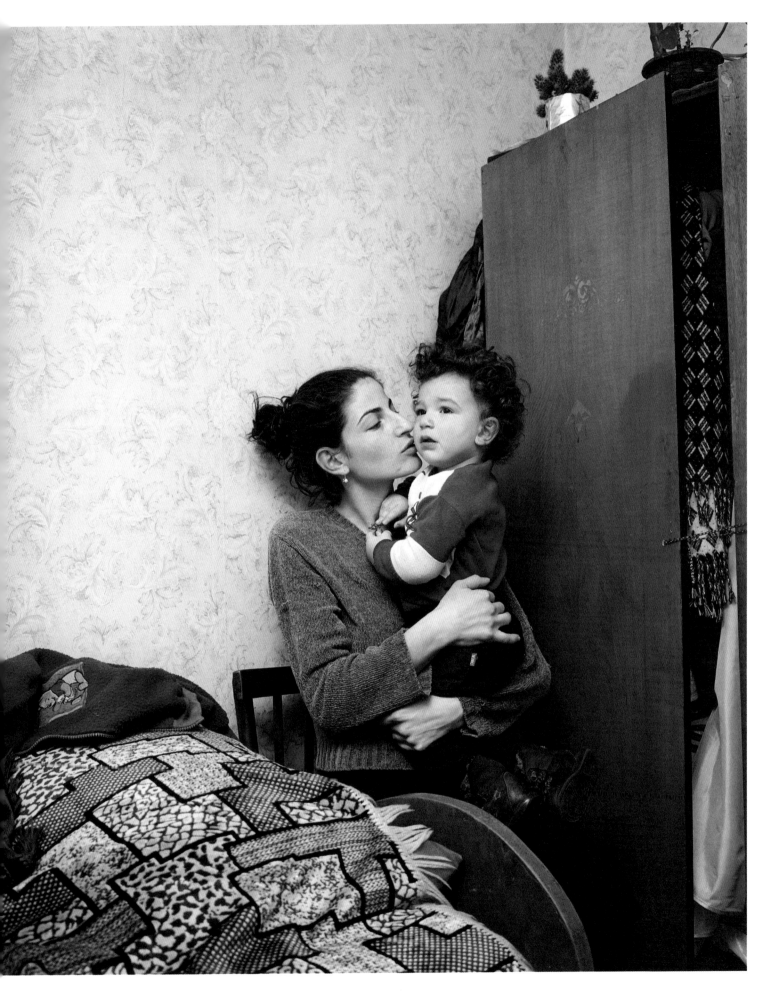

"Abkhazia seems farther away than ever."

Ketevan Gamisonia
Tbilisi, Georgia, 2013

Georgian Refugees

Twenty years after the war, when over two hundred thousand Abkhazian Georgians fled to Georgia, the lion's share of the refugees still lives in deplorable conditions, crowded into old schools, hotels, and communal apartments. Every Georgian president since 1993 has promised to end the frozen conflict so that the refugees can return home. That scenario seems increasingly unlikely, however, since the war between Georgia and Russia in 2008. Russia now recognizes Abkhazia as an independent country, and Russian troops guard Abkhazia's border with Georgia.

In one of Tbilisi's suburbs, two student apartment blocks are separated from the university by a deep ravine. The cable cars that once trundled back and forth between the two sides now dangle idly in the middle. The apartments' balconies have been sealed shut with scrap wood and agricultural plastic to create extra rooms—much-needed spaces for the large families who live here. The apartments can only be reached via endless concrete stairs. The electricity works for four hours a day and low pressure means that the upper floors have no running water. Outside, men trudge to and fro with garbage bags. In the parking lot they heap the garbage into piles and set it on fire. Residents have stuck a poster next to the exit of the complex. It reads "Auschwitz, building IV."

Although physically removed from their homeland, the Abkhazian refugees still dream of their land of milk and honey, the subtropical country of palms and mandarin trees on the Black Sea.

We are taken from apartment to apartment and, like the Pied Piper of Hamelin, the procession of curious children behind us keeps growing. In the late afternoon we visit eighty-four-year-old Ekaterina Dwaladze, who shares her small room with her daughter and son-in-law. She sits on her bed, opposite a small shrine. We tell her about our experiences in Abkhazia, about the people we met, and how the country looks today. She was a German teacher in Sukhum, she tells us. She uncorks a bottle of *chacha*, the headache-inducing and incredibly potent grape drink that is consumed whenever guests arrive. It makes the temperature more bearable—on the sixth floor in wintery Tbilisi the heaters are unable to compete with the cold. Through the windows we see the frost creeping up the hills; the worst is yet to come.

Ekaterina talks in German about her life. Her stories are familiar: Abkhazia as a small paradise, with its beautiful plants and trees and the ocean a short walk away; the mandarins in the garden, the porch around the house; the war they had all seen coming, but had never expected to be so devastating; her husband who had died of a heart attack the night before she fled. She refills our glasses as she speaks and keeps inventing reasons to drink another toast: to us, to good health, to The Netherlands, to the dead, to Abkhazia. She insists that we drain our glasses, while excusing herself with a small sip for each toast.

She dreams of Abkhazia every night. The last thing she wants is to die in this apartment in Tbilisi. The neighbors join us and several glasses later we are engulfed by the emotional stories of so many lost lives. All the children under fourteen, and there are many of them, were born as refugees.

Few people succeed in escaping refugee status. A handful work in construction or find jobs in a shop or market. The refugees have only had full Georgian citizenship since 2006. Prior to that, as displaced residents of Abkhazia, they were virtually excluded and could only vote for Abkhazia's de jure government—a president and several ministers in a suburb of Tbilisi—designed to keep pressure on Abkhazia.

We return three years after our first visit. It is distressing to see that the situation has not improved for any of them. Ekaterina, who had longed to go back to Abkhazia before she died, has passed away. Ketevan, one of the neighbors with whom we had raised a toast, had found Ekaterina in her room a few weeks earlier. Little seems to have changed for Ketevan either. She has had another child. We take another photograph of Ketevan in exactly the same place. It is only after we develop the photographs that we notice the differences. In those three years, the wallpaper and closet have been replaced. Her husband is a taxi driver, a job that everyone around Tbilisi with access to a car has. She is suffering from hepatitis B and requires expensive medical treatments, but money is scarce and it is unlikely that her financial situation will improve any time soon.

Another three years and the apartments are in an even worse condition. More electric cables have been slung through the hallways—a potential deathtrap in combination with the leaking ceilings. New walls have been erected in several empty walkways to create improvised apartments; the building seems to be getting fuller rather than emptier. Ketevan is doing better. She works long hours for a realtor and has recovered from hepatitis. This is our third visit and the third time we have seen new wallpaper in the house. There are new closets, a large flat-screen TV and the children are healthy and happy. Ketevan and her family now own their apartment, she says, what little good that will do them. Who would want to buy it? Few people manage to escape refugee status: the country is too poor and the opportunities too limited. And Abkhazia? That seems farther away than ever.

Ketevan and Ana

Tbilisi, Georgia, 2010

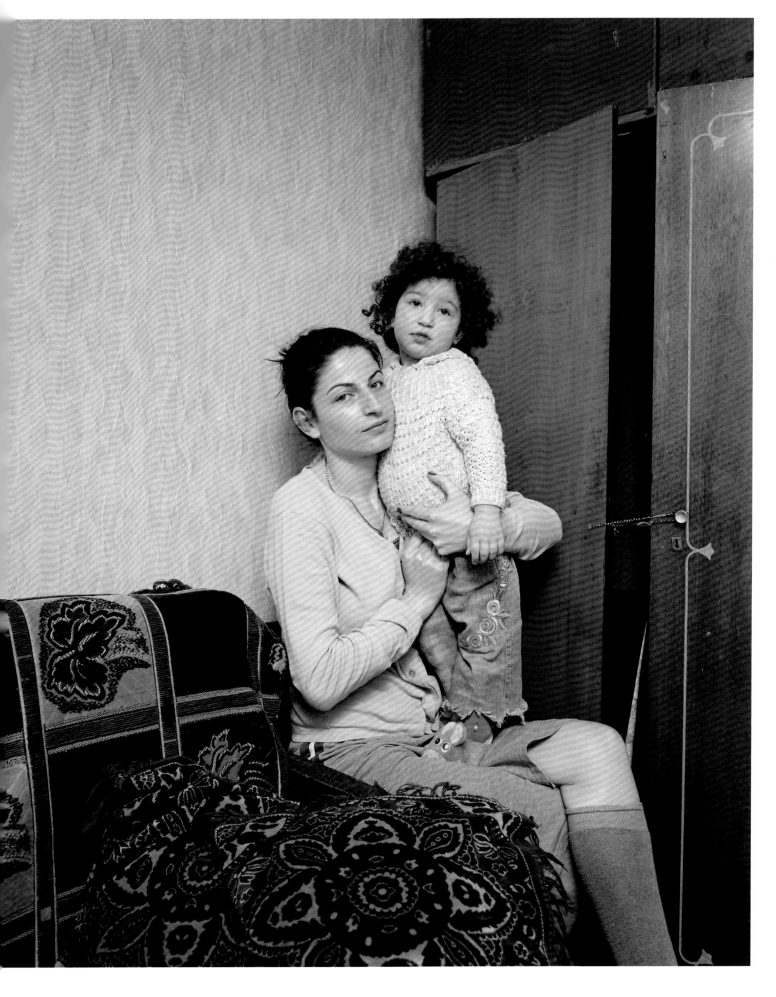

Glorious Past

This was once an orphanage to be proud of.
You could call it a mansion, situated a few
kilometers outside of the Georgian resort
town Batumi. With a good car, it takes more
than an hour to crawl up into the hills along
the poorly maintained, winding roads, but at
the end of the journey you are rewarded with
a fabulous view of the Black Sea and this
palatial orphanage. Since 1993 more refugees
from Abkhazia than orphans have lived here.
The building is slowly collapsing and the
refugees will have to find a new life, far from
the grapes and other fruit that grow in the
garden. But escaping the life of a refugee is
not easy.

Chakva, Georgia, 2010

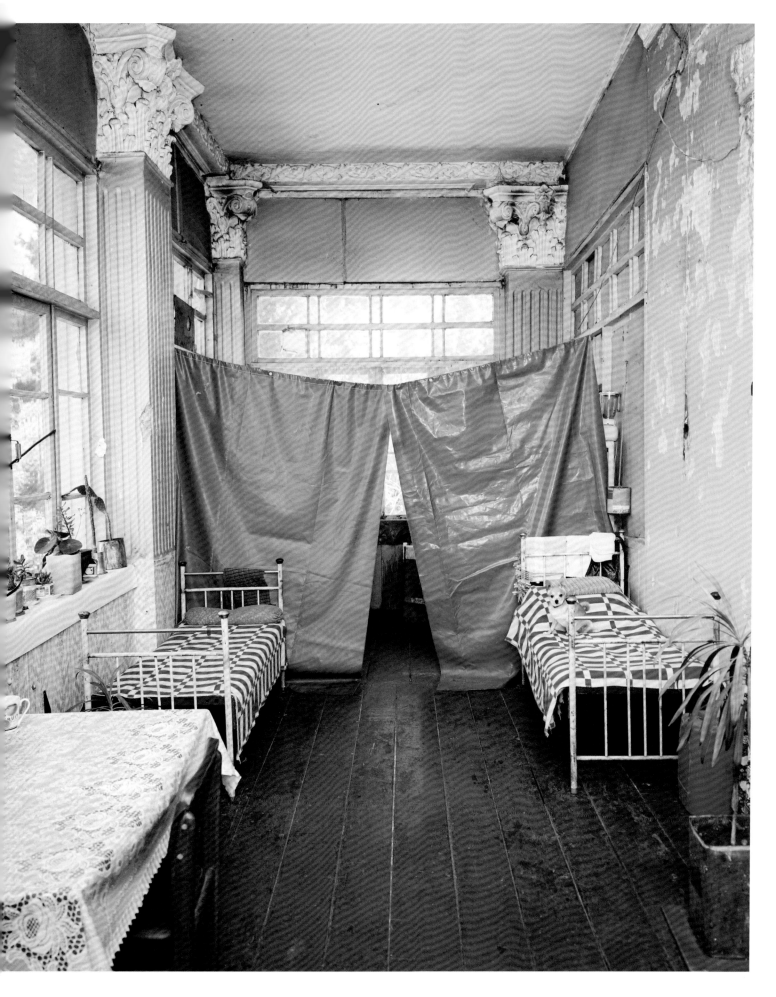

A Stone's Throw Away

On the other side of the river from Shamgona Island is Abkhazia. Sviadi and Lexo, two Georgian soldiers, crawl toward the riverbank and check that everything is as it should be. It says "police" on their uniforms, but also "special forces," in English. The grenades and automatic rifles suggest that they belong to the latter. At their signal we walk cautiously to a copse where we have a good view of the river. We look out at Abkhazia's Gali region and smoke a cigarette. Sviadi then gestures that we should be quiet. Very faintly we hear talking and the sound of an engine across the river. "Russians," he warns. I look through one of the soldier's binoculars. On the other bank is a small guardhouse. Perhaps someone inside is looking back at us. It is strange to look so covertly and conspiratorially at a country where a short time ago we were walking around freely.

Shamgona Island is still crowded with refugees. In Georgia it often feels as if time has stood still since they made their escape. These people fled in 1993 and turned the first school or hotel that they came to into a shelter. They slowly spread out across the country, first here, then to the cities of Zugdidi, Poti, and Kutaisi. "We thought it was temporary," says Mimoza Khurtsiluva, fifty-four, who gives us a tour of a blue wooden building that housed a kindergarten in the fifties. The building stands on stilts. You can see through the floor to the ground below. "We've now lived here for eighteen years. We get along with each other, but you also hear noises that you don't want to hear, and if I shake my head, the whole building shakes with me." The refugees receive thirty lari (about eighteen dollars) per month. There is little employment, so they help out on the land or run small stores at the side of the road. In an already impoverished country such as Georgia, refugees have even less chance of improving their situation.

Shamgona Island, Georgia, 2010

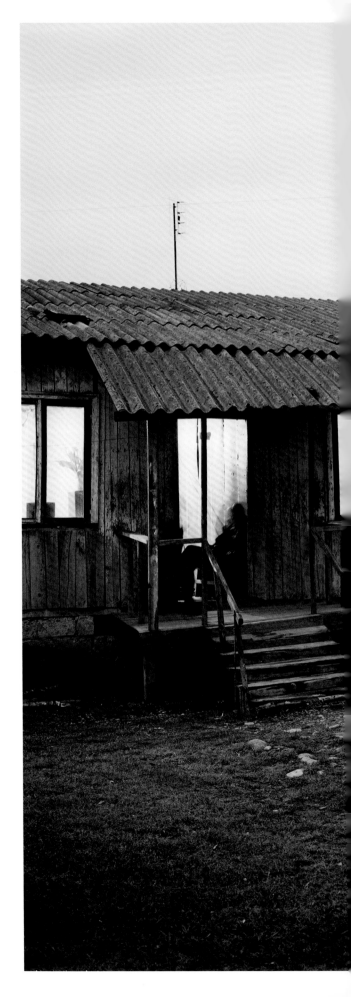

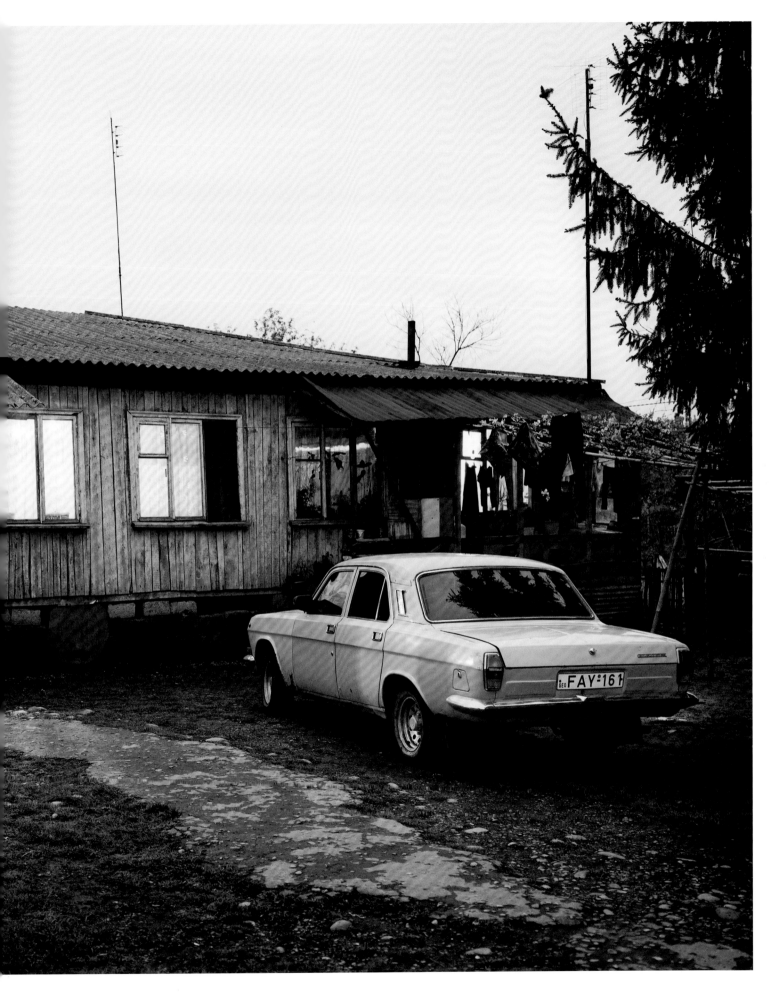

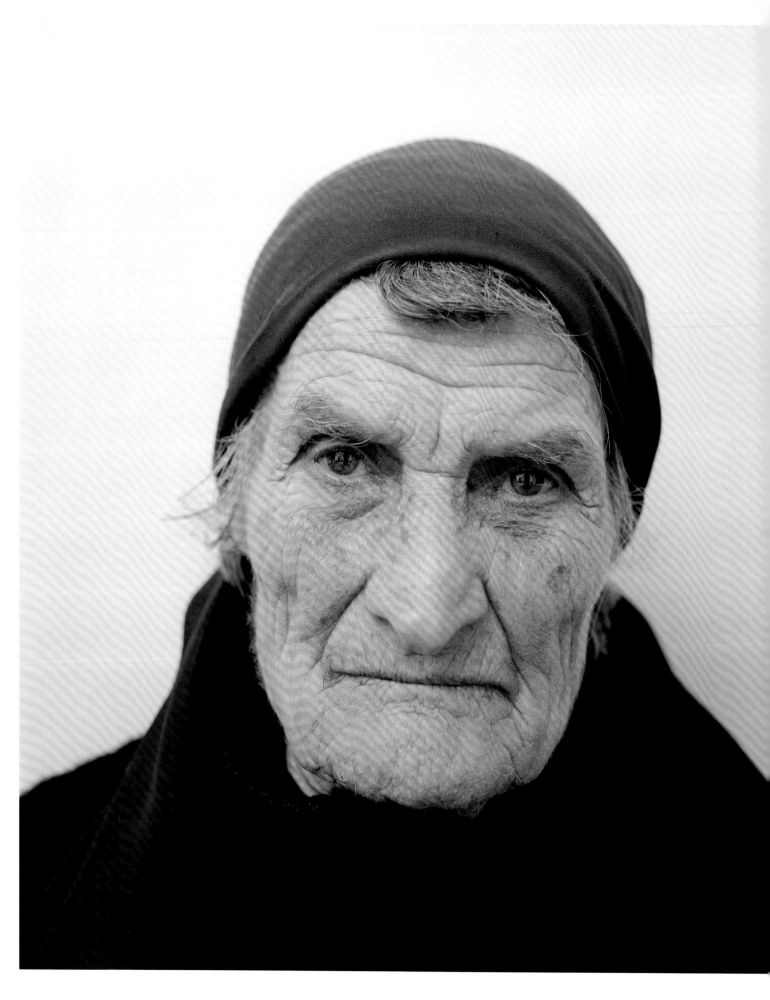

About to Move

After years of fighting legal battles to be
released from the mental hospital near
Kutaisi, Zhenia Kopaliani, eighty, finally
has the prospect of a new home, provided
by a number of NGOs that work with the
Saakashvili government.

Kutaisi, Georgia, 2010

Papuna Papaskiri

Tbilisi, Georgia, 2010

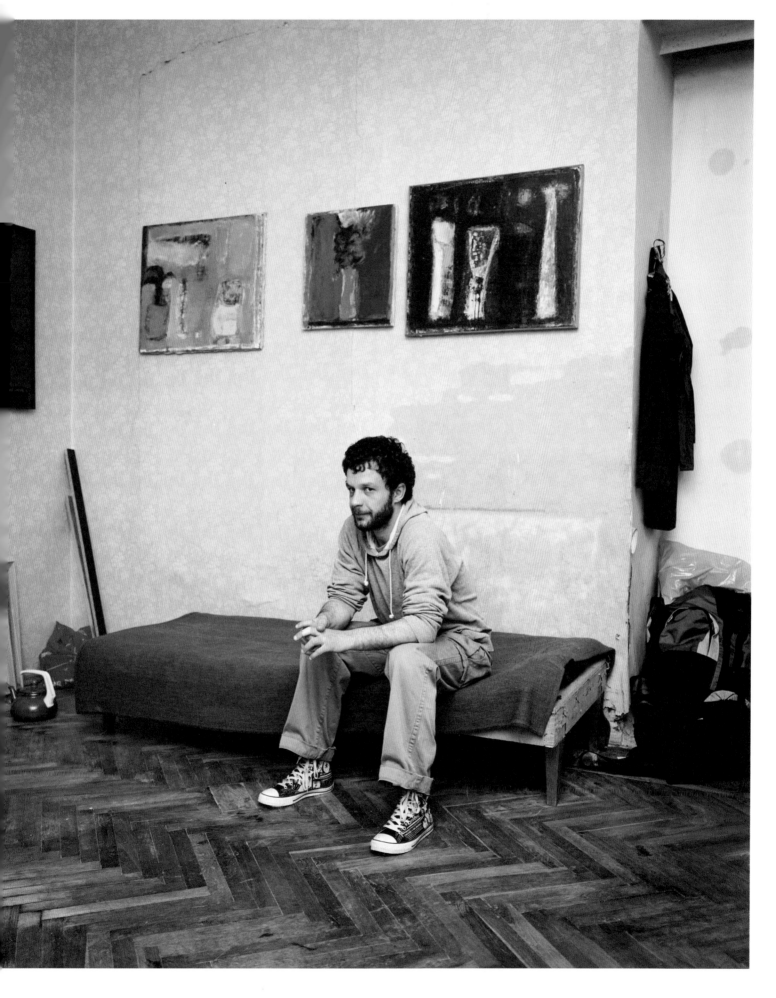

"I'll be disappointed if I ever return [to Abkhazia].... It will be a different country from the one I dream about."

Papuna Papaskiri
Tbilisi, Georgia, 2010

Artist-in-Exile

From the old center of Tbilisi, numerous narrow roads wind up through the hills between which the city is nestled. Where the incline is very steep, the roads become steps and the houses seem to cling to the rocks. One of those homes belongs to Papuna Papaskiri.

Papuna works as a designer for an advertising agency and is trying to launch a career as an artist. Several beautiful figurative still lifes and portraits hang on the wall. "Sales are increasing," he says, draining a strong cup of coffee and lighting cigarette after cigarette.

Not long before our first meeting, Papuna still lived with his parents in one of the many refugee apartments that fill Tbilisi. His parents remain there. "It's impossible to develop yourself in an apartment like that. With the best will in the world, you can't study, work, or think there. It's crowded, dirty, and noisy. Many of my friends are dead, often as a result of excessive drinking or drugs. I almost went the same way. I pulled myself up by my bootstraps. It was my painting that got me the job at the advertising agency and allowed me to rent this house. That was my salvation."

Papuna was seventeen when he was forced to flee Abkhazia. "I was one of the last people to leave Sukhum in 1993," he says. "We first tried to get away via the airport, but a plane that was taking off was shot down before our eyes. It was hell. We fled into the mountains with thousands of others. Through the Kodori Valley we finally made it to Svaneti in Georgia." His canvases, homemade furniture, and photos of Abkhazia litter the apartment. "I couldn't take anything from our house in Sukhum. I asked all my relatives in Georgia for photos that they had been sent, or of holidays they had spent with us. I now have a real picture of my youth again."

It took Papuna and his family seven days to cross the mountains. "It was a death march. Many people died on the side of the road. We survived by sleeping close to the fire. Even so, every morning my hair was frozen. It was indescribable. There were wild animals. We were robbed by the Svans, the mountain people who live there. My mother had, out of a kind of primitive instinct, stuffed all her pockets with *mwaba*, a sort of candied fruit. That kept us going. When we eventually reached Georgian villages again, Zviad Gamsakhurdia had arrived and brought the civil war with him.

"If I could, I'd go back right away," Papuna continues. The first bottle of wine—it is 9:30 a.m.—is uncorked and he shows us his childhood photographs. "I would have gone to study in Tbilisi anyway," he says. "I was young. I didn't mind adapting to the city. My parents suffered. They were forced from a comfortable life into a communal apartment in the big city. But the memories of Abkhazia now seem to be getting sharper.

"Night after night I watch films about Abkhazia on YouTube. Facebook is full of photographs and discussion groups about Sukhum and Gagra, for example. No one will ever stop missing Abkhazia. It's a different place, there's a certain magic attached to it. The way life is lived there no longer exists in Georgia."

It was only in 2012 that Papuna began to refer to Abkhazia in his painting. With another artist-in-exile he created an exhibition featuring the places and memories of his youth. "I'll be disappointed if I ever return," he says. "My house is empty and ruined. The country has been taken over by the Russians. It will be a different country from the one I dream about."

Double Dose of Bad Luck

Destruction in Abkhazia is widespread, but the country still has plenty of beautiful nature—wide beaches, forests, and rivers. Tkuarchal was hit doubly hard. Like every other mining town in the former Soviet Union, the mines here employ fewer men and the inhabitants have drifted away. Of the twenty-five thousand former inhabitants, only five thousand remain. The war made matters worse. Tkuarchal is truly destroyed.

Tkuarchal, Abkhazia, 2010

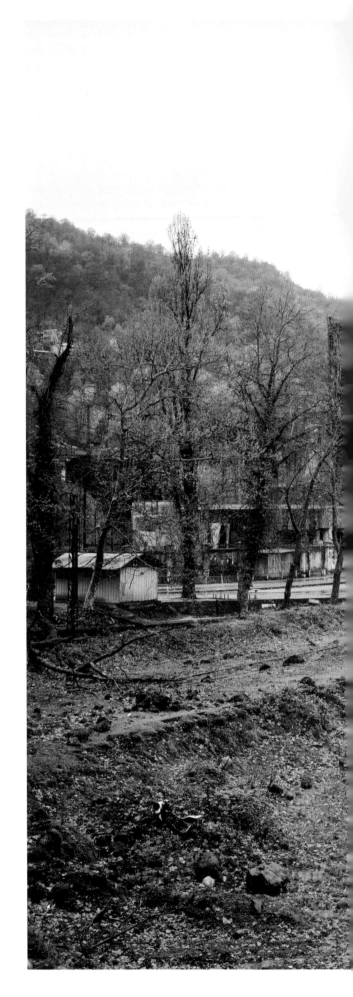

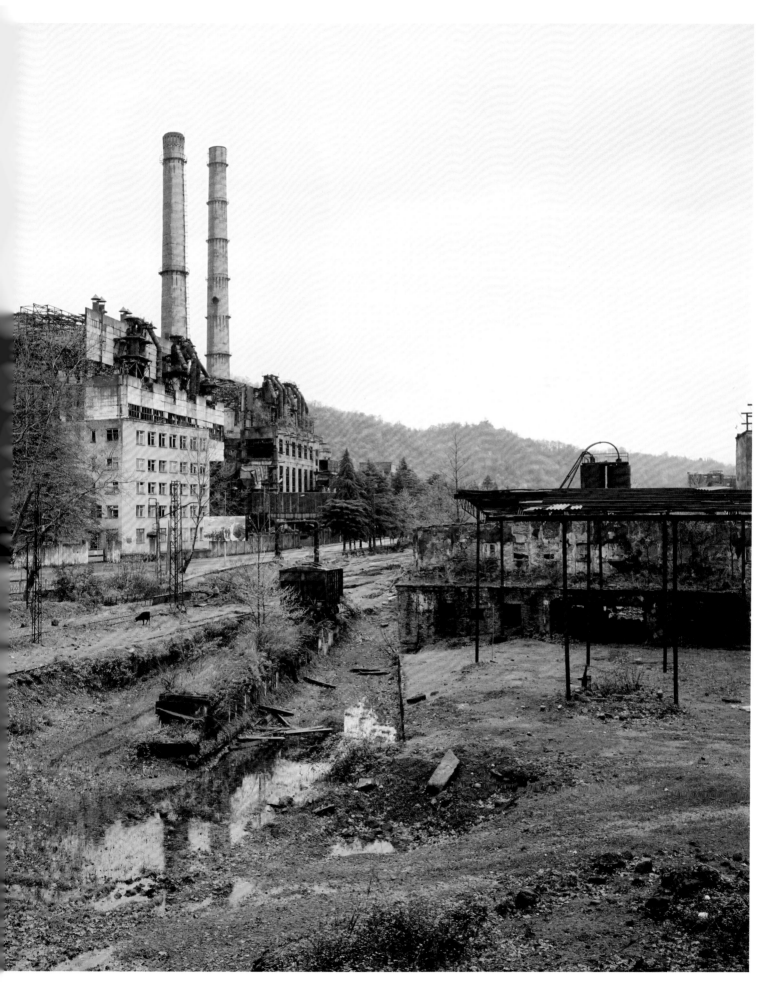

Mining Town

Tkuarchal, Abkhazia, 2013

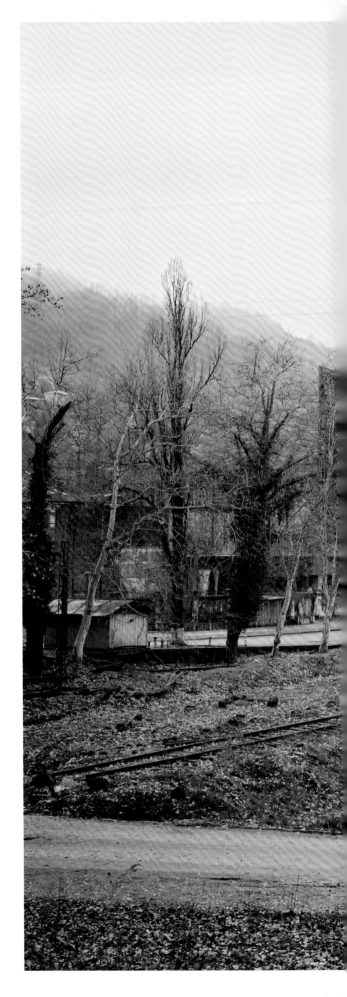

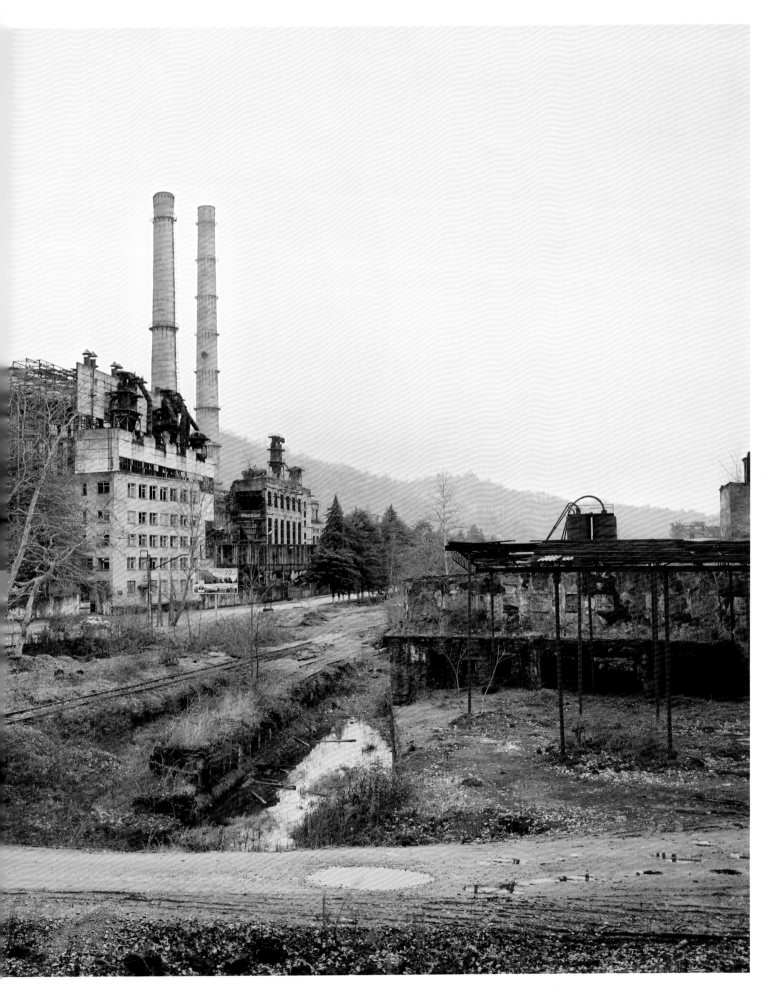

Empty House

Empty, abandoned houses are being
redistributed to returnees from Turkey.

Sukhum, Abkhazia, 2010

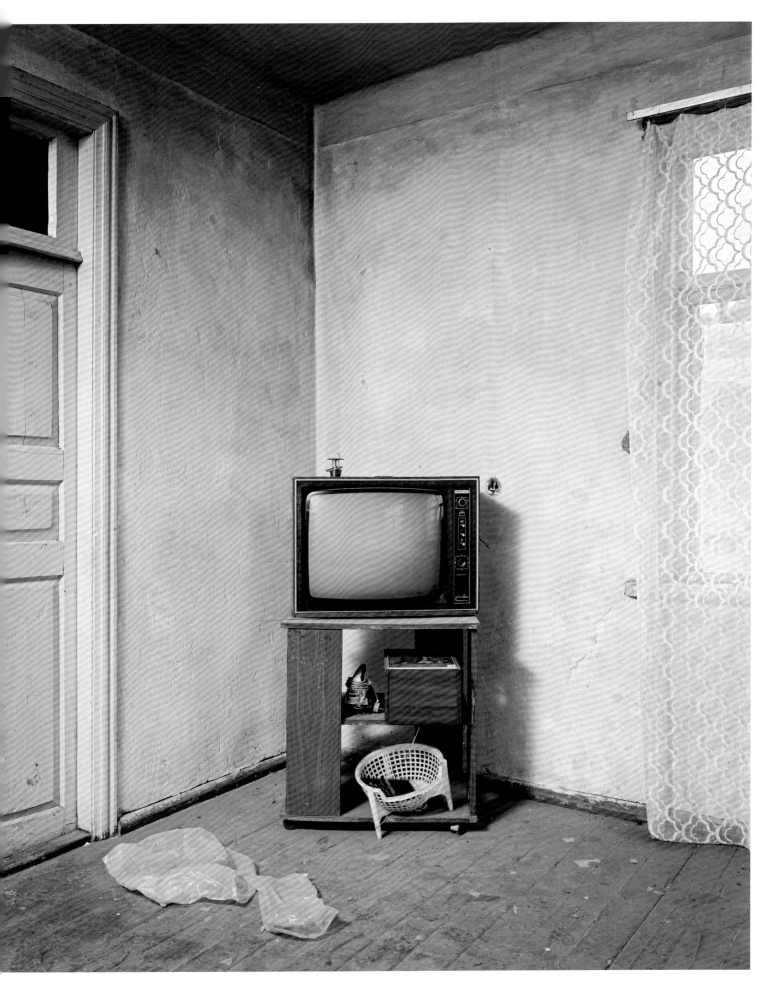

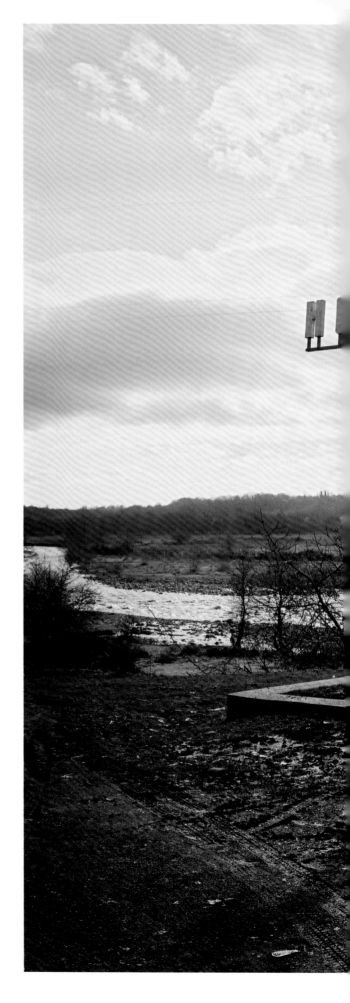

Ghalidzga River

A looming sign announces our arrival at the
mining town of Tkuarchal, located on the
Ghalidzga River; it serves as a reminder of
the recent, hopeful past, in which Tkuarchal
was one of the most prosperous towns in
Abkhazia.

Tkuarchal, Abkhazia, 2013

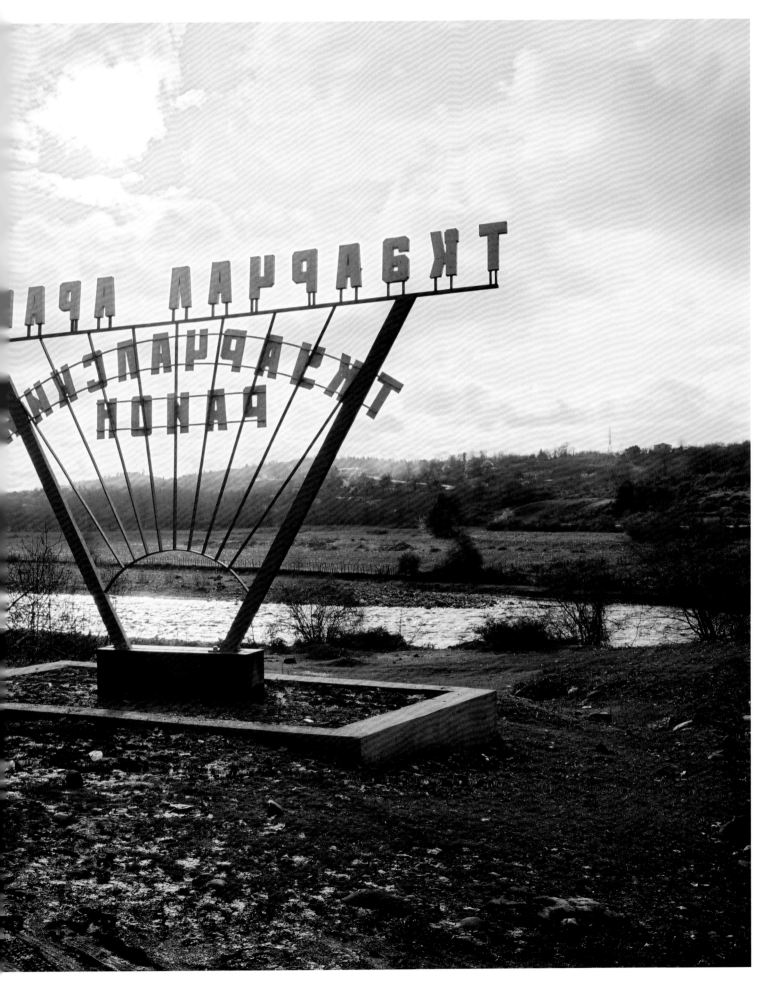

There is something compelling about these
empty houses, once home to Georgians,
Armenians, Greeks, or perhaps Abkhazians
who had fled their country. We poke our heads
inside and are moved by the ripped wallpaper
and the old newspapers stuck behind it. Or
we see a pair of old shoes, half disintegrated,
covered in dust.

The contents of the houses recall the previous inhabitants. We find photographs of a
man in a Soviet army uniform who is pulling
himself up on an industrial pipe and smiling
proudly into the camera. A large wooden box
is filled with cobbler's tools, and numerous,
homemade leather Michael Jackson sun
visors. They must have been a big hit in the
eighties. Judging by the handwriting in the
notebooks, an Armenian lived here. Who
knows what happened to this person. Did he
or she flee before the war or later? Is this person living in Armenia or elsewhere? Or did
an entire family perish in the fighting?

Found photograph, undated

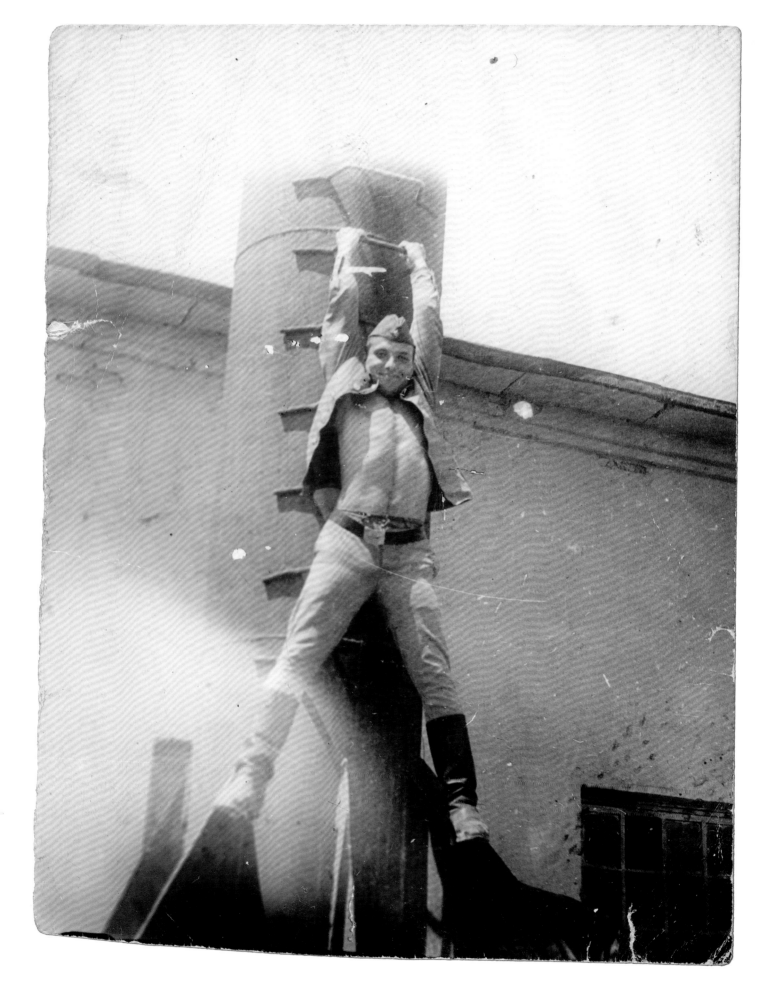

Commemorating the Past

The war, the genesis of modern Abkhazia, is commemorated in every school and public building.

Tkuarchal, Abkhazia, 2010

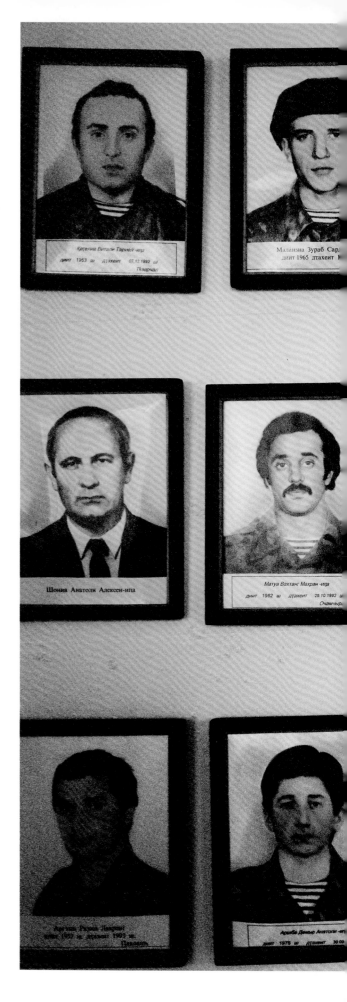

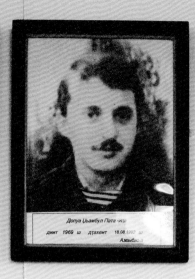

Доцуа Цьамбул Пата -ипа

диит 1969 ш   дтахеит   18.08.1992 ш
Ахьыбжьа

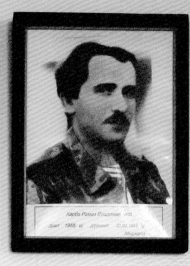

Карба Рамаз Владимир -ипа

диит 1965 ш   дтахеит   27.02.1993 ш
Мыркала

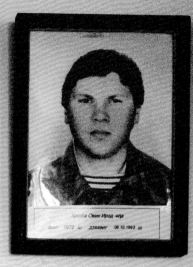

Хашба Омек Ирод -ипа

диит 1972 ш   дтахеит   08.10.1993 ш

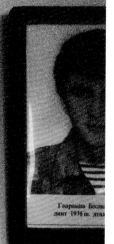

Гварамиа Бесли
диит 1976 ш. дтахеит

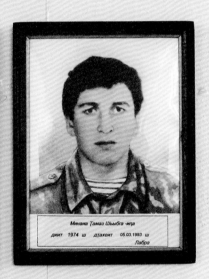

Минана Тамаз Шьыбга -ипа

диит 1974 ш   дтахеит   05.03.1993 ш
Лабра

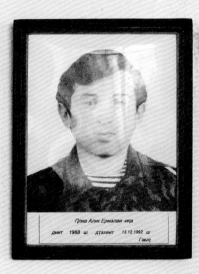

Плиа Алик Ермалаи -ипа

диит 1968 ш   дтахеит   13.12.1992 ш
Гаып

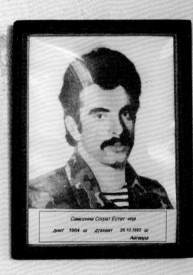

Самсониа Сограт Естат -ипа

диит 1964 ш   дтахеит   26.10.1992 ш
Аегаера

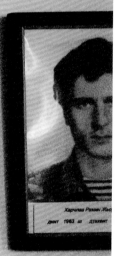

Харчлаа Рамин Жиуа
диит 1963 ш   дтахеит

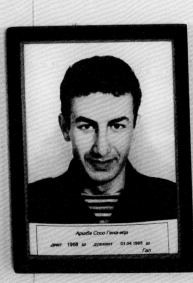

Аршба Сосо Гена-ипа

диит 1968 ш   дтахеит   01.04.1995 ш
Гал

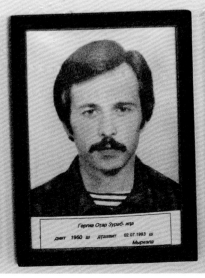

Герлиа Отар Зураб-ипа

диит 1960 ш   дтахеит   02.07.1993 ш
Мыркала

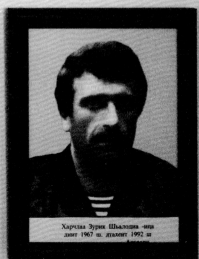

Харчлаа Зурик Шьалодиа -ипа
диит 1967 ш. дтахеит 1992 ш
Ахьыбжьа

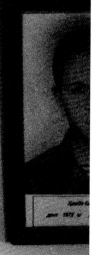

Хашба Б
диит 1972 ш

Theater

Tkuarchal, Abkhazia, 2010

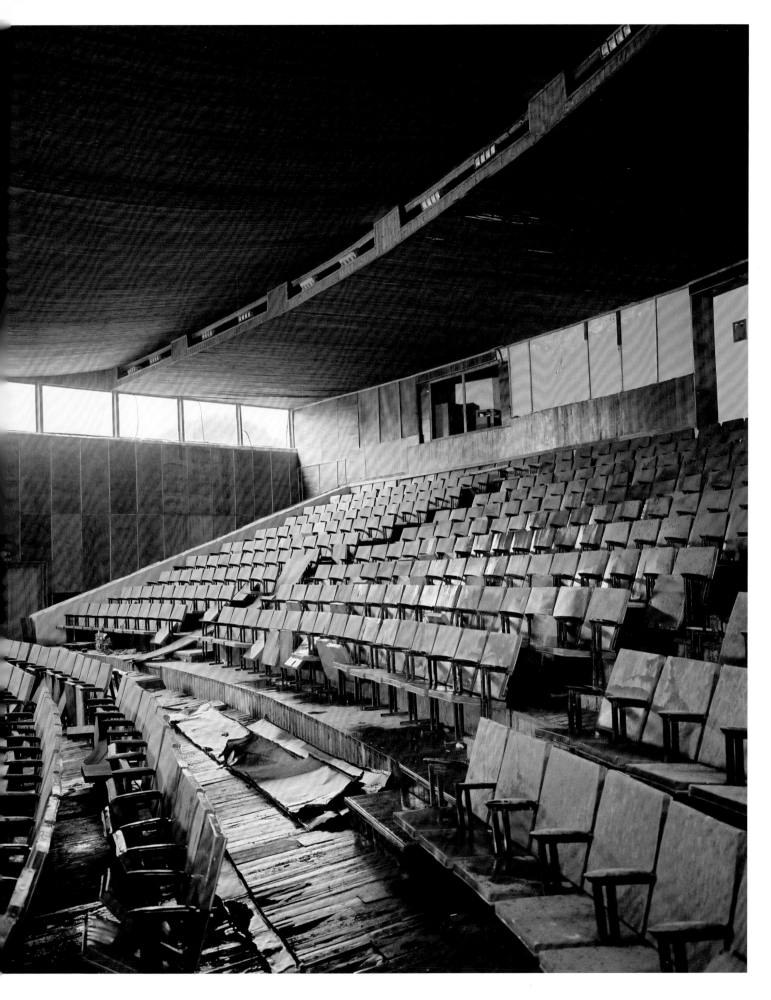

"I want to think, do, and dream Abkhazian. But I often think and dream in Russian and many of our traditions have been lost."

Angela Pataraya
Sukhum, Abkhazia, 2013

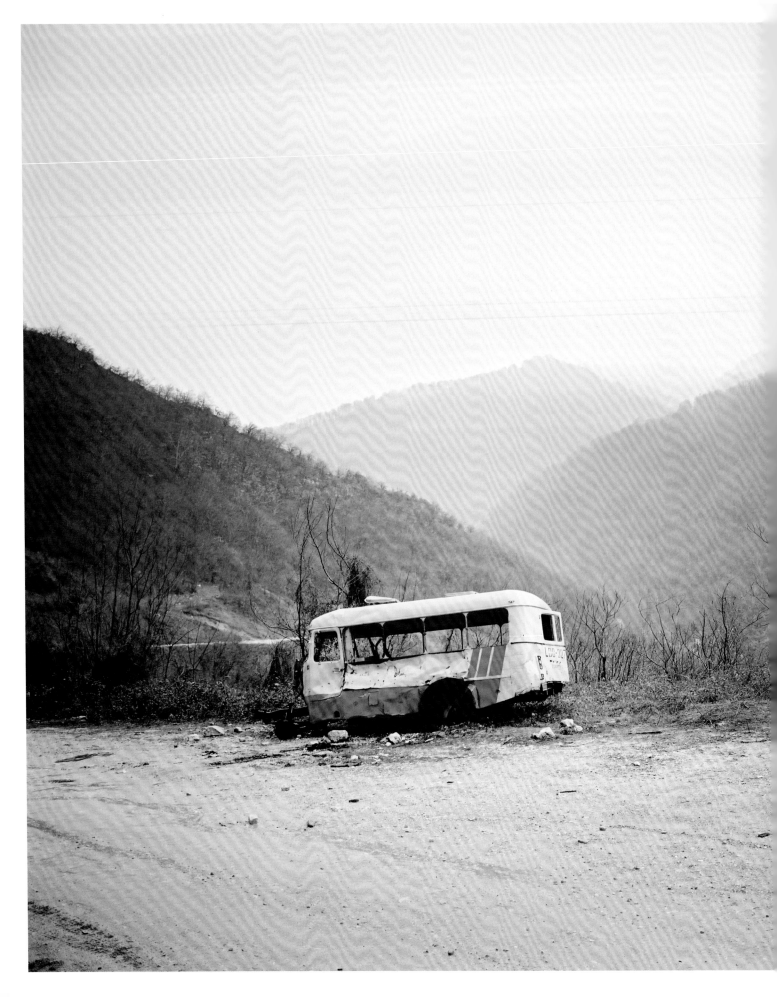

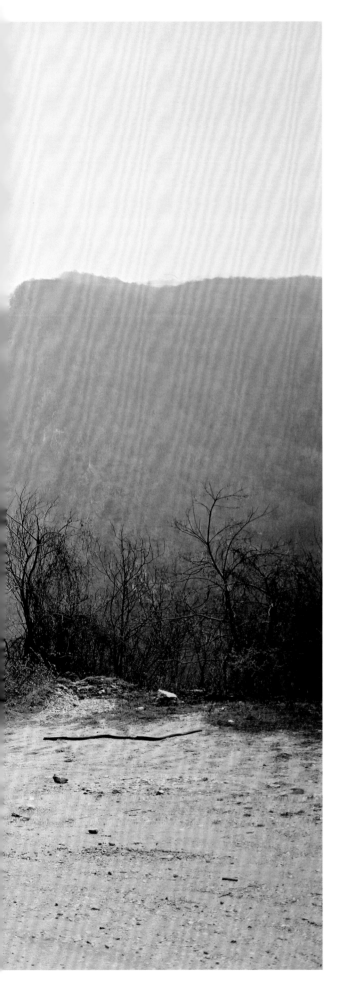

Kodori Gorge

In the shadow of the war between Georgia and Russia in 2008, a smaller war unfolded. With Russian support, Abkhazia captured the officially demilitarized Kodori Valley, a remote mountainous region on the border between Abkhazia and Georgia. Since then another two thousand refugees have entered Georgia.

Our small column of vehicles crawls along the road to the Kodori Valley. It takes us about three hours to cover forty kilometers. The route takes us past breathtaking rivers and ravines, remote villages with tumbledown cultural centers and schools, beehives, and the occasional goat. Here and there, a new spring has bubbled up from the ground and temporarily submerged the road. As we approach the Kodori Valley, we drive carefully past the first minefields and foxholes, over temporary military bridges, and through unlit tunnels toward the area that until last year was still in Georgian hands. An old United Nations post indicates the border. It is now an Abkhazian army post. Up to this point the infrastructure appears to be rather improvised. The military solutions are Russian and the villages—as elsewhere in Abkhazia—are largely bullet-ridden or abandoned.

On the Georgian side of the border everything changes. Barricades have been built and trenches dug at every possible point along the narrow mountain road. We stop by a large construction. The general traveling with us jumps out of his Gaz (the Russian-made vehicle of choice in this region) and invites us to look at the Georgian defenses with him. We inspect fresh trenches. The retreat must have been hurried. A soggy Georgian instruction manual lies in the mud. Next to it are bags of kosher, Israeli-made army rations. An abandoned bulletproof jacket bears a strangely precise set of washing instructions: "Do not dry or bleach, wash at 30 degrees." We discuss the bad road with the regional governor. "Fast buses will soon drive along here," he brags. "And we want to build a tunnel to Dombai in the North Caucasus as quickly as possible. Abkhazia is going to bring prosperity to Kodori."

Kodori, Abkhazia, 2009

Zashrikwa, Edrese, and Their Guns

Before the war the Georgian government established Azhara, a model village in the Kodori Valley. There is an international cash machine (vandalized). There is a brand-new school, paid for by UNICEF and USAID (vandalized). Signs are no longer in Cyrillic but in Georgian or English (crossed out). Azhara has been President Saakashvili's showpiece in Abkhazia. This is how it will be if you come back to us, Georgia wanted to make clear to Abkhazia: we are prosperous, friendly, and democratic.

But during the short war, the valley's Georgian inhabitants fled over the border. A few families refused to be driven out. At the home of the Aschuba family, the enthusiastic grandfather lets us in. "If I'd known you were coming, I would have killed a goat," he says, and goes down to the basement to fetch wine. His two grandsons, Zashrikwa, seventeen, and Edrese, fourteen, sit proudly with Kalashnikovs on their laps. They insist that we fire some shots.

Afterward, with ringing ears, we sample the vinegary wine. Grandfather Tariel, sixty-five, lives near Sukhum. Immediately after the war he made sure his family, who had fled, could return to Kodori. "I know Abkhazia; I know what a good country it is," he says. In halting Russian, he tells us about the escape to the Georgian city Kutaisi, when the first bombs fell. "We are mountain people. Borders don't mean very much to us. If I had to choose between a Georgian and an Abkhazian passport, though, I would choose a Georgian one."

Kodori, Abkhazia, 2009

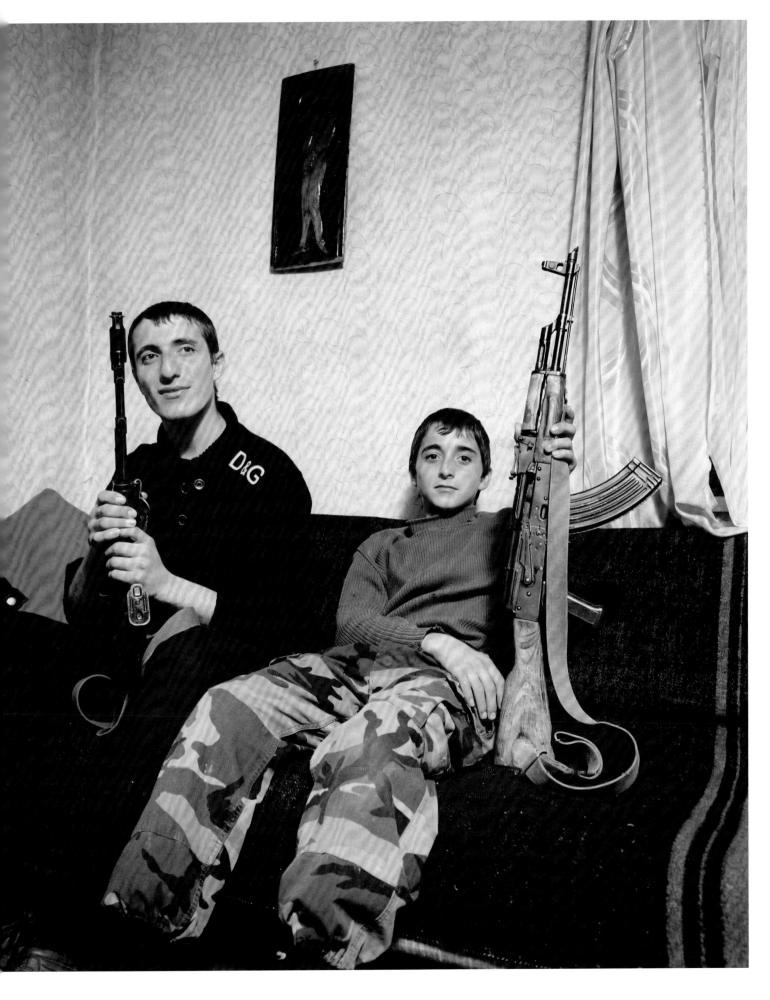

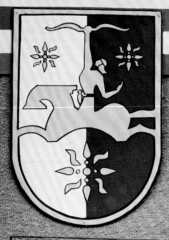

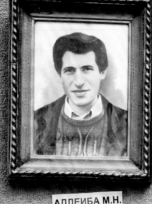

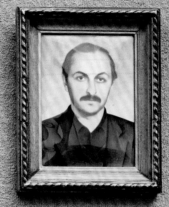

АСЦЕНА

АА

АДЛЕИБА М.Н.
1959-1993 ш
ЛЕОН ИОРДЕН

ИНАПШЬБА Б.Т.
1949-1993 ш
ЛЕОН ИОРДЕН

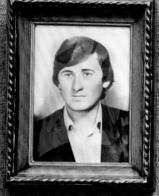

ЛАГӘЛАА Р.Ш.
1956-1993 ш
ЛЕОН ИОРДЕН

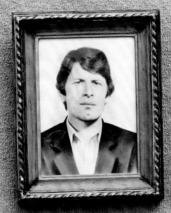

КАСЛАНЗИА Е.К.
1956-1993 ш
АГӘЫMШ0АРАЗ АМЕДАЛ

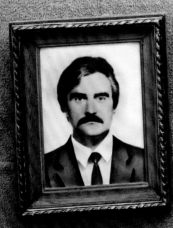

АДЛЕИБА В

1956-1992 ш

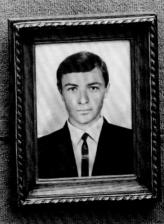

ШӘҚЬЕРИА И.К.
1972-1993 ш

ДЕ

War Is Everywhere

A cultural center displays a tribute to war casualties.

Sukhum, Abkhazia, 2009

War Is Everywhere

A Two-Hundred-Year Conflict

The entire North Caucasus is a region riddled with an assortment of conflicts, all rooted in the centuries-long struggle between the Persian shahs, the Ottoman Empire, and the Russian tsars. It was only around 1800 that Russia established a firmer grip on the region, but the population refused to surrender easily. The Caucasian War (1817–64) extended from Sochi in the west to Derbent, Dagestan, in the east. Imam Shamil and Imam Ghazi Mullah, two of the four great leaders of the uprising against the Russian occupation, were born here in Gimry. Almost everyone in the North Caucasus can recite their heroic deeds. Nearly two centuries later Gimry is once again at the center of the uprising against the Russians and their local henchmen. One of the girls who carried out a suicide attack on the Moscow subway in 2010 came from a neighboring village. A few weeks before our planned visit to Gimry, the police arrested a local boy on suspicion of helping the *boyeviks*, the terrorists, separatists, or bandits in the woods. This time the village decided to fight back and barricaded the main road through the mountains. It was soon blocked with a long line of honking trucks. The police changed tack. The boy was released and the village went back to sleep.

The road winds through stunning scenery. (The next *Star Wars* film should be shot in Dagestan.) We drive through villages, each with its own specialty: fridges, bread, fruit. Long valleys crowded with apricot trees form a picturesque contrast to the rocks in myriad shades of gray, black, red, and yellow. The scene soon loses its charm. Men with black balaclavas and large automatic rifles guard checkpoints. Barricades have been erected along the side of the road. Our driver has a cheerful face and an amiable bristly moustache. That may explain why we are waved through at every checkpoint. We twist and turn our way up to a large hydroelectric power station. We stop to photograph the village on the other side of the valley. Then two cars pull up and men in leather jackets get out. We are under arrest. "Can't we go to Gimry?" we ask the leather jackets. "Of course not," one of them replies curtly.

Gimry, Dagestan, 2012

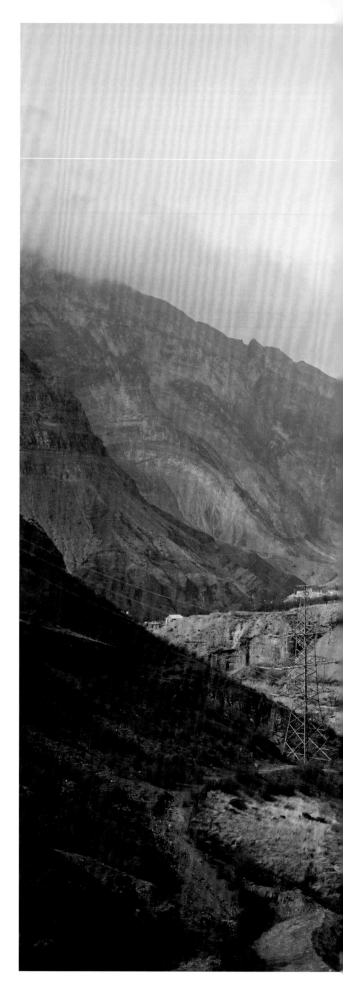

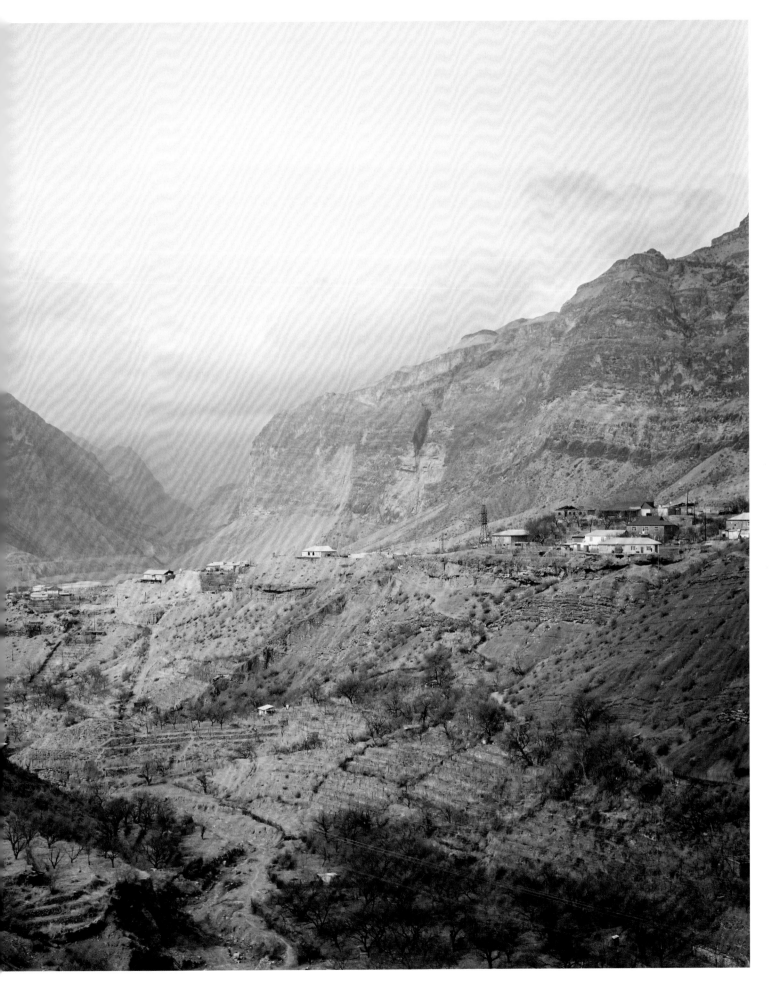

Provincial Town Becomes a Capital

In the old days, our South Ossetian guide tells us, Tskhinval was the most beautiful town imaginable. Houses were covered in grapevines and the vibrant Georgian capital, Tbilisi, was only an hour away. As breakaway South Ossetia's new capital, Tskhinval is now on its own. Following the war in 2008, much still needs to be rebuilt.

Tskhinval, South Ossetia, 2011

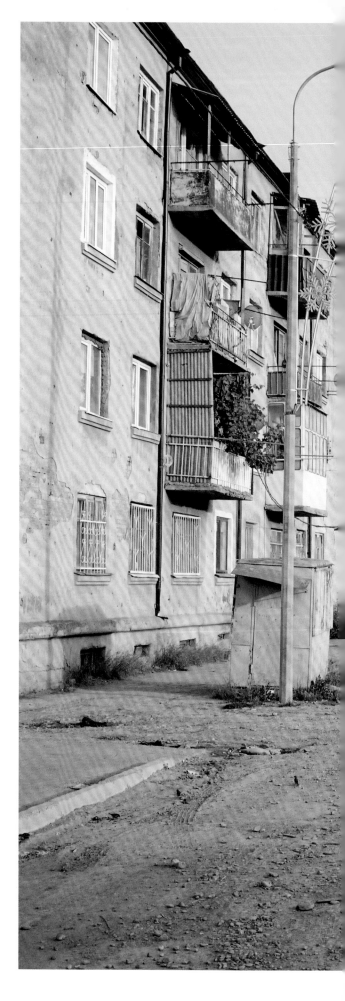

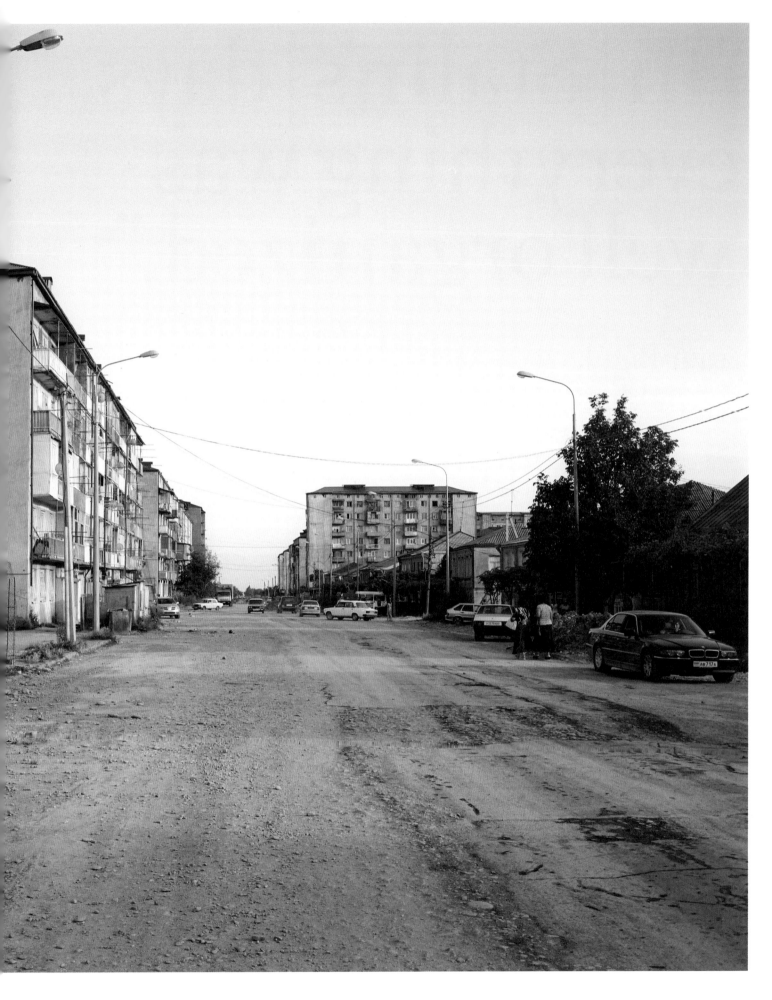

"In [Stalin's] days, everything was well organized."

Zaur Bigulaev
Khetakhurovo, South Ossetia, 2011

Survivors

Like a drop of water clinging to her northern brother, South Ossetia hangs off the southern edge of the North Caucasus, in the middle of Georgia.

During the Soviet era, South Ossetia was part of the Soviet Republic of Georgia. Today, hardly a trace remains of the many Georgians who lived there until the 2008 war. The villages that were known as Georgian have been so completely devastated that a stroll through them today feels more like a visit to Pompeii than to a recently inhabited village. Not a single person, dog, cow, or cat lives there anymore.

Despite the fact that South Ossetia, like Abkhazia, has been recognized by six nations (including Russia) since the war, it can hardly be called a country. Around fifty thousand people live in the provincial town of Tskhinval and the villages scattered around it. While it is only slightly larger than Luxemburg, South Ossetia can easily take six hours to cross via steep mountain ridges and poor roads. There is also a fast route, which takes twenty minutes, but it runs through Georgia and has been closed since the war.

In the center of Tskhinval, the fountain in front of the theater bombed by the Georgians is working again. Former South Ossetian President Eduard Kokoity's offices were just across from the fountain. In December 2011, the opposition, the courts, and allegedly Moscow succeeded with great difficulty in preventing him from serving a third term. Such a large proportion of the billions of rubles of support from Moscow had disappeared into the pockets of Kokoity's clan that even Moscow had to draw the line.

But not long before, in the summer, he had received us with a large grin in his office. He is a broad man, a former professional wrestler. Ruined by an excess of media training, he had few interesting insights to share with us during our half-hour visit. He did say this: "We have survived a Georgian blockade for the past eighteen years. Even though it is taking us a long time to build up the economy, we survive, even if that means being self-sufficient." The only way that this little country can become viable is by engaging with Georgia. "As equal partners," every Ossetian, including Kokoity, will insist. But it will be many years before Georgia is ready for that.

On the other side of South Ossetia, self-sufficiency is almost a fact. At the end of the six-hour journey through the mountains, in villages such as Leningor, the inhabitants live in virtual isolation. The border with Georgia is officially closed. Only the handful of Georgians who still live here can cross the border and sometimes smuggle goods back to South Ossetia. The economy has been largely ruined, but the fertile ground makes it possible to survive.

The brand-new Tbilisi-Gori highway lies a few hundred meters away. From Leningor it takes thirty minutes to reach the center of Tbilisi. From the Ossetian homes we hear the cars whizzing by, sometimes glinting in the sun. In the surrounding fields, the occasional Russian flag can be seen fluttering on the army posts that guard the new border. The tiny farmers' villages have been transformed into a little Berlin. The streets may not be separated by a dividing wall, but the villagers can tell us exactly where the border is. They do not dare to cross it. "Our phones are tapped and you never know when the Russians are nearby," says a woman, who will not reveal her name. "In the past we used to go to each other's birthdays, weddings, and funerals. Now we don't even greet each other."

Zaur Bigulaev, seventy-two, maintains the old cultural center. He is a modest man who shows us the sets that the schoolchildren use for the annual school play. Then he walks to his house, saying he wants to offer us something to drink. We soon understand that he has an ulterior motive: the house is half destroyed. A round hole in the outer wall of the bedroom is covered in plastic. On the other side, the wall is covered in carpets, as is customary here, but they are riddled with bullets or bomb splinters. "We're scared to death that the whole house will fall on our heads," says Zaur. "The structure is no good anymore." The house has been declared habitable, however, and so Zaur is not eligible for compensation from Moscow. He wrote dozens of letters but has now given up. The powerlessness of his situation brings him to tears. No one can help him. His life and his country are without prospects. On the wall of his veranda hangs a portrait of Joseph Stalin, son of Ossetia. "In those days, everything was well organized," he says.

Zaur Bigulaev

Khetakhurovo, South Ossetia, 2011

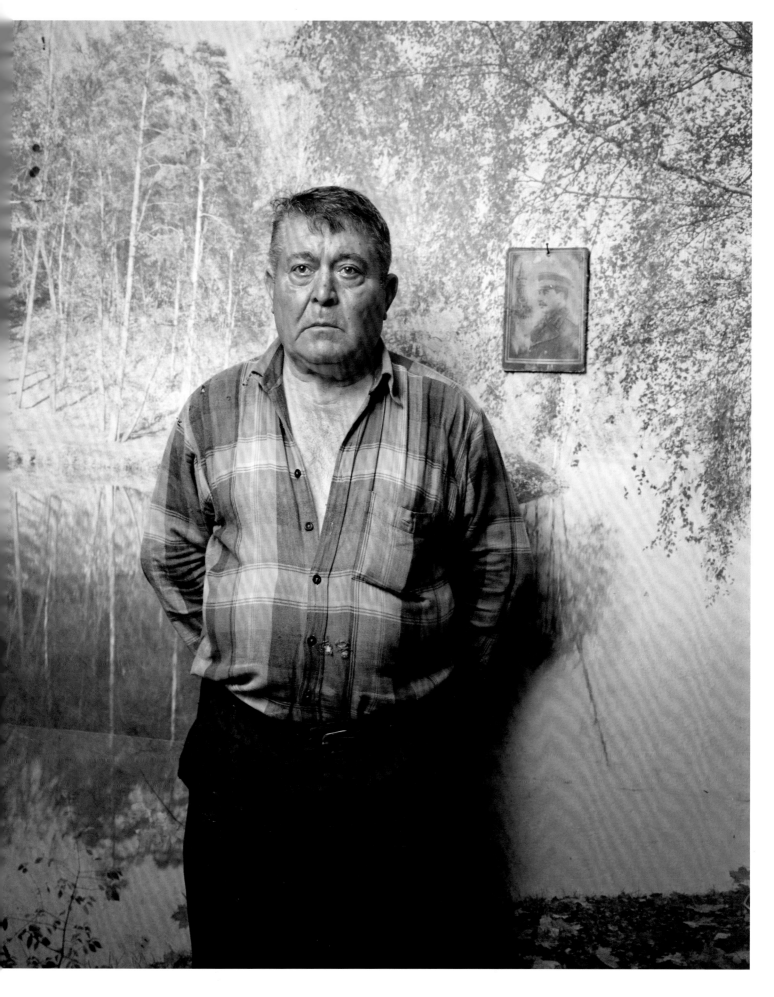

The Aftermath of War

These assorted household items belong to
Zaur Bigulaev, whose house was bombed
during the 2008 war.

Khetakhurovo, South Ossetia, 2011

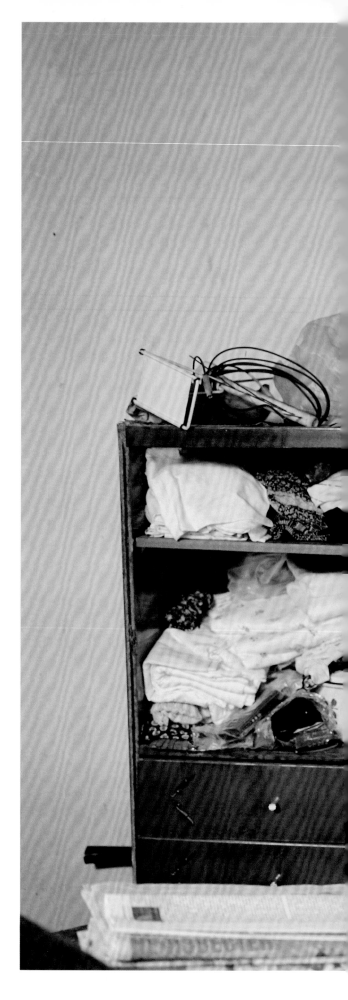

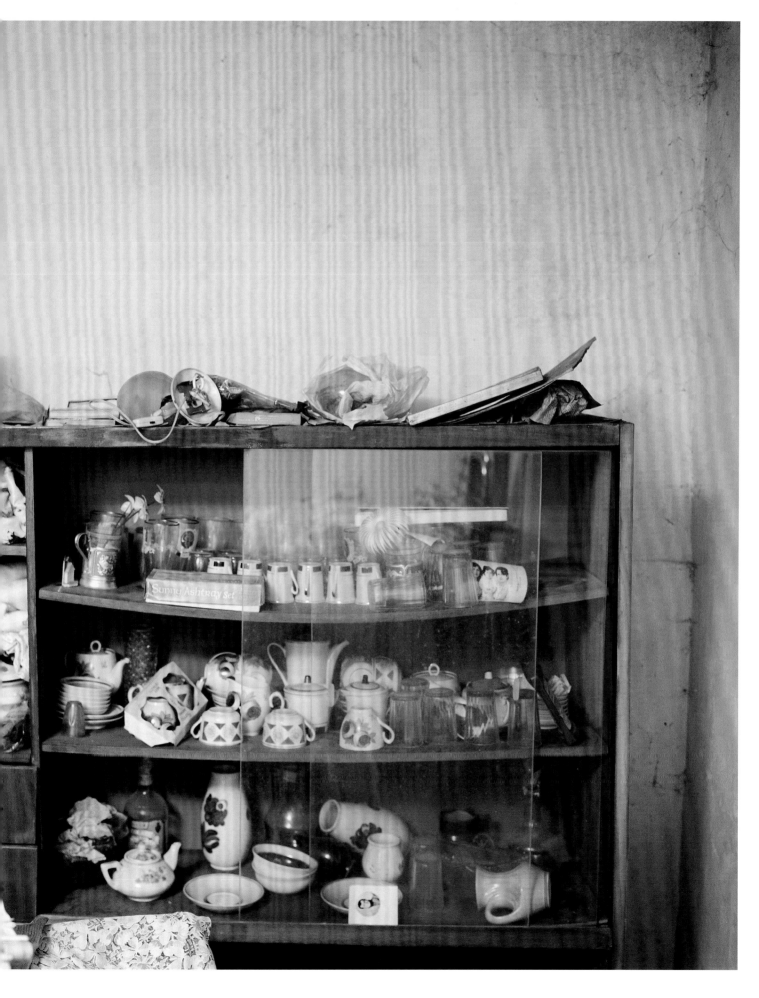

A Dying Breed

The Caucasus is a region of veterans. No other part of the Soviet Union sent so many men to the front, many will say, after which an argument will ensue over exactly which Caucasian people produced the most soldiers. Sochi is an important city for veterans. Thousands of war-wounded men were cared for in its numerous sanatoria. After the war, Sochi became a hot ticket for veterans. Those allowed to vacation here had done well for themselves. Many veterans stayed on in Sochi, where a large number still live.

Veterans in the rest of the Caucasus were less fortunate. They entered the turbulent nineties as old men. It was not uncommon for them to die in their homes or flee their native regions altogether. Roman Eloev, eighty-eight, was one of the latter. Born and raised in Gori, Georgia, where the August War of 2008 got close indeed, he now lives in a converted barn in South Ossetia. The third war in his lifetime (after 1941-45 and 1991-92) was too much for him. He is now a refugee in his own country.

Not long after this photograph was taken, we received a phone call from our contact in South Ossetia. The cold winter of 2011-12 had taken its toll on Roman. He was buried without friends and family in a small village in South Ossetia.

Leningorsky Rayon, South Ossetia, 2011

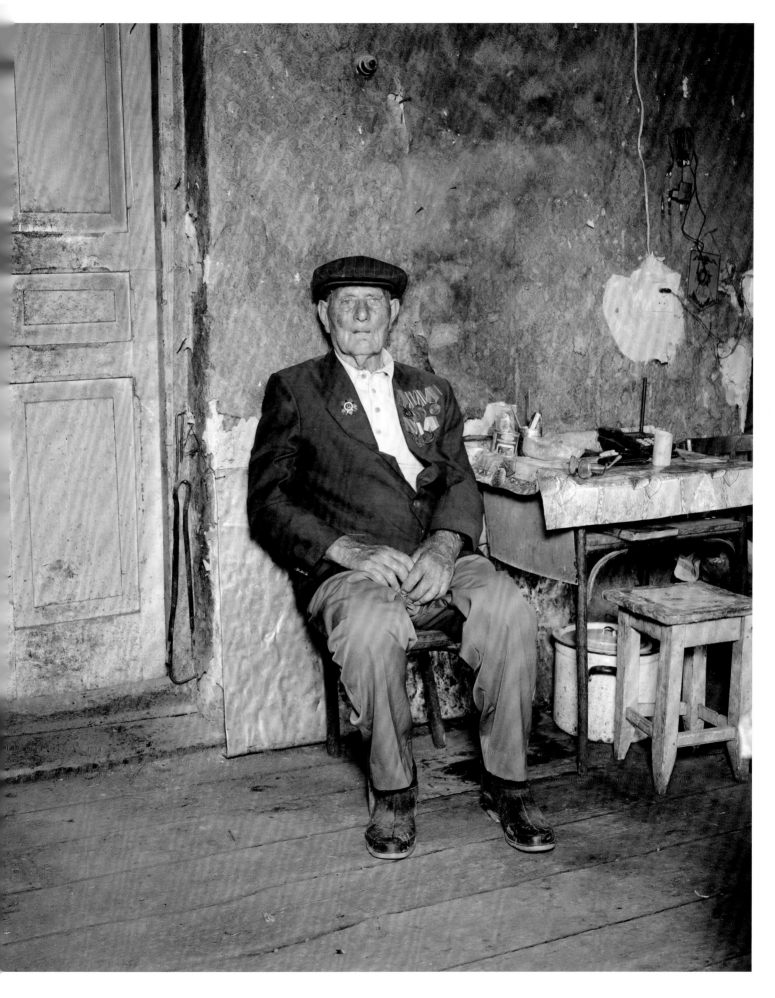

Monument to Russian-Georgian Friendship

This monument, lonely and rundown, towers above the military highway, a feat of engineering at the time of its construction, sometime between 1799 and 1817. The road was necessary for the Russians to conquer the Caucasus. It also made it easier for the Russians to protect the Georgians against the Ottoman and Persian empires, but consequently the Georgians forfeited their independence.

Gudauri, Georgia, 2013

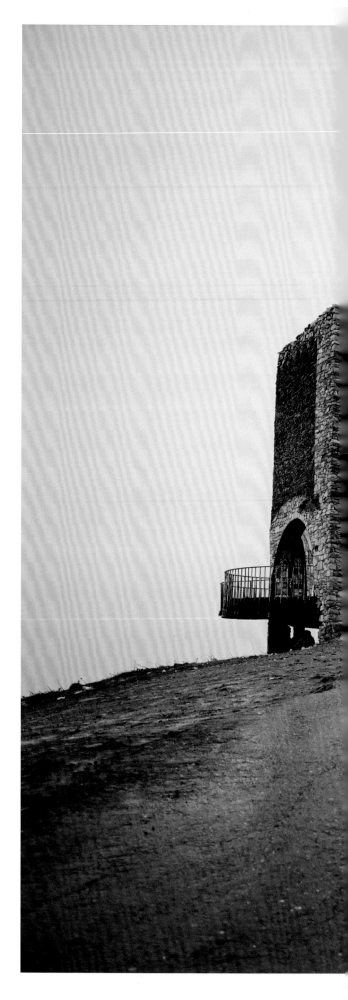

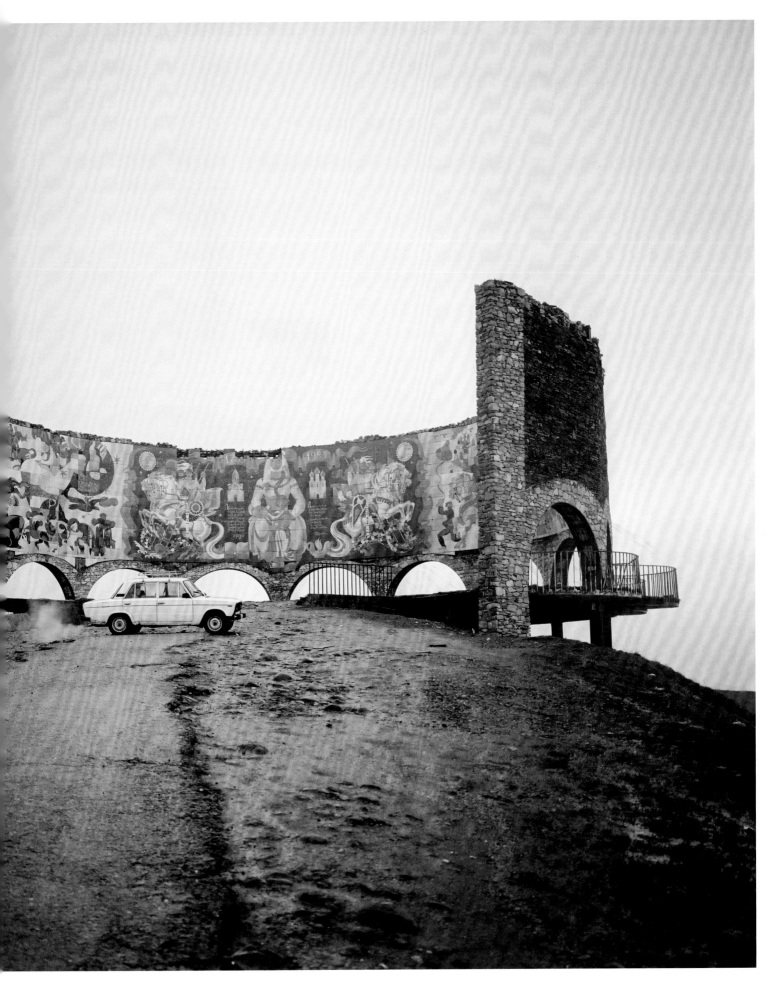

The Weak Stay Behind

The Ossetian refugees from Georgia and South Ossetia arrived in North Ossetia in 1991. The civil war drove them over the mountains from grim, nationalistic Georgia, where militias roamed the towns and cities. The most proactive among them found their way to Moscow, Vladikavkaz, and Europe. Some returned to South Ossetia. The disabled, the elderly, and those who lacked initiative or cunning still live in the sanatorium, twenty years after the war that forced them to leave their country.

Vezir Kozaev, seventy-three, owned a home in Tbilisi, but was driven out by his neighbors. Every so often he travels to Tskhinvali, "because you can still buy Georgian books there." He left Georgia in a hurry in 1991. "I never thought things would get that bad," he says, still surprised. He now receives a pension of 180 dollars a month from the Russian state. His wife has died; she never recovered from the skull fracture she sustained when they fled. "Luckily my children went to university; we do what we can," he says, before immersing himself in his book again.

Sanatorium 1st of May, North Ossetia, 2011

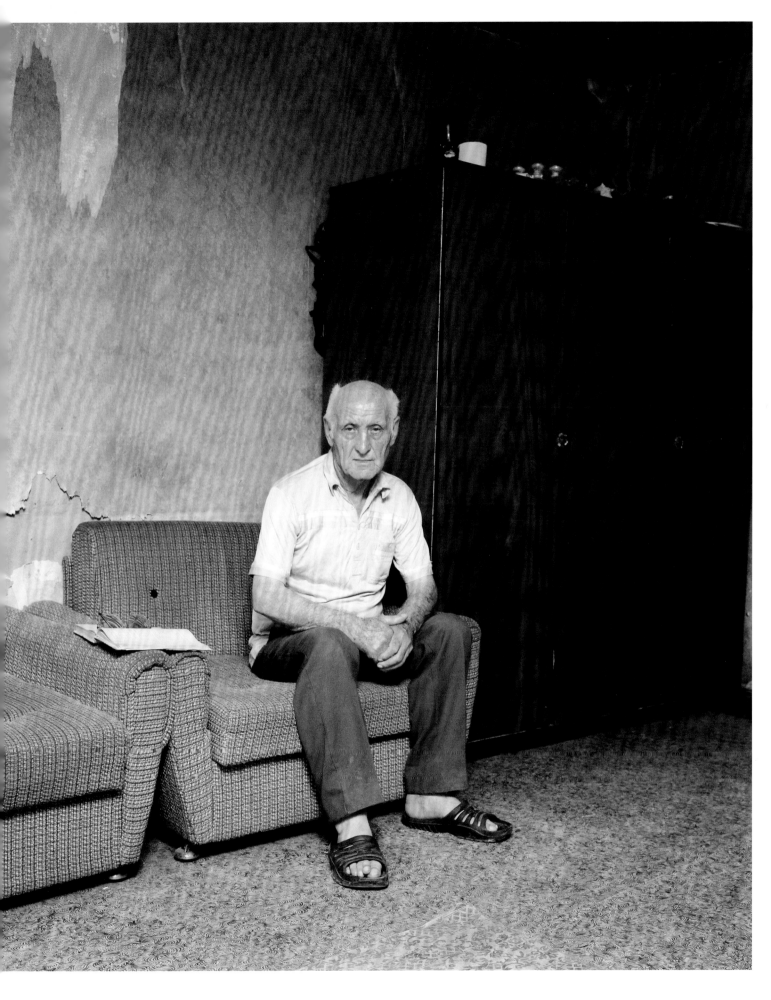

Up in the Mountains

The population in the mountains is declining.
The difficult farming conditions and long
distances to the cities are destroying the
villages.

Churzuk, Karachay-Cherkessia, 2009

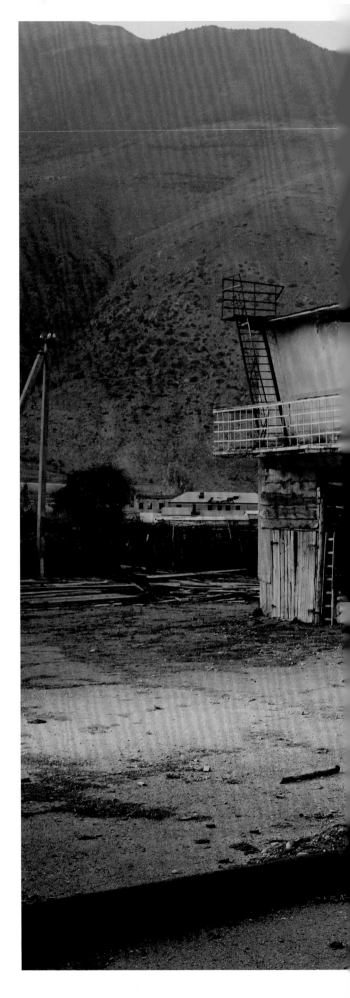

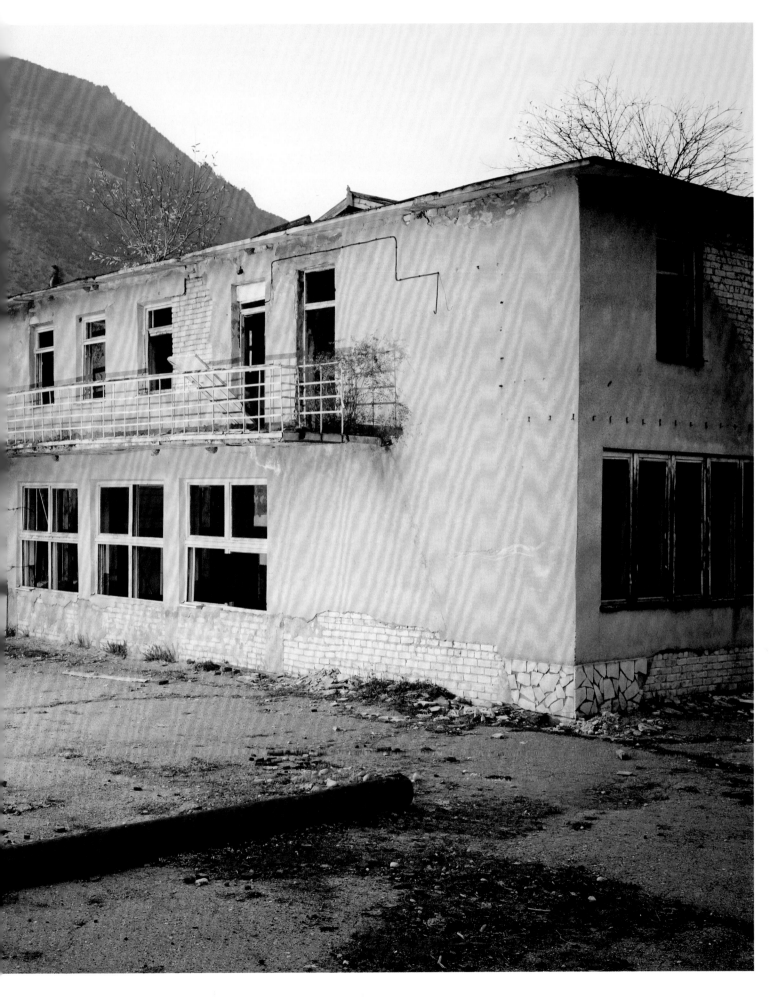

The Old Sovkhoz

After standing empty for ten years, this large, seven-hundred-hectare state farm has been bought by a businessman born in the village. Having made his fortune in Moscow in the turbulent nineties, he wants to give something back. The workers receive a minimum salary and a percentage of the profit. Like cowboys they ride on horseback over the rolling hills, the outliers of the mighty Caucasus Mountains on the horizon. In the late afternoon, a long procession of cows returns to the village. Most of the animals go into the farm's barn, but some turn left or right in search of their own individual stalls.

Krasny Vostok, Karachay-Cherkessia, 2009

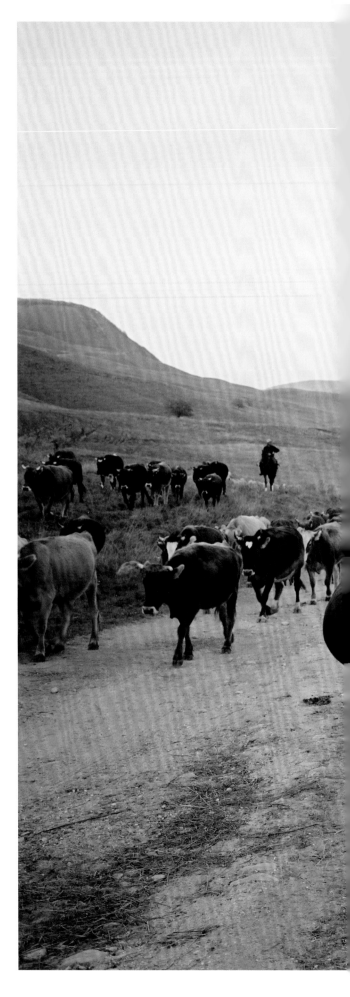

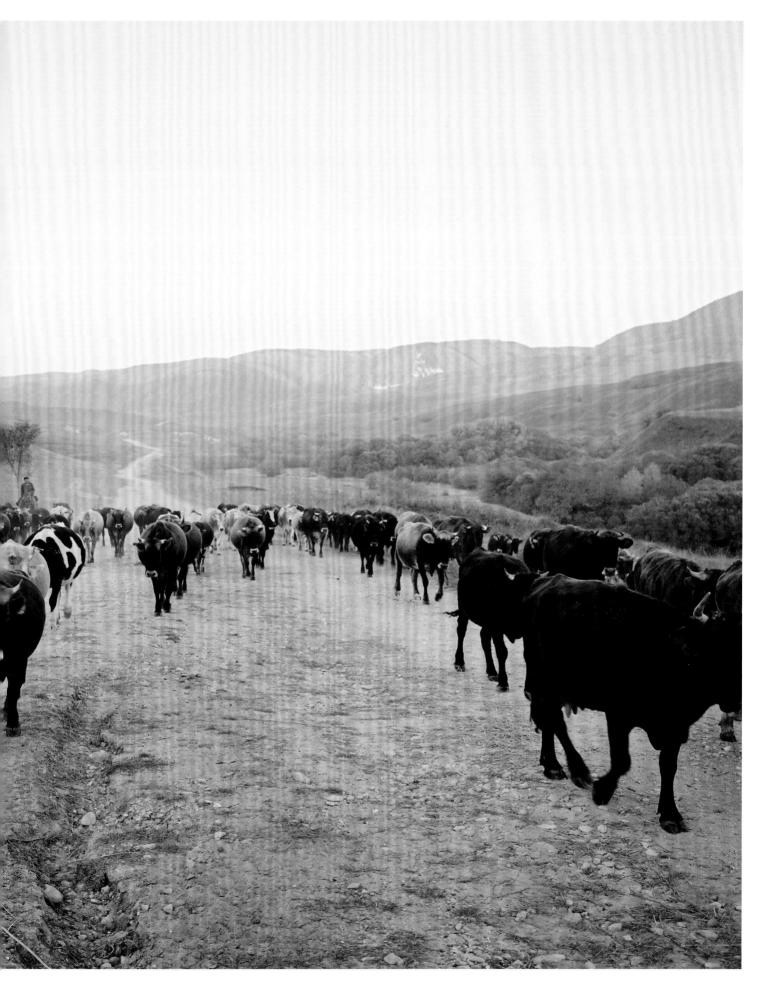

A Gift from God

Guests in the Caucasus are considered sacred, a gift from God. When guests arrive, everything else is put on hold. Bottles of drink are brought out, a sheep is rounded up and appears on the table as grilled *shashlik* in the evening.

Krasny Vostok, Karachay-Cherkessia, 2010

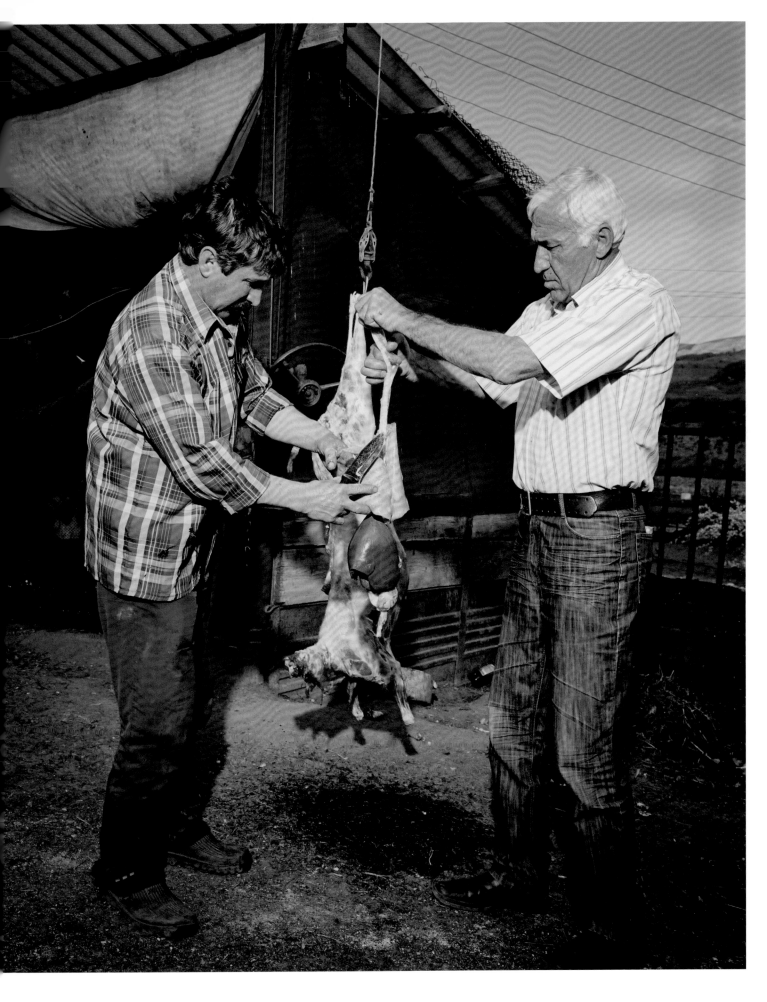

The Mayor

Taisya Makova was mayor of Krasny Vostok
until 2011.

Krasny Vostok, Karachay-Cherkessia, 2009

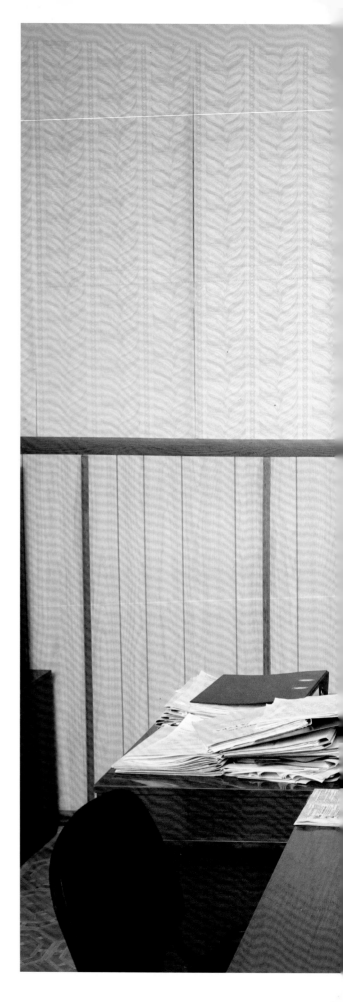

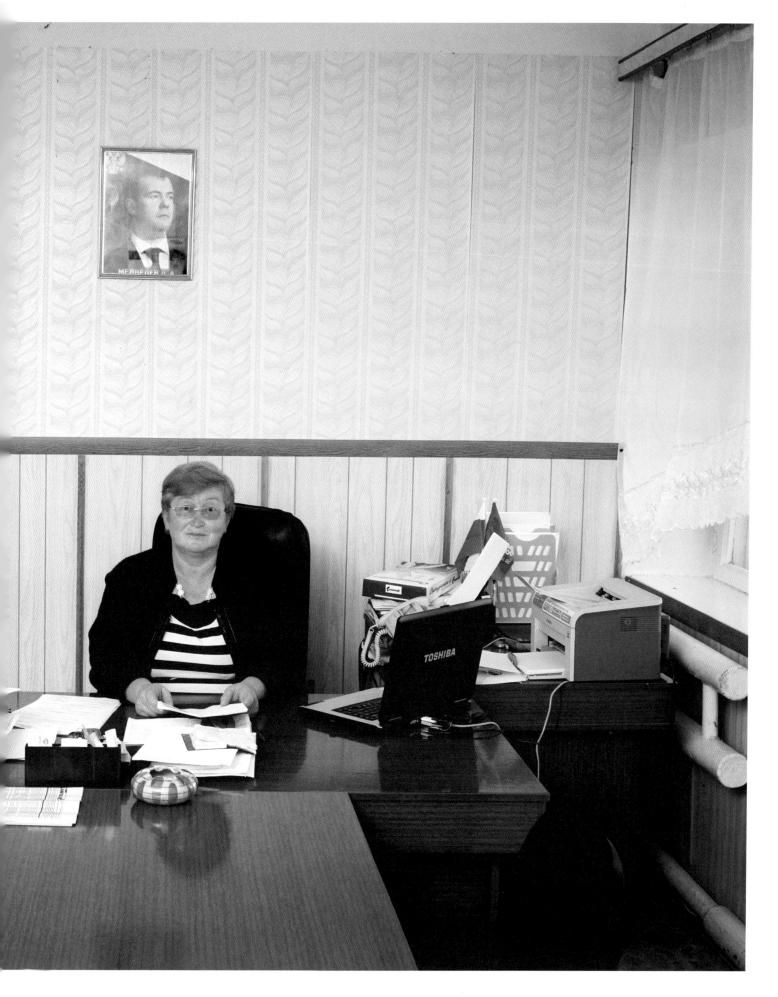

"There's a strong Islamic lobby.... They won't stop until we're all leading Islamic lives."

Taisya Makova
Krasny Vostok, Karachay-Cherkessia, 2013

The Red East Turns Green

Krasny Vostok is a tiny village in east Karachay-Cherkessia, the westernmost republic in the North Caucasus. It is only a small village in the North Caucasus, but the name appeals to our imagination: "The Red East." A small river flows north-south through the area. It has carved deep into the landscape, creating canyons south of the village topped with prehistoric forts. Shepherds, who bring their sheep and cows to graze here, gallop through the rugged landscape on horseback to find their livestock.

Along the road that runs west from the capital, Cherkessk, to the rest of the North Caucasus, you can find everything you need: a grocer, a mosque, and a garage. North of the road, on a hilltop covered in birch trees, sit the symbols of Russian authority. A small building houses the town hall, the post office, and the municipal cultural center. This is the realm of Taisya Makova, the mayor of Krasny Vostok, who welcomes us with open arms. This time we were lucky: on other occasions mayors turned pale and would have preferred to dive under their desks than to speak to two foreign journalists. After all, you never knew where it might lead.

Two civil servants work at the town hall, staffing the records office and supporting the mayor. When the occasional villager walks in, the mayor puts on her other hat and opens the safe in the office at the end of the hall. This is where she collects the payments for phone, gas, water, and electricity. "It isn't a very stressful job," she jokes, as there is rarely gas or water in Krasny Vostok.

Taisya was elected in 2008 with 80 percent of the vote, she tells us. Her principal election platform was gas and water. "If you vote for me, it will be here within a year," she promised. And people believed her. Taisya is from a well-known family in the village. She was head of the town's chapter of Komsomol, the Soviet youth organization, before she became director of the school. "It was a tough experience," she says of Komsomol. "It's a shame young people no longer get the attention they did during Soviet times." She has lost almost three and a half pounds since the elections. The economic crisis also hit hard. The council's budget plummeted dramatically. "I haven't been able to fulfill any election promises," she sighs. "After the elections, the regional head told me, 'If you don't drink like crazy, your job will drive you crazy.'"

But Taisya loves it. Her phone starts ringing early in the morning. Residents are constantly calling to report a gas stoppage or a plumbing problem. The mayor then calls her handyman (and uncle), who drives around the village in an old Lada to locate the fault. Every day begins with a visit to the school. "At the very least, the gas and electricity there need to work," she says. She slides her papers off the table and walks out of the building. She wants to show us the state of the village twenty years after the factory closed. Taisya has ambitious plans for her village. She wants to replace the old shoe factory with a mineral water bottling plant. And ten years after it was abandoned, the sovkhoz—a seven-hundred-hectare state farm—has finally been bought by a businessman who was born in the village.

A little flag of Vladimir Putin's United Russia party takes pride of place on Taisya's desk, replacing the red Soviet Union flag that was there some years before. It all seems to make little difference to life in Krasny Vostok. Lost in Russia's hinterland, the village gets by as best it can.

Less than two years later, a small revolution seems to have taken place in the village. The mayor has resigned and "a clique around the imam," as she puts it, has taken the reins. Little else has changed. The water and gas still do not work. The sovkhoz has again been abandoned and the factory is not yet operational. But Taisya is scared. "There's a strong Islamic lobby. As soon as they feel a bite, they reel in the new converts. They won't stop until we're all leading Islamic lives.

"Faith," she continues, "is something personal, something you keep to yourself. Those modern Muslims like to show off. We had to fight to prevent them from building a third large mosque, sponsored by Arabs, next to the school."

Taisya associates political Islam with suppression and violence, and that violence is creeping closer. The neighboring republic, Kabardino-Balkaria, is regarded as the new hotbed of the North Caucasus, but so far Karachay-Cherkessia has remained largely peaceful. The regional capital is Uchkeken, where Taisya moved to work for the school inspectorate after resigning as mayor. "There's been a counter-terrorism operation in Uchkeken for almost half a year," she says. "I've seen people shot in the street. That never used to happen. The imam here in the village was educated in Cairo," she adds ominously, "at a special place where they 'breed' bearded men."

The imam in question, Mohamet Adzhibekov, presides over the upper mosque, on the hill next to the abandoned shoe factory. He does not have a beard, but is dressed in a long white robe and turban. It is shortly after Friday prayers, and he and several other mosque elders are enjoying grilled chicken and cups of cola. There were few worshippers that day, perhaps eighteen or so of the village's 1,300 inhabitants. It does not seem like an impressive figure, but the imam is elated. "Everything is changing for the better. More people are coming to the mosque than before. We're gaining influence in the village, and finally making it clear that those old traditions, such as drinking alcohol or taking drugs, are incompatible with Islam.

"Politics isn't for me," continues the imam and recently elected village head. "We're not too concerned about life now. The afterlife, that's what it's all about. That's what we're trying to prepare people for. I've been elected but we have little room to maneuver. We'll never be able to introduce Islamic laws. We can make rules, as long as they don't conflict with national laws. We can ensure that people who pray too little or drink too much are no longer greeted on the street, are ostracized. But we can't prohibit the sale of alcohol."

The imam's greatest example is the Chechen leader Ramzan Kadyrov. "He's succeeded in implementing the Islamic model within the confines of Russian law. The crooks are afraid of him. All the corruption you find in Russia is impossible under him." Mohamet believes that an Islamic village and country will be a reality one day. But there is a lot to be done. "We're still looking for an inspiring leader for our girls. They are already Muslim but they don't come to the mosque. We need time. You can't eradicate all those old Caucasian traditions overnight. It will take at least a generation."

The New Head of the Village

Mohamet Adzibekov is the imam in Krasny
Vostok's central mosque. "The fact that fifty
billion dollars is being pumped into Sochi
is so frustrating," he says. "In the West, if
governments don't act in people's interests,
they revolt. But Russians are obedient."

Krasny Vostok, Karachay-Cherkessia, 2013

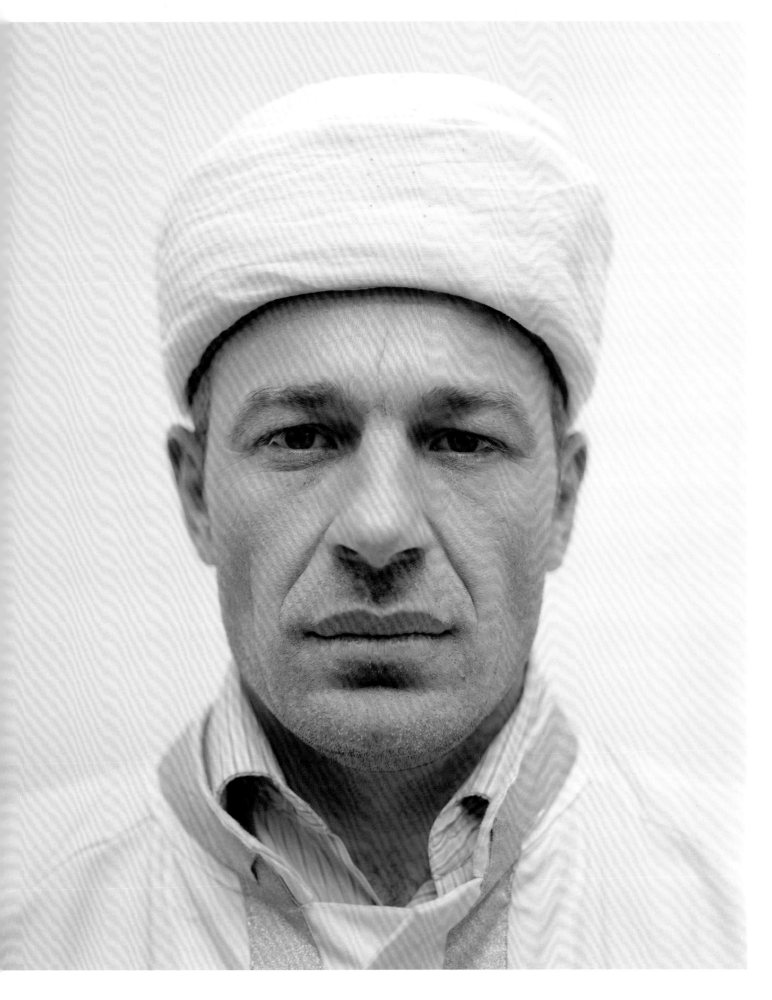

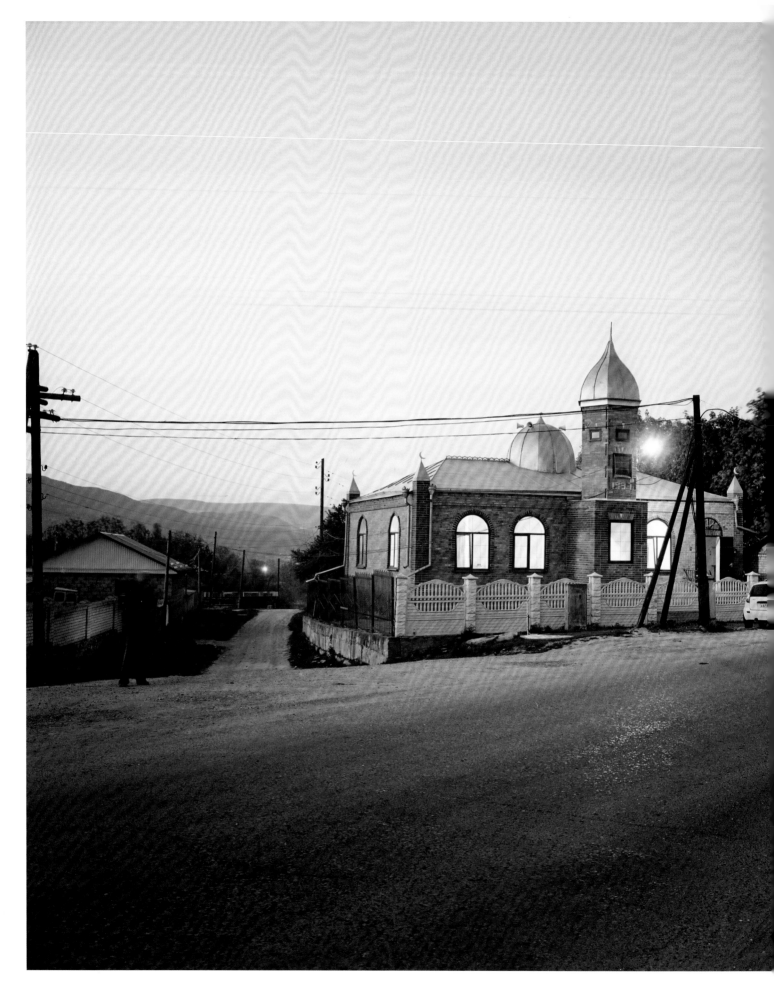

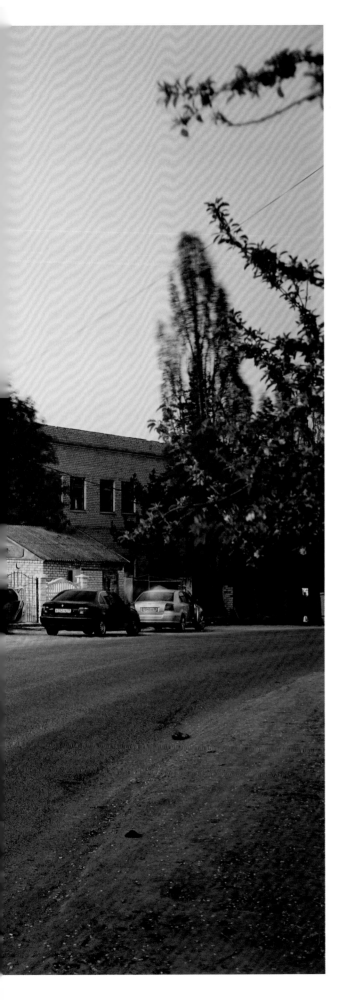

Mosque in Krasny Vostok

The upper mosque is situated on the main road between Cherkessk and Kislovodsk. Late in the evening, a party of wedding guests from Uchkeken stops at the mosque to say a quick prayer as they pass through. The women stay outside and dance exuberantly to music blaring from the cars.

Krasny Vostok, Karachay-Cherkessia, 2013

While in Sochi millions of dollars are being pumped into the Olympic Games, on the other side of the mountains time seems momentarily to stand still.

A New Generation

Veronika, twenty-two, and Viktoriya, twenty-four, live in Pyatigorsk, a small town not far from Krasny Vostok. The girls live on their own and are trying to build careers.

Years ago their mother, Stella, was plucked from the street by her husband, Georgy. While he held her captive in a neighboring village—as is the tradition—his friends negotiated the wedding with Stella's parents. True love never played a role in the marriage. Not for her, in any case. He adores her. But they make a good couple. Thankfully, says Stella, her daughters are growing up in a different era.

Veronika tells us about her former boyfriend, whom she dumped after two years because he became too controlling. That kind of behavior is unnecessary, her mother believes. Her Georgy still gets jealous. "He sometimes keeps me at home," she says, "because he is afraid of losing me."

Veronika and Viktoriya gently stroke their mother as she talks. They love both their parents deeply. Whenever they go to another town, or to a party, they always tell their father. Their mother would never allow them to go. But when Georgy looks at his watch in the evening and suddenly says, "I wonder whether the girls are back yet," Stella knows exactly what is going on.

Stella says her daughters are too materialistic when it comes to finding a husband; they are too focused on money and status. Veronika admits this is true: "I want a husband with a house, a car, and a good job. Apart from that I can support myself. A good husband will leave me alone."

In the bathroom Georgy throws a bucket of lukewarm water over his head, then sits down at the table with a twinkle in his eyes and opens a bottle of vodka. The conversation shifts back to the sheep, the village, and his daughters' careers. "You know what you should write down?" he says. "You're in the mountains. There are no deep rivers here. We aren't very complicated."

Krasny Vostok, Karachay-Cherkessia, 2010

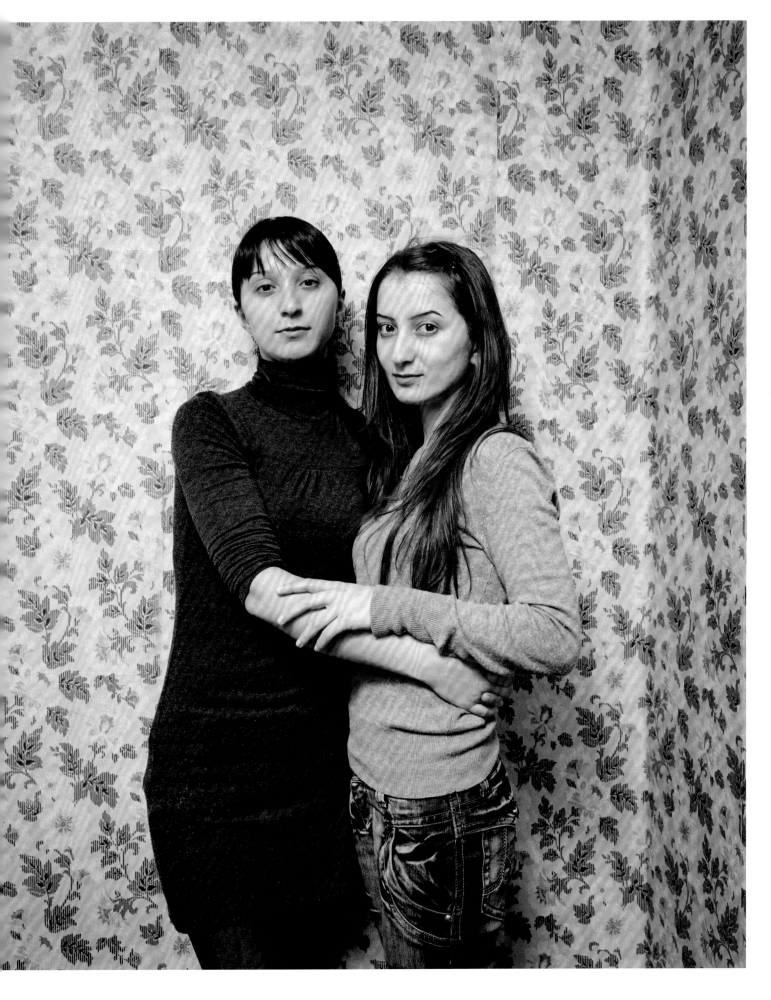

Looking Back

Like many other schools in Russia, Krasny Vostok's elementary school has turned a second-floor hallway into a museum commemorating World War II, or the Great Patriotic War as it is called here. The school's veteran—employed here for sixty-three years—personally selects the pupils who have to polish the small monuments and the glass exhibition cases. As soon as visitors set foot in the museum, the veteran waves his hand and, as though by military order, the sound of marches echoes through the hall.

The school is beautiful. It is the kind of place where the staff is so enthusiastic that even Lenin's slogans still seem shiny and new. "During the Soviet Union our school director was a committed Communist," the young teacher Irina tells us. "He stayed on and made sure that the whole school remained in the same state, with all the Soviet traditions. That's why the little ones here are still called *Oktyabryata* [Little Octoberists] and the older ones Pioneers. We still receive the uniforms and red scarves of Zyuganov, the leader of the Russian Communist party."

Krasny Vostok, Karachay-Cherkessia, 2009

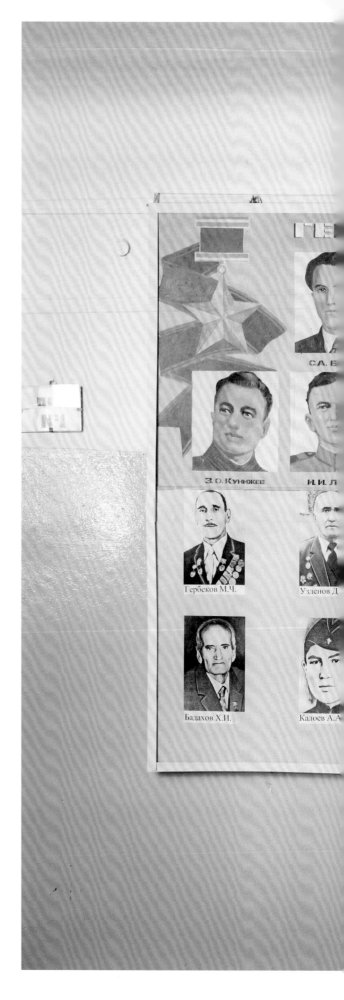

И КАРАЧАЕВО – ЧЕРКЕСИИ

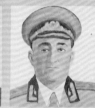 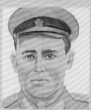 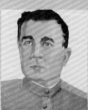 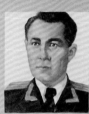 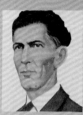 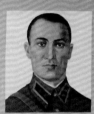

Х.У. Богатырев   Г.Д. Бутаев   Енжиевский А.А.   А. Б. Казаев   Карданов М.А.   О.М. Касаев

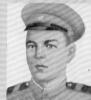 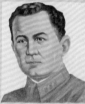 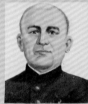 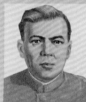 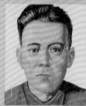 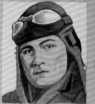

В. П. Леонов   И.И. Лободин   И.П. Меркулов   Ф.Т. Смельянюк   Д.И.Панченко   Д. А. Стариков

Каракетов Ю.К.   Биджиев С.Л.   Хаиркизов К.А.   Кумуков Х.С.   Чочуев Х.А.

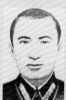 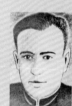 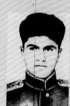 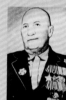 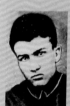

Голаев Д.Н.   Камалдинов Ф.Г   Хабеков У.Х.   Ижаев А.М.   Карданов О.М.

Rolling Hills

Eltarkach, Karachay-Cherkessia, 2013

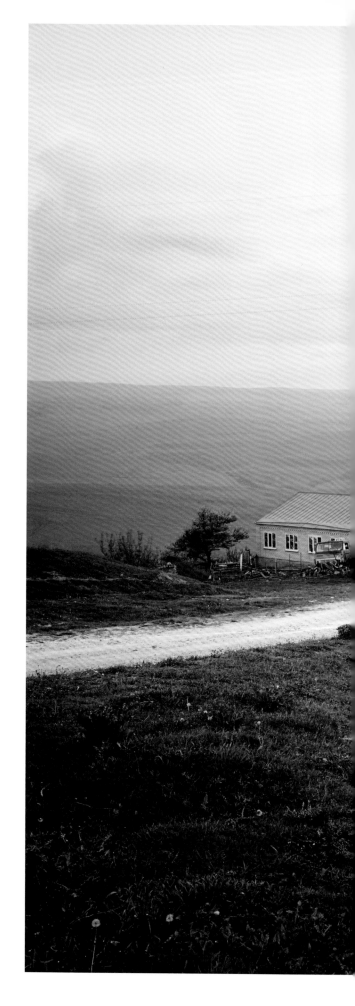

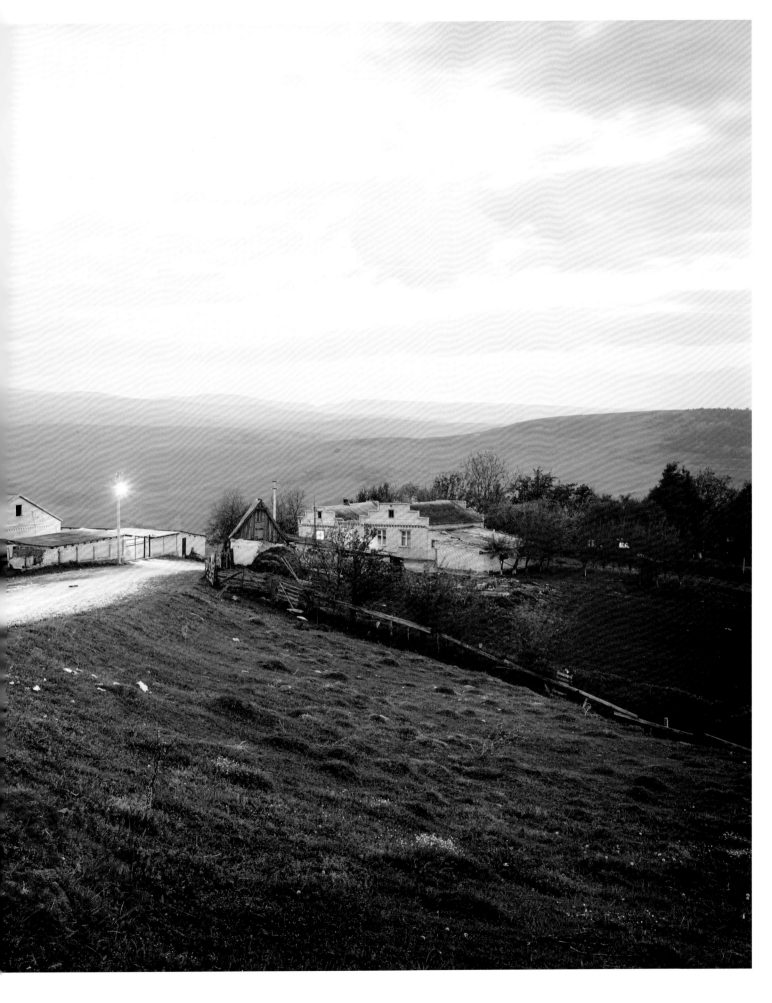

Recovering from the Wars

In the early nineties, Eset Umarov was driven out of Kazakhstan by nationalistic Kazakhs. She fled to Chechnya, the country from where her parents had once been deported under Stalin. "Then war broke out here, too," she says. "Thousands of Russian soldiers passed by." Six years after the second of two wars in Chechnya, she is still repairing her house.

Ishchersky, Chechnya, 2012

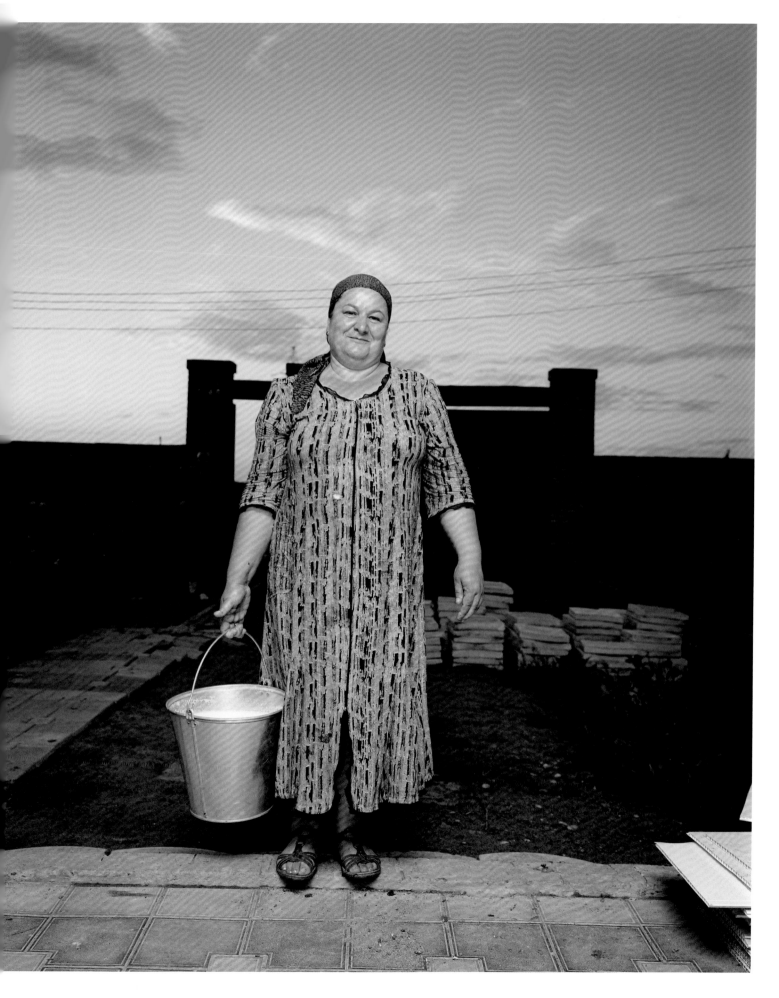

A Colonial Town

Grozny—"the terrible"—has lived up to its name in recent decades. The city was founded by the Russian General Yermolov with the aim of terrorizing and subduing the rebellious mountain people. The name now strikes fear into even the bravest Russian hearts. Tens of thousands of Russian soldiers lost their lives here and across Chechnya. The city, not yet two hundred years old, was almost completely destroyed until the pro-Russian Ramzan Kadyrov came to power.

Found postcard of Grozny, undated

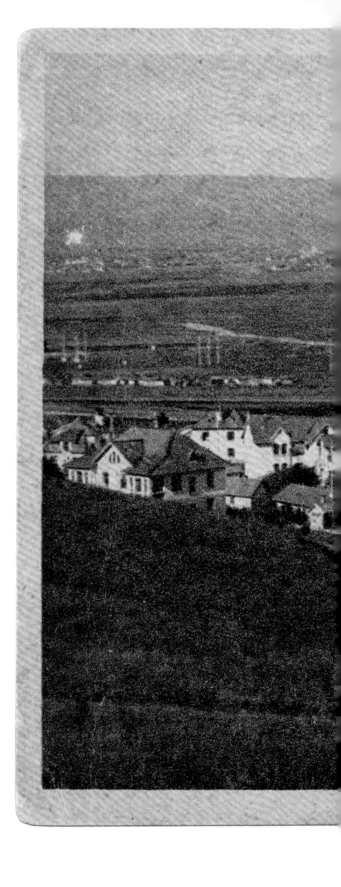

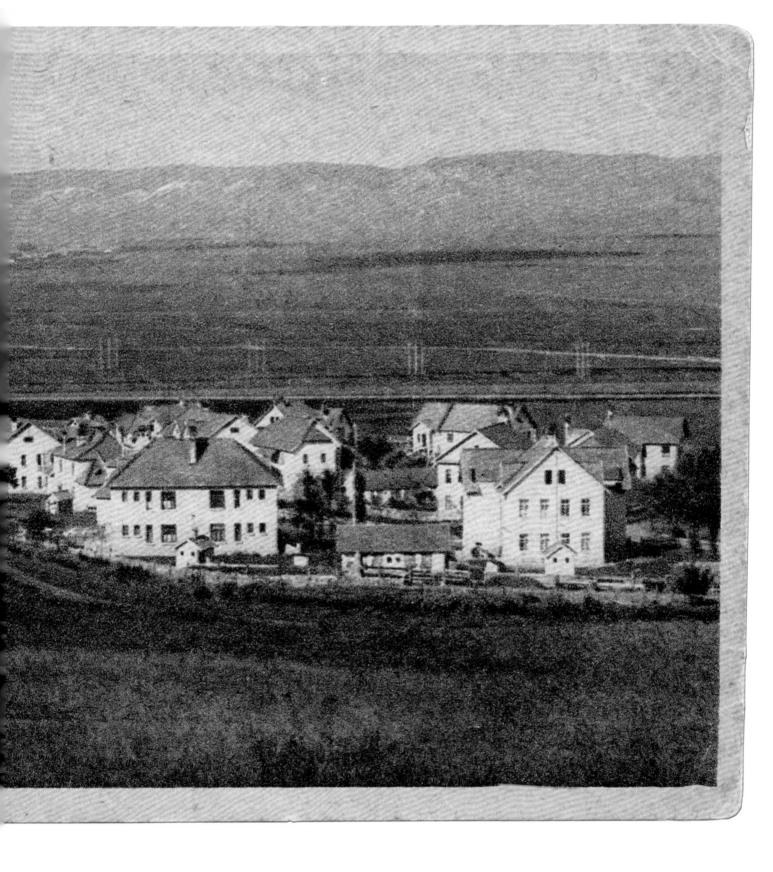

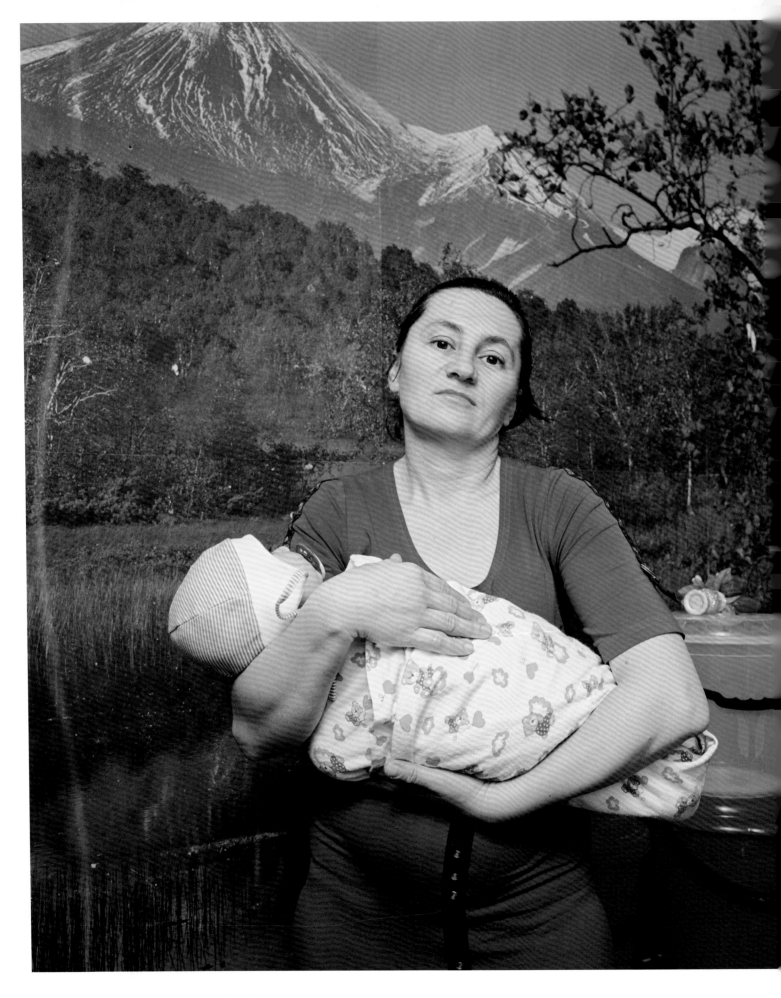

Refugee in Your Own City

In the center of Grozny, which has been largely rebuilt, we come across a ravaged apartment block. The building is surrounded by a pool of mud, as the only tap is outside and permanently running. Luisa, forty-two, and her three-month-old son, Rashik, live on the second floor. Around them the city's new buildings sparkle in the sun, while on his farm the Chechen leader Ramzan Kadyrov frolics with imported lions and Hollywood stars, photographs of which are broadcast to the world via an extremely active Instagram feed.

Grozny, Chechnya, 2011

Appeasing the Dictator

Thirteen-year-old twins Stanislav and Vladislav are Cossacks. Their father, Nikolai, represents the Cossacks in Naurskaya. This village was once on the frontline of the conflict between Russia and Chechnya and the Cossacks were pawns. Cossacks living in modern Chechnya are now obliged to comply with the local government. The twins may have inherited their father's diplomatic skills. It was a stroke of genius when the two boys recited a poem in Chechen in front of a Chechen audience that included President Ramzan Kadyrov. Following the recital Kadyrov stood up and cheered, and the entire audience cheered with him. The boys were immediately handed the keys of a luxury apartment in the capital, Grozny. Nikolai beams with pride when he tells his sons' story, then reveals his own triumphs: on the weekends he sometimes heads into the mountains with Chechen special forces to hunt down separatists. There's nothing like it, claims the former winemaker.

Naurskaya, Chechnya, 2012

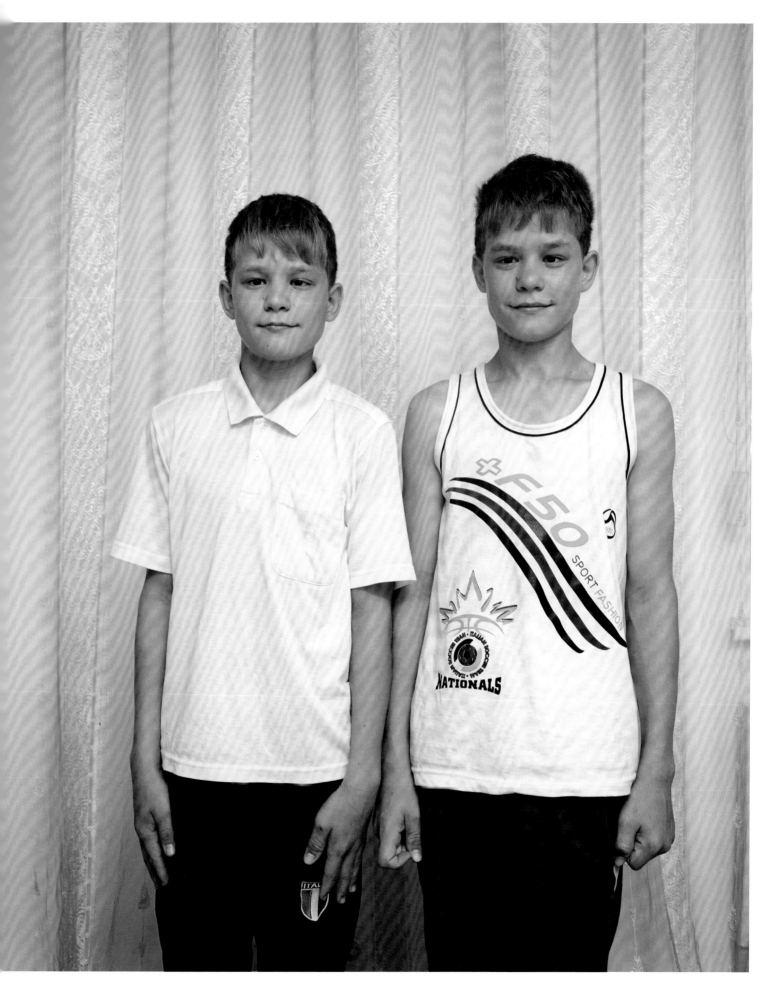

Dubai of the Caucasus, Under Construction

Big, bigger, biggest is Ramzan Kadyrov's motto. His grand plans, designed to transform Grozny into nothing short of the Dubai of the Caucasus, include "Grozny City," a complex of skyscrapers, the enormous Akhmad Kadyrov Mosque, and the wide Vladimir Putin Boulevard that he hopes will attract the world's leading brands. He has invited celebrities Gérard Depardieu, Ruud Gullit, Vanessa-Mae, Hilary Swank, and Jean-Claude Van Damme to the country and flaunts expensive racehorses and cars. All of this is financed with local oil revenues, subsidies, and loans from Moscow. As long as he keeps the peace in Chechnya, he is left to his own devices.

Grozny, Chechnya, 2011

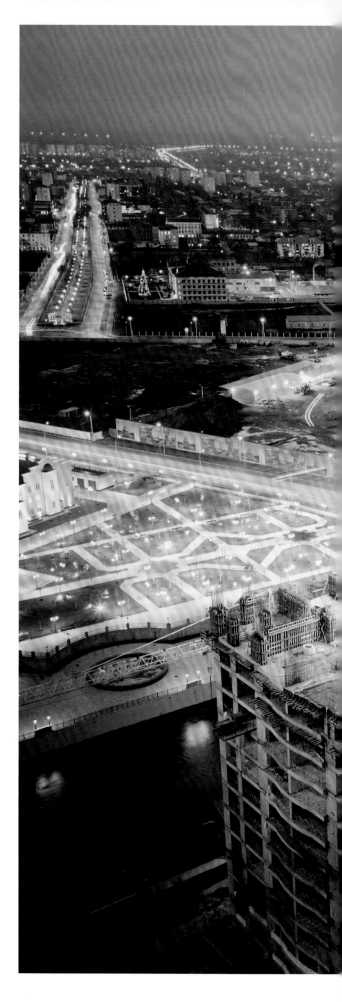

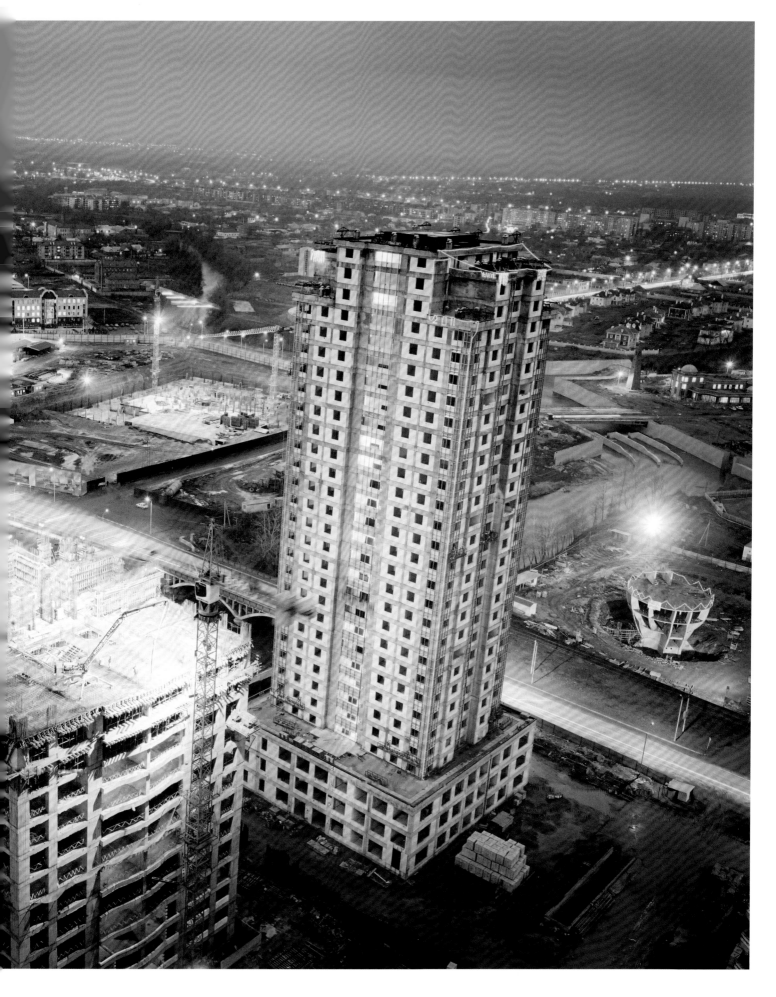

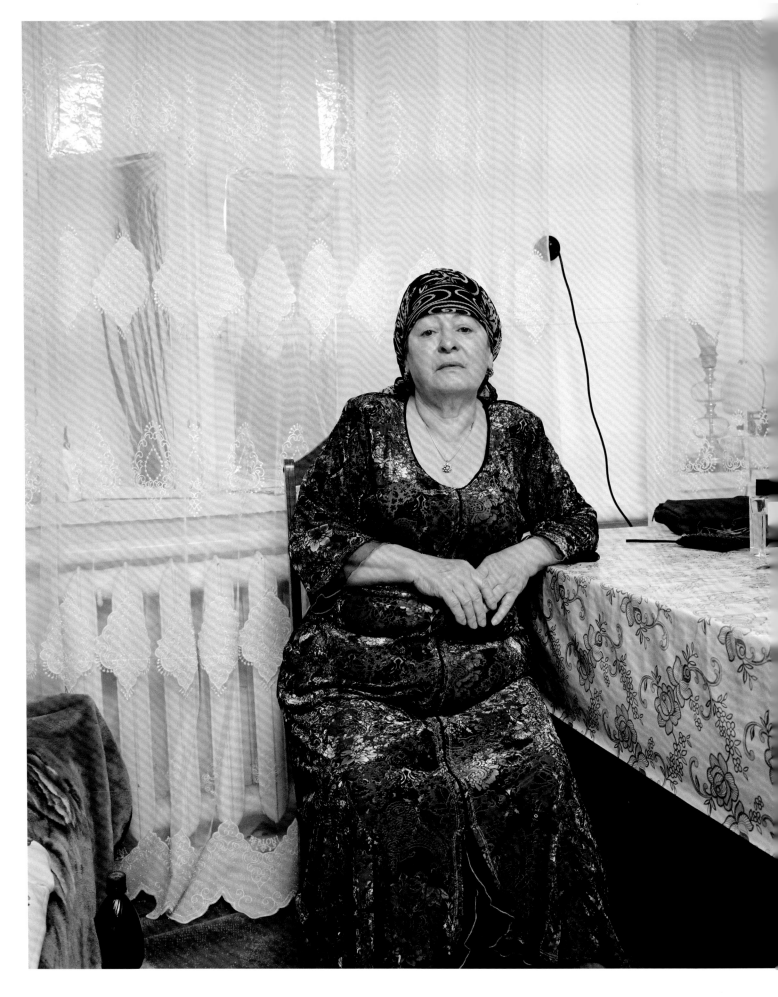

No Way Back

Lis Ismailova, sixty-four, lives with her relatives, the Katziev family, in Ingushetia. For decades she lived in the Chechen capital of Grozny, until she was forced to flee during the Second Chechen War (1999–2006). She cannot return. Her apartment was destroyed and as an ethnic Ingush she is not eligible for compensation from the Chechen government.

Ekazhevo, Ingushetia, 2012

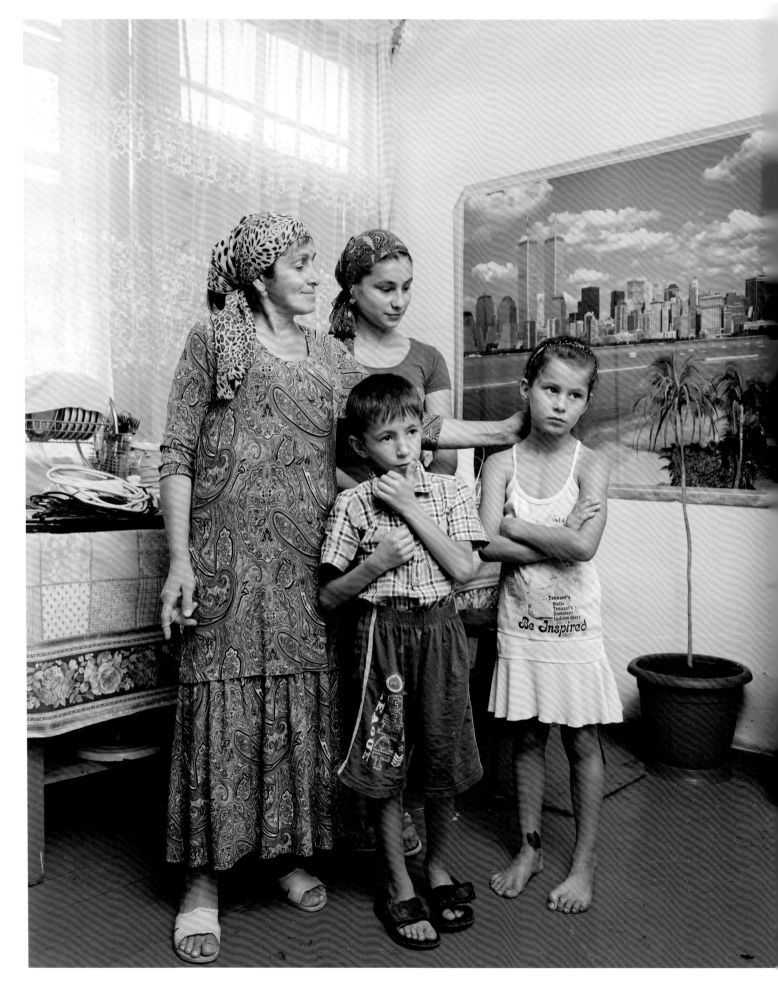

Dreams of Peace

The Katziev family dreams of peace. The past few years in the village of Ekazhevo, Ingushetia, have been difficult. The father of the family, a policeman, was shot by insurgents and is unable to work. An aunt from Grozny also lives in the Katzievs' small, crumbling house. She fled during the last Chechen war. As she is ethnically Ingush and not Chechen, she is not eligible for a new apartment in Grozny. A neighbor hobbles by on crutches. His foot was blown off by a bomb. Another neighbor recently lost his home when it was destroyed by tanks. The disabled inhabitant supposedly supported the insurgents. Nobody in the street believes it. We join the Katzievs for fresh mutton, homemade cheese, soup, and honey. This is just one chance encounter in the North Caucasus, where every front door hides another story.

Ekazhevo, Ingushetia, 2012

Kadyrov's Dream

Not long after this photograph was taken, fire broke out—the result of human error—in one of the skyscrapers in the Grozny City complex. Chechen President Ramzan Kadyrov returned from his vacation angry and disappointed. He promised to rebuild the tower and that it would be bigger and better than before. And the people who had made jokes about it on the Internet? They stood contritely behind him at the press conference and would be made— as Kadyrov put it—to lick the building clean.

Grozny, Chechnya, 2012

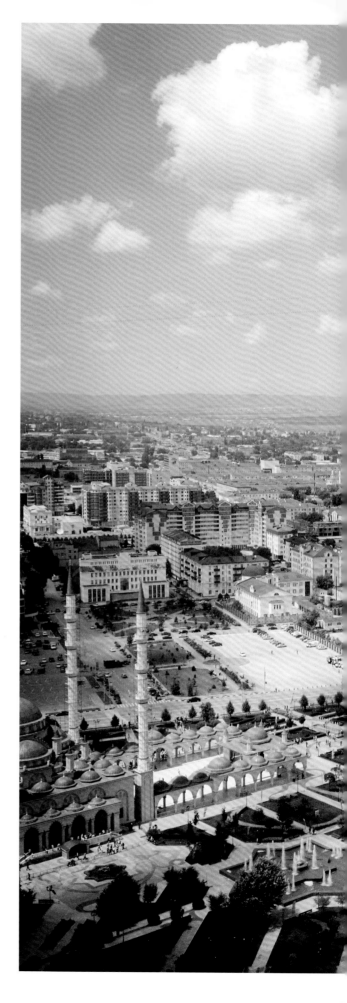

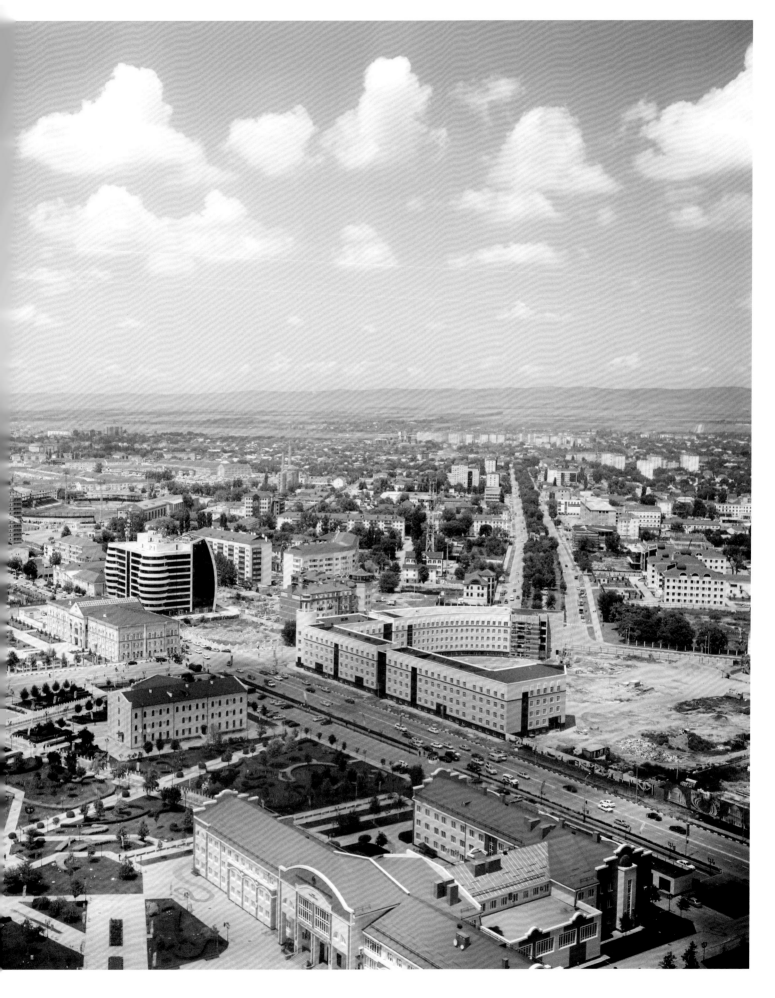

Hotel Svetlana

Postcard of Sochi during the Soviet era, 1970s

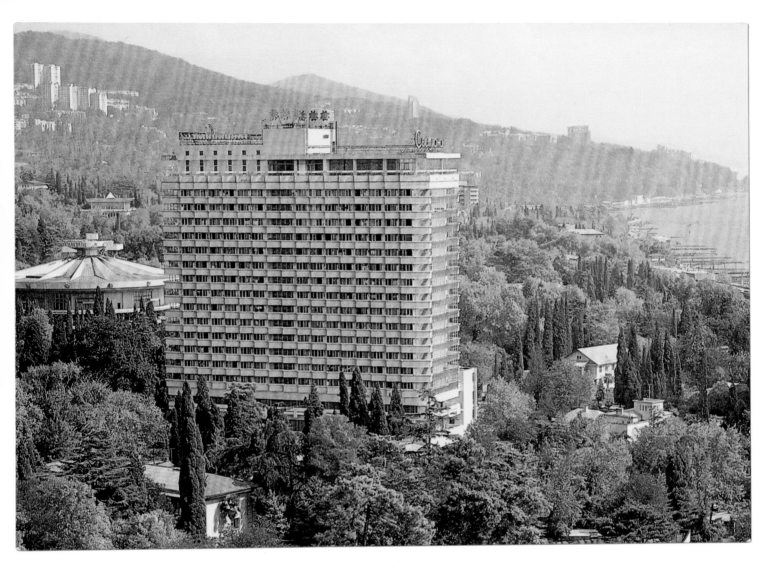

Hotel Svetlana

Sochi, Russia, 2012

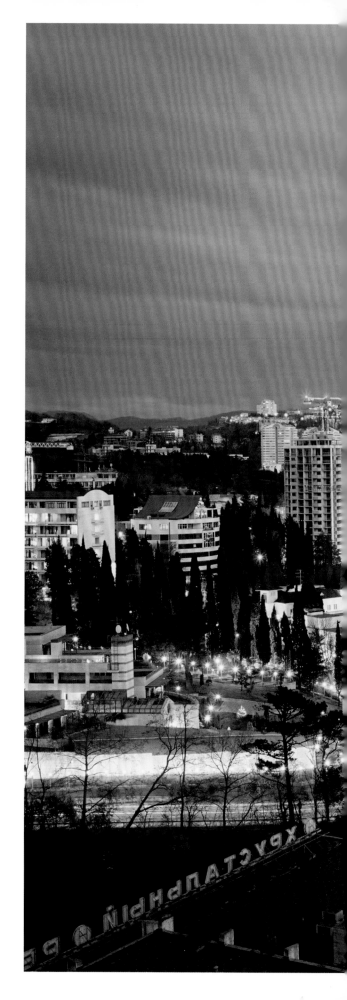

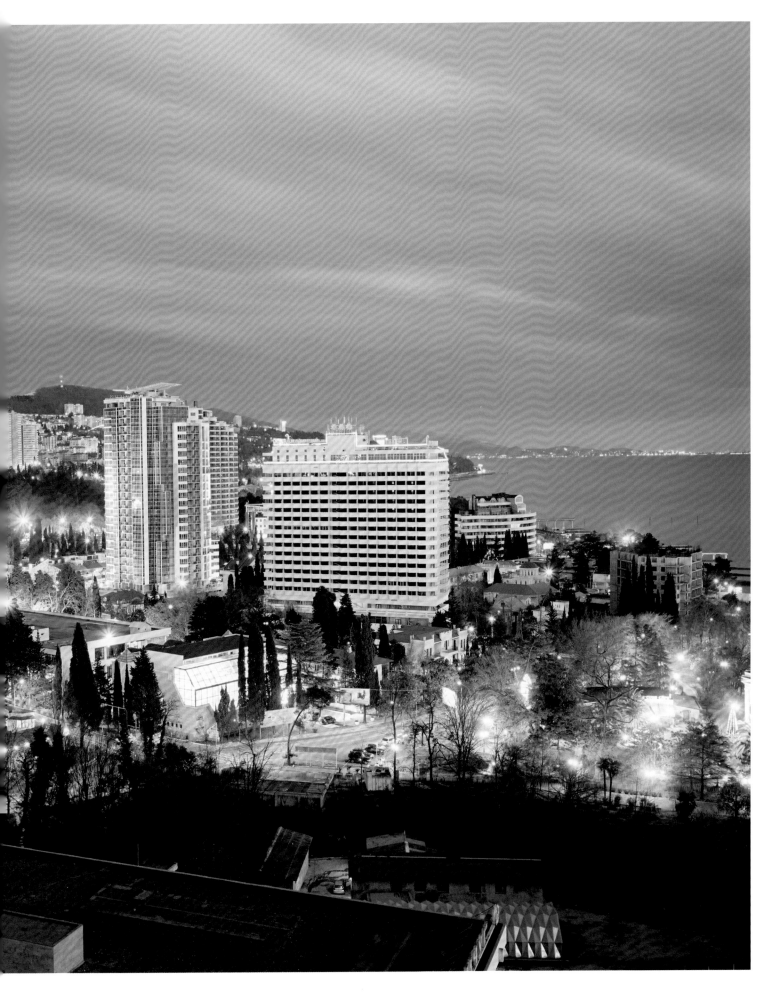

Restaurant Olymp

Lyana Tatevosian, twenty-five, and guitar player Viktor sing "Vino kachnulos' na dne bokala" (The wine swirls at the bottom of my glass).

Novomikhailovsky, Sochi region, Russia, 2011

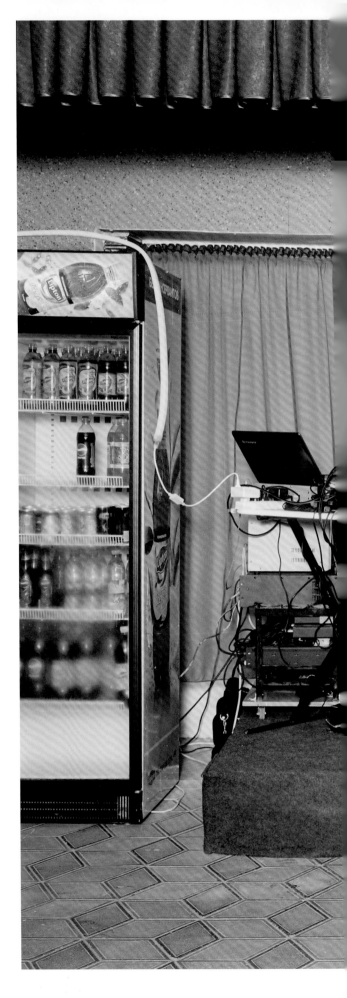

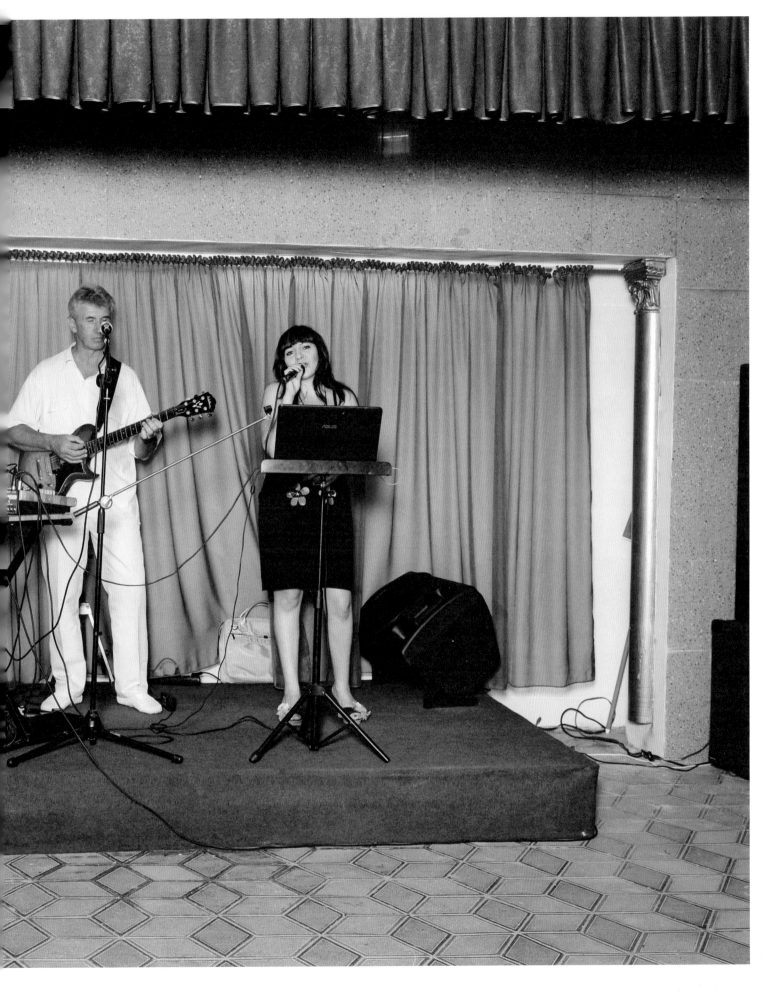

"Sochi used to be much prettier. These days crooks from Moscow come here to build and sell."

Viktor Alexeyevich
Murmansk, Russia, 2009

Sochi Singers

Viktor Alexeyevich approaches us on the beach. A retired shipbuilder from Murmansk, he has happily made use of the opportunity to relax in Sochi for years. "Sochi used to be much prettier," he says. "These days crooks from Moscow come here to build and sell skyscrapers and apartments, although it used to be such a small, lovely town. You can't even see the sanatorium from the beach anymore. Still, it's better than Murmansk."

There are thousands of others like Alexeyevich in Sochi: Russians of the Soviet old guard who sometimes travel for days by train, car, or (if they can afford it) plane to get here. One girl told us that summer in her Siberian village lasts just two weeks, when everyone is eaten alive by mosquitoes. Sochi is paradise in comparison.

That paradise is designed for eating, bathing, and amusement. To this end, the roads leading to the sanatoria, the promenades, and the towns and villages strung along the coast are crammed with stores and restaurants. First-time visitors will be struck by the barrage of noise that hits them from all sides, and the sometimes-ludicrous ways in which entrepreneurs attempt to relieve them of their spending money.

On one promenade a throne is draped with leopard skins. Sitting on the throne is a black man—a negro, to use a politically incorrect term still common here. He is wearing a short bamboo skirt and crown and is holding a spear. On the street in front of him, his lackeys (also black) carry spears, daggers, and leather pouches for their cell phones. One has a bag tied around his waist for tips. Parents hoist their crying children onto the throne for a photograph with the negro king while drunken men look on.

The smell of sunscreen, sweat, alcohol, and roasting meat pervades the air. On the beaches, perspiring men with baskets of blackberries, popcorn, and corn advertise their wares. Respectable families and drunks carrying large bottles of beer walk side by side. In the streets and alleys behind the beaches, clouds of smoke from grilling *shashlik* drift upward. On the promenades, voluptuous girls lure visitors to the attractions: throwing darts at balloons, shooting guns, having the skin on your feet nibbled off by special fish, parasailing, banana boating—the options are almost endless.

A young man named Vasya is sitting on a concrete seawall dotted with pebbles and rusty piers that run into the ocean. A cameraman from Moscow, he has just completed an assignment in Abkhazia, farther to the south. He is now enjoying a short vacation in Adler, on the Russian side of the border. His older girlfriend, Yulia, has come with him. Her nipples are covered with two silver stars; topless sunbathing in Russia is not permitted. "Look around you," Vasya points to the stone desert. "It's fantastic." The waves break on the beach, making a magical sound as they retreat and drag the pebbles with them. The sound almost drowns out the *popsa* (Russian pop) and house music coming from various telephones and ghetto blasters. "There aren't many good nightclubs, but hey, we Muscovites are spoiled." Yulia's only reservation is "all the Caucasians" who live here. "We're from Moscow and the culture here is very different. There are more Muslims."

Our conversation is cut short by a passing train. The woman next to us introduces herself as Ekaterina. "Sochi is the Florida of Russia, but cheaper," she says. "My daughter lives in Kansas and we bought an apartment together in Sochi, for me to retire to. It's heavenly. The climate is subtropical but you can hike in the cool mountains whenever you want."

Every self-respecting restaurant has a singer. Restaurants forced to share the limited space on the riverbank—such as at Sochi's desirable Riviera Park location—have built special singing booths of corrugated glass to direct the sound toward their own venue. They make little difference. Restaurant Romashka is filled with a cacophony of different songs. Many guests seem to appreciate this, however, and choose the exact spot where the sound converges. Two songs for the price of one. And why not?

The restaurants farther from the promenades attract older visitors and families. The dance floor in Novy Afon is empty. An exhausted group huddles around a table. The music renders most conversation impossible, but the guests do not seem to mind. After a long scorching day on the beach, in the amusement parks, gardens, and stores, most of them simply enjoy losing themselves in the dramatic lyrics of chansons and *popsa*. "My soul cannot sleep without you," issues almost cheerfully from the speakers. Satisfied heads bob up and down. "I am beaten and crushed, and this is my last letter to you." At the table, the guests drink a final toast.

Bar Proletarski

Sochi, Russia, 2011

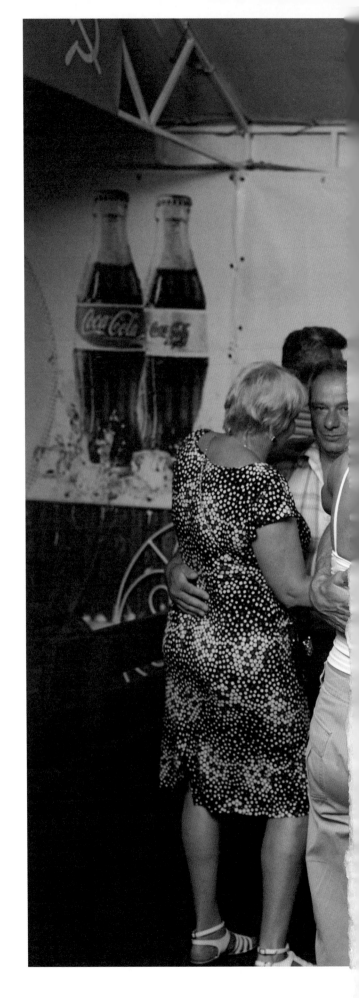

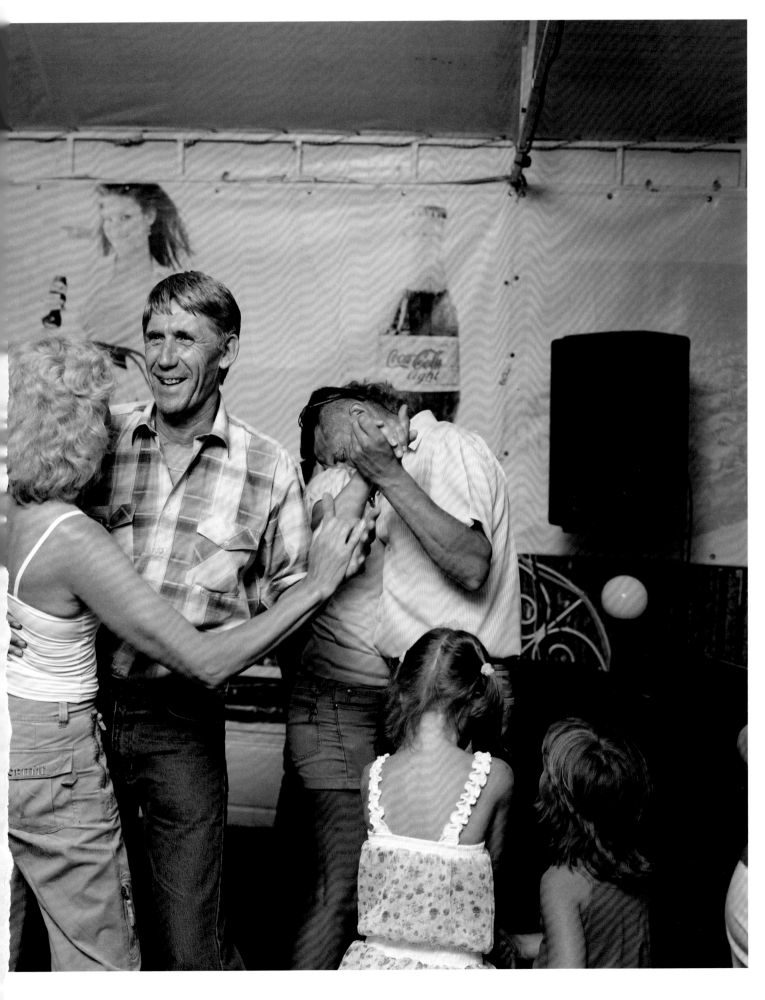

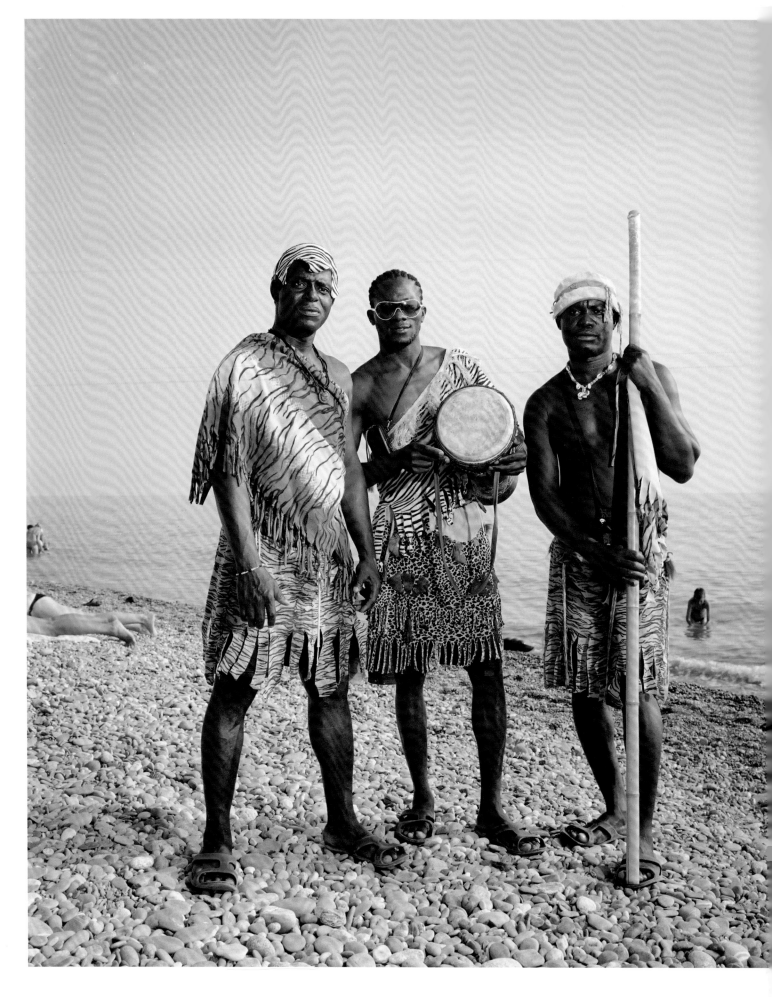

African Kings

It costs one hundred rubles to have your picture taken with a real African king. Dressed in tribal clothing, black students from Moscow's Friendship University earn extra money working in Sochi in the summer. They sometimes build thrones on the boulevards, with ostrich feathers, leopard-skin cushions, and real spears.

Loo, Sochi region, Russia, 2011

The smell of sunscreen, sweat, alcohol, and roasting meat pervades the air.

Tatiana

In 2013, the official website of the Sochi
Chamber of Commerce reads: "It is not a
secret that every year millions of Russians
tend to spend their holydays [sic] in Sochi, to
enjoy the gentle surf of the Black Sea warm
waves, the beauty of the mountains, to improve their health, to make a tour of Sochi,
and to save vivid impressions about their
relaxation.... Sochi will relax your body and
your soul."

Sochi, Russia, 2011

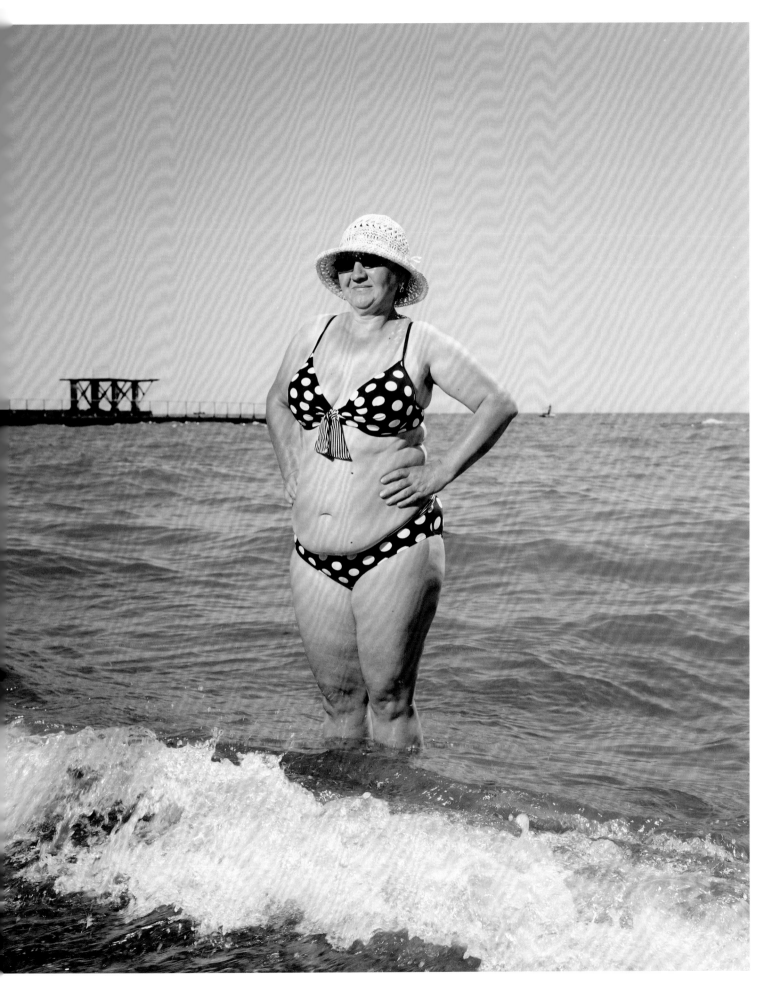

Vacation in Sochi

Khava Gaisanova (second row, on the right) was born in Kazakhstan the eldest daughter of parents exiled from Ingushetia. She returned to the North Caucasus in 1975 and chose the warm waters of Sochi for her vacations.

Holiday snapshot from Sochi, 1970s

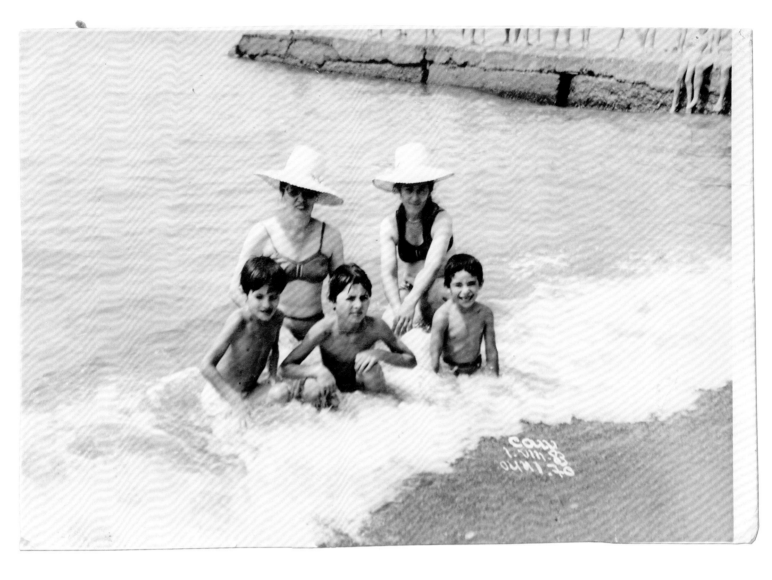

213

A Changing Past

Khava Gaisanova's parents were exiled by
Stalin from Bazurkina, Ingushetia, in 1944.
When Khava returned in 1975, the village was
renamed Chermen, North Ossetia. Stalin
and his cronies' geopolitical games had been
effective. Immediately after the fall of the
Soviet Union, war broke out between the
Ingush and the North Ossetians. It was the
first of many conflicts in the region.

Chermen, North Ossetia, 2011

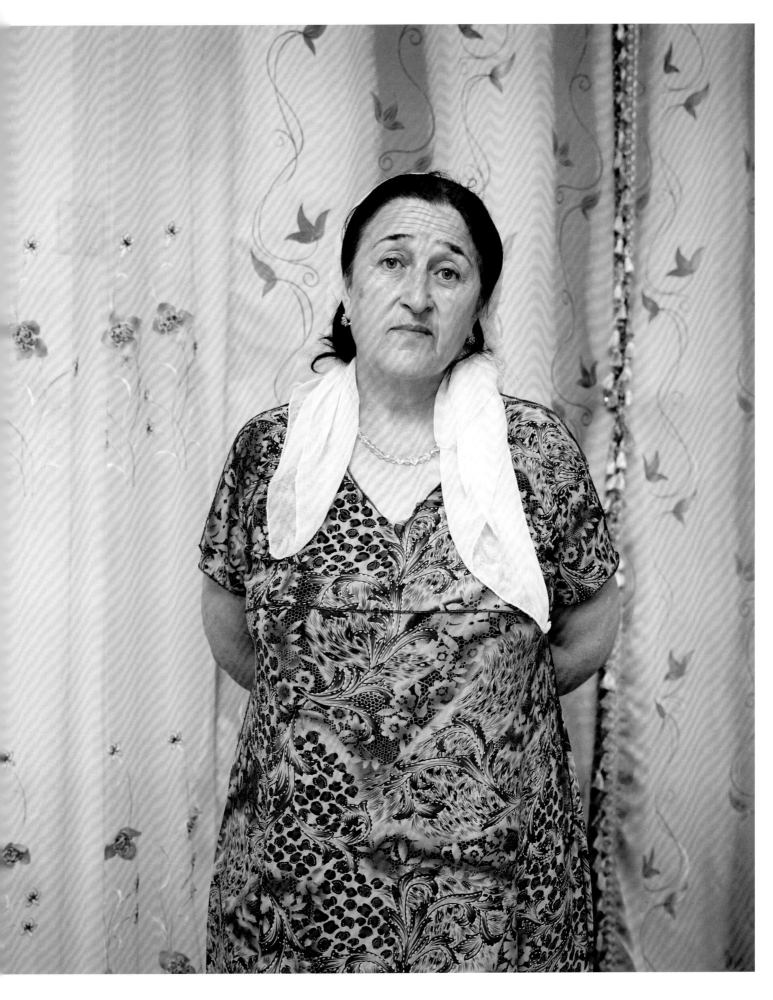

Mukhazhir Gaisanov, Missing

"My husband had gone shopping in Vladikavkaz with a neighbor," says Khava. "They then intended to drive to Ingushetia together to buy a new car with an Ossetian license plate. They never got there. They were probably arrested by men posing as the police, or stopped by the real police. I don't know what happened. No one knows what happened."

Mukhazhir's car was found the same day, in the street near the interior ministry and police headquarters. Residents had alerted the authorities. A car with an Ingush license plate parked in an area like that was suspicious. There had been a spate of bombings and residents were afraid that this car, too, would explode. "I got everything back," says Khava. "All their important documents were still there, except my husband's driving license. That's our only clue; that someone asked for his driving license. Otherwise the car was clean. There was no trace of blood, nothing that indicated any violence."

Chermen, North Ossetia, 2012

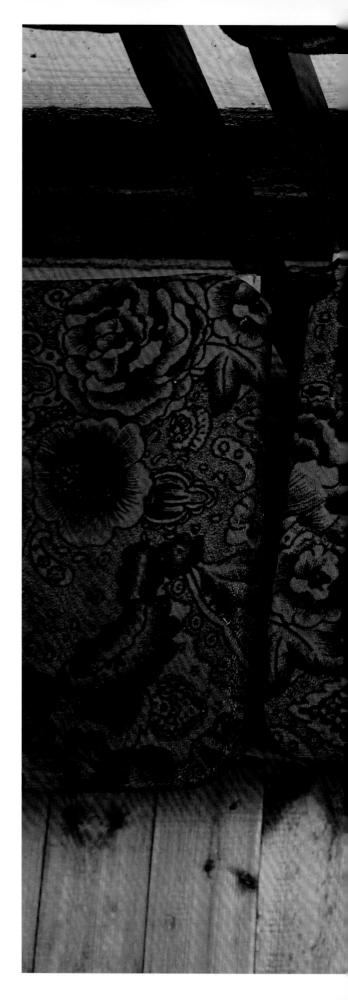

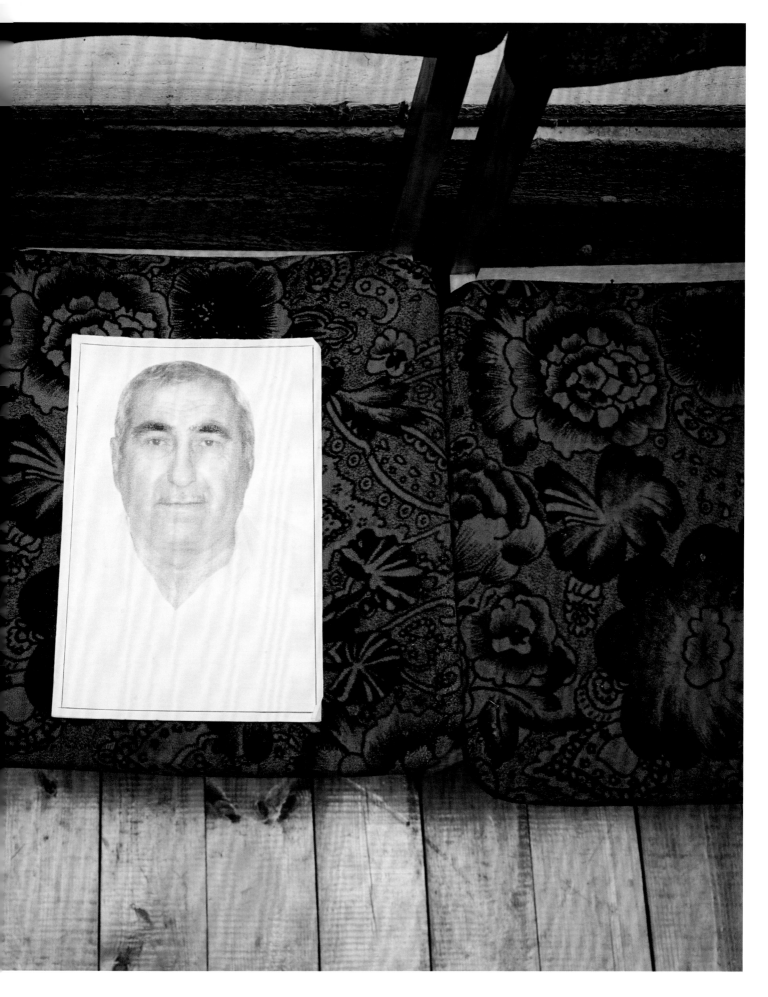

Dreaming of a Town Without Muslims

"The Ingush are Muslims," says Taimuraz
Tsirigov. "Their aim is for every Muslim to
kill an orthodox Christian in his lifetime.
We'll always live separately, like the Jews
among the Muslims in the Middle East. Until
the next conflict, that is," he says menacingly.
"Our ancestors were true fighters. I'm an old
man, but I'll be the first to defend myself.
I'll never renounce part of my motherland
to anyone."

Chermen, North Ossetia, 2011

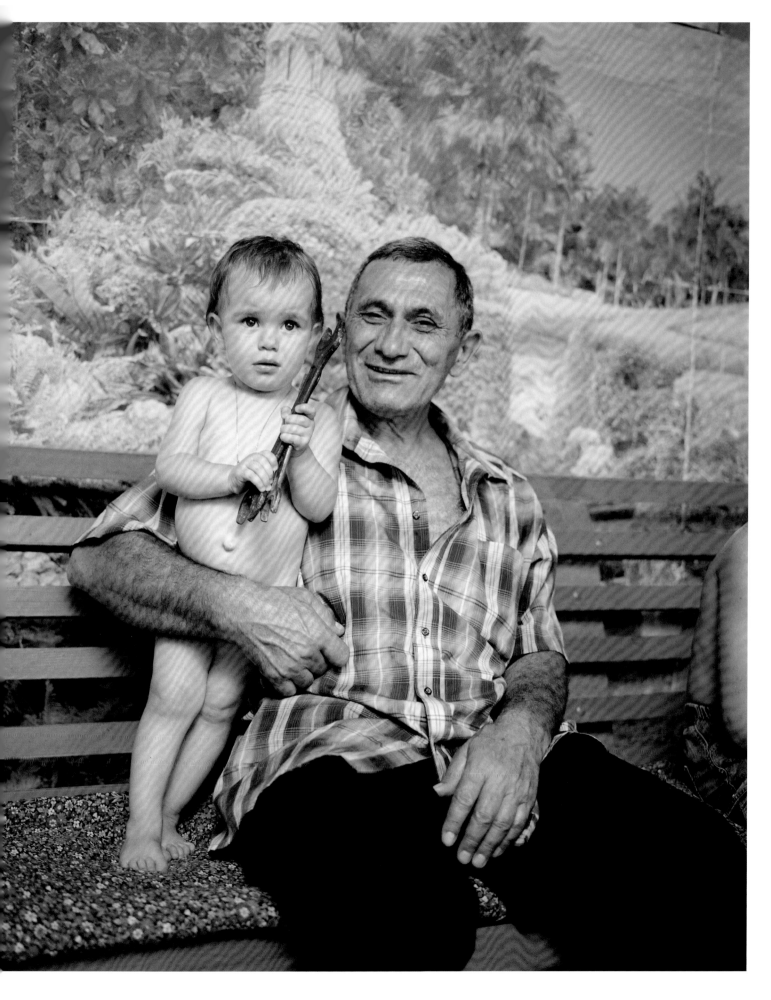

"We'll always live separately, like the Jews among the Muslims in the Middle East."

Taimuraz Tsirigov
Chermen, North Ossetia, 2011

Missing

Photographs and documents belonging to those who went missing during the 1992 East Prigorodny Conflict between North Ossetia and Ingushetia are preserved in the Deportation Museum.

Nazran, Ingushetia, 2012

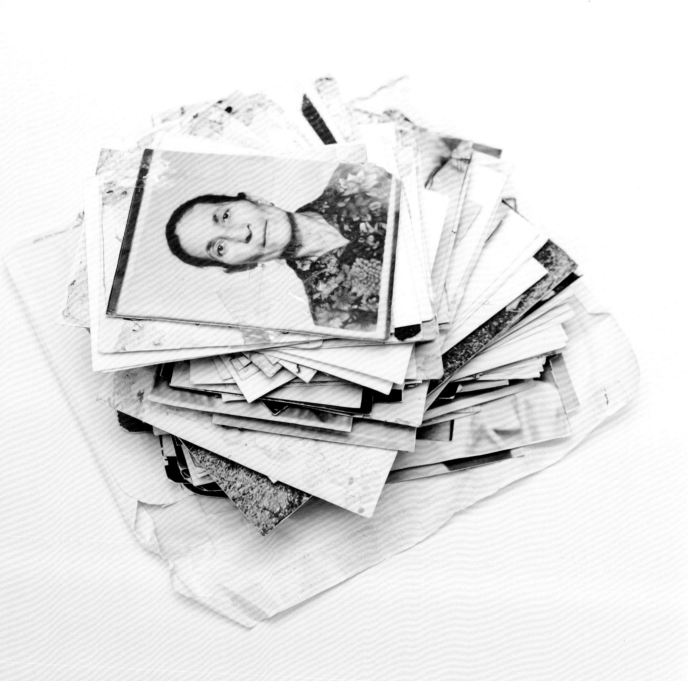

Bad Timing

Gamat-Khan Kartzoyev heard an explosion nearby. "In my naïveté, I went toward it. Just as I arrived, a second bomb exploded. The Ossetians were bombing the crossroads. I only regained consciousness in the hospital. When the conflict started, I thought it would stay small. But the Soviet Union deployed its entire arsenal: planes, tanks, grenades, machine guns. I was working in Vladikavkaz so I had a lot of Ossetian friends. Now I rarely see them. They're afraid of us and we're afraid of them."

Kantishevo, Ingushetia, 2012

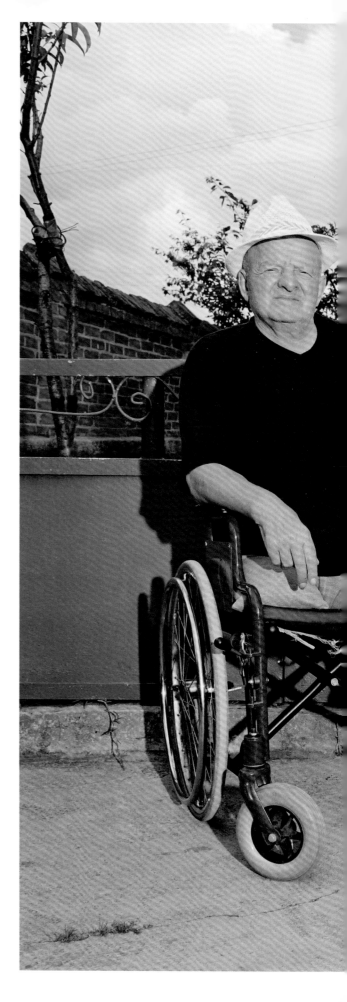

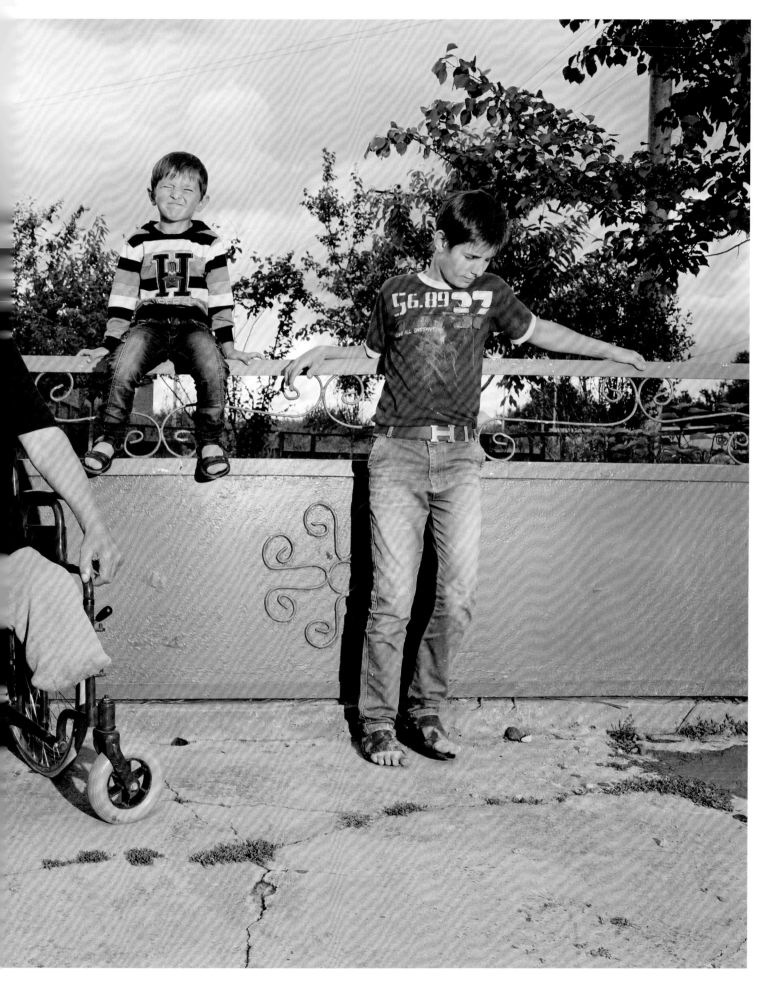

How to Shoot

Weapon-handling instructions are posted on the notice board of the combined elementary and high school in Sogratl, in the mountains of Dagestan.

Sogratl, Dagestan, 2012

Огневая подготовка

РУЧНЫЕ ГРАНАТЫ РКГ-3, РГД-5, Ф-1

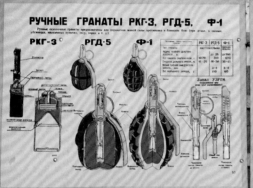

РКГ-3 **РГД-5** **Ф-1**

ПРИЕМЫ МЕТАНИЯ РУЧНЫХ ГРАНАТ

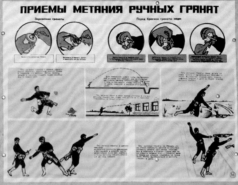

7,62-мм АВТОМАТ КАЛАШНИКОВА (АКМ)

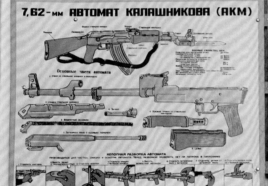

7,62-мм РУЧНОЙ ПУЛЕМЕТ КАЛАШНИКОВА (РПК)

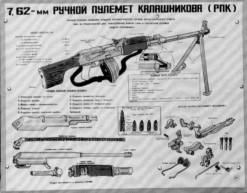

Порядок ЧИСТКИ и СМАЗКИ ОРУЖИЯ

Чистку и смазку оружия производится в следующем порядке:
ПОДГОТОВИТЬ МАТЕРИАЛЫ ДЛЯ ЧИСТКИ И СМАЗКИ;
РАЗОБРАТЬ АВТОМАТ;
ОСМОТРЕТЬ ПРИНАДЛЕЖНОСТЬ И ПОДГОТОВИТЬ ЕЁ ДЛЯ
ИСПОЛЬЗОВАНИЯ ПРИ ЧИСТКЕ;
ПРОЧИСТИТЬ КАНАЛ СТВОЛА, ГАЗОВУЮ КАМЕРУ, ГАЗОВУЮ
ТРУБКУ, СТВОЛЬНУЮ КОРОБКУ, ЗАТВОР, ГАЗОВЫЙ ПОРШЕНЬ С ПОМОЩЬЮ
ШОМПОЛА С ВЕТОШЬЮ (ПАКЛЕЙ), СМОЧЕННОЙ В ЖИДКОЙ РУЖЕЙНОЙ
СМАЗКЕ, И ДЕРЕВЯННЫХ ПАЛОЧЕК;
ПРОТЕРЕТЬ ВСЕ ДЕТАЛИ НАСУХО, ДЕРЕВЯННЫЕ ЧАСТИ ОБТЕ-
РЕТЬ СУХОЙ ВЕТОШЬЮ. ПОСЛЕ ЧИСТКИ МЕТАЛЛИЧЕСКИХ ЧАСТЕЙ ОРУЖИЕ
СМАЗАТЬ.

МАТЕРИАЛЫ

ПАМЯТКА по уходу за ОРУЖИЕМ

Оружие должно содержаться всегда в полной исправ-
ности и быть готовым к действию. Это достигается
умелой чисткой и смазкой, правильным хранением,
сбережением и своевременным устранением поломок.
Чистка производится
- после стрельбы боевыми или холостыми патро-
нами-немедленно после окончания стрельбы;
- после наряда или занятий;
- в боевой обстановке и на длительных учениях-
ежедневно в период затишья боя и во время
перерыва в учениях.
- если оружие стоит без применения - не ре-
же одного раза в неделю.
Солдаты и сержанты осматривают оружие
ежедневно, перед заступлением в наряд, перед выхо-
дом на занятия. В боевой обстановке - периодически
в течение дня и перед выполнением боевой задачи.
При осмотре убедитесь в наличии всех частей оружия, и проверьте нет ли на наружных частях ржав-
чины, трещин, отколов и побитостей. Проверить
состояние смазки, наличие ремня и принадлеж-
ности, магазинов и сумок для них, штыка-ножа
Предохранять оружие от попадания в ствол
посторонних предметов, что при стрельбе приводит
к раздутию или разрыву ствола.

The Glorious Mountains

Great Russian writers such as Pushkin, Lermontov, and Tolstoy were fully engrossed by the Caucasus. The Caucasus represented the mountains where humans and animals still lived in harmony, where nature was as fearless as man. The struggle in the Caucasus was against the noble savage, a civilizing mission, a task for Russia. At the same time, it held up a mirror to Russia. While civilization had brought calm to Russia, the Caucasian was still a real man, a fighter, someone whose honor mattered. In both Pushkin's poem "The Prisoner of the Caucasus" (1820–21) and Lermontov's poem "Demon" (1829–39), Caucasian women are portrayed as mysterious, fairytale beauties; the women from *The Thousand and One Nights*, but in Russia's very own Near East.

The Romanticism of the nineteenth century persists in twentieth-century folklore. The fierce guerrilla fighters of the Caucasian War are translated into tableaux of supernaturally healthy, powerful, noble warriors who rise above the common hustle and bustle, sitting proudly on horseback. The women—firm, dignified types with large bosoms—are engrossed in crafts such as jewelry making, pottery, or fruit preserving.

Tolstoy's final novel, *Hadji Murad* (1912), begins with the eponymous protagonist finding a beautiful raspberry-colored thistle on his land. When he tries to pick it for his wildflower bouquet, the thistle is so tough and strong that he has to tear it off filament by filament. Such a life force, the writer reflects: man has subdued most of nature, but this one thistle refuses to give up. Tolstoy pursues his meditation and uses the thistle as a metaphor in his short history of the Caucasus.

Chokh, Dagestan, 2011

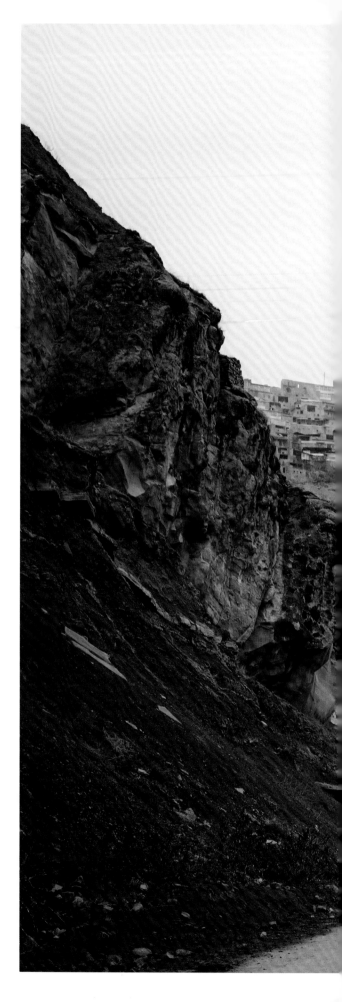

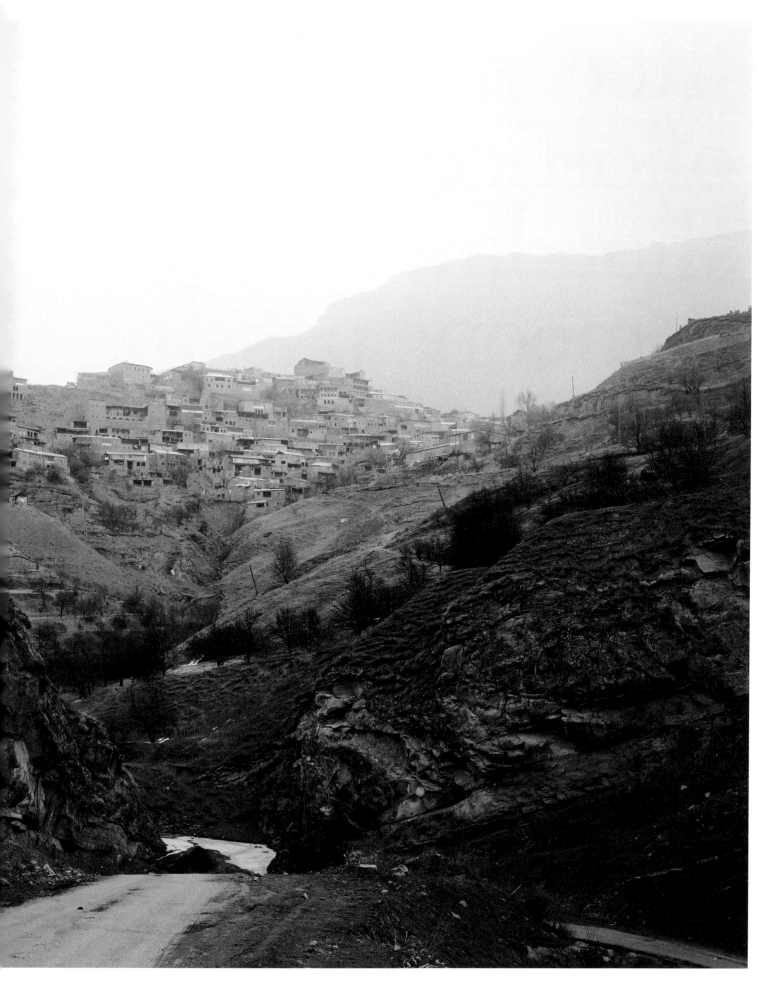

"Recently, a couple of officers were shot down by someone passing on a bike. We never practiced that scenario."

Anonymous
Makhachkala, Dagestan, 2012

Policemen Under Fire

Hamzad Ivloev was at his post, as usual. Night fell and most policemen went home. Hamzad was on the night shift with his colleague Magomed. "You go to sleep," he told Magomed, "we'll switch halfway." Hamzad was standing behind the concrete wall of the small guard post in the village of Troitska in Ingushetia. From there he had a view of the access road to the village. He would occasionally go and sit inside, fighting sleep.

At three in the morning he woke up Magomed and collapsed onto the bed. But he did not get much sleep: less than fifteen minutes later Magomed looked out of the window and saw a group of armed men with masks. "I was woken by Magomed calling for reinforcements," Hamzad remembers. Then Magomed stormed into his room and screamed: "Get out!" Total chaos ensued. Hamzad ran to the neighboring house with a shotgun to take up position there. Magomed was behind the concrete wall on the street side. "We didn't know how many men were going to attack us, so I had taken lots of grenades with me," he says. He describes how he saw the *boyeviks* (separatist fighters) go down one by one, while Magomed and he miraculously managed to stay out of the line of fire. "They threw Molotov cocktails and they had a grenade launcher. Their guns were much more modern than ours."

It seemed to take forever for the reinforcements to arrive. "Most of the *boyeviks* had probably fled by then," says Hamzad. "We stayed at our posts all that time. It was pitch dark."

When the reinforcements arrived, Hamzad knew instinctively that there was something wrong. He panicked and called out: "Stop!" He was sure that there was a hidden trap somewhere, and there was no better place to plant an improvised explosive device than on the gate. The officers climbed over it with difficulty. "I called out, maybe three times, that we had to be careful, that we had to look around, that we had to scout out the surroundings. Three times Magomed replied that everything was clean. Then I saw the grenade. The terrorists had placed it in a glass in such a way that it would only detonate after it was moved. One of the new officers, Adam, had knocked over the glass and was crouching on the floor covering his face with his hands as he waited for the blast. I started shouting: 'Get out everyone, there's going to be an explosion!' No one seemed to respond. Magomed was three meters farther away; in total there were five people near the grenade. And me. I must have shouted three or four times that everyone should get out. It seemed like they didn't know what to do, or they didn't hear me—their brains weren't working. Everything was muffled.

"Most grenades explode within six seconds; this one must have taken fifteen seconds. I asked God for forgiveness and lay down on the grenade.

"When the explosion came I could still see. I saw that my hand had been ripped off. I wanted to go and look for my friends but everything became light and I couldn't see anything. I touched my eyes and felt blood. Later it turned out that my rifle had absorbed a large part of the blast because it had been right on top of the grenade." His colleagues, Adam, Magomed, and the others, got off lightly and were released from hospital after just a few days.

Local authorities are not keen for foreign journalists to tackle this subject. We ask why and argue sympatheti-cally that it will generate understanding for their position, their struggle. We get no answer, but we do get a phone call to inform us that we are not to visit police officers in Ingushetia anymore.

Agent X lives in the Dagestani capital, Makhachkala. We are not allowed to use his name and, worse still, we have to stop the interview halfway through when his father and uncle break out in a cold sweat. Agent X was on the scene of a large bomb attack on a police post in Makhachkala and sustained injuries to his neck, arm, chest, and leg. "We receive training on terrorism attacks," says X. "Sometimes it works, sometimes it doesn't. No one knows when it's going to happen. Recently, a couple of officers were shot down by someone passing on a bike. We never practiced that scenario." Then X is not permitted to talk anymore and his father and uncle affably explain why they want to remain anonymous. "Once you get into the media," they say, "everyone can suddenly find you. The authorities get upset because you've come out with your own story, the terrorists can find you; we prefer to remain anonymous. It's bad enough as it is."

Hamzad Saved Cowards

Hamzad, forty-four, sits on the edge of his sofa bed in the small town of Karabulak. He lost his legs and an arm when the checkpoint he was guarding was attacked by rebels "from the woods." He is now bedridden. He can hardly see and his hearing has been badly damaged but his mind is as sharp as ever. His two daughters frolic about around him while he listens to the radio. He is embittered. He does not know why he sacrificed himself. He goes over and over that fateful night in his mind. Why did the others not react? "I saved cowards," he says. He will soon move into a new house, which he was already working on before everything went wrong. But it will not change much for him; there, too, his life will be reduced to a sofa bed and a radio.

"Still," says the amputee police officer, "I'd do it all again. My son has also joined the police academy. For the fatherland. Only God knows when it will be safe. One day there will be peace." Hamzad is not the only unemployed and wounded police officer who is stuck at home. Police officers are on the front line of the fight against the rebellions in Dagestan, Chechnya, Ingushetia, and Kabardino-Balkaria. Their guard posts are targets. Their homes are targets. Wherever they walk, eat, and drive are targets.

Karabulak, Ingushetia, 2012

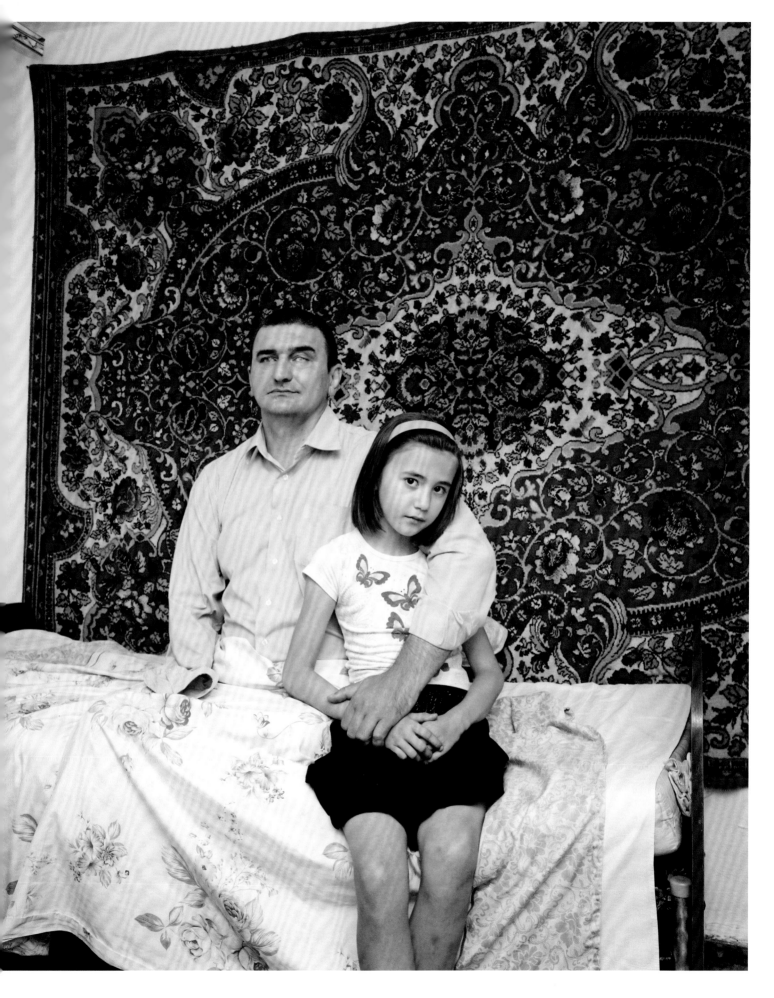

Salman Was Abandoned

In 2008 policeman Salman Aliev, thirty-five, was guarding a border post between North Ossetia and Ingushetia in Russia's North Caucasus. He was shot in the head by a sniper, in the continuing rebellion against the Russian regime. He is bitter about how his colleagues from the neighboring republic reacted to the attacks. "We were standing at the traffic circle in Chermen, on the border. The Ossetians didn't help, only the Ingush tried to save me. The Ossetians had already sought cover."

Nazran, Ingushetia, 2012

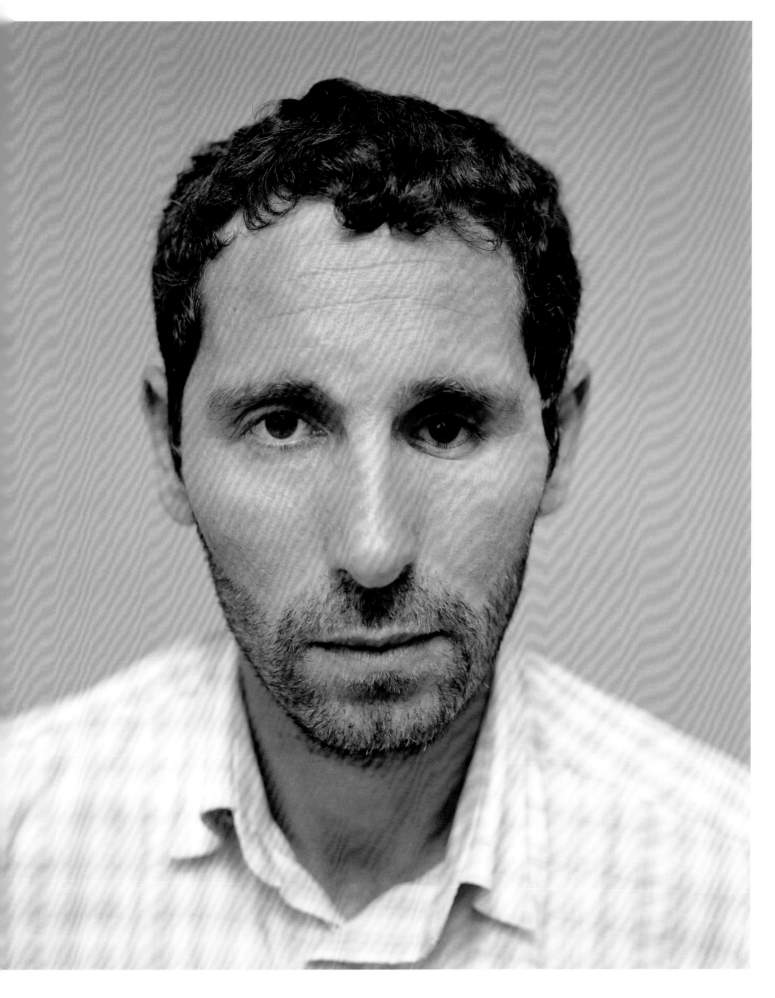

Born as Refugees

Milana, Rizvan, and Ravida Dezaurov were born as refugees. Their father fled from the Prigorodny District in North Ossetia to Ingushetia and found shelter in a communal building that had previously housed prisoners carrying out community service. The other refugees are slowly drifting away, allowing the Dezaurov family to take over their vacant rooms instead of being confined to the single room in which they had lived until recently.

Karabulak, Ingushetia, 2012

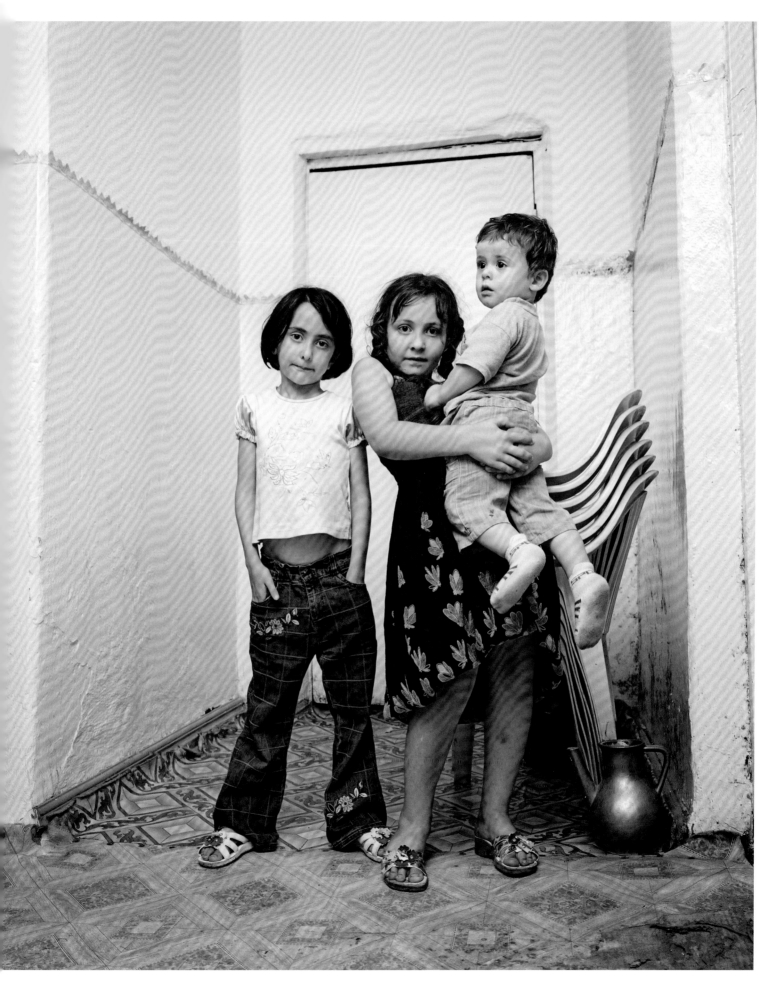

Imran Dzhambekov, Missing

One evening Imran Dzhambekov was dragged from his home by masked men in government vehicles. The license plate numbers were written down and the vehicles were traced, but Imran was never heard from again. He joins the growing army of missing people in the North Caucasus. Disappearances plague all the republics, whether they have experienced two decades of war and armed insurgency, such as Chechnya, or a few years of unrest due to the rise of radical Islam, such as Kabardino-Balkaria.

Imran's parents moved heaven and earth to find their son. His mother, Zainap, voiced a fiery protest that landed her in jail. She has since been released and was awarded significant damages by Moscow, which was forced to pay out by the European Court of Human Rights for the unlawful abduction of her son and for her own unlawful detention in appalling conditions. The family is using the money to build a small store, and continues to talk to as many reporters as possible in order to organize protests. "I'm too old to be scared of this government," Zainap says.

Goity, Chechnya, 2011

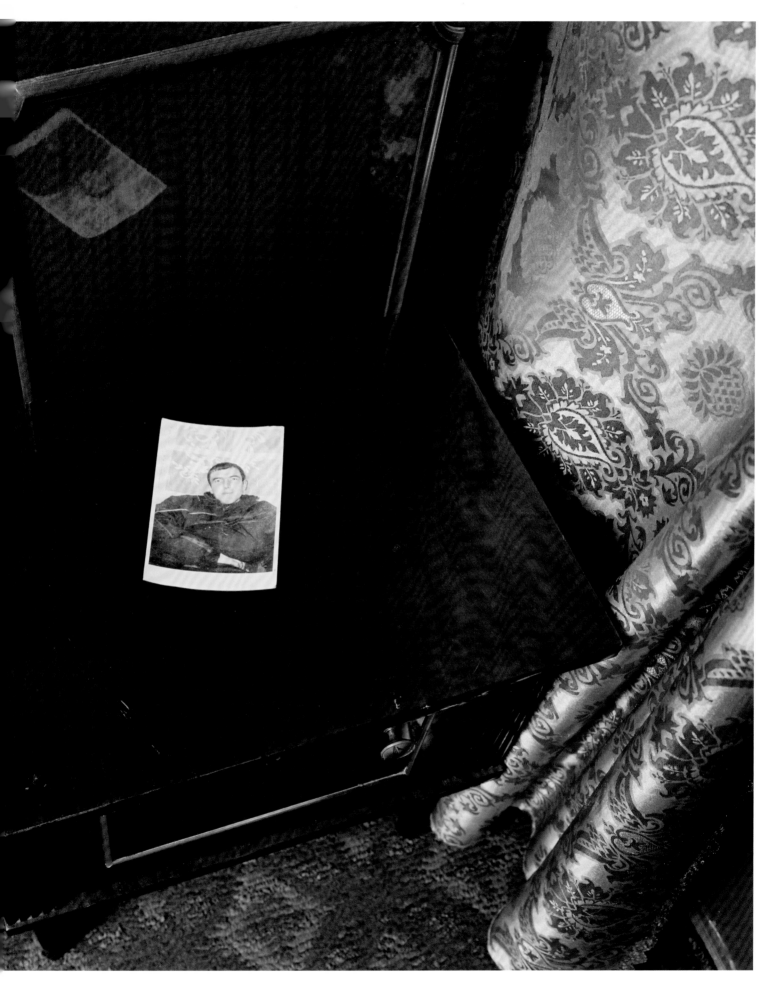

The Lawyer

Lawyer Adipgerey Umarov has an office in Khasavyurt, a troubled market town in western Dagestan and the wrestling capital of the Caucasus. Umarov is sixty-seven years old, but has no intention of retiring anytime soon. His office, located on an unpaved road in one of the suburbs, is filled with piles of papers and cupboards overflowing with files. His caseload is dominated by incidents related to the separatists in the mountains and woods. He takes a pessimistic view of the situation. Two of his current clients are men who assisted the separatists and, despite turning themselves in, have been harshly punished. "No one will ever come out of the woods if this kind of sentencing continues," he says. "It makes all the policies introduced to encourage young men to leave those groups completely worthless."

The struggle against the separatists is already difficult, he says. "The *boyeviks* offer an idea—something to fight for. They offer a lifestyle, a way out. They are winning the battle of ideas with the government, and that's extremely worrying. Poverty, corruption, and unemployment are rife and traditional Islam and the political elite are feeling each other out." Umarov believes that only the country's leaders have the power to bring about change, but adds that none has ever made any serious attempts to do so. "The elite earn too much money from the situation. They are overloaded with subsidies from Moscow. Half of the army and the Russian FSB receive huge allowances to work here. People have a vested interest in maintaining the status quo." It is the most commonly heard argument throughout the Caucasus: why so much violence? Because "they" have a financial interest in maintaining it. On the other hand: how do the *boyeviks* survive? Because they receive support, Umarov says. "Georgia, the West, Arab countries, everyone has a stake in continuing instability in Russia.

"I have three children," Umarov continues. "I hope it will never happen, but I can truly imagine why they might go into the woods. The police break all the laws. Can you imagine? Sympathy for the *boyeviks* in a family where the father is a lawyer and the mother a judge!"

Khasavyurt, Dagestan, 2012

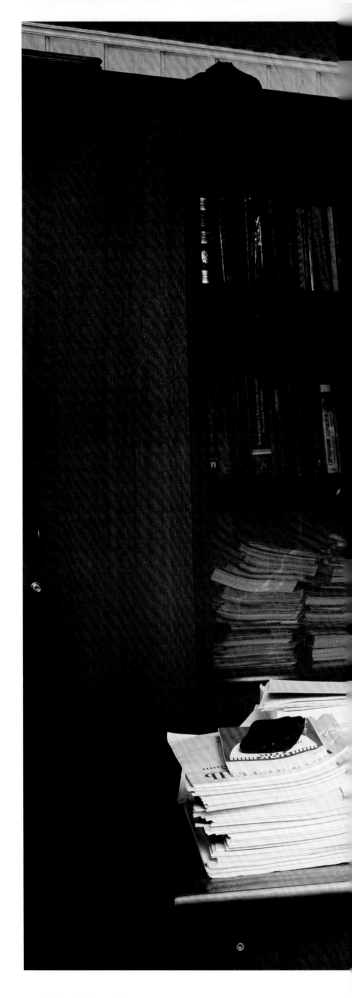

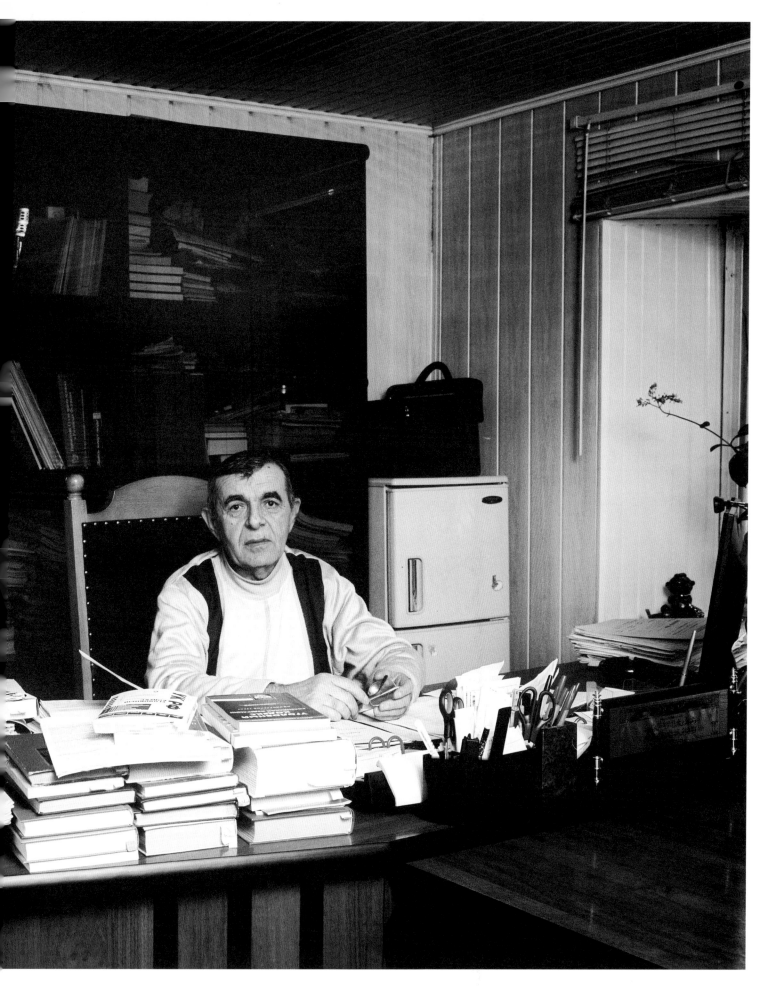

"Human rights are actually very well defined here. But that's on paper. As soon as you run into a uniform and a gun, it's over."

Human rights lawyer Amir
Chechnya, 2011

Afraid of the Police

"Every time the electricity is cut in the evening, we know we have to watch out," says Zainap Dzhambekova in the small Chechen village of Goity. "It means someone is being picked up. It still happens." In 2002 Zainap's doorbell rang in the middle of the night and several masked men, whose identities are still unknown, got out of government jeeps. Her son Imran was taken away and nothing has been heard from him since. There are plenty of stories like this in Goity: knock on any door and people will tell you about how they lost their son, father, brother, or neighbor.

It is widespread in the North Caucasus: fear of the police, fear of the security forces, fear of anyone in a uniform. Trust in the authorities is incredibly low. At checkpoints, internal borders, or roadblocks, drivers make a price assessment and stick a few rubles—sometimes as few as fifty ($1.50)—into their ID or driver's license before handing it to the police officer with a congenial smile. When officers come to your home, it is best to get out quickly. If you see them in the street, you avoid walking next to them: you could become collateral damage in an assault. You would not be the first. At the same time, the police department is one of the most sought-after employers, as are all other public-sector agencies. The great poverty, the privatized economy that has not been rebuilt since the fall of the Soviet Union, and the billion-ruble subsidies from Moscow mean that a public-sector job offers the greatest chance of social security plus the occasional kickback.

A journalist in Dagestan once explained how a conflict is solved there. "People first see whether they can bribe the civil servants or the police. If that does not work, only then do they consider going to court. People here prefer fighting with their neighbor than officially resolving a case. Compare that to England," the journalist said dreamily. "Two quarreling parties have a cup of tea together, play a game of chess, while a judge settles their dispute. That's civilization."

"You'll be surprised if I tell you that human rights are actually very well defined here," says Amir, a human rights lawyer in Chechnya. "But that's on paper. As soon as you run into a uniform and a gun, it's over." Amir mainly devotes himself to cases like that of Zainap's disappeared son. "We sometimes achieve small victories—people are released or we win a case at the European Court of Human Rights in Strasbourg. But the chance of achieving justice here is very small."

His Kabardino-Balkar colleague Rustam Matsev confirms this. "In fact," says Rustam, "you stand virtually no chance if you are picked up." He sums up what happens in most cases. "First you are tortured for three days in order to extract the first piece of evidence against you. Then they bring in witnesses who tell a story and invent a burden of proof, like the discovery of so-called explosive materials, grenades. Then they draw up an indictment, in which they very carefully instruct the judge on the charges he is to bring. And at some point after that, the lawyer is allowed to come in." His profession must feel pretty useless. "In 0.01 percent of the cases a plea leads to a different verdict," Rustam admits.

That is what happened to one of Rustam's clients, Muradin Berov, sixty-eight. He speaks to us on behalf of his son, who is recovering in Moscow. Muradin has a garage, where his son also used to work. He shows us a video on his phone. We see the exterior of the garage and three cars driving up to it. A group of men get out, walk up to Muradin and his colleagues with a determined air and gesture for them to go inside. A man pulls a revolver from his pocket, looks around nervously, and enters the garage. Inside—shot by a different camera—one of the men leads the way and looks into the office to see whether there is anyone in it. There is an exchange of words and within a minute the group walks outside again, where a bewildered mechanic is still scratching his head. Muradin's son, Inali is pushed into a car as a desperate, pleading Muradin follows.

"It wasn't an arrest," says Muradin. "They were wearing normal clothes, not uniforms." Muradin quickly changed into his best suit, loaded the tapes from his surveillance cameras onto a hard disk, and jumped into his car. He was turned away at the police station, where they rejected his hastily written letter. He sped through Nalchik, on to the public ministry, and from there to the offices of the city's public prosecutor, where they finally accepted his letter. Inali was kidnapped at 6 p.m. At 11:30 p.m. Muradin finally sat down with the prosecutor. "He watched the video in disbelief," he says, laughing bitterly, "and he told me: 'Those attackers are crazy.' But when he phoned the police they still kept denying any involvement. It was at that moment, more or less, that they broke my son's back."

"There is only one way out for men who have been picked up," says Rustam. "But it is reserved for a lucky few." He looks at us over the top of his glasses and emphasizes every word: "Never admit anything under torture. Whatever they do to you, however they treat you, keep saying that you didn't do it, that you're innocent—however strange that may sound in the Caucasus. That is the perverse thing about the lawless judicial system here. It's still a judicial system and they need your consent. Without your 'yes' they don't have a case. They can still murder you or make you disappear, but a consistent 'no' is my only chance of getting anyone released."

That is exactly what Inali did. He denied everything. At 11 a.m. the next day he rang his father and said that he had just been released from the police station. A taxi driver brought him home, where they discovered the physical toll of a sixteen-hour police kidnapping. Inali could hardly move. He was suspected of stealing six thousand rubles from a car. But in the end the keys they had planted on him as proof did not fit the stolen car. "The police officers tied his hands behind his back and hit him almost continuously," his father says. "He had to spread his legs, and they kicked him in the balls. He was covered in large bruises. They used electric cords on him. Two vertebrae were broken. We washed him and took him to a hospital as soon as we could. And from there to Moscow, where we have more faith in the doctors."

While Inali has clearly been tortured and has proclaimed his innocence, his case remains open. He could be picked up again at any moment, which is why the family thinks it might be better for him to stay in Moscow. Outside, between the drab 1950s flats, Muradin waves goodbye. "I'm sixty-eight," he says. "I studied Marxist-Leninist theory and philosophy. I smoke and I drink. But I have a very small beard. If they want, they can make me a terrorist within five minutes."

Tortured Clients

One of Rustam Matsev's most notorious cases is that of Aslan Emkuzhev (depicted in the photos here). Aslan was tortured to death by security forces while being interrogated—although initially it was reported that he had been killed during an antiterrorist operation. He was suspected of being a Salafist (an adherent of an orthodox branch of Islam), an allegation that Matsev disputes, in part, on the evidence of these photographs.

He walks us through the variety of cases he has dealt with, describing the procedure one should follow if someone should go missing. "As a lawyer or a family member, you should try to attract as much attention as possible to the situation. I should alert any and all NGOs, the European Court of Human Rights. Only a lot of noise can save a person who is about to disappear for good."

Nalchik, Kabardino-Balkaria, 2012

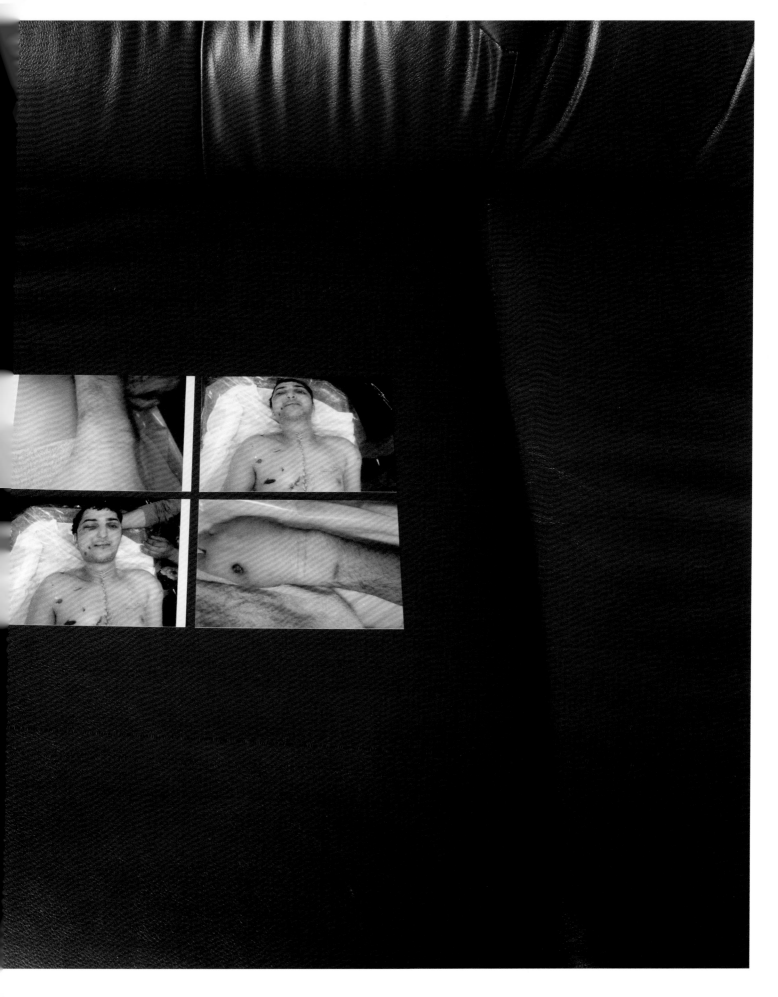

Electing Putin

If election percentages are any indication of the degree of loyalty toward the central government in Moscow, then the republics in the North Caucasus are loyal indeed. Almost nowhere else in Russia is President Vladimir Putin elected by such an overwhelming majority; at the same time, the country is faced with a rebellion against Russia, the ideological underpinning of which enjoys fairly broad support. A teacher tells us furtively why he is voting for Putin today: "My principal ordered us to do so this morning." If the number of votes required still falls short, movies on YouTube and reports from election monitors provide an explanation for the discrepancy: election fraud is committed on a national scale.

Makhachkala, Dagestan, 2012

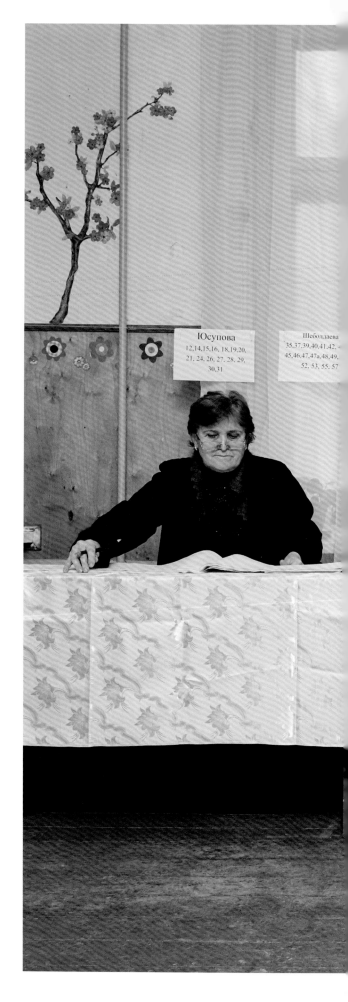

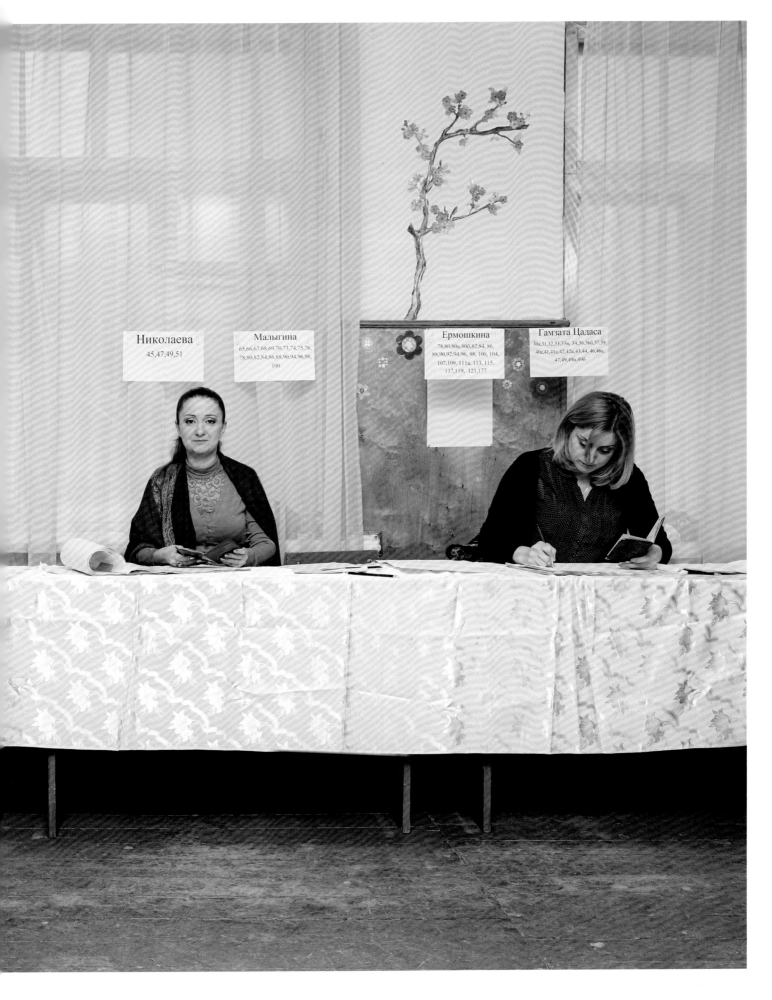

Nargiz

Nargiz Zaidova, nineteen, has lost both her brothers to terrorism and the fight against it. She asserts that she witnessed police officers planting a grenade in her family's basement as a pretext to arrest her eldest brother.

Derbent, Dagestan, 2012

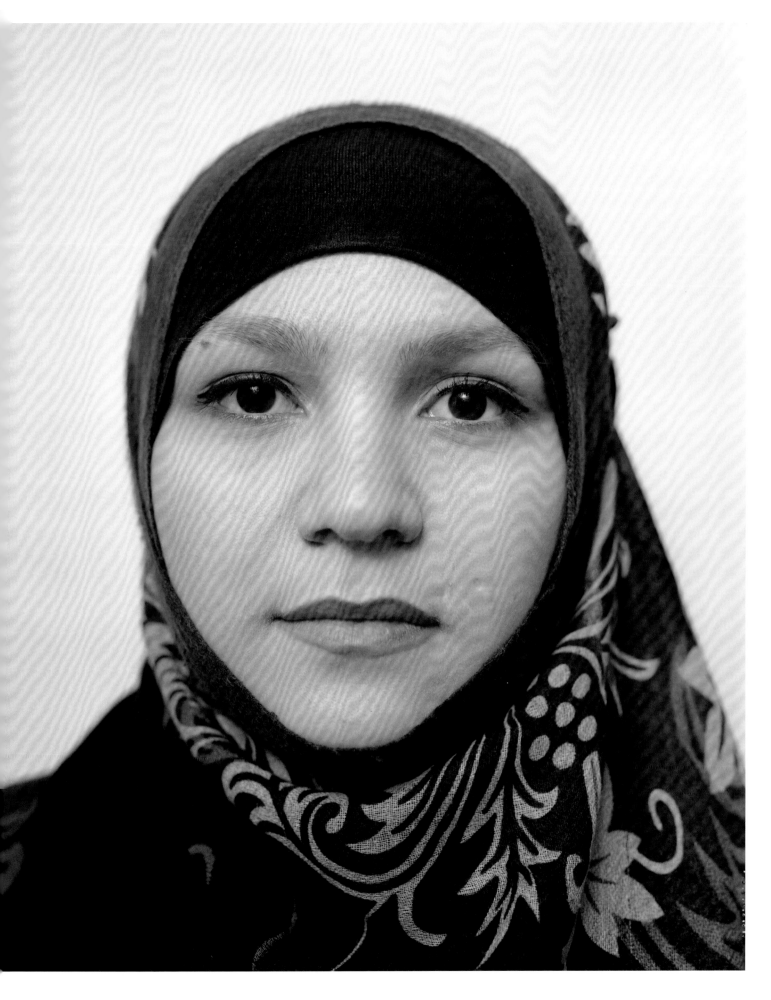

Farewell Letter

"I'm going into the woods. I'm joining the Mujahedeen brothers. Don't register me as missing; it will only result in unnecessary unpleasantness for you. I can't come back. I ask you not to stop [my sister] Nargiz from saying her prayers."

Derbent, Dagestan, 2012

"I'm going into the woods. I'm joining the Mujahedeen brothers."

Farewell note to mother, Derbent, Dagestan, 2010

Into the Woods

"He was unemployed and he was religious," Shamil's mother sighs, "but we never expected this." She searches in a photo album for the letter she found under her pillow on that fateful day. *"I'm going into the woods..."* it begins. "Shamil was the Dagestani national judo champion," she tells us. "He was such a good boy. It must have been well organized. We called all his friends, but nobody knew a thing. He turned his telephone off straight away. A few months later we heard that he had been killed during a military operation." She shows us a newspaper article with a picture of an overturned truck, peppered with bullets.

Shamil's father jumps to his feet. "Everyone and everything is corrupt," he shouts bitterly. He reels off a long list of all the things he believes are wrong. "The elections are rigged, the police are corrupt. Everything can be bought, even the coastline if you want it. At the same time, they celebrate their weddings with hundreds of limousines, champagne, and gold bars. Here, if your father's a judge, then you become a judge. But nothing works. All of the services and facilities are improvised. If you want to visit a mosque, you're branded a terrorist and thrown into prison without trial. It sometimes still feels like it's 1937," he laments, referring to the Great Terror under Stalin. "One of our sons is dead and the other is locked up. We can't denounce the government. They were the ones who planted the grenade in my cellar, which they used to put my son away. If I take action, they'll lock me up, too."

This is not a radical Islamic family. The father is a cabinet joiner and they live in a reasonably modern, middle-class house. Daughter Nargiz goes to school, is modern and assertive, and is not kept away from male visitors. The fact that even this family sympathizes with the militants in the woods, despite losing a son to them, is telling. Simply put, this is not the type of family one would expect to support the Islamic radicals.

But the appeal seems to be growing. Videos of militants battling through knee-high snow and jubilantly laying ambushes can be viewed via shaky Internet connections across the Caucasus. In a seventeen-minute interview, martyr Amir Supyan explains how to prepare *plov* (an Uzbek rice dish) in a makeshift field kitchen. In another video, an injured militant mumbles his prayers while a comrade treats his gunshot wound. The images depict a sort of Islamic Boy Scouts' eagerness, combined with the heroic allure of war. A wide range of websites and blogs supplies a complete multilingual news service for anyone interested. The Caucasian rebels also receive support from radical Islamic movements around the world. The conflict in the Caucasus is no longer an isolated cause; it has become part of what is seen as a global fight against the repression of Islam by Christian terrorists. The words used to describe Russia on one prominent militant website, Kavkaz Center, are almost comical. The site's headline reads: "Russian alpha-male Putin undergoing surgery on his back." The regime of Chechen President Ramzan

Ухожу в лес, присоединяюсь к братьям - лудиа-худам, Не давайте в розыск у вас будут лишние лишние неприятности и я не смогу спускаться. Просьба к вам не мешайте Кыргызке делать намаз.

Into the Woods

"Come and join us, our life is good," the stream of photographs and videos from the woods seems to say. The images shown here were tweeted by Kavkaz Center, the insurgents' news and propaganda channel. The person on the right of the top-right photograph and the left of the bottom-right photograph is Dokka Umarov, the self-proclaimed emir of the Caucasian Emirate he hopes to establish in the North Caucasus and possibly beyond. The words and images don't only depict the good life, however. Countless collages glorifying Islamic martyrdom show grinning fighters alongside their equally grinning corpses. They believe those who have died have seen heaven. Still other photographs and videos show wounded fighters being nursed, or crimes being committed against Muslims around the world—anything to win support for the Caucasian Emirate.

Images selected from the Kavkaz Center Twitter feed, Caucasus, 2012

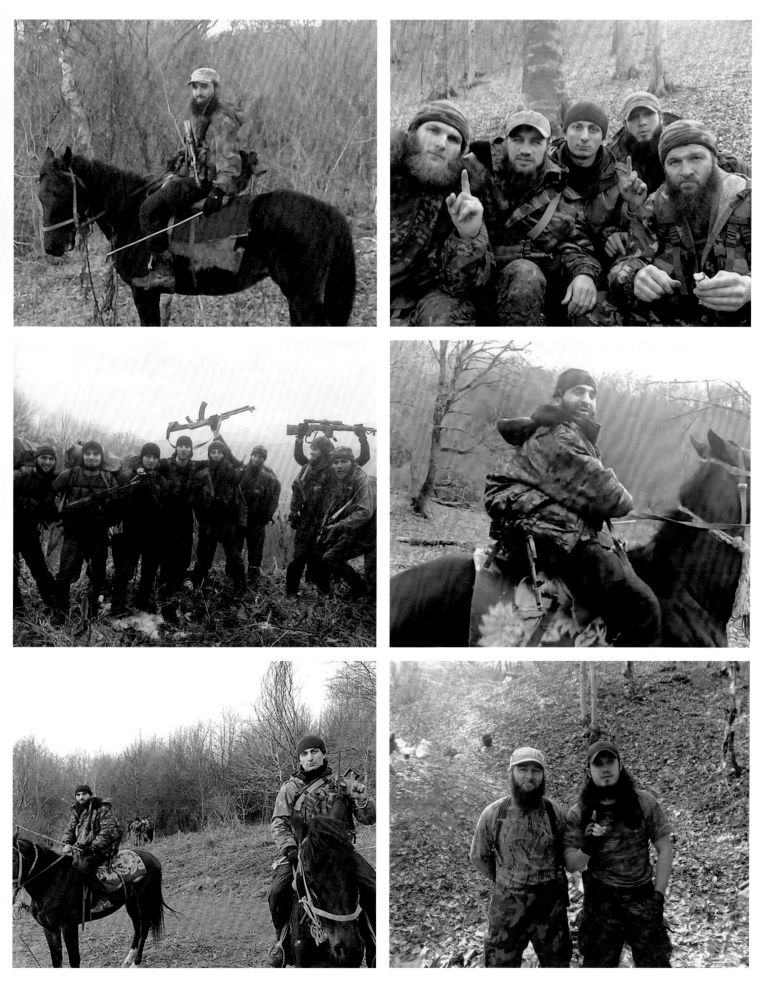

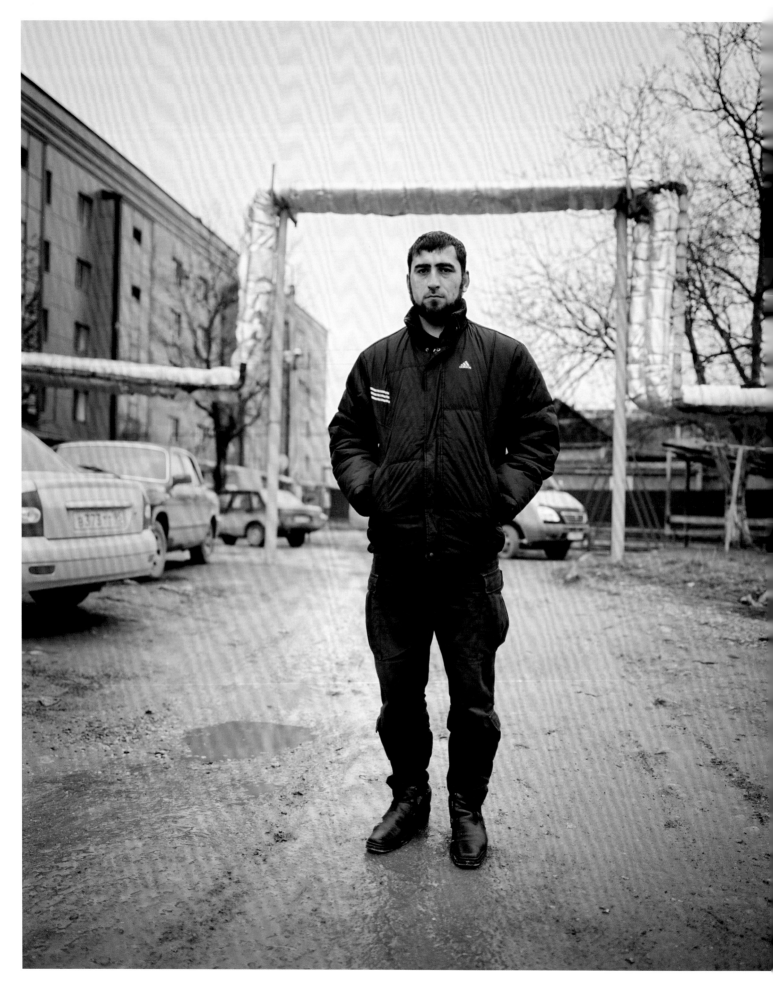

Living with Uncertainty

"One brother is still in prison, the other has just been released. We sit at home, without work." Urus-Martan is a hotbed of "Wahhabism," as the government calls this branch of radical, orthodox Islam. "We identify with the Wahhabis," Isa Nenkayev admits, "but we wouldn't call ourselves that. There's a difference between religion and terrorism. Russia wants to ensure that it remains peaceful until 2014, so that visitors to Sochi don't stay away. Sochi is only six hundred kilometers from here. What will happen after that? No one knows. In the meantime, they calmly kill anyone who might disturb the peace."

Urus-Martan, Chechnya, 2011

Decapitated

Safudin Shibzbugov is the father of a murdered police officer. In 2010, he discovered his son's body at the side of a road. "I had to bury him without his head," he tells us. "Terrorists hacked it off and took it with them. They lured him to a nearby village under false pretenses and then decapitated him and a colleague." The heads were later found in a fridge and buried alongside the men in their graves. Safudin had previously discovered a picture of his son's head on a radical Islamic blog. He confesses that he has not told his wife. He wants to spare her the horrific details. "They're now doing everything they can to destabilize us before the Games begin in Sochi," Safudin says. "They know that a bomb there would be extremely damaging for Russia."

Baksan, Kabardino-Balkaria, 2011

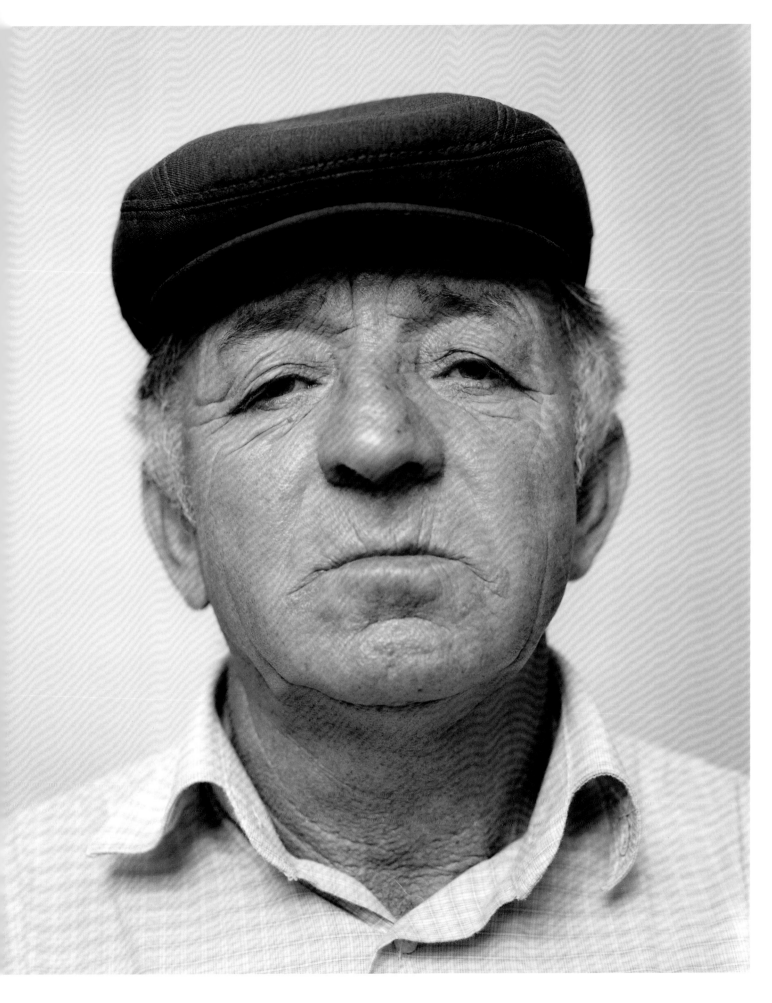

Dreaming of Switzerland

In 2007 the then-mayor of Shatoy proudly announced that within a few years the Chechen mountain town would become the Switzerland of Russia. "We'll open spas," he said to the *Guardian* newspaper, "and very soon thousands of people will be able to enjoy our nature."

We visit Shatoy in 2010 to see the extent to which the mayor's promises have been fulfilled. As we approach the mountains, we drive through a landscape dotted with foxholes and small fortifications. Everything looks derelict or abandoned, but deeper into the mountains soldiers are still entrenched on the hillsides.

At the checkpoint just outside the village, we are told that we cannot simply enter the area. "You have to wait," says the soldier on duty. Several cars screech to a halt and an officer gets out. He says that we have to accompany him to Shatoy. We are breaking the law and the Federal Security Service of the Russian Federation (FSB) wants to talk to us. The illusion of a Chechen Switzerland in the mountains vanishes in an instant.

Later the same afternoon, after questioning by the local FSB and a friendly farewell, we speak to the new mayor. He is nervous about our arrival. It is not long before two armored vehicles pull up in the parking lot and what appear to be officers from one of the security forces monitor us closely. "The authorities are like shepherds," he says, proudly reciting the propaganda jingle of his leader, Ramzan Kadyrov. "They guide the people in the right direction. Our ancestors prayed for a president who would help them develop. And look, our prayers have been answered."

"What happened to the previous mayor?" we ask. "His idea for a Switzerland in Russia hasn't really materialized." The mayor cuts the conversation short. Political affairs are off limits and only result in trouble. We leave the turbulent mountains and drive back to the plains of the North Caucasus.

Shatoy, Chechnya, 2011

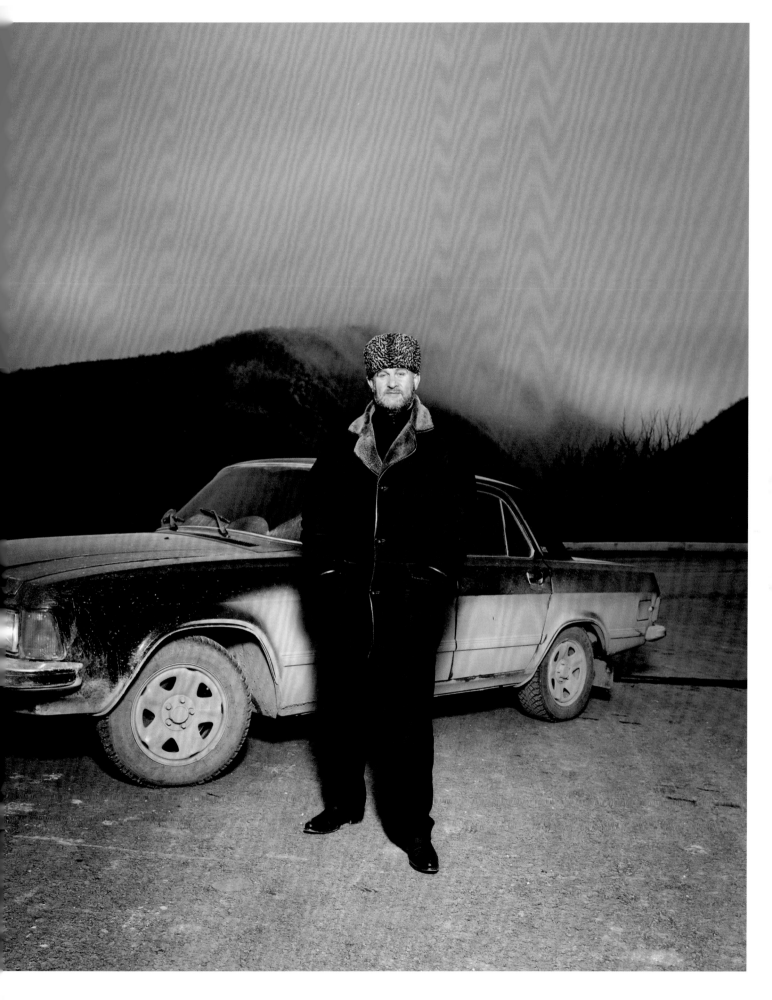

Shamil's Fort

Shamilkala can literally be translated as "Shamil's Fort." The town high in the mountains of Dagestan is named after Imam Shamil, the greatest resistance fighter the North Caucasus has ever known. A modern town due to the hydroelectric power station in the nearby valley, it is better known for the incessant bombings, kidnappings, and murders that plague the area. Not far from the infamous Gimry, which has rebelled against Russian domination for two hundred years, this is the seat of the local government and police. The buildings are heavily guarded and disguised as forts. Outside the police station, where we are held for hours by officers suspicious of foreigners in this unstable region, two bearded men run a small store. One of them is covered in wounds. "Boom," he says, indicating an explosion. When we say that we have been denied access to Gimry, the men think for a moment and then offer to take us there via a goat path. The spirit of independence and contempt for the state is clearly evident here, no less so among these men who run a store specifically for the police.

Shamilkala, Dagestan, 2012

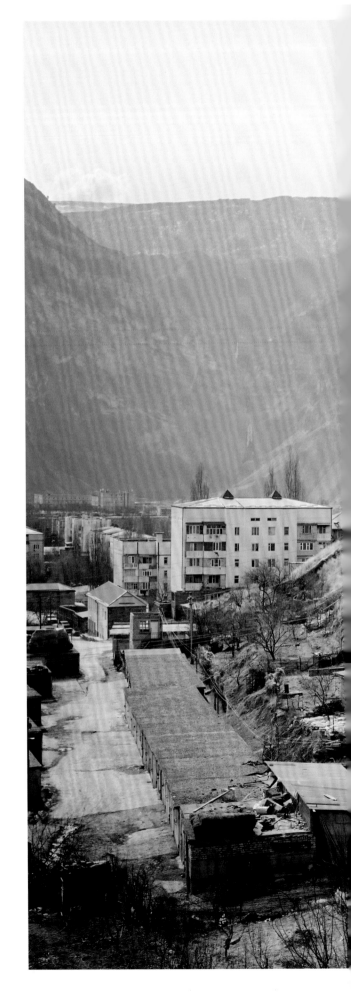

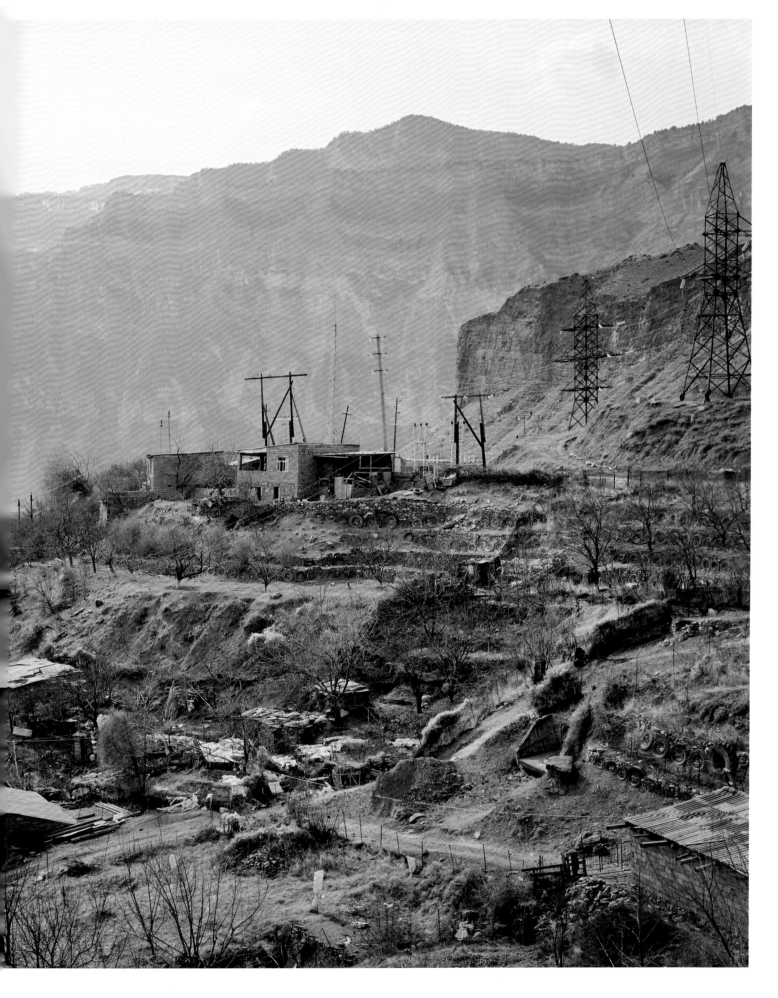

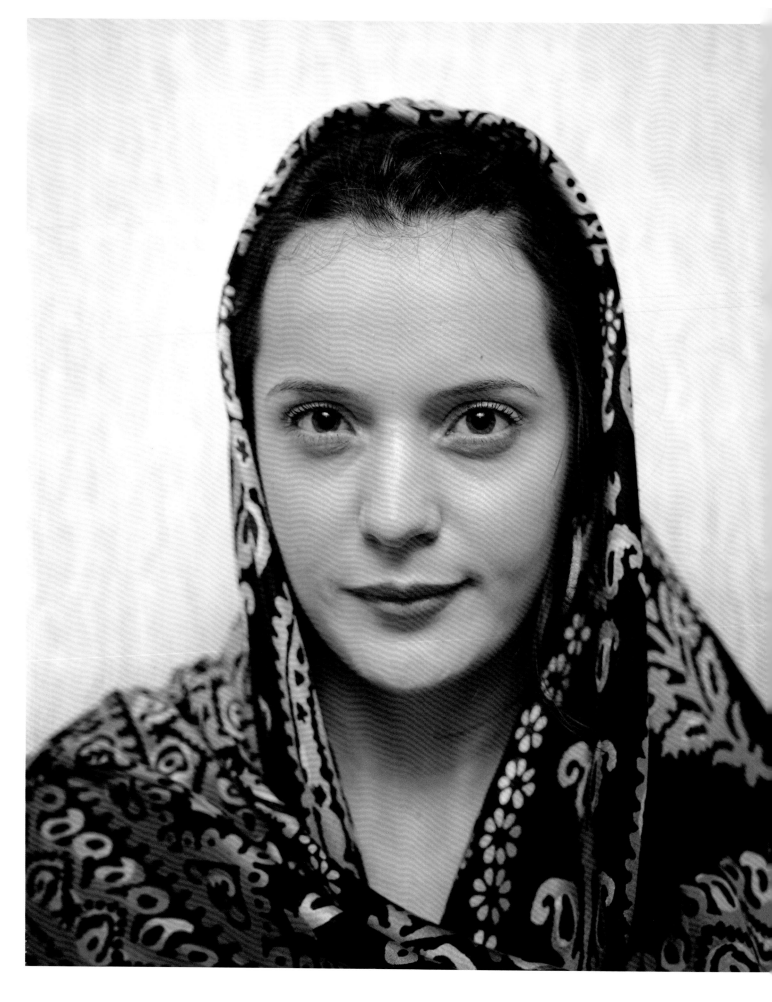

Amina, Nineteen

The truth is, we don't know much about this girl. She is called Amina, is nineteen years old, and lives in a mountain village in Dagestan. That's where our information stops. Rob and I had just spent a whole day in custody, where we had been interrogated continuously by various security services, from local police officers to aggressive antiterrorist forces. In the end we are forced to leave the mountains and return to the capital Makhachkala. Embittered and exhausted, we accept our driver's suggestion to take a break at the house of his friend, who is a traffic cop. While the cop regales us with stories, in the adjacent kitchen Amina and her almost identical niece are dressed in traditional Dagestani costumes. The abundant meal we are served is accompanied by a potent mix of spirits. The stories become more and more fantastical, but all we can do is stare into the kitchen.

Levashi, Dagestan, 2012

Born to Fight

The Caucasus is the birthplace of champions. At every Summer Olympics it is almost a given that the Dagestanis, Chechens, Ossetians, Georgians, and other Caucasians will win half the medals for wrestling and boxing. "We fought and fought," coach and former champion of the Soviet Union Magomed Magomedov says of the region's history. "Wrestling is in our blood. Wrestling is politics, culture, philosophy, and art. In this life, only the very fittest survive in Dagestan. Life is a struggle, and wrestling is a struggle in itself." And so the men keep wrestling, because no other sport offers as many opportunities for wealth and success. Champions are rewarded with money, cars, political positions, and international travel. Wrestling is a way out of the Caucasus.

Khasavyurt, Dagestan, 2012

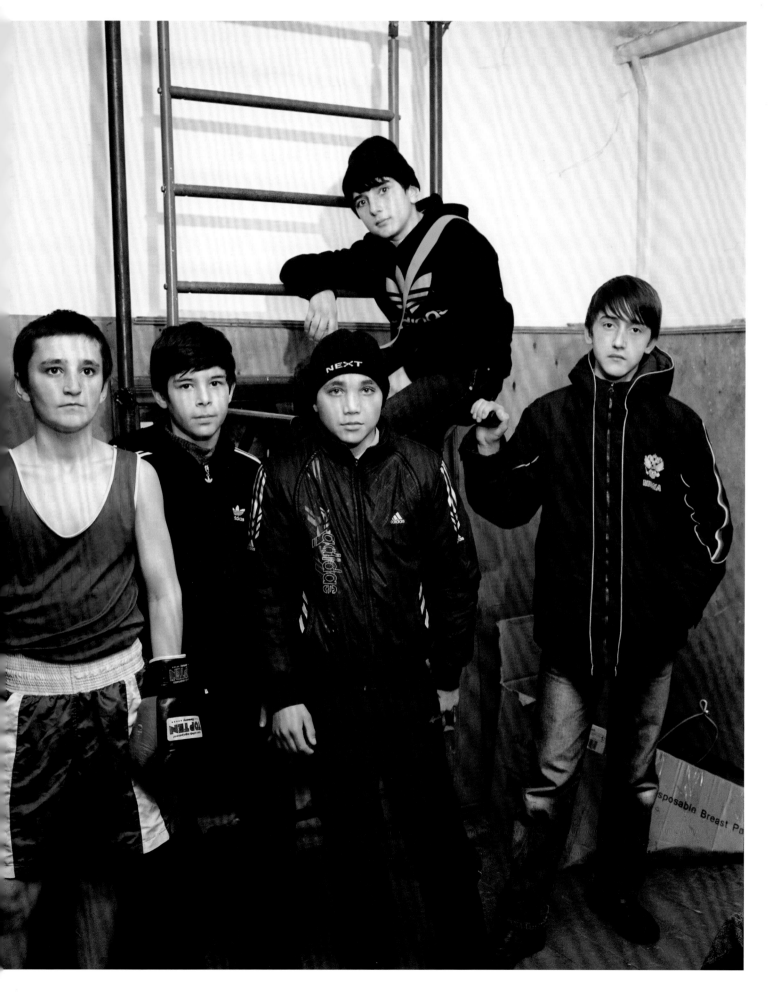

"If I were young and naïve, and unaware of the consequences, I would join the militants in the woods."

Saidakhmed Nasibov
Kirovaul, Dagestan, 2012

A War of Words

In late August 2012 Saidakhmed Nasibov was dragged from his car and shot dead in front of his wife, daughter, and sister-in-law. He was the last surviving male member of his family. His three sons and numerous nephews had already been killed by the shadowy, masked security forces that roam the North Caucasus, arresting and killing people seemingly at will.

We had met Nasibov a few months earlier and talked with him about his sons and religious beliefs. He was a Salafist, an adherent of an orthodox branch of Islam. The Salafists want to live pure lives, establish Sharia law, and reject the Caucasus's traditional Islam, which has—they say—been corrupted by money and politics. Nasibov sympathized with the terror-sowing radicals in the mountains, but chose to wage his war using only words. In Dagestan it is easy to become a target of the eternally suspicious security forces and authorities. Too many people have already been illegally imprisoned, tortured, killed, or have simply disappeared over the years. For an outspoken figure like Nasibov, it was only a matter of time before the masked men would come after him.

Kirovaul, Dagestan, 2012

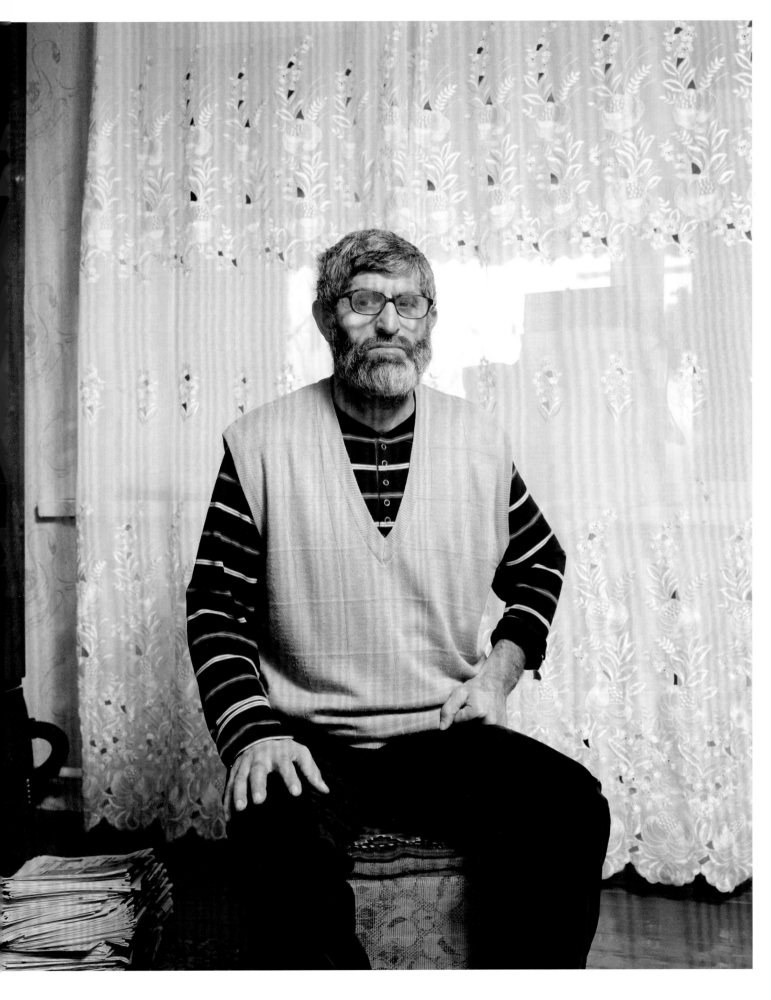

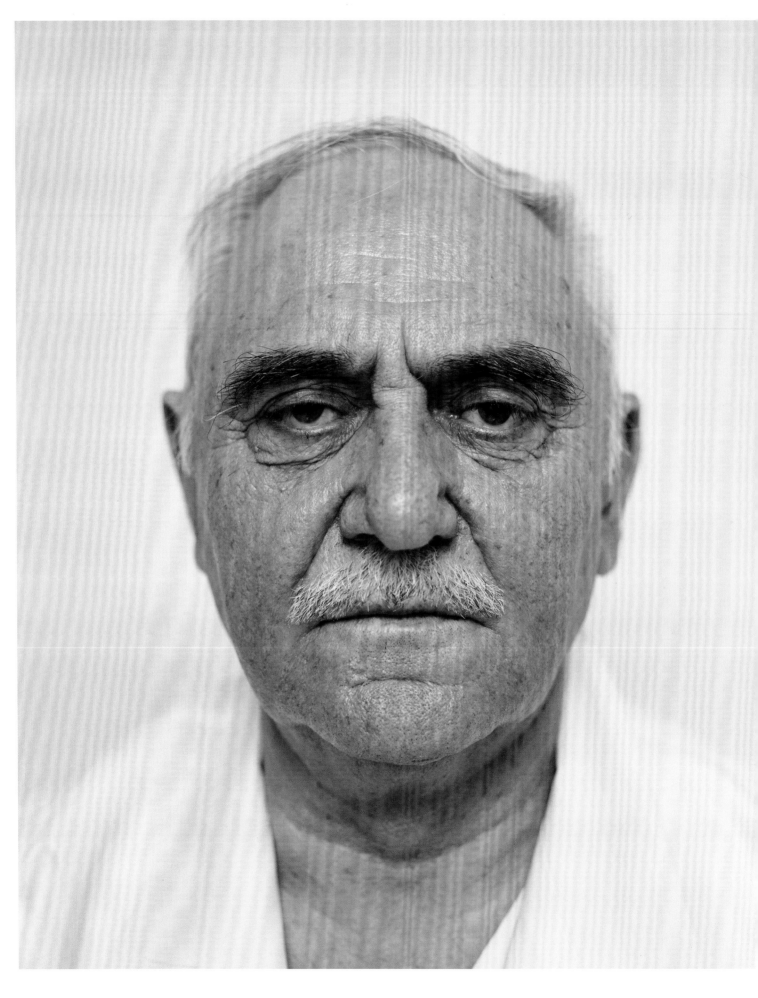

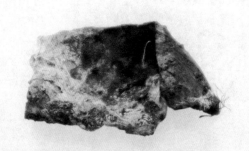

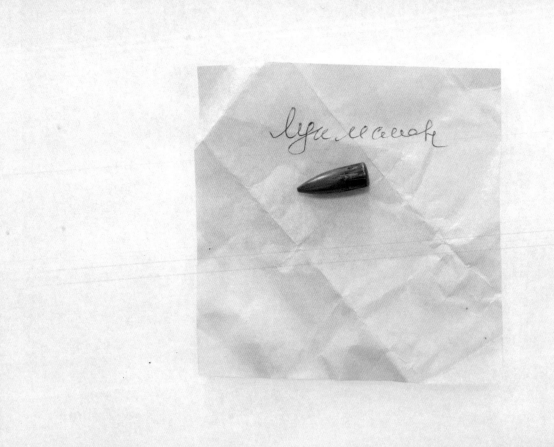

Magomed Omarov is the chief physician of the central hospital in Makhachkala, Dagestan. Every time violence erupts on the streets of his city, a bomb explodes, or people are shot, he and his team are there to treat the victims.

Since taking the job in 1990, Magomed has seen it all: the civil wars, the rise of terrorism. "There are just too many weapons in the former USSR," he bemoans. "There was a saying in the early 1990s: sell your last cow and buy a gun to protect yourself. With all the guns in our country, you could form a colonial army." In his desk drawer is the palpable evidence: fragments of bullets and knives that he has removed from his patients' bodies (depicted in the adjacent

Makhachkala, Dagestan, 2012

Yareksu

Opposite Isita Azieva's house in Yareksu is the first monument in the Caucasus commemorating the deportations in World War II. Yareksu is predominantly Chechen. Like the Balkars, Ingush, and Karachay, the Chechens were also deported to Central Asia, as punishment for rebelling against the Russians and to prevent them from collaborating with the Germans.

Yareksu, Dagestan, 2012

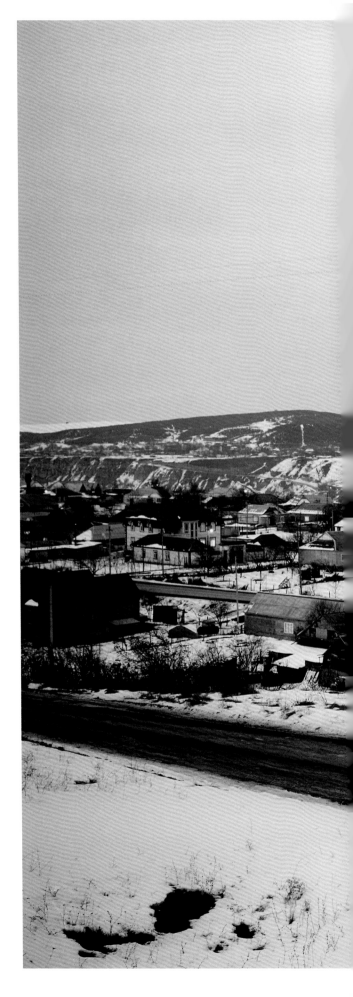

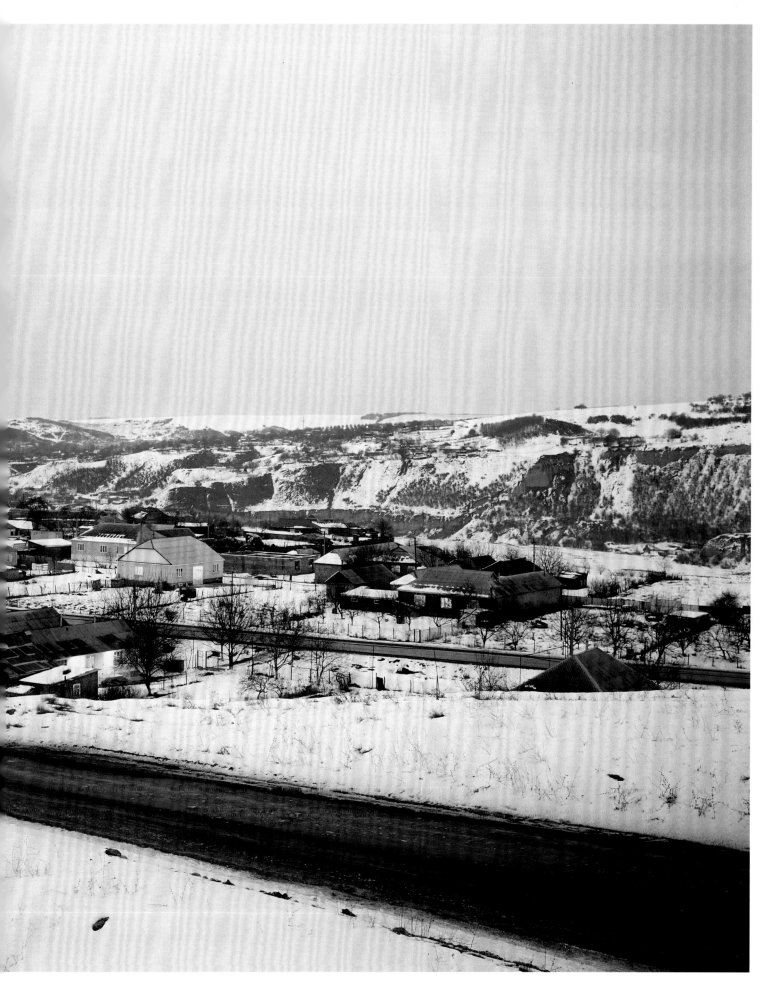

Missing Husband

Isita Azieva, twenty-eight, from Yareksu, is
married to Ismail Gayrbekov, thirty. Ismail
has been sentenced to fourteen years in a
prison camp near Murmansk. Two years ago
he was convicted of assisting terrorists and
murder. The latter charge is false, says Isita.
He is guilty of the former, but he was forced
to do it. Twice he transported terrorists in
his car, and twice he brought them food. His
family would suffer, they said, if he refused.
Ismail turned himself in to the police, after
a shooting incident in his village left two
policemen dead. In doing so he became the
perfect scapegoat. Under torture he was
forced to make a full confession.

Yareksu, Dagestan, 2012

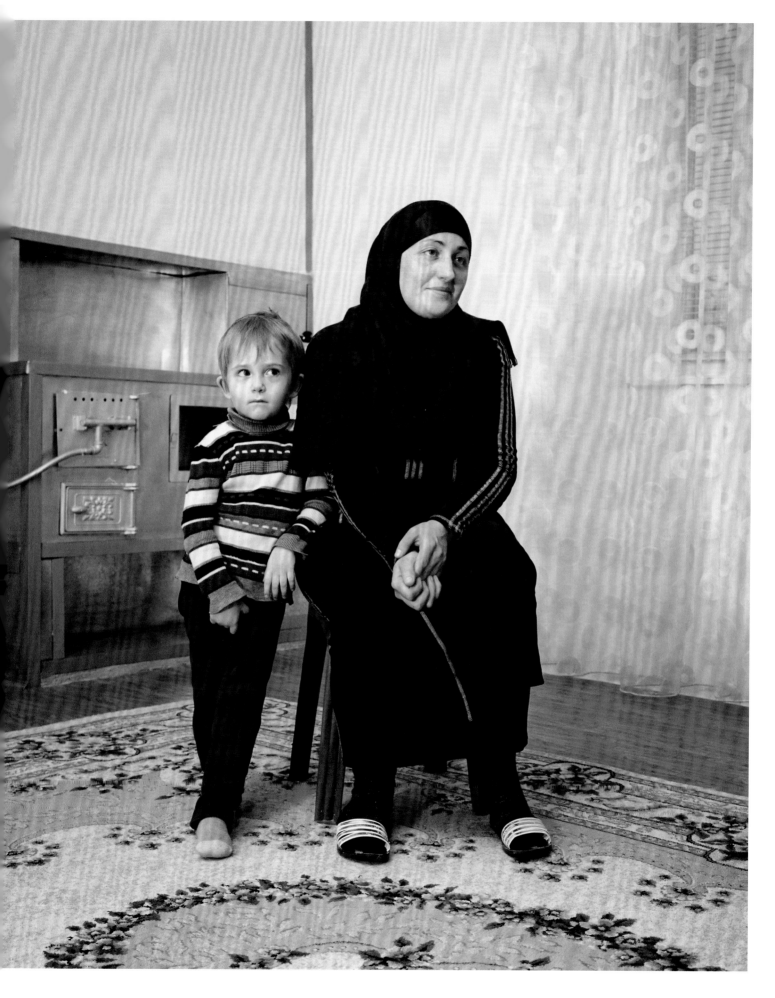

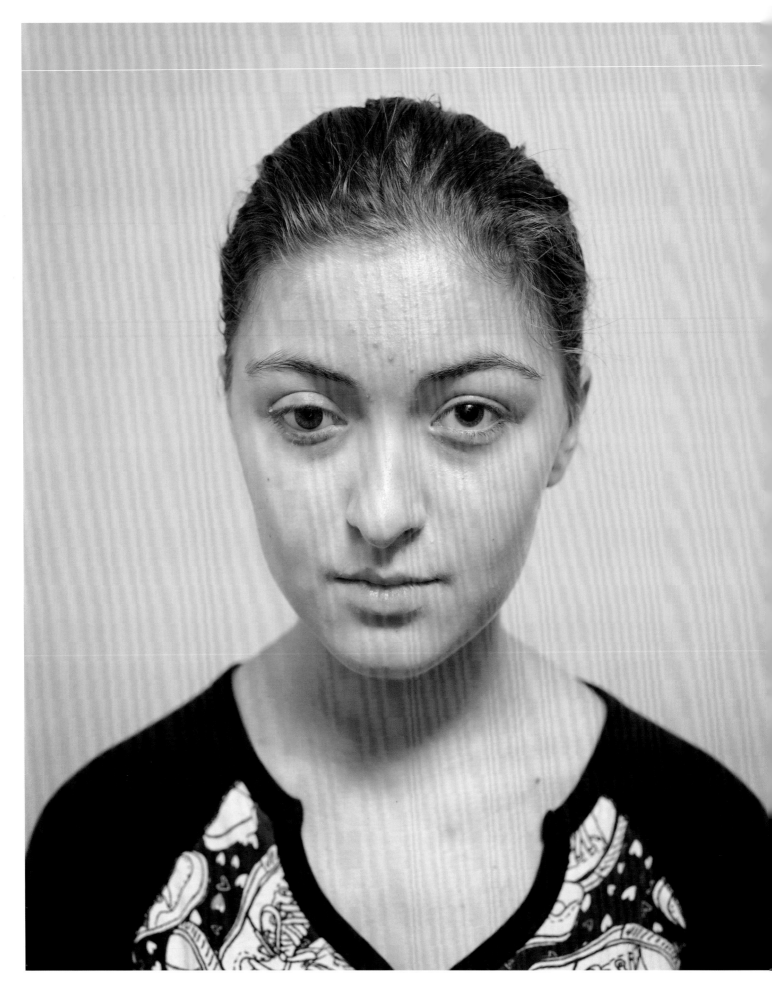

Ilona

Beslan, North Ossetia, 2011

"Sometimes when it's dark at night, I become para- lyzed with fear. I see masked men entering my room."

Ilona
Beslan, North Ossetia, 2011

On September 1, Our School Died

"Today we're going to do something nice," said forty-seven-year-old Aleta Khasieva to her Year Ten children at 9 a.m. "It will be a day that you'll remember forever!" It was September 1, the first day of school, and a day that has been widely celebrated in Russia for as long as anyone can remember. Less than ten minutes later, dozens of terrorists, mostly Ingush and Chechen, stormed the school and ushered more than a thousand adults and children into the gym.

Of all the attacks carried out as a result of the unrest in the Caucasus, the Beslan school siege in 2004 was perhaps the most dramatic. Beslan is located in North Ossetia, less than a thirty-minute drive from Vladikavkaz and only a few minutes from Ingushetia. The small, sleepy town of about thirty thousand inhabitants is known mainly for the large, steel-gray complexes that surround it. These buildings are the vodka distilleries that brought fame to North Ossetia and, in the 1990s, enabled a handful of local vodka oligarchs to prosper. The trains from Moscow, Grozny, Sochi, and Vladikavkaz pass through here, dividing the town into three areas.

School Number 1 is located next to one of the railway lines. The playground is dilapidated and partially overgrown with grass. The buildings stand empty—eerily empty. The outbuildings also look derelict and smell of urine. The full extent of what happened here only becomes apparent when you walk around the corner: the roof of the gym has been shot off and the windows of the main school building are boarded up. Wreaths have been laid in front of the gym, where a tragedy of terrible magnitude once unfolded. The names of the victims and survivors, interspersed with wishes and hearts, have been scratched into the walls. On the weathered wooden floor, between the cracks and bullet and shrapnel damage, the faded lines of the basketball court are barely visible and a basketball hoop still hangs from the wall. It recalls video images from the siege that showed wires strung from the basketball hoops connecting makeshift bombs around the room. In this tiny gym, no bigger than the basketball court itself, hundreds of school children, parents, and teachers were held captive. Photographs of the more than three hundred victims who died here line the walls. It is a poignant collection, depicting pupils dressed in their Sunday best, ready to start the new school year.

If it was the captors' intention to hold hostage as large a group as possible, they could not have chosen a better day. On September 1, children make a special effort to dress up, encouraged by fathers and mothers, grandmothers and grandfathers, and are treated to large bags of sweets. The start of the school year is celebrated across Russia, which made the siege all the more shocking.

"Since the siege, I'm no longer able to enjoy life," says Aleta. "Everyone in the Caucasus dreams of diamonds or a new fridge, but those things don't matter to me." She sits at her kitchen table in a luxurious apartment in the small town. Following the siege the village was completely rebuilt with money from the government, churches, and Islamic aid organizations. New schools, playing fields, and an enormous hospital have been constructed. "What I saw is difficult to describe. We were packed into the gym like cattle. There were babies who had come with their mothers and grandmothers, as well as pupils aged six through eighteen. Some children could only laugh manically due to the stress. Others talked extremely loudly, too loudly, which was strictly forbidden by the terrorists. Many children who had come to school by themselves, or whose parents had escaped in the initial confusion, were on their own. I tried to be kind to them and calm them down like a mother would. I still dream about it. It isn't as if it happened yesterday, but that's how it feels."

We talk to Ilona, who was eight at the time and lost her mother and brother. She now lives with Aleta and her father, Igor. "I was a little girl," she says. "I didn't understand the seriousness of the situation. It was as if I was having a bad dream. Now that I'm older, I often think back to those three days. I mostly wonder what I would do if it happened to me again. Then I realize that I wouldn't be able to do anything. That's absolutely the worst feeling there is."

Ilona lost sight in her right eye as a result of the explosions. Her father found her later in the hospital. She has no idea how her mother and brother died. "I can only talk about it with my best friend, and nobody else," she says. Talking to us causes her visible distress. "I remember the terrorists well. The men had full beards. The women were the worst. They were the most aggressive and dressed completely in black. Sometimes when it's dark at night, I become paralyzed with fear. I see masked men entering my room. Then I try to fall asleep as quickly as possible."

Ilona's new mother, Aleta, strokes her hair lovingly. "I'm still angry," Aleta says. "When I left the hospital I never wanted to teach again. But the director convinced me. I thought about my pupils who had been through the same ordeal. I went back, but I'd rather emigrate to a place where citizens have rights and their government represents them.

"Beslan will never be the same," she believes. Her husband, Igor, enters. He is an ambulance driver and during the siege he waited outside the school for three days, ready to assist if necessary. The entire time, he faced the uncertainty of not knowing whether his family was alive or dead. When asked a question about the siege, he breaks out in a sweat and searches haltingly for words. Aleta nods and says: "He can't talk about it." She tells us how the trauma of the siege lives on, even among children who were not involved. "We now have a new school. When the children arrived for the first time they saw the high windows in the gym. 'We'd never be able to escape through those,' they said, and refused to take part in sports." A few years ago, the security forces stationed at the school since the siege went on strike. They had not been paid for months. "When the pupils found out, they ran away as fast as they could," says Aleta. "The same thing happened when the fire alarm was tested, and again when we heard about a bombing in Vladikavkaz. Everyone in our school is a wreck. On September 1, our school died."

A Monument

It is tucked away in a corner of the small memorial room in the rebuilt Secondary School No. 1 in Beslan, along with a few other items of clothing. We fall silent as the German teacher pulls a shirt from the pile. It looks as if it has just been ripped from a child's body, bloodied and grim. "This was my daughter's shirt," the teacher says. "I'll always cherish it." With the other memories of the old school, the attack, and the outpouring of support from around the world, it is part of a monument to the children of Beslan. But perhaps most of all it is a monument to the daughter of the teacher, who maintains the memorial. She lovingly strokes the photographs of her daughter.

Beslan, North Ossetia, 2011

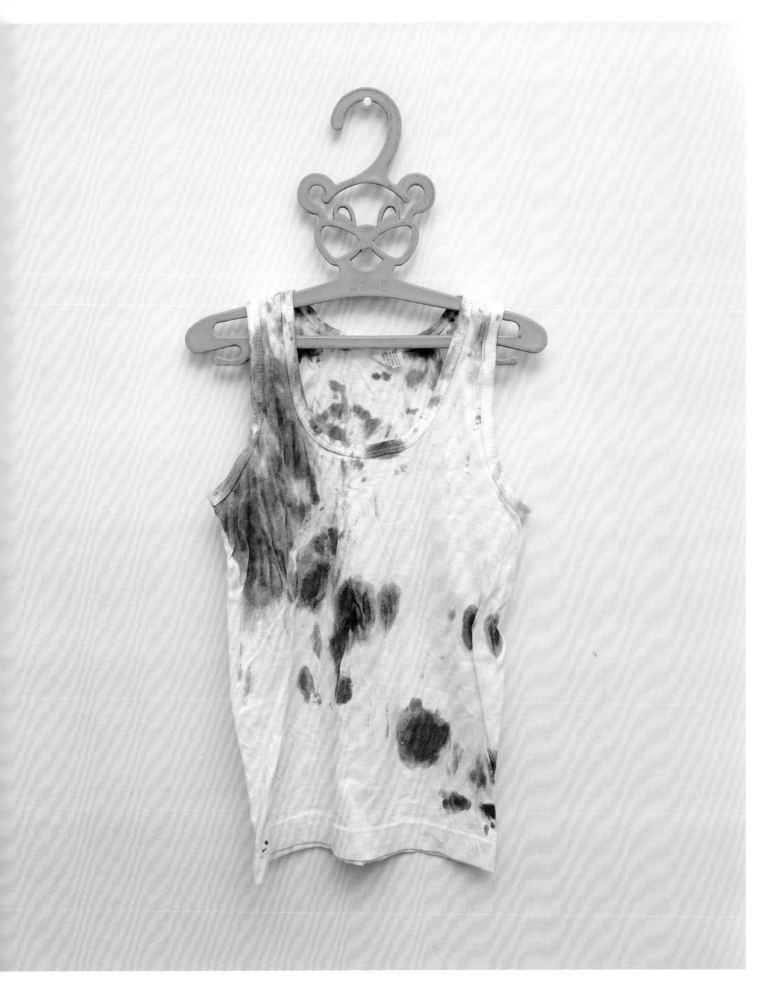

Gymnasium

This basketball court was the epicenter of the horror that unfolded on September 1, 2004, and the days thereafter, when Beslan Secondary School No. 1 was attacked. On the walls, cracks and holes serve as a reminder of the bullets and shrapnel that ripped through the building. Portraits of children dressed in their Sunday best adorn the walls. More than three hundred people died here during the hostage crisis that September. The attackers were predominantly rebels from Ingushetia and a number of other republics. Their goal was to achieve Chechen independence. After nearly a decade of war, that goal is still a long way off.

Beslan, North Ossetia, 2011

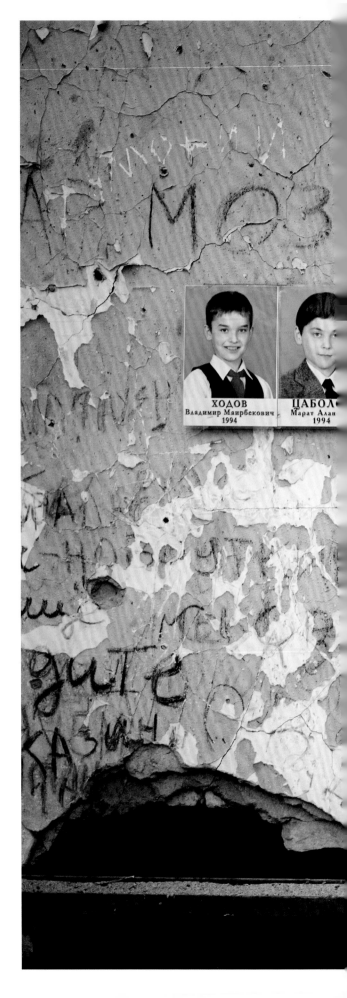

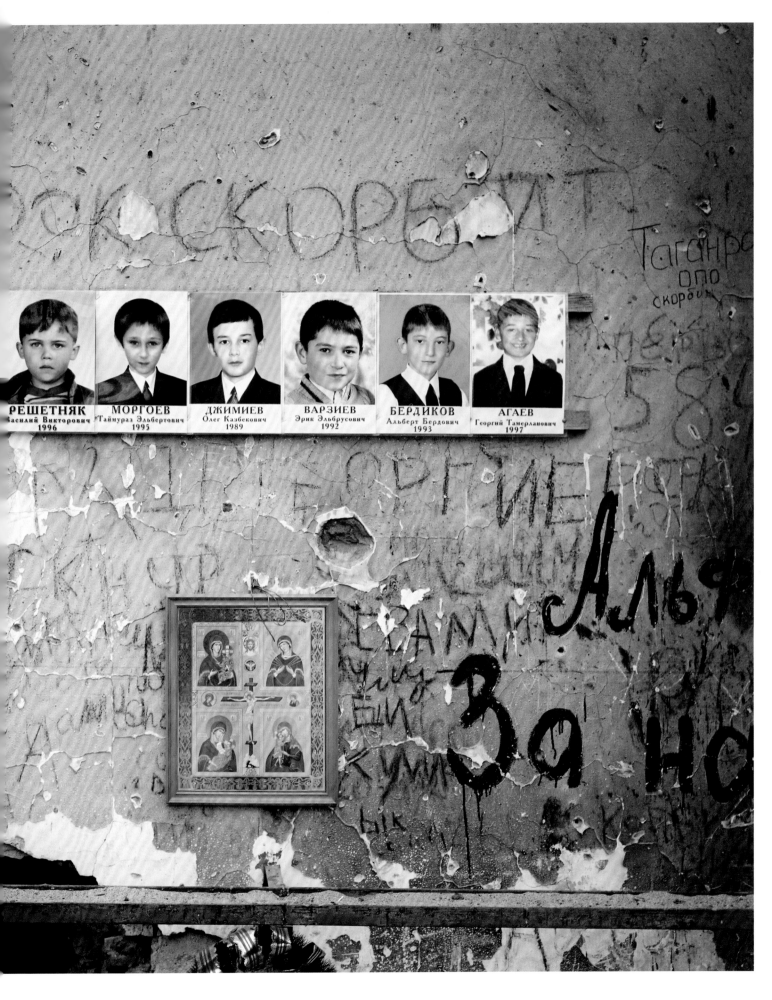

Friends

Guram and Vakha, ages thirty-six and
twenty, respectively, are good friends. It is a
remarkable friendship because Guram is
Ossetian and Vakha is Ingush, and they live
in the ethnically divided village of Chermen,
where fierce fighting erupted in the nineties.
The men help each other out. Guram repairs
Vakha's car and in exchange Vakha drives
Guram around. When Vakha has to cross
into Ossetia, he takes Guram along for the
ride: if the Ossetian police stop them, Guram
can ensure that Vakha is not arrested.

Beslan, North Ossetia, 2012

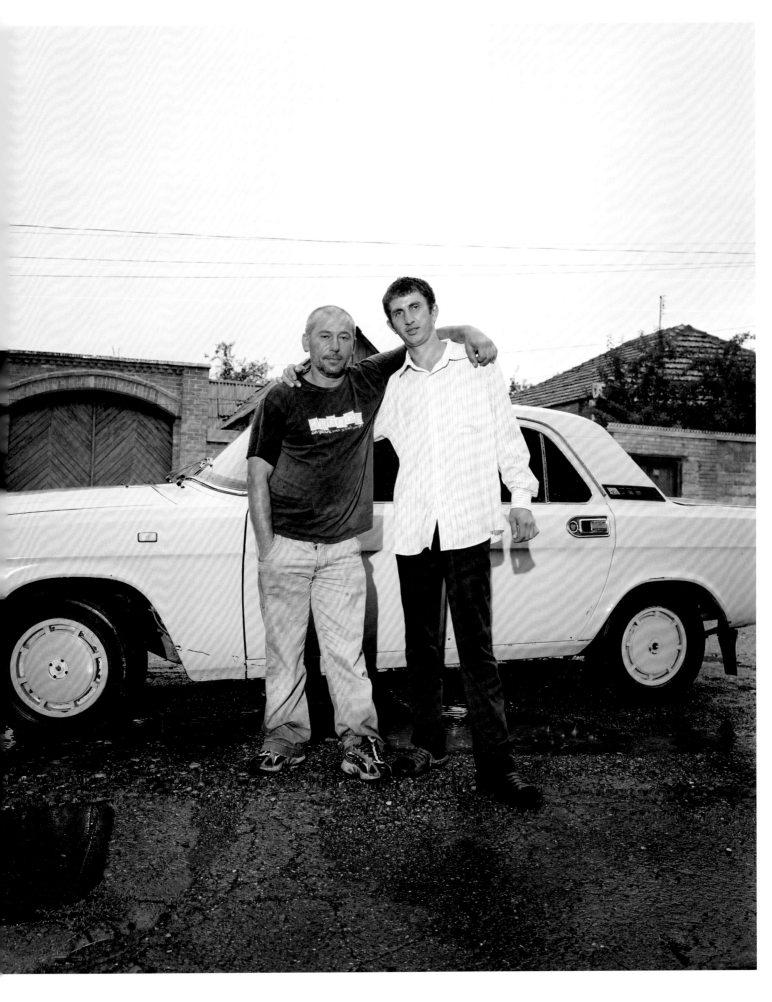

Rebuilding

Twenty years after the war, Abkhazia is still recovering. Abkhazians have been isolated for so long, they can't do anything about it. Money is scarce, but now that a small amount is trickling in again, schools and roads are being rebuilt. They are the backbone of the country and so the Abkhazians are beginning with them, the minister of foreign affairs tells us. Like this boarding school, which is being restored one building at a time.

Kaldahuara, Abkhazia, 2010

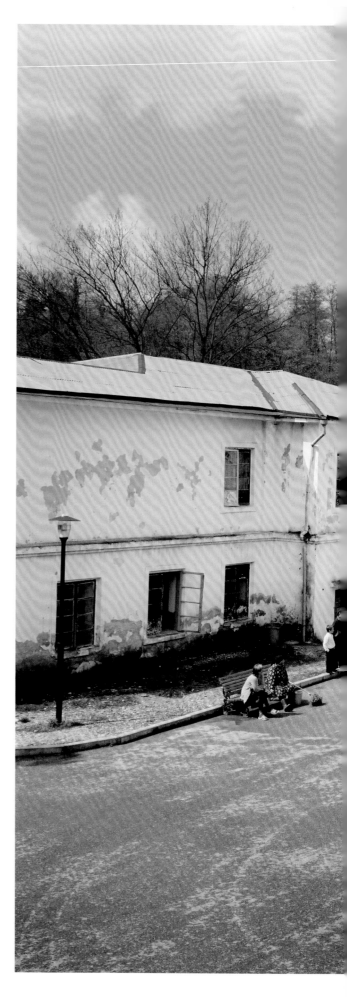

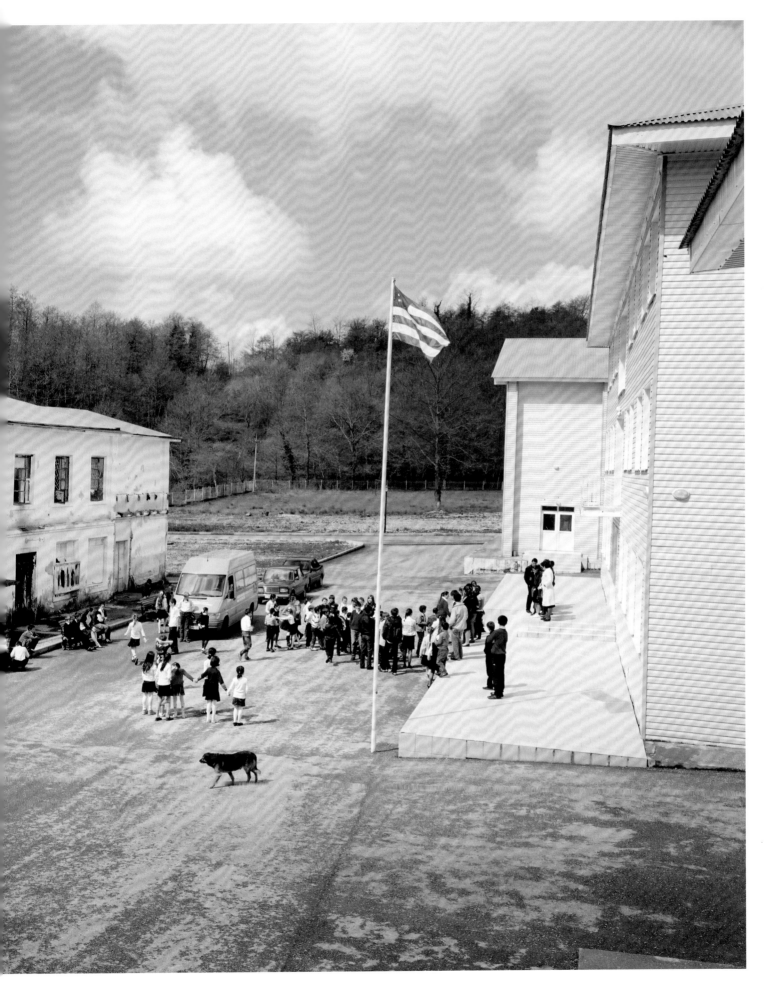

The Next President?

At a school in empty, desolate Tkuarchal,
seven-year-old Ainar introduces himself. He
dreams of becoming his country's president
and a singer.

Tkuarchal, Abkhazia, 2010

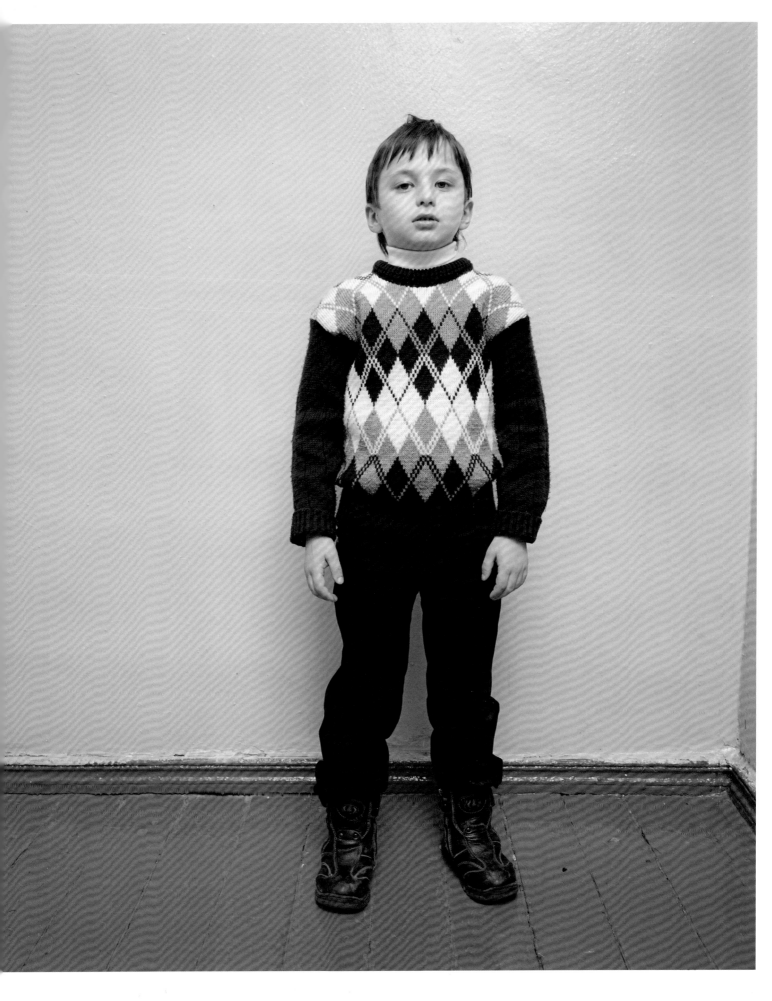

Remembering the War

Perhaps the greatest obstacle to Abkhazia's development is the last war: although it ended twenty years ago, it still maintains its grip on the country. The younger generation complains that you're no one if you didn't earn your stripes in the war. If only the older generations would just step aside, a public servant remarks. But the memories of loved ones who lost their lives are still fresh. The war is commemorated seven times a year.

Sukhum, Abkhazia, 2013

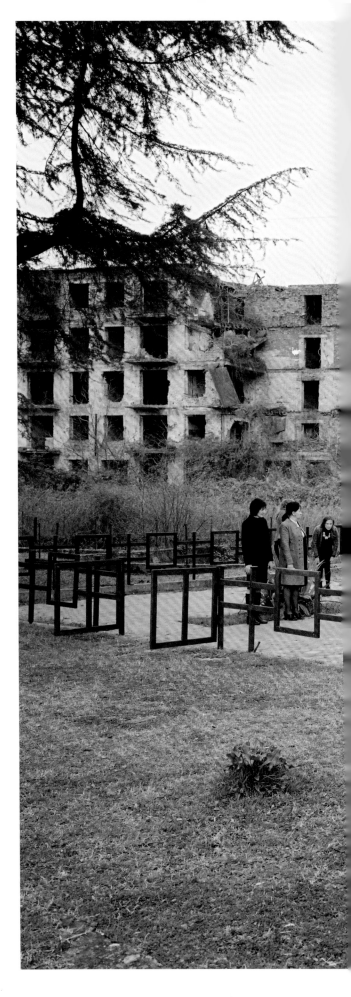

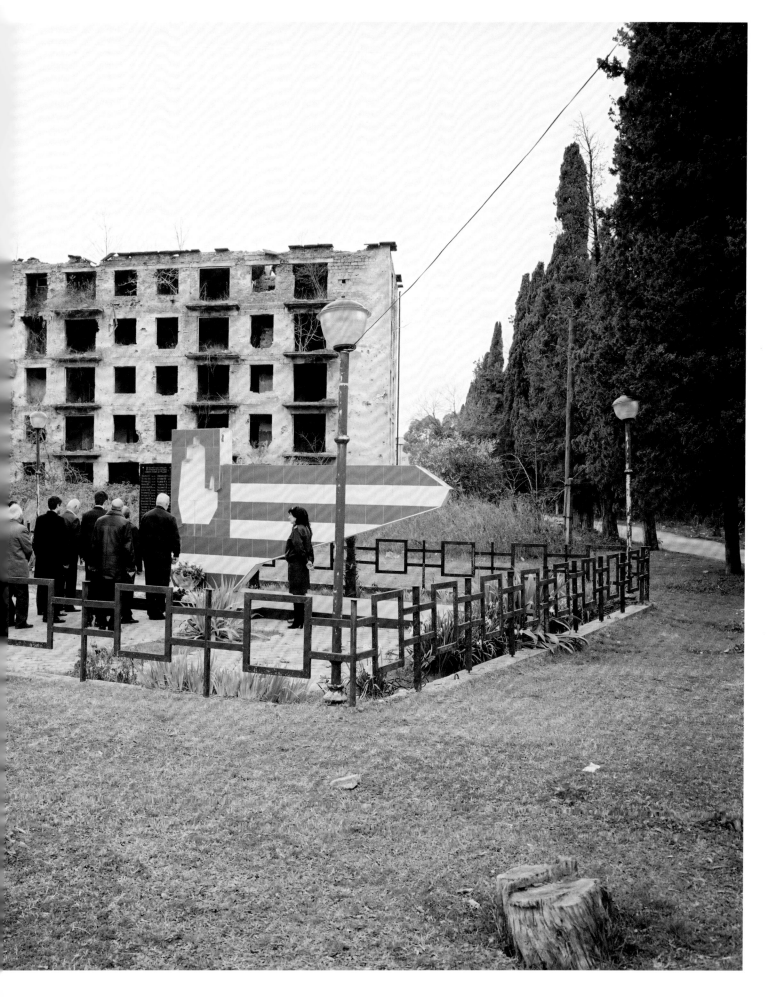

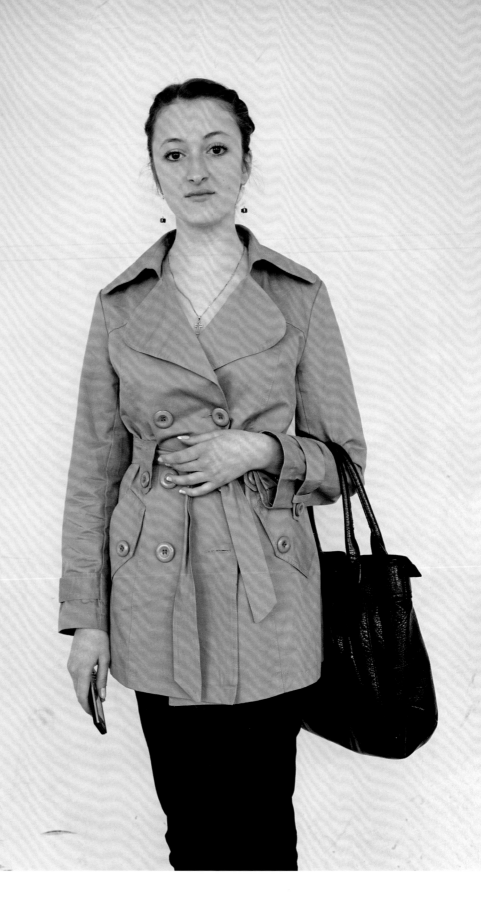

Looking Outward

Milana Vozba is young and ambitious. She wants to raise the standard of local journalism and takes advantage of every opportunity offered to her. She studied in the United States on a peace scholarship and attended summer courses at Radio Free Europe in Prague. She is frustrated by the slow rate of change in her country and blames it on the amateurism of policymakers and the widespread corruption.

Sukhum, Abkhazia, 2010

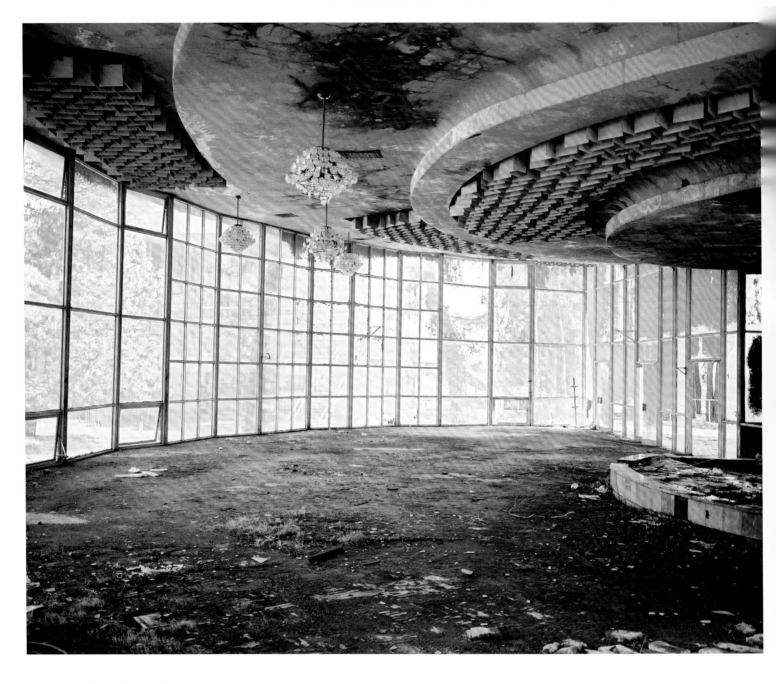

The Ballroom, Unchanged

In the center of the seaside resort Pitsunda, between the ramshackle high-rise hotels and pine trees, is a long-abandoned ballroom. It epitomizes the romance of decay. "Not for long," the mayor assured us. Sochi 2014 will put Abkhazia on the tourist map. Nonetheless, when we returned to Pitsunda and revisited the ballroom in 2013, not much seemed to have changed.

Pitsunda, Abkhazia, 2009 (left) and 2013 (right)

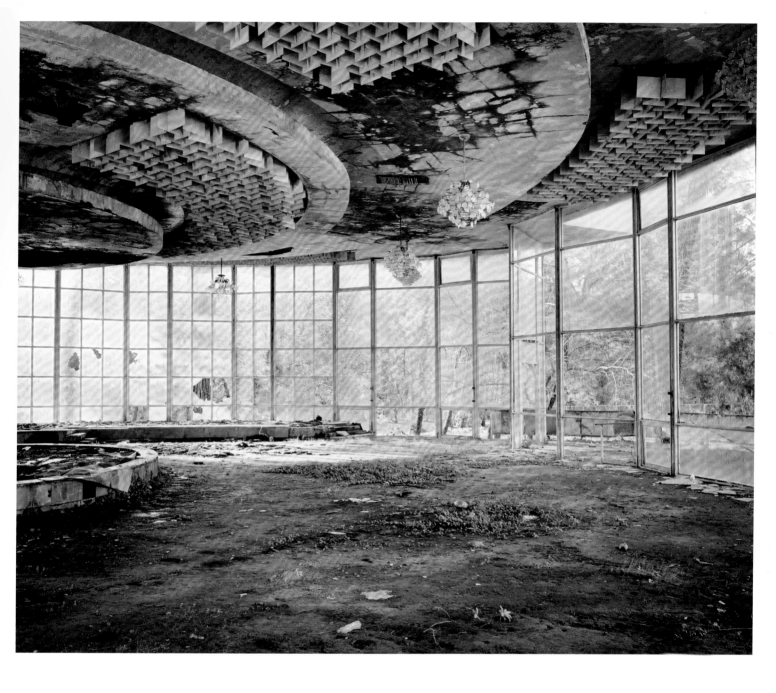

Fighting for Recognition

Viacheslav Chirikba, Abkhazian Minister
of Foreign Affairs

Sukhum, Abkhazia, 2013

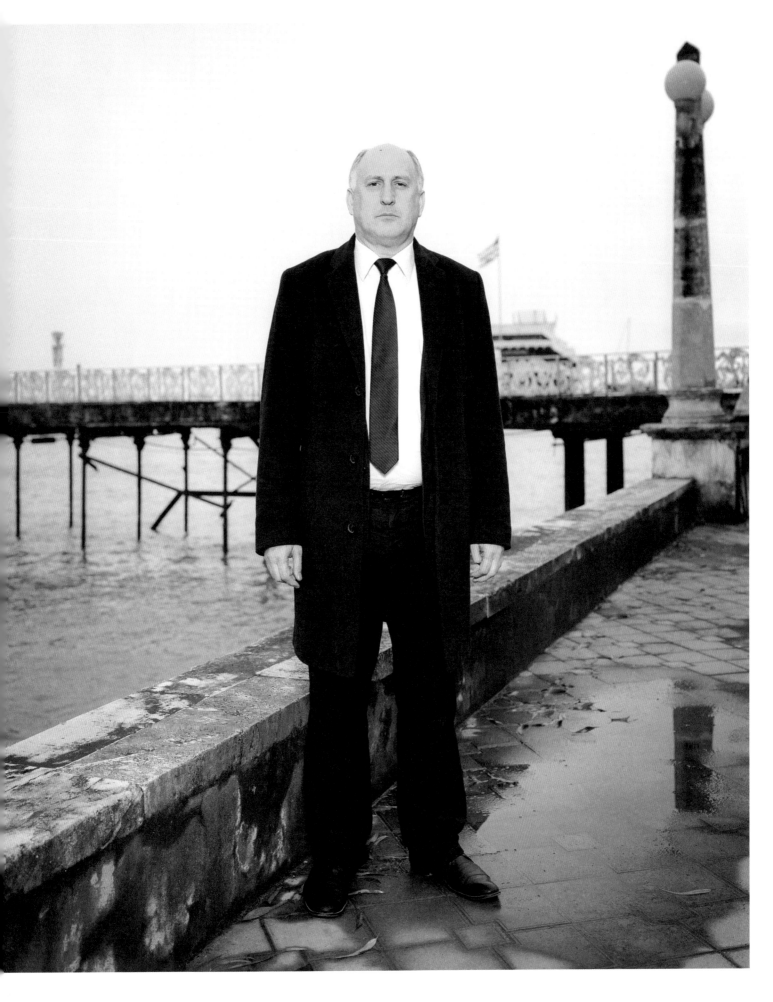

"There's an ongoing crusade against Abkhazia. It's as if the Cold War mentality still prevails."

Viacheslav Chirikba
Sukhum, Abkhazia, 2013

Diplomat Without a Country

The position of Abkhazian Minister of Foreign Affairs is possibly one of the most hopeless in international politics. Only three major countries—Nicaragua, Russia, and Venezuela—recognize Abkhazia, and rumors circulate that recognition by the Pacific Islands Nauru, Tuvalu, and Vanuatu was the result of a deal with Russia.

The hopeless position is currently filled by Viacheslav Chirikba, a balding man in his late forties. With a tiny ministry of barely twenty people behind him—little more than a corridor in a small building full of ministries—he is tasked with convincing the world that Abkhazia really exists, is viable, and deserves official recognition. "It's hard," the minister tells us in the lobby of Ritsa, an old hotel on the waterfront of the capital, Sukhum. He is in a hurry because he has to pick up his children from day care, but decides to send his driver instead. "A bloc policy has been established. It's as if the Cold War mentality still prevails. People think if Russia is the only country to lend us real support, there must be something wrong with us. But our aim is to remain independent—to become a small, tourist-driven country that is independent and on good terms with all its neighbors. It's difficult to achieve, but that's our goal."

Several years ago, Chirikba's predecessor still believed that a contemporary version of the domino theory would guarantee recognition of his country. After Russia recognized Abkhazia in 2008, a young Maksim Gvindjia traveled the world and saw the whole of Latin America fall for his charms. Chirikba interrupts me when I mention this. "Yes, and then the European Union came along and told everyone—South America, Belarus, Kazakhstan—that it would impose sanctions on them if they recognized us." His frustration is audible. "There's an ongoing crusade against Abkhazia. That's despite the fact that recognizing us would be beneficial for Georgia as well. The border could be opened again and refugees could travel back and forth." His use of the word *travel* is no accident. Except in the south, Chirikba does not see Georgian refugees returning permanently to Abkhazia.

"Of course we are still fighting for recognition, but it is now perhaps more important to disseminate accurate information, to show that we are no longer a conflict zone, to organize exchanges and kick-start our economy."

In the late eighties Chirikba studied in Kharkov, Ukraine, and Moscow, but he found the Soviet Union's clammy grip increasingly oppressive. "My ego wanted freedom," he recalls. "I wanted to speak English with English people, to see other countries." That opportunity arose when he was invited to finish his PhD in Caucasian languages in The Netherlands. Soon after his arrival, war broke out in Abkhazia. So began the minister's career, as a plenipotentiary diplomat for Abkhazia in Western Europe. "I actually had two jobs," he says. "During the day I taught at the university, and the rest of my time was spent calling, faxing, giving lectures, and attending peace talks." To illustrate this, he has brought along an old newspaper. In the text below a youthful photograph of him, he patiently explains his country and the issues with Georgia to the public, which, in the early nineties, was ignorant of the dozens of post-Soviet nations that had appeared seemingly overnight.

Chirikba eventually spent more than twenty years in The Netherlands. It has shaped him, he says. "I experienced the nineties, the golden age of Western Europe. It amazed me that everyone was satisfied with their life. The unemployed, the elite, all sectors of society. . . . For me that was a hallmark of a healthy society: everyone had a niche and was satisfied with their place in it."

The minister has taken The Netherlands and the Northern Europe he witnessed then as a model for his ideal Abkhazia. "Our country is not Northern Europe, so there's a different mentality here, but it has still remained a model for me. A state should be social and so its first function is to protect and care for its children, parents, immigrants, disabled, and sick. At the same time we Abkhazians have our own characteristics. Our traditions, language, and culture must be preserved."

We walk outside. The interview has run over and Chirikba's driver has been sent home. The minister hesitantly starts his car. "I've driven in Europe," he says, "but it's different here. They drive like maniacs. Look!" He jumps up. "Did you see that? He didn't even indicate before turning." Life in his homeland is not always easy, he admits. "The culture is different from The Netherlands, it's more Mediterranean. All those big cars are the horses of the past. They're not Calvinists here," he winks. "Some things are deeply rooted in the national character, like the drinking. I can't stand it. I have to try and refuse when I'm yet again offered *chacha* or some other drink."

Sukhum

Sukhum, Abkhazia, 2013

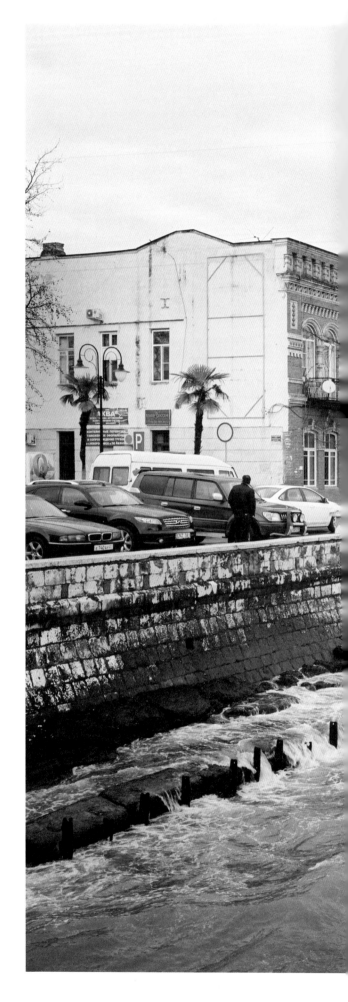

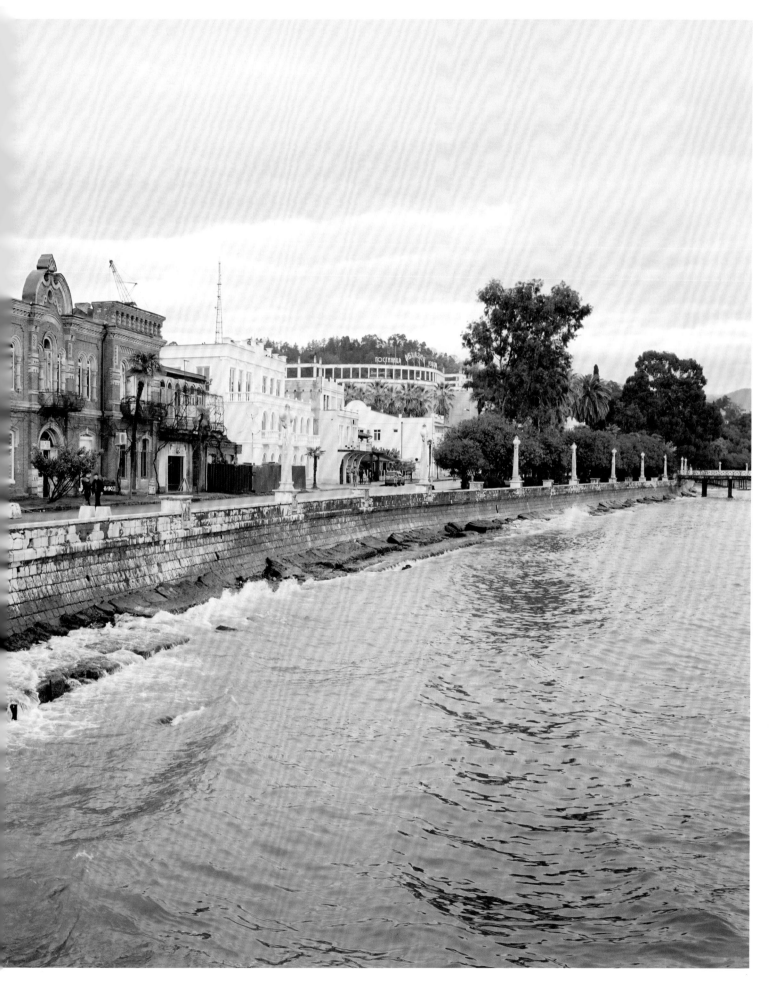

Liquor Store

The day after a bombing, workers have already cleaned up most of the debris. New bricks and cement have been delivered and unloaded. For the owner, Beslan, it is business as usual: this is the fifth time that his liquor store has been blown up. "The terrorists support Islamic Sharia and so reject liquor stores," he says. "It's primarily poor boys who go into the woods because they can make good money. We're vulnerable, and they know that." But that doesn't deter him from reopening. "We're almost on the border with Chechnya," he says. "There's never a shortage of customers. For New Year's Eve, half of Chechnya comes to buy drinks from us."

Ordzhonikidzevskaya, Ingushetia, 2012

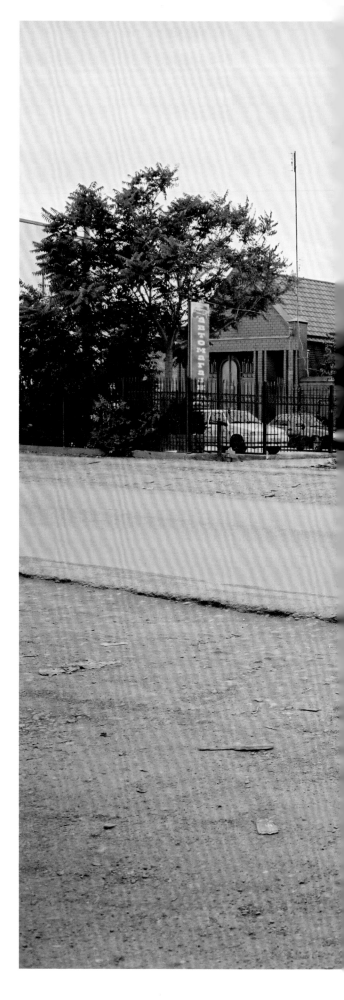

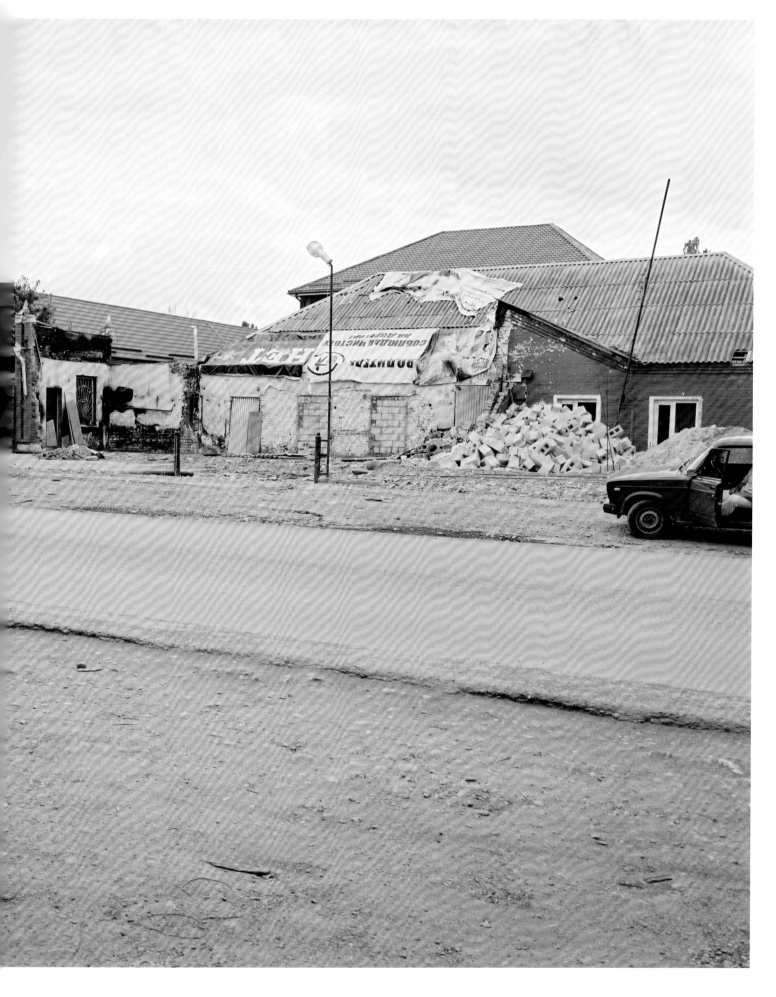

An Attempt at Orthodoxy

Terik Bairamukov, thirty-four, is on a mission to convert his village to Islam. He attended Islamic college in the regional capital and runs the lower mosque near the river in his village, Krasny Vostok. The village council has been largely Islamic for some time, which is a step in the right direction. But the neighbors, a bunch of miscreants, stole the microphone from his minaret. Only when someone dies do they come to his mosque to announce the name of the deceased through the loud-speakers. Terik now occasionally sings on the street when it is time to call the faithful to prayer. He is a patient man. "Everyone here was raised in the Soviet Union. Alcohol, media propaganda, and luxury keep them away from Islam. But the next generations will finally make our village Islamic."

Krasny Vostok, Karachay-Cherkessia, 2013

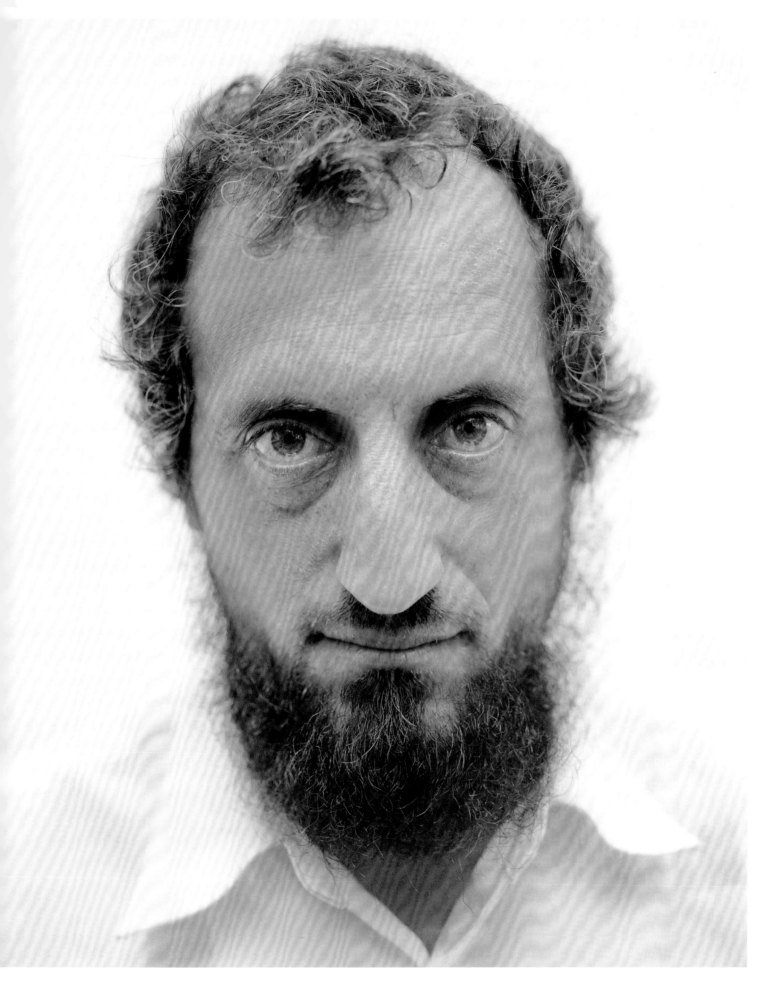

Tatiana Grigoryeva, fifty-three, has had to tell her story so many times to various investigation teams from the police and the FSB that she now recounts it almost automatically. From memory, she draws the layout of the subway carriage and the location of the bomber on a piece of paper. "I heard someone in the carriage sobbing like a child. I was sitting by the first door, at the back of the carriage. The woman who detonated the bomb was between the third and fourth doors. There was a lot of smoke and I was afraid I would suffocate. I walked outside pushing the man in front of me. He couldn't walk, but somehow I was able to push him along." Tatiana was confronted with complete silence. It was as if everyone had frozen, she tells us, even though the platform was filled with people who were undoubtedly panic stricken. "Perhaps my ear drums were damaged, or maybe it was shock." On the platform she saw a sign: exit to the city. She continued to push the man toward the exit, up the long escalator.

Tatiana later heard that a delay in the subway service had caused the suicide bomber to panic. Her bomb was on a timer and she realized that she would not reach her target–the subway station under the Ministry of Internal Affairs–on time. Tatiana thinks that was perhaps why she overheard the girl crying. Tatiana is still astonished: "She was just seventeen years old, from Dagestan."

Sketch of the 2010 subway bombing in Moscow

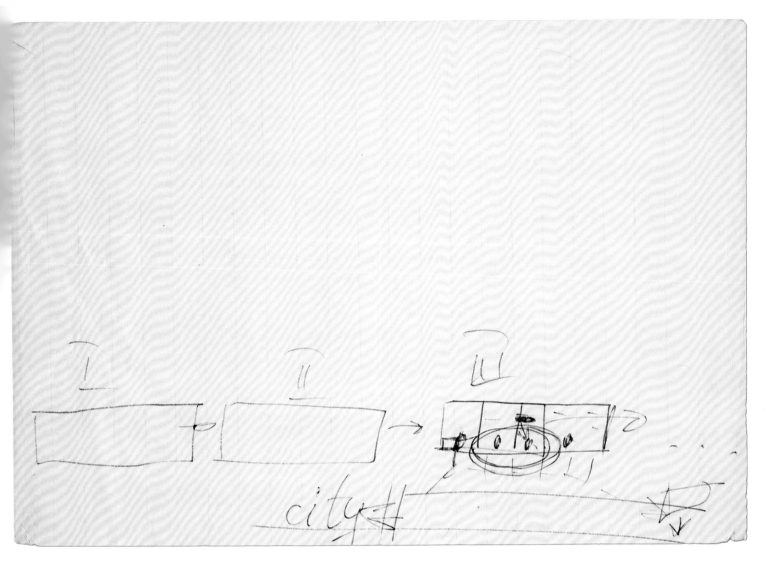

city #

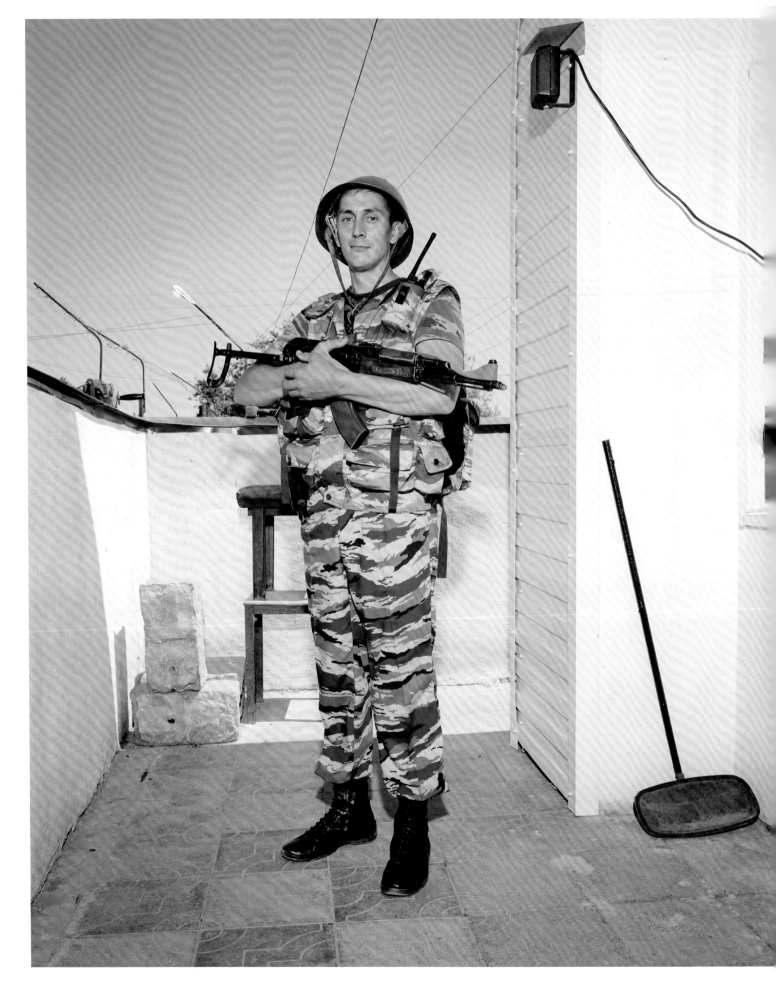

After the Bombing

With a multiethnic team of soldiers from
Russia and Tatarstan, Aleksandr Magomedov
guards this checkpoint on one of the access
roads to Makhachkala. It was here that a
suicide bomber blew up himself and the van
he was driving in May 2012. Minutes later,
while police officers, soldiers, and bystanders
attended to the victims, the bomber's sister
drove into the crowd and blew up her car.
Fourteen people were killed and more than
one hundred were injured. A month after the
attack much of the damage has already been
repaired; holes in the street and surrounding
walls are the only evidence of the force of the
explosions.

Makhachkala, Dagestan, 2012

"Most people in the Caucasus don't know that democracy doesn't mean you can do just anything at the expense of others."

Nazi Madgeva
Vladikavkaz, North Ossetia, 2011

If You Come with Guns, the Same Guns Will Kill You.

Nazi Madgeva, fifty-eight, sells herbs at the gates of the central market in Vladikavkaz, the capital of North Ossetia. You are not supposed to sell anything here; that privilege is reserved for the shops and stalls in the market. But so many women from the surrounding villages try to earn a little extra money that authorities turn a blind eye. The women know each other well: next to Nazi, Vera and Lela sell lemons.

They recall one fateful afternoon in 2010. It was noon and a woman had just told Nazi that she should pack up her herbs because her stall was illegal. Nazi protested halfheartedly but soon gave in, knowing that she would be back the following morning. She packed up her things—the herbs, some lettuce, a folding table, and a little stool—and walked to her storage space, just outside the market. "At that moment," Nazi remembers, "it felt like an endless wave of electricity was being pumped through me. My head was smashed against a metal wall. I didn't hear the explosion, because I immediately lost consciousness. I just lay there and when I woke up I saw terrible things."

"They should cut off the hands and feet of the people who did this," says Lela furiously. She remembers the moment as if it were yesterday. "Everything was flattened in the space of a second. I was lying on the ground without knowing how I had ended up there with a heavy metal construction on my back. I couldn't get up. My sugar level plummeted; I am diabetic."

Outside the market gates, near the place where Nazi and Lela still sell their wares today, a car was on fire. This was the third attack on the market in ten years. In total more than eighty people died and two hundred were injured.

"Why do they do this? It's a genocide against the Ossetians," says Nazi. "We're normal people. We have nothing to do with this. My neighbor died in front of my eyes. The baker over there was critically injured. And the perpetrator was an Ingush, a Muslim. I'm always told to be friendly to other nations, but when I try to make contact with my neighbors, I never really know what they think of me, what goes on in their hearts."

The ladies start clamoring all at once. "We're Christians, we are peace loving!" one of them says. "We can also wage war," cries another.

"My favorite expression is: 'if you come with guns, the same guns will kill you,'" says Nazi. "Most people in the Caucasus don't know that democracy doesn't mean you can do just anything at the expense of others."

Vladikavkaz's Central Market

North Ossetia is accustomed to attacks. As a Christian and pro-Russian republic in the North Caucasus, it is a convenient target within easy reach. Since the attack on the central market, a special lock has been constructed and all bags are checked. Whether this is enough to withstand car bombs detonated outside the market remains to be seen.

Vladikavkaz, North Ossetia, 2011

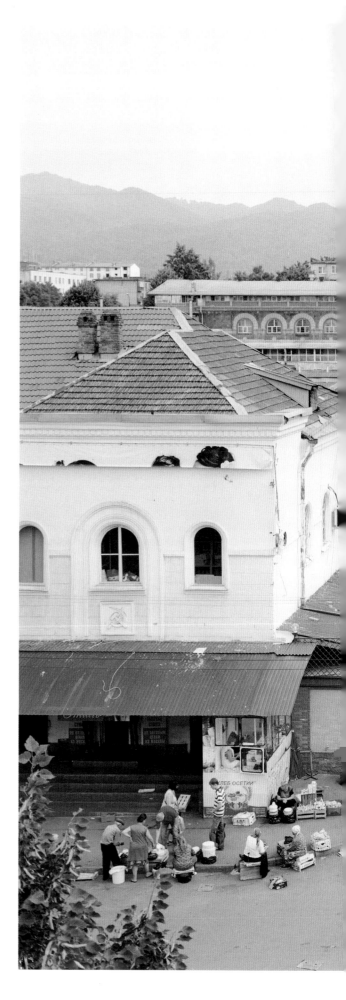

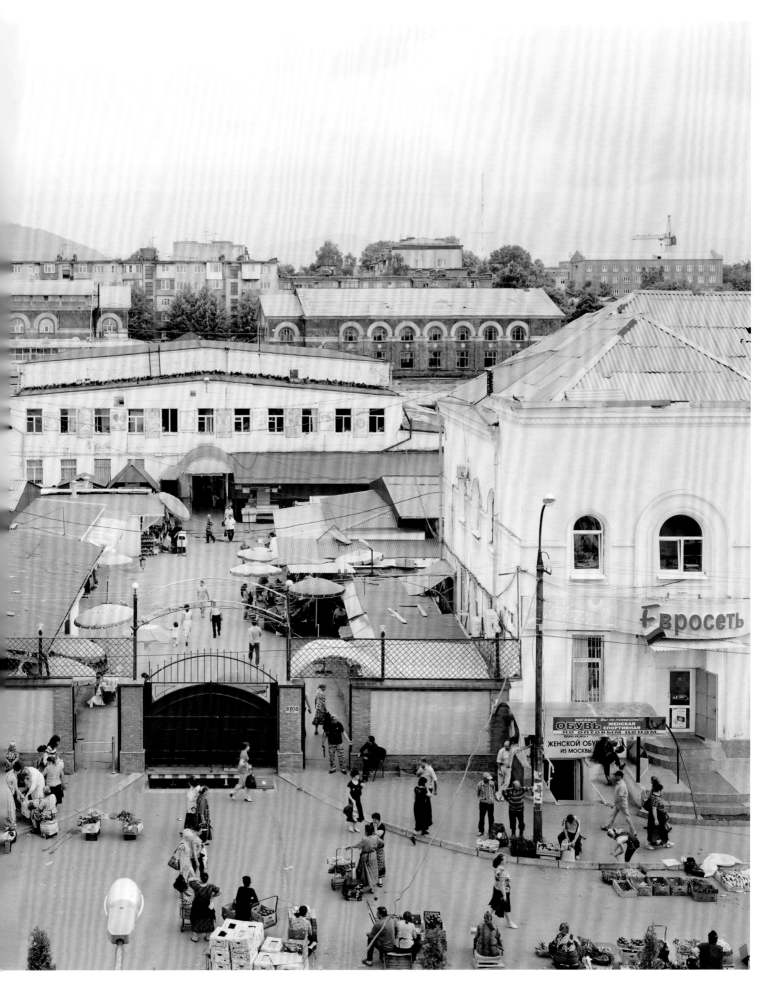

From Sovkhoz to Stadiums

In fits and starts the old sovkhoz, cabbage fields, and surrounding villages are being replaced by immense building sites, storage depots for materials, or new structures such as the Bolshoi Ice Dome ice hockey stadium. The landscape has changed almost beyond recognition, making it increasingly difficult to orient oneself. Only the small cemetery and the hills in the background remain as fixed reference points in the tangle of workers' huts, machinery, railroad sidings, Olympic villages, hotels, and facilities under construction.

Adler, Sochi region, Russia, 2010

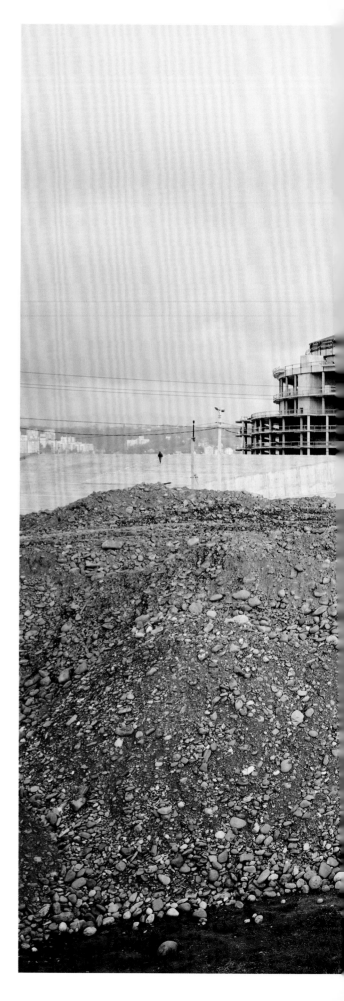

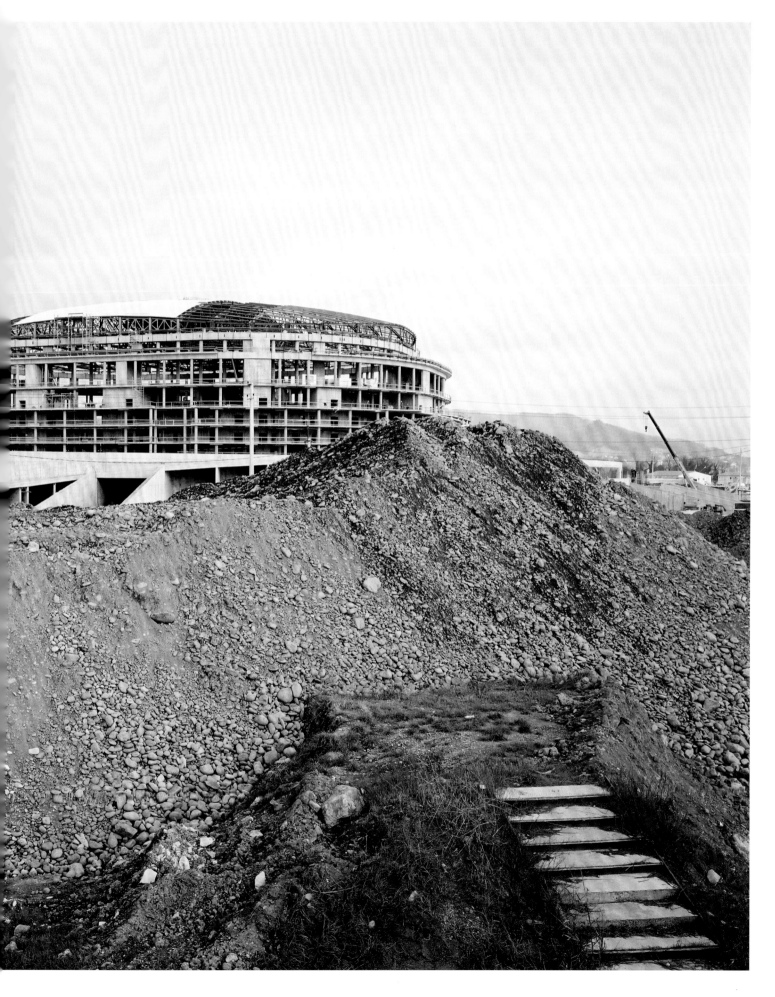

Fired for Protesting

While the cost of the Olympics has risen to a staggering fifty billion dollars, the Games' lowliest employees are barely paid. The first riots broke out in 2010. Movies shot on cell phones, showing the appalling conditions in the workers' villages, went viral on YouTube. Laborers complained that they had not been paid for six months. Organizers blamed the subcontractors and promised to rectify the situation, but the instigators of the protest are now unemployed. Ivan has slept in a cowshed next to the construction site for weeks. "Our boss changes every month," he says. "He receives a certain amount from his superiors at the Moskonversprom Company or one of its subcontractors and makes sure that most of it goes into his own pocket. So it's completely unclear to us where we should collect our pay. Not at Moskonversprom or one of its subcontractors, because they've outsourced the job again." He is trying to buy a bus ticket back to his family in Azov, a town relatively nearby. Most of the victims are migrant workers from Central Asia who have fewer rights and less courage to stand up for themselves. They continue working, in the blind hope that everything will be all right.

Adler, Sochi region, Russia, 2010

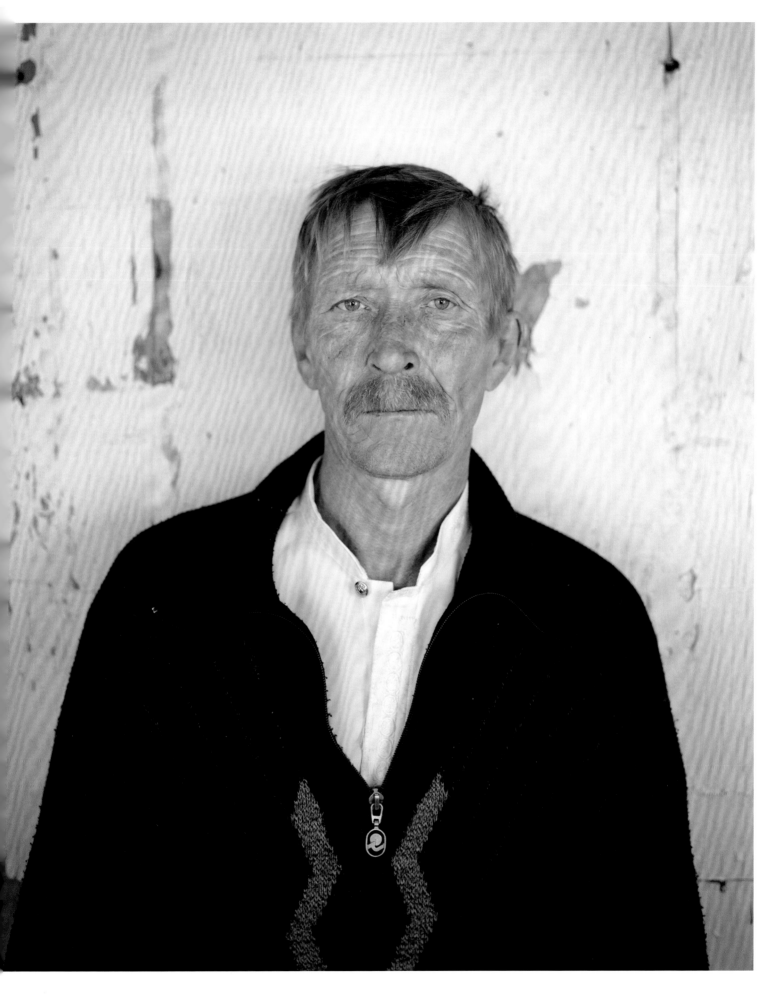

Ivan's Cowshed

In his improvised accommodation, fired laborer Ivan keeps his possessions in a bag on the wall. "Striking is pointless," he says. "Workers like me are a dime a dozen."

Adler, Sochi region, Russia, 2010

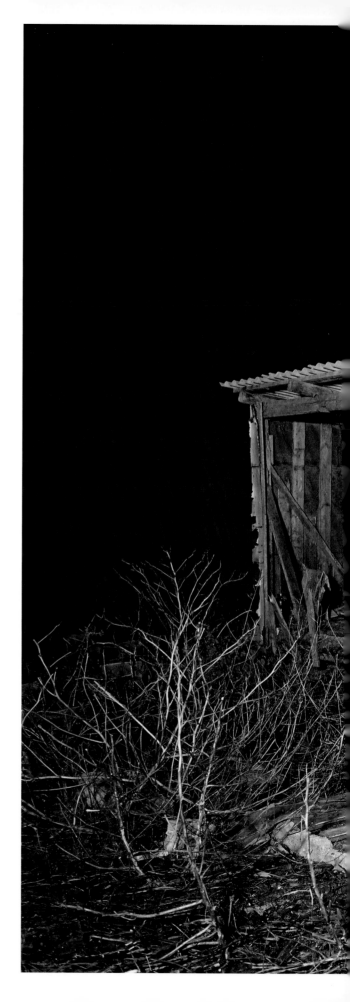

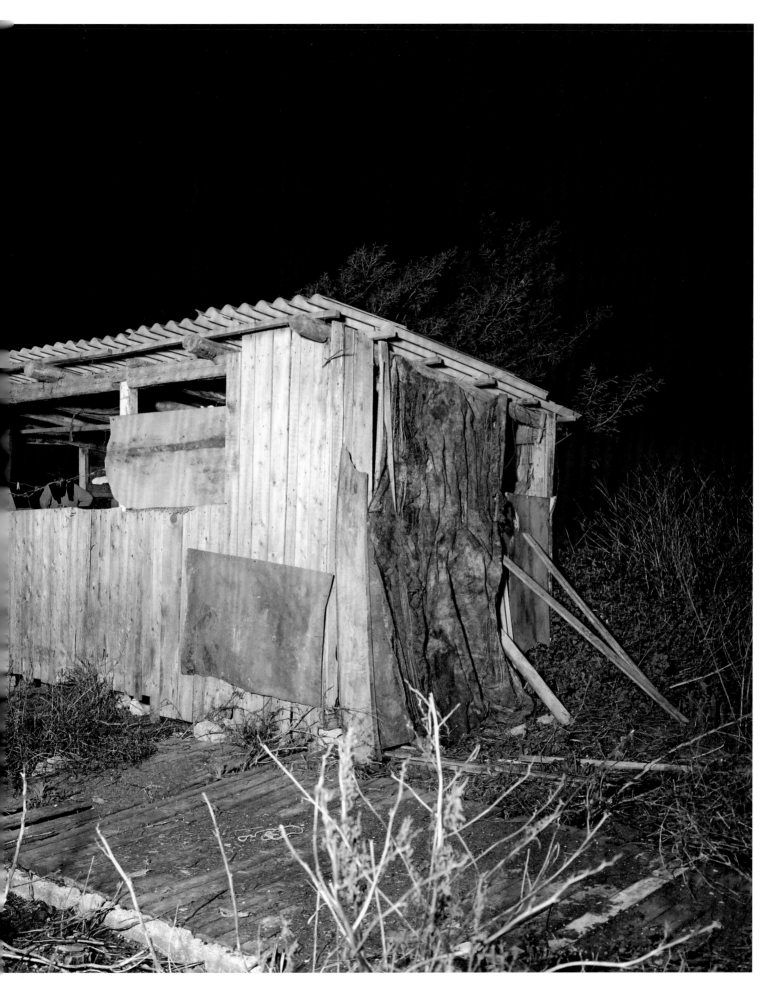

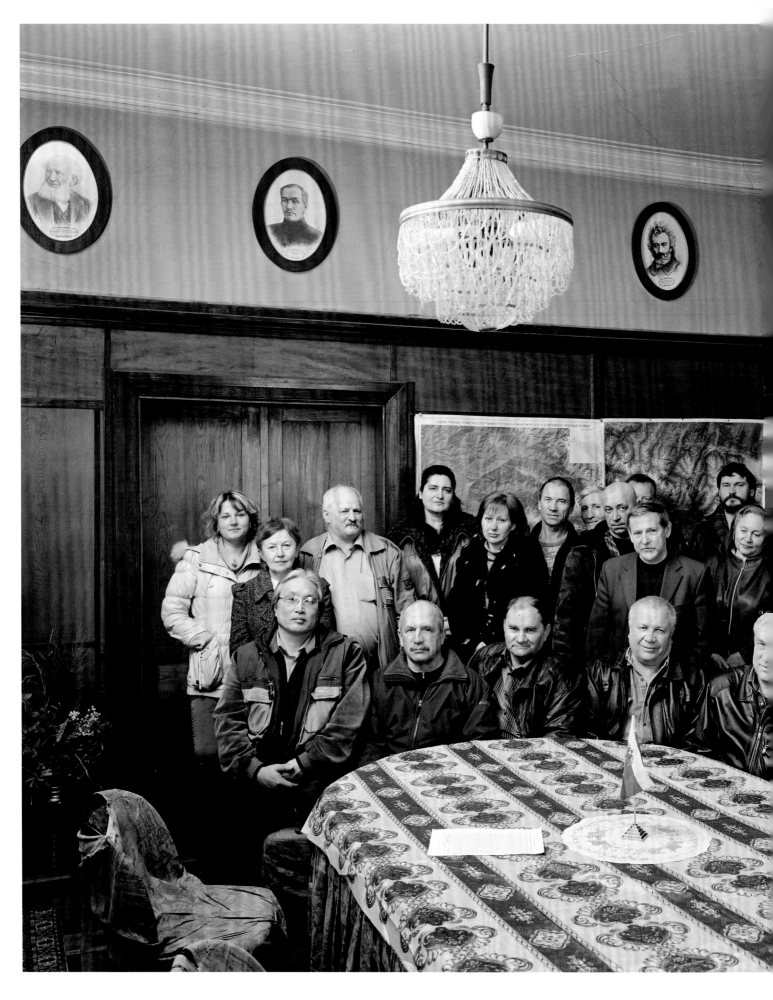

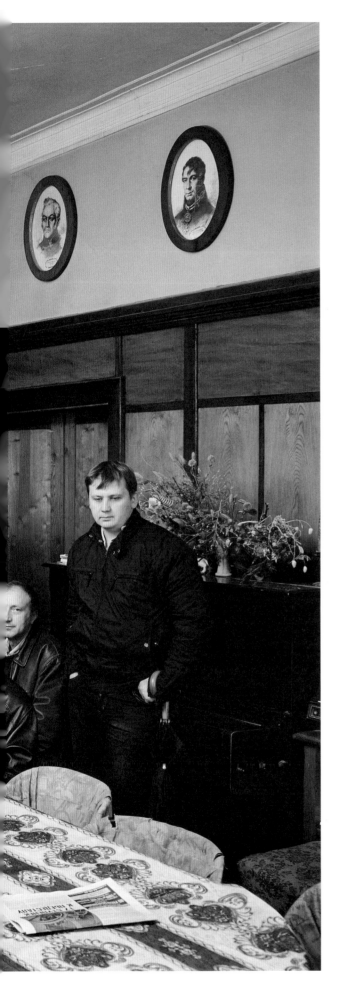

Civilized Protest

They can curse like troopers and yell if they have to. Yet these protesters aren't rabble-rousers but geologists, lawyers, environmentalists, and concerned citizens. They gather every two weeks in the Geographic Society, where they discuss the latest Olympic plans and decide how they can limit the environmental damage, contest the forced removals, and ultimately keep the Games out of Sochi, at least partially. They talk hopefully about the possibility of moving the ice skating rinks farther north, at least to a city where it is cold in the winter. Then off they go, carrying files bulging with cases on land ownership, expropriation, protected trees, and theories about underground lakes that in due course will swallow the skating rinks whole.

Sochi, Russia, 2009

"The Olympic Games in the subtropics—it's a fraud!"

Boris Nemtsov
Sochi, Russia, 2009

The Activist

Katya Primakova was perhaps the first person we met in Sochi. She was our guide and driver in this changing city. And she hated the change. When we talked to a worried resident of a village that had been singled out for demolition to make way for the Olympic infrastructure or to an activist who was flitting nervously around a tree for fear it would be cut down, Katya would stand back, often dressed in a crop top that revealed a healthy belly, and smoke a cigarette. But in the car to the next demonstration or meeting she would provide cynical commentary on what had been said, or the developments taking place in Sochi—though the cynicism was always directed at the government and the Olympic Games.

Katya has worked her way up from a florist to a journalist at the local paper. She is proud of her achievement but by no means satisfied. She is now studying law, a decision motivated by what she saw in her work as a journalist. One day she hopes to be able to take on cases herself. She is increasingly becoming an activist. When she speaks to the people in the sovkhoz (state-owned farms) who are being evicted, she talks clearly, using simple language, and has the patience to repeat herself if necessary. She will keep fighting, no matter how much patience is required. The government continues to lie and must be corrected at all costs. One of our trips with her is a visit to workers who have been forced to sleep in the fields since they were turned out of their homes for complaining about unpaid salaries.

Most Russians affiliated with the government and the Games dismiss Katya's objections. Of course there is corruption, of course things go wrong, but just wait until the Games are here. Then everything will be great. Yes, sixteen hundred homes need to be demolished, but did anyone criticize the Games in Beijing after the event? More than a million people were turned out of their homes there. It won't matter as long as the event is a success. A Russian may take his time to saddle his horse, but woe betide anyone who tries to overtake him once he is in the saddle.

Katya explains that before 2007 there was a semblance of a protest against the havoc that the Games threatened to wreak on the city. Then, she says, Mayor Anatoly Pakhomov arrived. He placated the protesters by saying that no one had the right to demolish homes. The initial momentum was never regained. By lying through his teeth, the mayor effectively suppressed all dissent.

Another meeting in Sochi in 2009, attended by national heavyweights Boris Nemtsov and Garry Kasparov, attracts mainly oddballs. A woman in an enormous fur coat who introduces herself as a Putin supporter says that she is now siding with the opposition because of the Games. The editor of a small Christian paper proclaims that the rise of feminism is a sign that the end of days is nigh. A few people tell harrowing stories of how their harvest was seized when their sovkhoz were taken away virtually overnight. Someone whispers that they should not support Nemtsov, because he is a Jew aspiring to world domination. Katya leans against the wall in her crop top, texting on her cell phone and surveying the chaos. She is still proud that her struggle is making it into the international media and that Nemtsov, the former prime minister of Russia, is now running for mayor of her city: for just a moment, she is at the center of history

in the making. "The Olympic Games in the subtropics—it's a fraud!" Nemtsov exclaims to loud cheers.

A few days later an activists' meeting is held at the Sochi branch of the Russian Geographical Society. The participants are excited: there is momentum! Katya suddenly takes the floor, together with her best friend, Alyk Le, a Russian of Korean origin. They talk about corruption, about old family-run hotels that are being destroyed to make space for hotels for the rich, and about public beaches that are being sold to billionaires. Once again, the activists sense an opportunity. Nemtsov said that the Games should be organized throughout Russia—in Moscow, Krasnodar, and Volgograd—not just here. But Nemtsov has little influence in Putin's Russia. He suffers a crushing defeat in the mayoral election and departs soon after for Moscow.

A few months later Alyk Le is disgraced on a Russian website, which releases a strange clip showing him talking to Nemtsov and getting in and out of a delivery van. The images are accompanied by a tapped phone conversation, which allegedly exposes Le as a Korean spy who has come to sabotage the Sochi Games on behalf of PyeongChang, South Korea, a rival competitor for the event. The clip insinuates that he was negotiating with Nemtsov to move the Games to Korea at the last minute.

We continue seeing Katya. The villages have been cleared; the tunnels dug. Katya keeps on fighting, for every tree if she has to. Each time the stories she shows us are smaller and more hopeless, as the stadiums rise steadily on the surrounding skyline.

It is 2013. Katya has just had her fourth child. The infrastructure for the Games is almost complete and the streets are lined with Russian flags and Olympic logos. Katya looks at us slyly as she admits her change of direction. She now works for the Games and has an administrative position at one of the larger companies operating in the area. She sees our surprise. "If you can't beat them, join them," she says.

If You Can't Beat Them, Join Them

Katya Primakova, twenty-eight

Adler, Sochi region, Russia, 2009

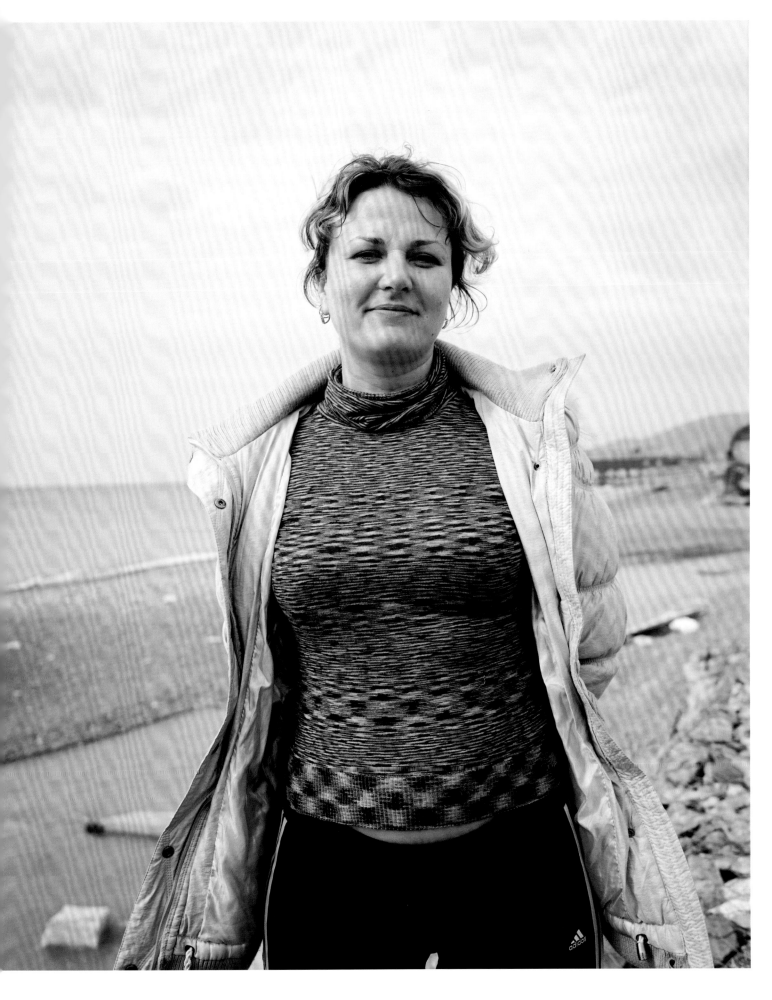

Almost Done

Almost all the Olympic facilities are complete. They have to be, because the International Olympic Committee (IOC) is paying increasingly frequent visits to Sochi. The first test events were held in the winter of 2012. The tone of the IOC's remarks is becoming increasingly concerned. Putin's response, during a visit to the city in early 2013, was a show of authority. He fired the deputy head of the Russian Olympic Committee, which is responsible not only for developing the ski slopes around Sochi but also for turning the mountains of the North Caucasus into the tourist resorts of the future. It is all part of his plan to lift the North Caucasus out of the economic doldrums, he says, as tourism brings prosperity and development. During the same visit, it became clear that the Games had exceeded the $50 billion mark. "Cost increases might occur during construction, but they must be justified," Putin was quoted as saying on *Russia Today*. "The most important thing is to make sure that nothing was stolen and that there are legitimate grounds for the additional expense," he stressed.

Adler, Sochi region, Russia, 2012

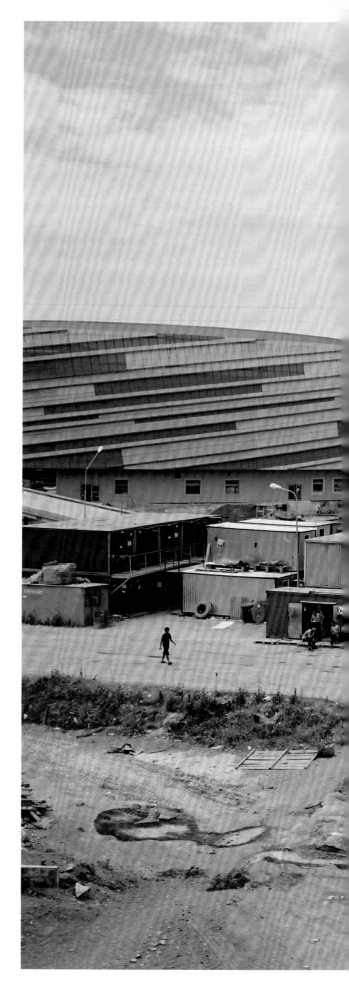

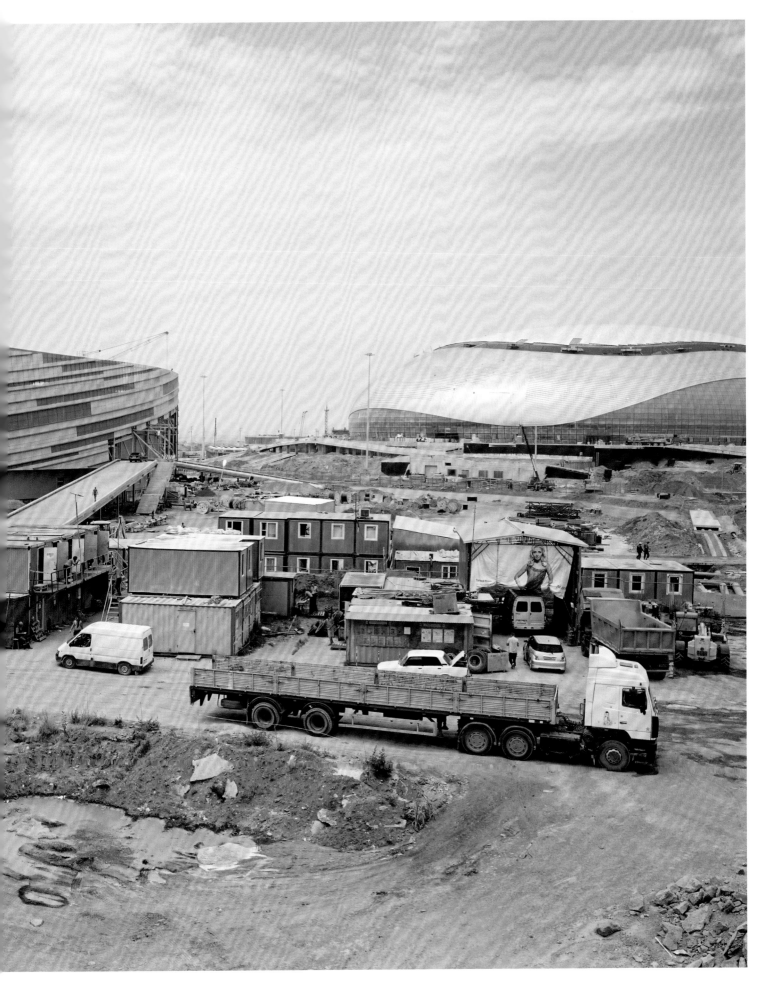

"The Olympic family is going to feel at home in Sochi."

President Vladimir Putin
Guatemala City, Guatemala, 2007

Gennadi Kuk

The road to Krasnaya Polyana is spectacular, winding past steep gorges, fast-flowing rivers, unspoiled coniferous forests, and through impressive tunnels. The modest village is beautifully situated between pine-covered hills and snow-capped mountains. In the nearby valley the Russian gas company Gazprom has invested in a large hotel with new lifts up to the ski slopes. Gennadi Kuk, eighty-one, who had joined us in the village, sighs as he observes the damage inflicted on the forests and valleys. Wide roads have been built, the river has been channeled, and menacing bulldozers stand ready for yet more work. "My God, this still has to happen to me," he mutters.

Behind his house he unbuckles his belt, hooks it to a cable and swishes over the swirling river. His land is on the other side of the water and this improvised "cable car" is the fastest way for him to reach it. He has taken up the fight against the local authorities. "I'm a thorn in their side," he says. He proudly shows us his land, an elevated pasture with burial mounds and the remains of old watch towers dotted here and there. "This is a world heritage site from the Bronze Age," he says, "and now a delivery road for the railway is going to be built through the middle of it." He walks around the burial mounds. His grandfather had once been able to acquire the land; now, thanks to eminent domain, it has become part of the ongoing development in advance of the Games. "We've never disturbed the burial mounds and now they're going to disappear. It's not that I'm against these Games. It's the way in which they're being realized. Local residents are supposed to be updated on progress every three months, according to the IOC, but the local authorities behave like spies, they never show their faces."

Krasnaya Polyana, Sochi region, Russia, 2010

ЗАРЕГ... № 74/

«01» сентября 10 г.

СЧ ...
СЧ по ... граду
Центрального району
г... ... г. Сочи

Дежурный _____ Николаев (С.С.

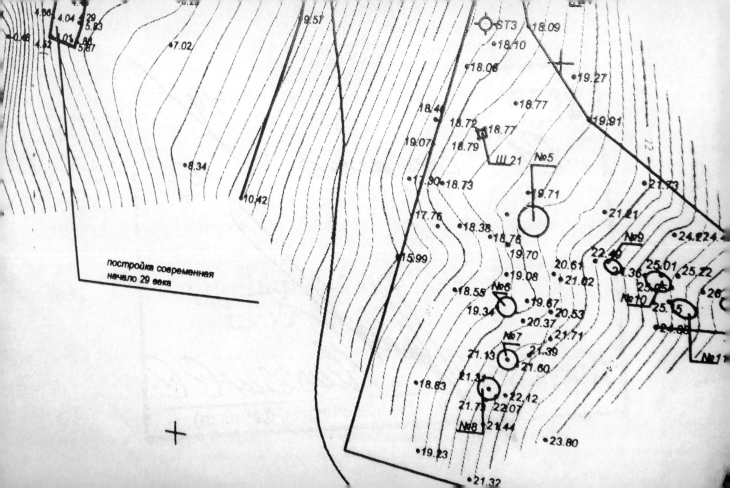

постройка современная
начало 29 века

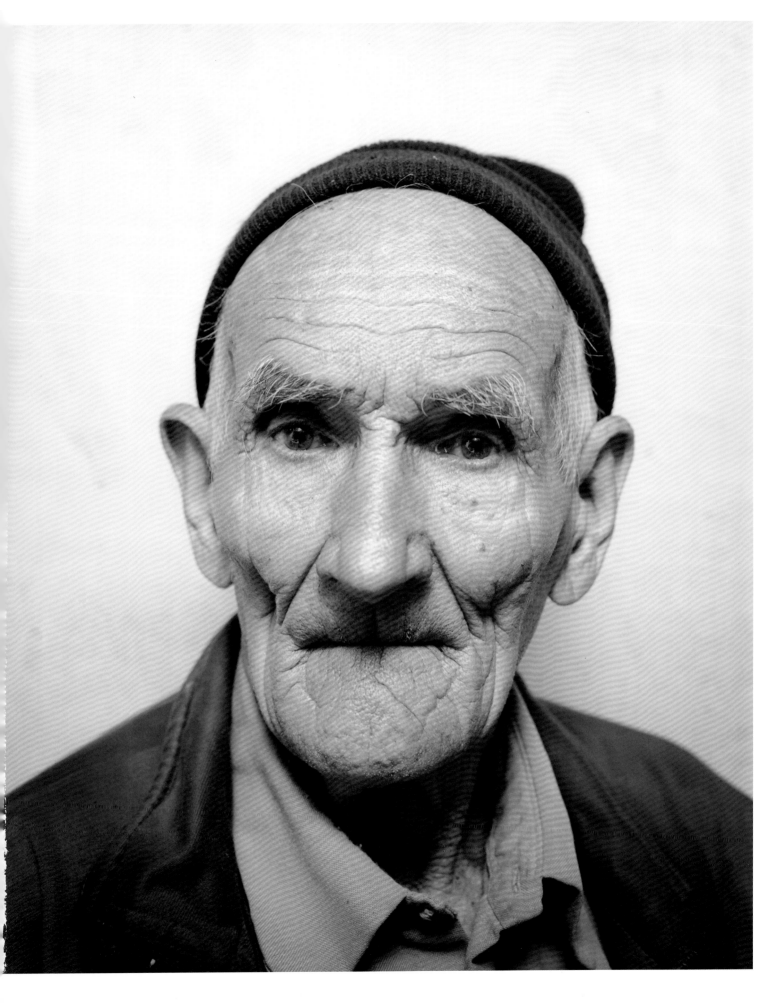

Slow Progress

In February 2013 Putin and the International Olympic Committee began to express shared concern. The mammoth operation on which Russia had embarked in 2007 was moving too slowly. Too many hotels, roads, and Olympic venues were still unfinished, including the ski jump in Estosadok. Putin came, saw, and demanded to know who was responsible for the delays and considerable overspending. The vice president of the Russian Olympic Committee, Akhmed Bilalov, was singled out and fired the same day. Not wanting to become a scapegoat for the cost of the Games, he and his brother, who was working on Olympic construction sites, hastily fled the country. A few months later Bilalov claimed to have been poisoned when a high concentration of mercury was found in his body.

Estosadok, Sochi region, Russia, 2010

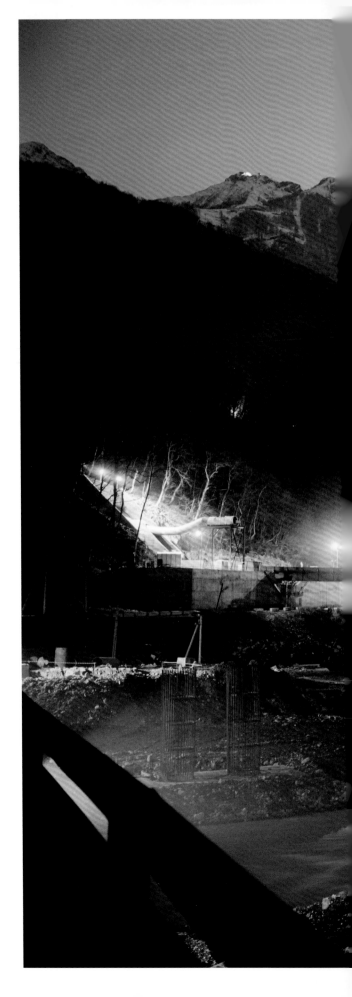

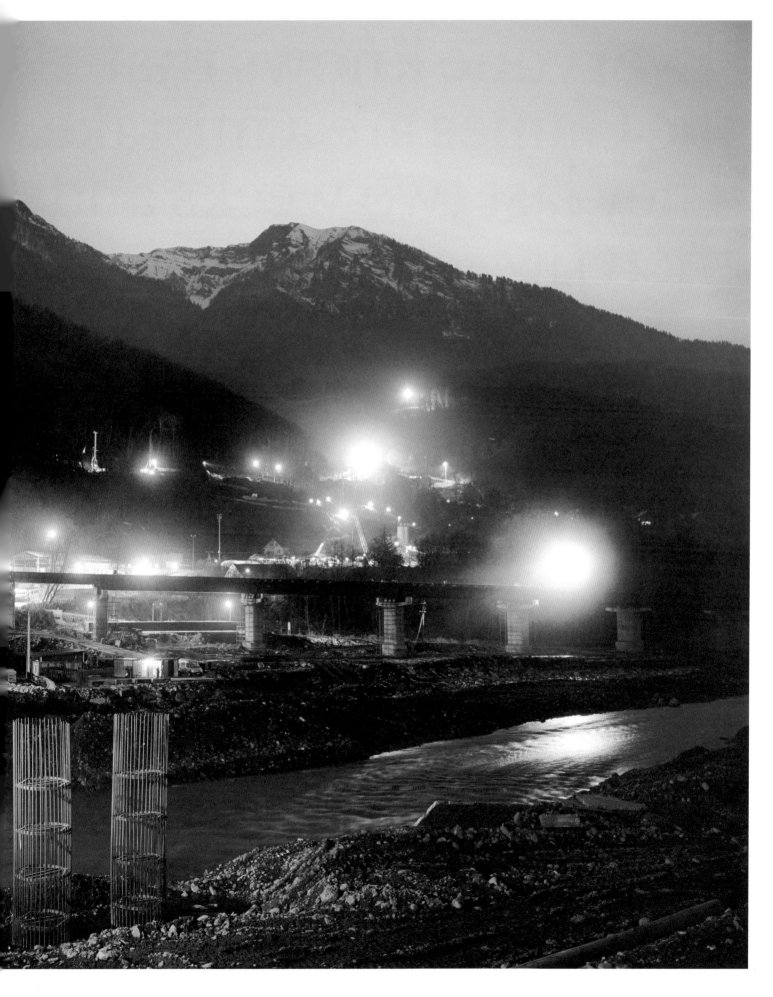

"Everyone knows that the Games are a mistake. They last two weeks and then *fweeet*..."

Vladimir Sorokin
Krasnaya Polyana, Russia, 2010

The Ski Lift Builder

Vladimir Sorokin walks through Krasnaya Polyana with a big grin. *His* village. There comes another helicopter with its characteristic chopper sound. Vladimir looks up briefly. *His* helicopter. A large empty bag hangs from it. "24/7," he laughs. These are the years of plenty.

Vladimir has lived in Krasnaya Polyana for twenty-five years. He moved here after finishing college in Riga, Latvia, and became the local ski lift pioneer. "There was absolutely nothing," he tells us in his office, which looks more like a site hut, with people constantly rushing in and out. He seems to prefer having meetings in his four-wheel-drive jeep, juggling a cell and a satellite phone.

It all started with heli-skiing. Vladimir brought people from around the world to the Caucasus to ski off-piste. His son grew up with it and plans to be at the start line in 2014, he says proudly. The first ski lifts were only built in the 1990s, and of course it was Vladimir who imported the technology. He is now so uniquely experienced and efficient, he says, that he is being asked to erect lifts around the world. "Others need six helicopters and are at it for weeks; I get by with less and I'm faster," he grins.

We drive through the village in his jeep. He disapprovingly points out newly built villas situated on the most scenic or strategic spots. He shows us the enormous wooden chalet belonging to the Russian president. In a forested area where construction is banned, one villa after another appears. "Minister, minister, colonel, member of the Duma...." According to Vladimir, they all live in illegal houses that were obtained through corruption. Some were even built and delivered for free, as a small addendum to a signed contract.

Vladimir effortlessly sums up all the problems with the Games: the weak ground on which the stadiums are being erected and the fact that literally all the infrastructure needs to be built from scratch. He lets it all wash over him; at the end of the day it does not make his life less interesting. He skis with Putin—he recently skied into Abkhazia by mistake, he tells us—and rubs shoulders with Russia's billionaires and sports stars. Above all, it is a mad adventure for him. "Of course you always worry that it won't be ready in time for the Games. That's the same everywhere. But we'll make sure that everything is ready here." He is also aware of the ecological problems associated with the construction, but, well, that's not his department. He is a foreman and manager, the Olympic Committee decided.

"Actually," says Vladimir, "the intention was to bring the Skiing World Cup to Sochi. Under Putin's influence that suddenly became the Olympic Games. That's not a problem for us in Krasnaya Polyana; it will only affect Adler and Sochi." Ultimately, Vladimir does not want to get hung up on the Games. "Everyone knows that they are a mistake. They last two weeks and then *fweeet*," he whistles, "they're gone. Regular Games cost $2.5 billion; ours cost $12.5 billion." A few years on and the price tag for the Games has soared to $50 billion. "We have to look beyond the Games. How do we make this region interesting in the long term? How do we get tourists to come here in the summer?" His goal will only truly have been reached when Krasnaya Polyana becomes a vacation destination for tourists from around the world, who come for skiing in the winter and hiking in the summer. The Games are only a temporary highlight.

Summer, says Vladimir, is essential for the village. "We can live off the forest, that's how we used to live. You can bring down nine bears during an evening in these forests, there's that many of them out there. The place is full of fruit, nuts, and berries. We can make everything from the forest, even coffee."

The Russian Dream

Rosa Khutor is an odd mix of Stalinist neoclassicism and Alpine village. It is the last Olympic village in Krasnaya Polyana's long valley, built by the oligarch Vladimir Potanin's investment companies. Modern, eclectic, and flashy, it is a small embassy of planet Moscow in the Caucasus, President Putin's dream of a new Russia become reality.

Rosa Khutor, Sochi region, Russia, 2013

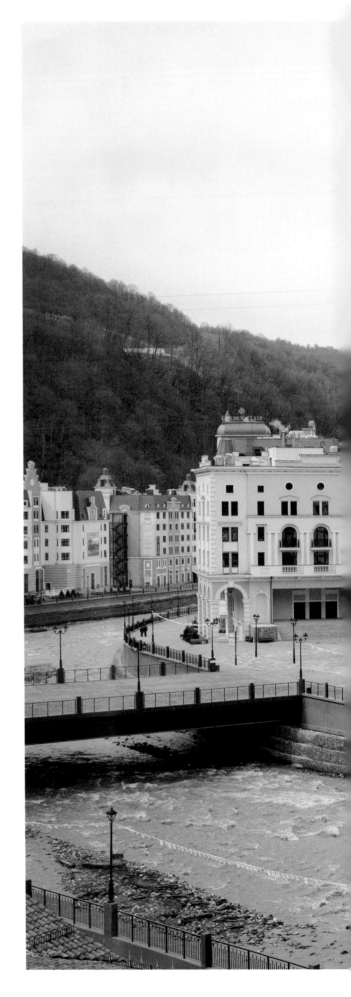

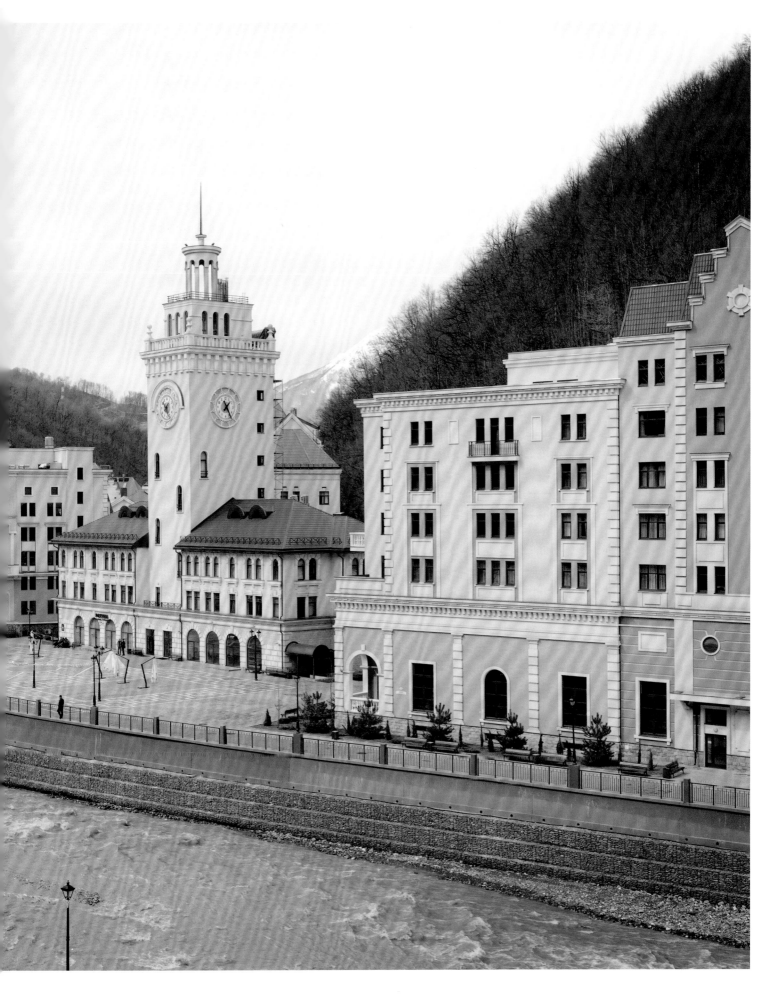

Restaurant Eurasia

In Restaurant Eurasia, Marika Bayur sings melancholy Russian chansons. Although the waiters are dressed in Asian, Turkish, and traditional Russian garb, in an effort to reinforce the restaurant's cosmopolitan character, customers only want to hear old-fashion songs about love, longing, and loss.

Sochi, Russia, 2011

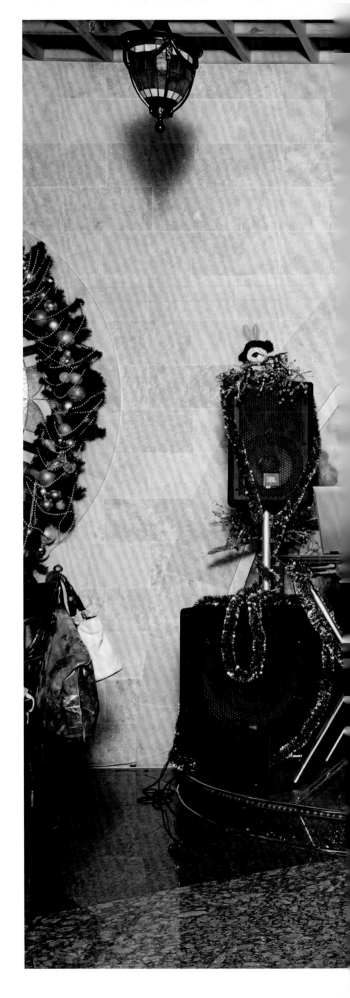

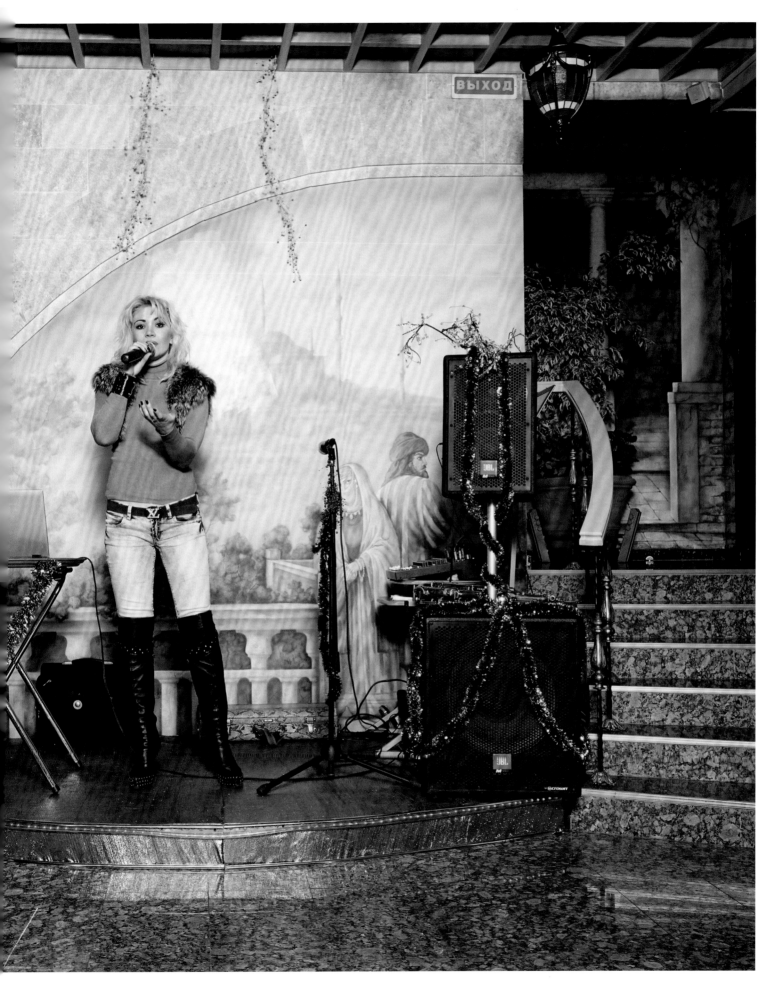

Officially Ready

All the test events and championships in Sochi have been declared a success. The stadiums are complete. The Russian Minister of Foreign Affairs Sergei Lavrov declares that the Games will be safe. Officials from a variety of international sports federations cautiously declare that they're looking forward to the Games.

A sense of restlessness in the North Caucasus prevails, however. In a few months, the Games will be over, leaving a vacuum in the region. Local leaders fret about their future. What will become of the many breakaway and semi-independent republics, closely kept under the ever-attentive eye of Chechen strongman Ramzan Kadryov? What will become of the subsidies that have bolstered the economy over the past five years?

Adler, Sochi region, Russia, 2012

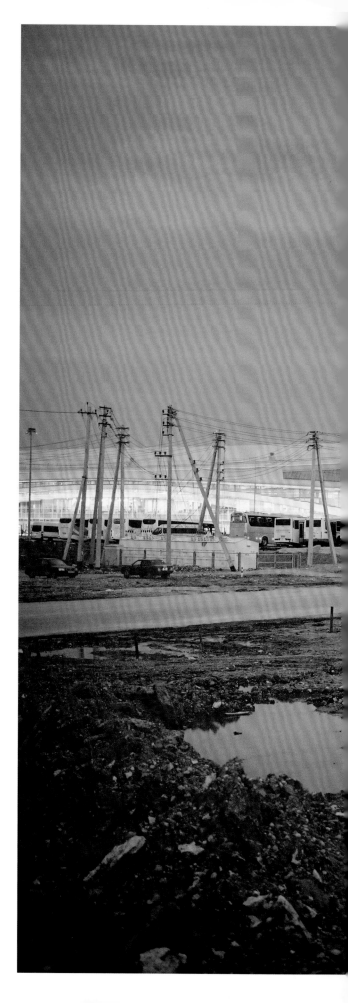

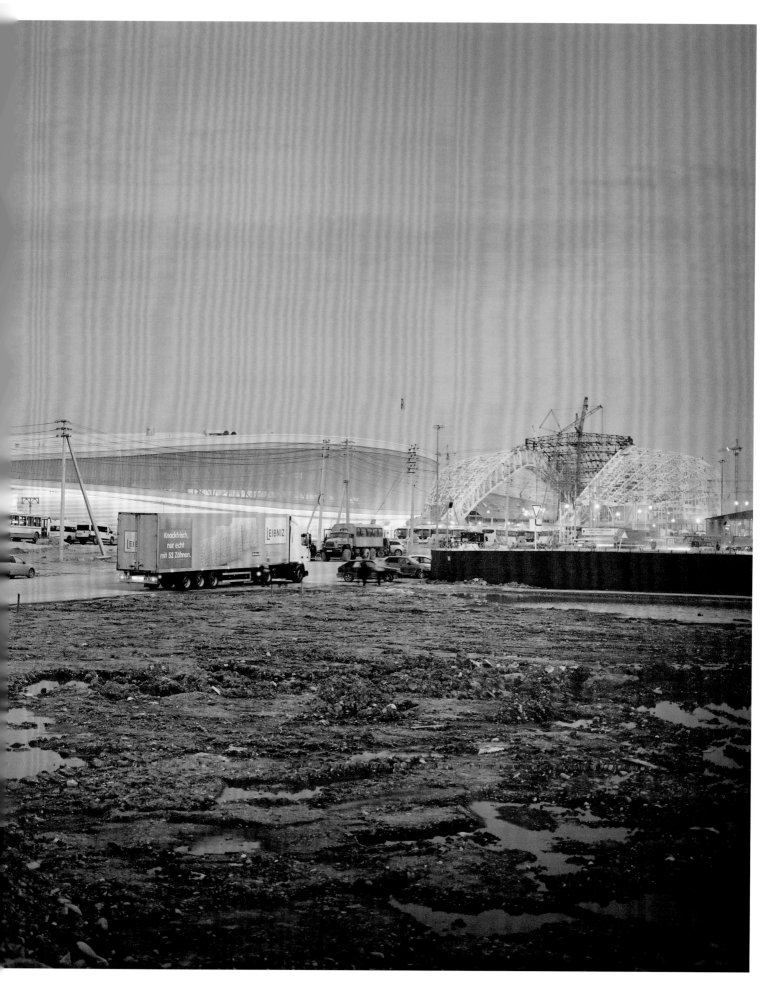

Striptease Dancer

Elena, thirty-one, has been a dancer at Art
Klub, the strip club on the first floor of the
monstrous Hotel Zhemchuzhina, for eighteen
months. Loud music, sweaty bodies on the
pebble beach, and striptease are perhaps more
at home in Sochi than the sporting spectacles
of the Winter Olympics. The coming years
will prove what survives of both. Elena hopes
to have left the profession by then. She makes
good money as a full-time dancer, but her
real dream is to start a family and raise
healthy children.

Sochi, Russia, 2012

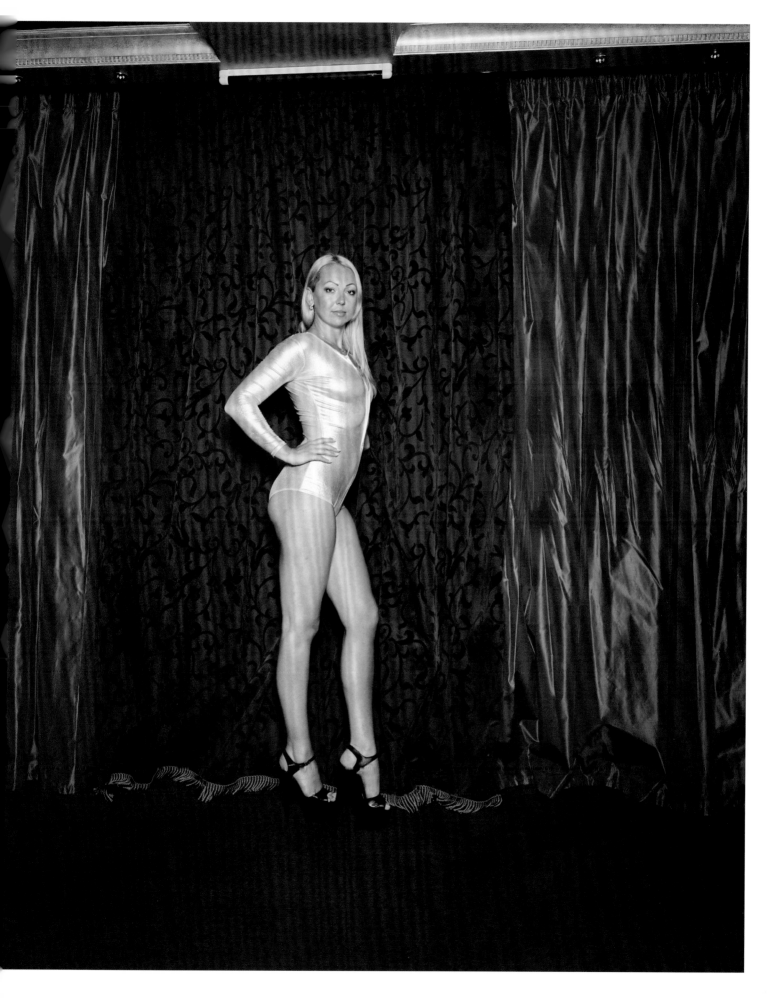

Five years behind the scenes of the Sochi Project

Moscow to Sochi by Train

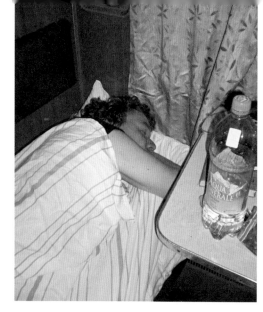

The train ride from Moscow to Sochi takes thirty-seven hours. To properly describe a region, it is best to approach it overland, in order to get a feel for the changes in scenery, climate, people, and architecture, rather than being dropped in the middle of it by plane. Most of the other passengers on the train appear accustomed to the length of the journey: their brain activity seems to slow and they lounge in comfortable clothes on the foldout beds. An endless supply of bottled water, wine, spirits, and food—such as dried fish and sweet sticky rolls—appears from large bags. We are less prepared and have to rely on a poorly equipped buffet car. Devoid of any of the romance of rail travel, our compartment is little more than four rickety, white, plastic garden chairs in an unkempt carriage.

"Do you want any women?" asks the Moldovan in charge of the buffet car. We are wrestling with plates of sausage and colorless, tasteless barley. The train is like a sauna and all the windows have been expertly disabled. "We have very cheap women." The Moldovan eyes up one of the attendants, a blond Russian who looks like she outgrew her clothes a decade ago. She is quite different from the two smartly dressed Caucasian train employees who attend to our compartment. "How cheap?" we ask. "Four hundred euros," the Moldovan says, leaning toward us; he just might be in luck.

We laugh. Amsterdam is even cheaper! The Moldovan is incensed. "But for four hundred euros you'll have her forever!" We have to think about it. The woman behind the counter saves us the trouble. "We don't have any cheap women on board," she says. The Moldovan gives up and asks us for cigarettes. Dutch cigarettes, that is. French Gauloises are good, too. Outside, a virtually unchanging landscape of vast fields,

half-wooden houses, and occasionally the typical post-Soviet town in all its picturesque drabness passes by. The mighty peaks of the Caucasus Mountains stretch to the horizon and, as we approach Sochi, the train chugs between the Black Sea on one side and steep hills on the other, from resort to resort.

Moscow / Sochi, 2009

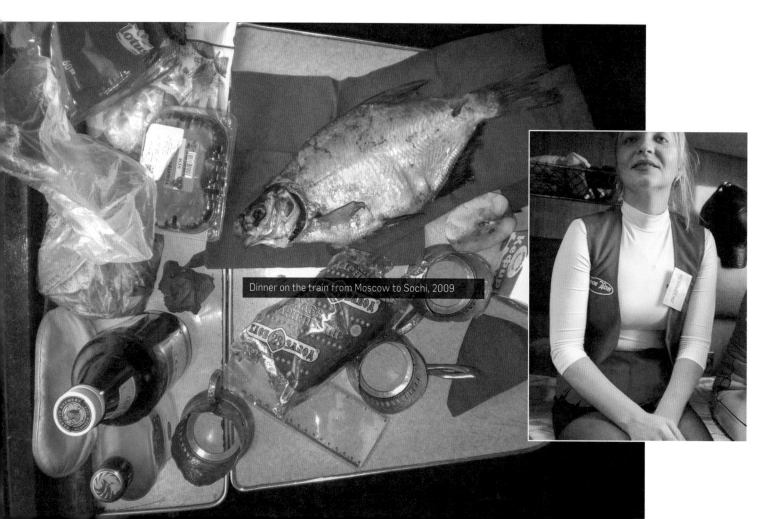

Dinner on the train from Moscow to Sochi, 2009

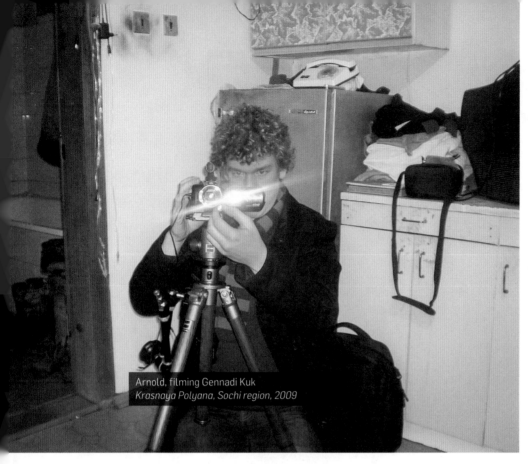

Arnold, filming Gennadi Kuk
Krasnaya Polyana, Sochi region, 2009

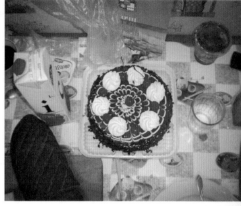

Arnold gives Rob a sickly sweet
Russian cake for his birthday
Sochi, 2009

The First Offense

Foreign travelers in Russia have to register in every city they visit. Hotels usually take care of this, but in Sochi we are staying in an older woman's apartment and do not consider it worthwhile spending a day on the bureaucracy. Our decision is now costing Rob dearly. At the Abkhazian border he produces all his documents but appears to be missing one. Arnold is called back from no-man's-land and his exit stamp is canceled. Despite frantic attempts by our Russian assistant to bribe almost every customs official with whom she comes into contact, we are mercilessly sent back over the border. Bored, we hang around a shed in which the head of customs is typing up documents. "There's a crisis on," she says. "I have to be careful not to lose my job. The rules have become much stricter."

We are sent from this hut to another, where a retired fighter pilot who supplements his pension with a government job directs us to a branch of Sberbank twenty kilometers away to pay a fine of forty-five euros. Only then are we allowed to leave the country, with a stern warning and an official report in which we acknowledge that we have broken the law and will not do it again. After a five-hour delay, we say goodbye to a Russia in which the rules are no longer quite so easily circumvented, and without further ado are waved across the border by an overweight Abkhazian in an ill-fitting uniform.

Sochi, 2009

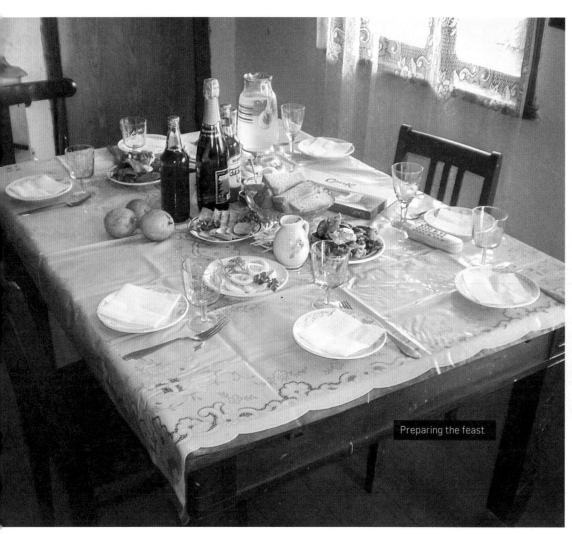

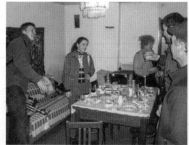

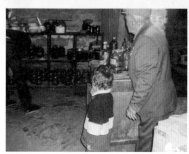

Preparing the feast

Raising a Toast with Mikhail Dzadzumiya

One of the most drunken encounters during the five years of the Sochi Project is with Mikhail Dzadzumiya in the village of Vladimirovka. [pp. 72–73] Mikhail's basement is filled with preserved fruit and vegetables and the equipment he uses to make his own wine and *chacha*, the potent local grape distillate. The table is set and plates and glasses are soon overflowing. The fact that Arnold is taking antibiotics for an infected tooth makes little difference to the family. Mikhail's *chacha* is more effective than antibiotics anyway, they say. Arnold should follow the host's instructions. Toast after toast is raised and songs are sung that bring even our assistant, Dina, to tears. Roaring drunk, we make several attempts to leave, but our host won't hear of it. His charming granddaughter is brought in to refill our glasses and push us gently back toward our seats. At some point during the carousing, Rob is so drunk that he has difficulty reaching the outdoor toilet. Only when Mikhail, with his grandchild on his shoulder, falls over, are we finally permitted to leave. Well, not before we have downed another two full glasses of red wine and a final shot of *chacha* for the road. In the car back to Sukhum, our drunken babble quickly turns to silence. At home, Rob is just able to locate a drawer somewhere before his upset stomach empties itself. The area around Arnold's infected tooth has now swollen to the size of a tennis ball.

Vladimirovka, Abkhazia, 2009

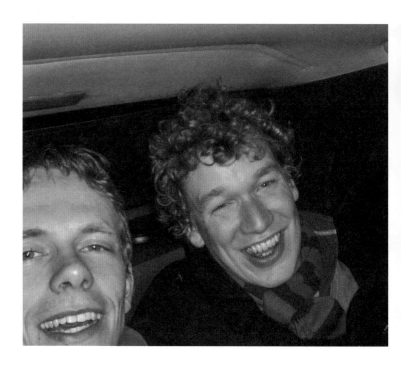

Dentist

Arnold has to go to the dentist. But Abkhazia is not the first country in which you would want to undergo medical treatment. Knowledge and equipment date from the Soviet era and little maintenance seems to have taken place in the intervening years. We have no insurance in this unrecognized country. Still, Arnold needs assistance and it can't do any harm for the dentist to take a look. Without asking any questions, an elderly man with a concerned expression pokes around in Arnold's mouth. He takes some X-rays in a dark room and submerges the results in a series of murky, chemical-filled jars. Outside, we struggle to discern any teeth in the inky images that the dentist gives us. Luckily, we pass an enormous banner advertising Vitadent, a newly opened private clinic in Abkhazia. For eight euros, Arnold is treated in a hypermodern room filled with stunning and highly professional dental assistants. We can continue our trip.

Sukhum, Abkhazia, 2009

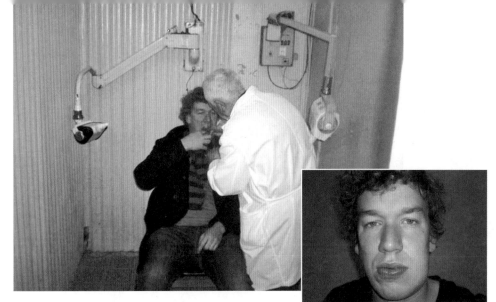

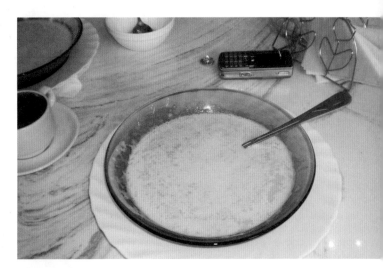

Breakfast in Hotel Ritsa
Sukhum, Abkhazia, 2009

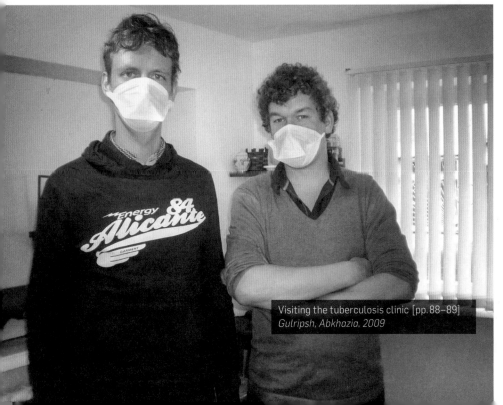

Visiting the tuberculosis clinic [pp. 88–89]
Gulripsh, Abkhazia, 2009

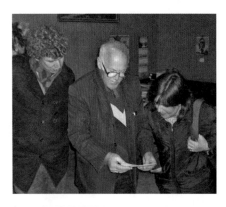

РЕСПУБЛИКА АБХАЗИЯ
ГК «АБХАЗСВЯЗЬ»

ПИЛИЯ
Эдуард Константинович
Генеральный директор

384900, Республика Абхазия   Тел. +(99544) 26-27-43 (р.),
г. Сухум, пр. Мира 108   26-30-30 (дом.), 70-00-98 (м.)
                                                          Факс. +(99544) 26-27-40

Life's Work

We find ourselves in the post office in Sukhum by chance, one of so many chance encounters during our travels. Before Rob can take a photo of one of the employees, we first have to ask the director for permission. The enthusiastic Eduard Konstantinovich Piliya does not pass up the opportunity to show us his work of the past forty-five years. When we return to Sukhum in 2013, we discover that a short circuit has burned the post office to the ground. The traumatic event struck Piliya hard. Less than a month later, he died of a heart attack. [pp. 70–71]

Sukhum, Abkhazia, 2009

Ringing Ears

Arnold decides that we have to go into the mountains, to the Kodori Valley, where six months earlier the last armed conflict between Abkhazians and Georgians took place. With a special permit in our pockets and a gaggle of government officials in our wake, we bump along a barely intact road. It takes us more than three hours to cover forty kilometers. The journey takes us past breathtaking rivers and ravines, remote villages with tumbledown cultural centers and schools, numerous beehives, and the occasional goat. At the home of the Aschuba family [pp. 138–39], the grandfather enthusiastically lets us in. "If I'd known you were coming, I would have slaughtered a goat," he says, and goes down to the basement to fetch wine. The two children proudly cradle Kalashnikovs in their laps. We have to go outside and shoot a few rounds before sitting down, with ringing ears, to the vinegary wine.

Kodori, Abkhazia, 2009

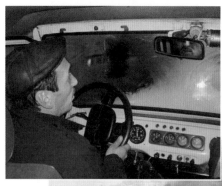

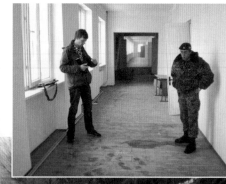

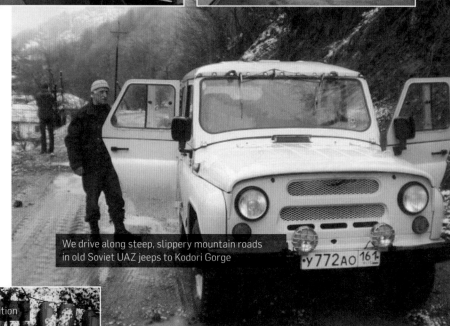

We drive along steep, slippery mountain roads in old Soviet UAZ jeeps to Kodori Gorge

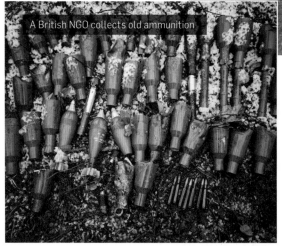

A British NGO collects old ammunition

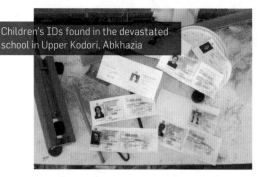

Children's IDs found in the devastated school in Upper Kodori, Abkhazia

No-Man's-Land

In 2009 the only way to enter Abkhazia is through Russia. The border between Georgia and Abkhazia is tightly closed and guarded by Russian troops. To travel from Abkhazia to Georgia, you have to go back to Russia and then enter Georgia via one of its other neighbors, such as Armenia or Turkey. It is a detour of several thousand kilometers. We ask the Abkhazian and Georgian Ministers of Foreign Affairs why we are not allowed to cross that particular border. Both ministers claim that their country is not the problem, but that the other country will not let us through. To put this assertion to the test, Arnold comes up with the idea of asking both ministers to instruct their own border guards to let us cross their (internal) border. Armed with two letters, we go first to the Abkhazian and then to the Georgian border posts. Many startled expressions and telephone calls later, we are finally let through. This photo was taken in no-man's-land: the bridge over the Inguri River. A year later our trick no longer works.

Between Abkhazia and Georgia, 2009

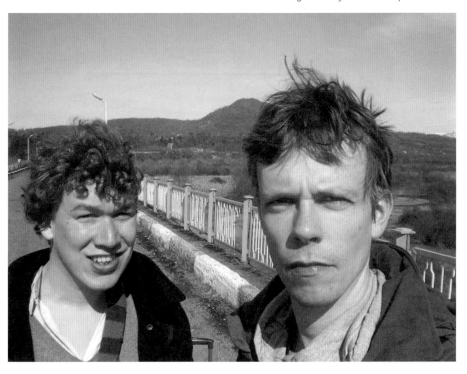

Border Toilets

After crossing the border at Zugdidi, between Abkhazia and Georgia, in 2007—our very first trip, long before we started the Sochi Project—Arnold needs to go to the toilet. This is not an uncommon occurrence as border crossings in the Caucasus can take a while. While Arnold is busy, a rat scurries out of the hole in the ground. Arnold's face is ashen when he returns. Two years later, Rob is caught short in Gali. After his experience in Zugdidi, incidentally, Arnold is even less impressed with these toilets.

Gali, Abkhazia, 2009

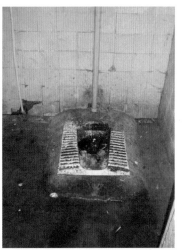
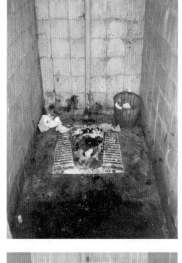
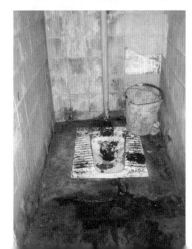
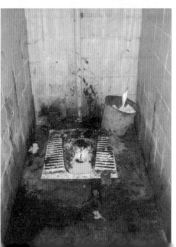

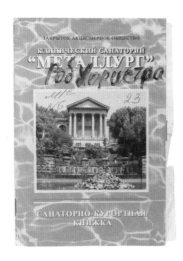

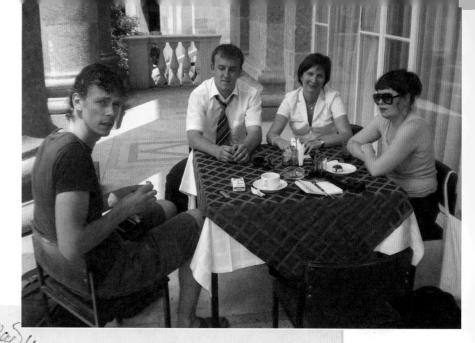

Прочие сероводородные процедуры
(дата, температура, концентрация, переносимость)

Физиотерапевтические процедуры

Каб. №_____

(57)

9 40
10/10
12/10
13/10
15/10

Подпись лечащего врача_____
8

9

Our treatment diary for Sanatorium Metallurg

Sanatorium Metallurg

We first visit a sanatorium, the institution that brought Sochi fame as a seaside resort and spa town, in the summer of 2009, and decide right away to devote our first annual publication to it. A few months later we check into Sanatorium Metallurg, where we aim to spend ten days immersing ourselves in sanatorium life. On the first morning of our stay we undergo a medical test. Since nothing is wrong with us, we agreed on in advance the physical symptoms we would claim to have to avoid being prescribed only gentle exercise and rest. Arnold complains of upper back pain and arrhythmia, while I say I have trouble with my lower back and right knee. We are overjoyed when we are prescribed a regime of mineral baths, clay treatments, and massages, interspersed with medicinal tea and healing water. [pp. 38–45, 48–49]

Sochi, 2009

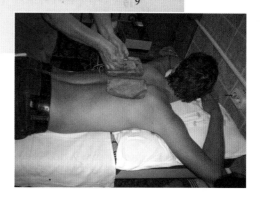

Rob undergoes his daily treatment for a fictional back problem

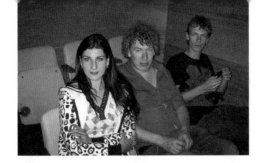

Bella Ksalova

For one reason or another we are unable to find an assistant in Karachay-Cherkessia, until we discover Bella through *Caucasian Knot*, one of the few local, independent news services in the North Caucasus. Full of confidence, she sends us a message saying that she also speaks English. This turns out to be an overstatement, but with a few quick phone calls she is able to organize a translator for us. And so with Bella from Cherkessk in tow, we travel to Karachayevsk and villages such as Krasny Vostok. On our last day, Bella refuses to let us work— she has a surprise for us. She takes us into the mountains for a picnic in the scenic Arkhyz Valley and on to an astronomical observatory. At the end of the day she puts us on a train to Nevinnomyssk and follows up with a text message saying how much she will miss us. We had agreed to see each other again a few months later. At least that was the plan.

Cherkessk, Karachay-Cherkessia, 2009

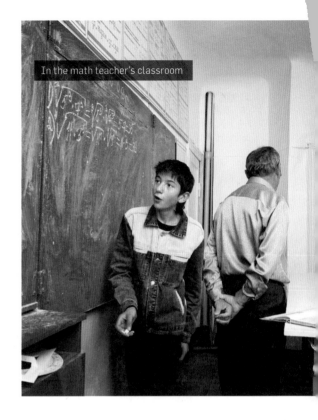

In the math teacher's classroom

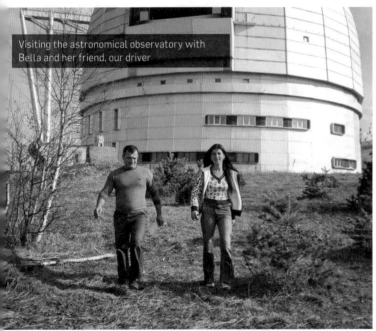

Visiting the astronomical observatory with Bella and her friend, our driver

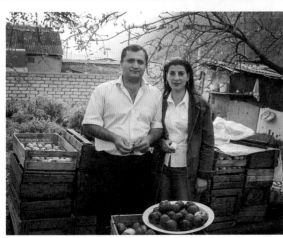

Closed Object

With Bella we study the map of Karachay-Cherkessia. We could go anywhere, but we have few concrete plans. Bella tells us stories about the different regions of her republic. Then we discover Krasny Vostok, which literally means "The Red East." We have to go.

We visit for the first time the next day. In all respects it is a perfectly normal Russian village. There is a defunct factory in the center. The sovkhoz has been divided up between the villagers, the youth have left, and the town has slowly bled to death.

In the local school, the harvest festival is about to begin. A girl dressed as a cucumber and two boys dressed as a green cabbage and an onion, respectively, run nervously through the building. We imagine the fantastic photo story the event will produce, until the math teacher—the type with tinted glasses and sweat patches under his arms—accosts us: "Do you have permits for this?" he barks. "Do you know that this school is a closed object?" This, in the peculiar vocabulary of bureaucratic Russia, means it is an off-limits site. We have spent enough time in Russia to know that it's over. The math teacher stomps off to find the director, who calls the mayor. The mayor calls Karachay-Cherkessia's presidential administration, and they call the federal government in Moscow. No one in Russia dares to take responsibility, and somewhere at the end of the line someone always says no. We are forced to leave. Rob has to hand over his film (of course he gives them blank rolls) and, with many apologies, we are waved out of the village. [pp. 160–177]

Krasny Vostok, Karachay-Cherkessia, 2009

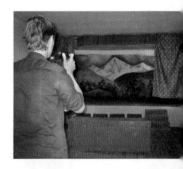

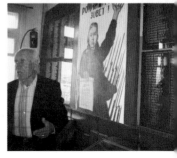

Gennadi Kuk

In 2010 we visit Gennadi Kuk, who had recorded a video message for our website a year earlier. We are curious to find out how his fight to stop the construction of a railway line through land that is filled with prehistoric graves, towers, and shrines is progressing. Gennadi's improvised cable car over the fast-flowing water is still there. He wants us to use the cable car to reach the other side, but we worry that it will be unable to hold our weight. Gennadi is still fighting, that much is clear, but he is doing so without support. [pp. 330–31]

Krasnaya Polyana, Sochi region, 2010

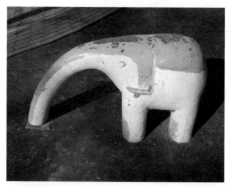

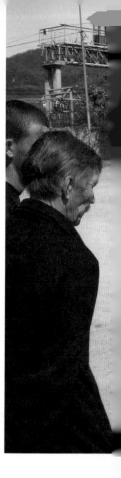

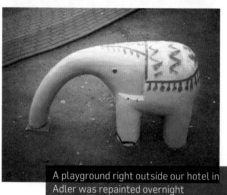

A playground right outside our hotel in Adler was repainted overnight
Adler, Russia, 2010

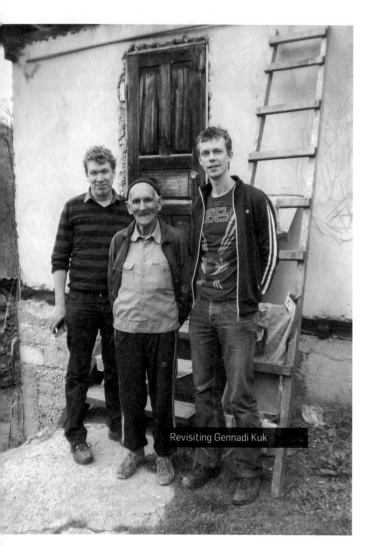

Revisiting Gennadi Kuk

Illegal Border Crossing

In 2010 Abkhazia is only accessible via the Russian border. Georgia does not recognize this as a legal border crossing because it regards the Abkhazian-Russian border as the Georgian-Russian border. The penalty for making the crossing is up to four years in prison. Fortunately, an Abkhazian visa is issued as a loose piece of paper and does not appear in your passport.

Still, we are taken aside at the Georgian border later in the trip. The customs officials discover that we left Russia overland at Sochi and could only have entered Abkhazia— in their minds, Georgia—which is illegal. We are able to pass thanks to a contact at the Georgian security service who had previously helped us to visit Abkhazia without any problems.

Georgia, 2010

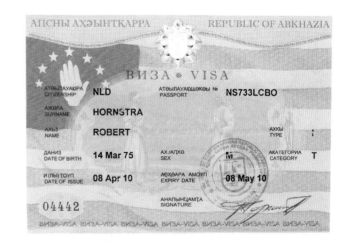

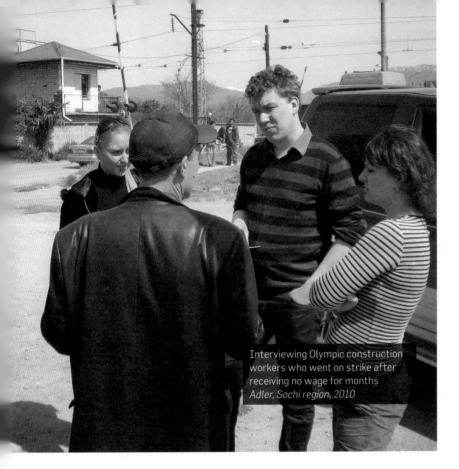

Interviewing Olympic construction workers who went on strike after receiving no wage for months
Adler, Sochi region, 2010

On the day that we wanted to visit Nikolay Zetunyan [pp. 80–84] for the second time, our interpreter, Khibla, lost her voice. She sent her younger sister Milana, which turned out to be a fortuitous decision. Unlike Khibla, who works for the presidential office, Milana is far more outspoken. We become friends with her on Facebook and notice that she is elected president of the Abkhazian student union and sets up volunteer initiatives. We decide to visit her again before the end of the project. [pp. 62–63, 292–93]

Eshera, Abkhazia, 2010

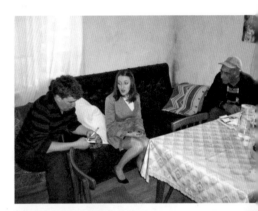

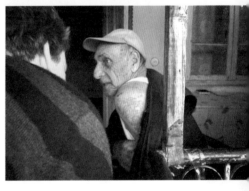

Nikolay Zetunyan shows us the tattoo on his left shoulder of his wartime girlfriend

Angela

Angela belongs to a new generation of Abkhazians. She is modern and outward-looking [pp. 63, 66–67, 134]. But when she is harassed by a group of men in a bar, she is powerless. One of the men hangs over a couch, puts his camera on the armrest, and points his lens at her. The flash fires three times in painfully slow succession. In a second Angela gets up, walks around the man, runs outside, and calls her brother on her cell. "You have to come, now. No, right now. Yes, it's serious. No, I really want you to come," she convinces him. This insult must be avenged.

As if a shot had been fired, the four men jump up from their seats and rush outside. Four other men stride purposefully toward them. The eight become a shapeless mass of black jackets, caps, and hair. They shake hands, kiss one another on the cheek, and slap one another on the back. They know each other, as does everyone in this country. Angela pushes through the crowd and hauls her brother from the group. She quickly tells him what happened. He approaches the offending photographer and consults with him briefly. He then explains to Angela that peace has been restored. He apologizes on behalf of the offender. "Ok, I'm satisfied," Angela says. "They've offered a sort of apology."

Sukhum, Abkhazia, 2010

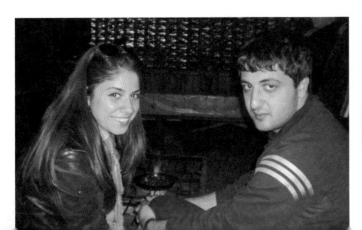

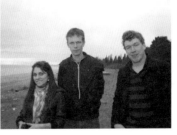

New Cell Phone Number

Our unexplained eviction from Krasny Vostok in late 2009 still rankles. What did such an innocent-looking place have to hide? We decide to go back for answers, but this time we want to be prepared. Before we leave we try to contact Taisya Makova, the mayor with whom we had spoken on our previous visit. In The Netherlands it takes a matter of seconds to find the telephone number of a local town hall. In Russia things are not quite as straightforward. Our search lasts four weeks and ultimately results in nothing. We find out afterward that Taisya has a new cell phone number.

We go to Krasny Vostok anyway, on spec. The mayor recognizes us from our last visit, offers us accommodation in her sister's house, and for the first time in her life organizes the registration of two foreigners. The latter act takes her so long that she almost misses the regional antiterrorism meeting. We stay five days and continue our journey to Georgia ten pounds heavier thanks to the generous cooking of the mayor's sister. [pp. 164–67]

Krasny Vostok, Karachay-Cherkessia, 2010

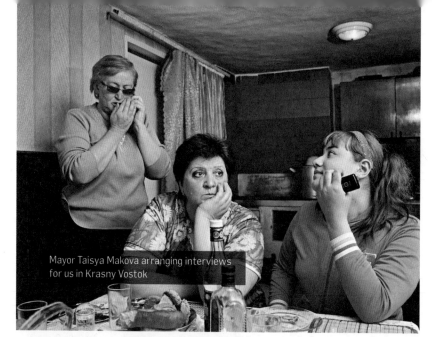

Mayor Taisya Makova arranging interviews for us in Krasny Vostok

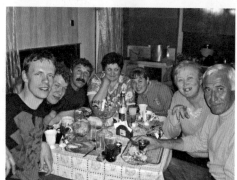

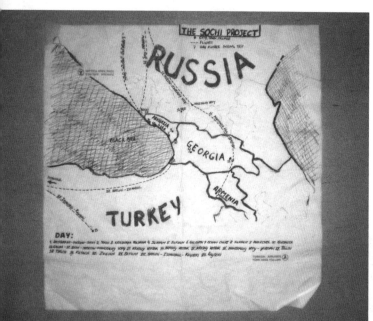

Itinerary

We want to travel from the North Caucasus to Tbilisi in Georgia, which is literally around the corner. Since the last war between Georgia and Russia, however, all the border crossings between the two countries have been tightly sealed and flights have been suspended. As a result, we are forced to travel hundreds of miles (via Moscow and Yerevan, Armenia) to reach the other side of the border.

Istanbul, Turkey, 2010

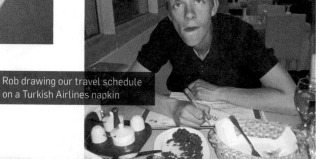

Rob drawing our travel schedule on a Turkish Airlines napkin

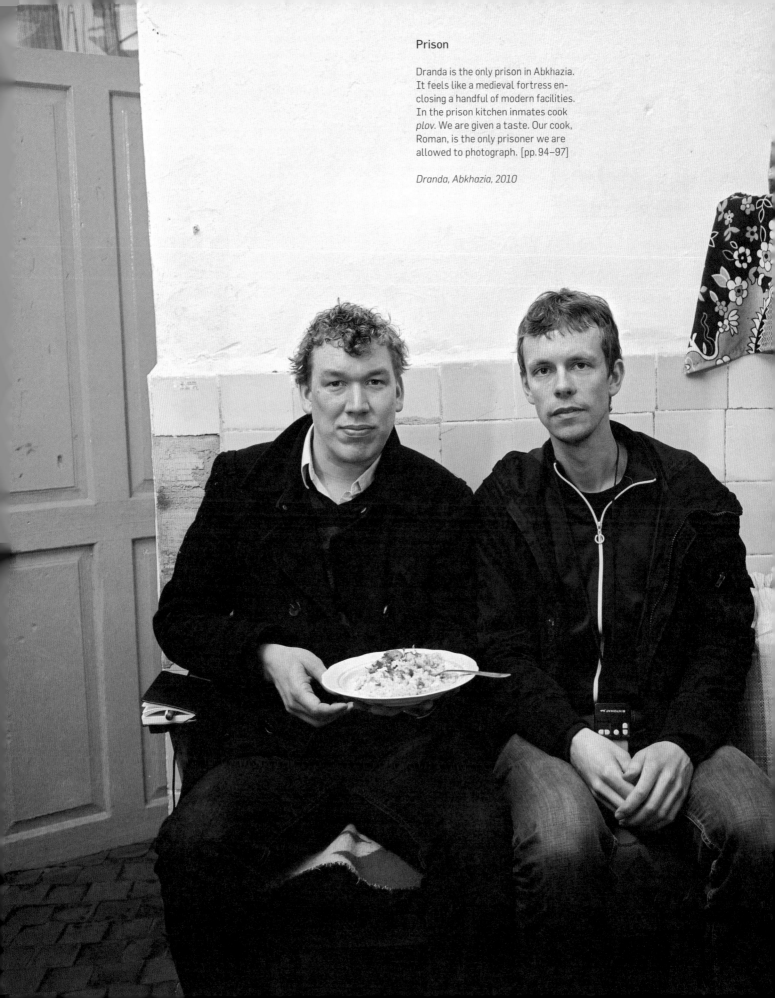

Prison

Dranda is the only prison in Abkhazia. It feels like a medieval fortress enclosing a handful of modern facilities. In the prison kitchen inmates cook *plov*. We are given a taste. Our cook, Roman, is the only prisoner we are allowed to photograph. [pp. 94–97]

Dranda, Abkhazia, 2010

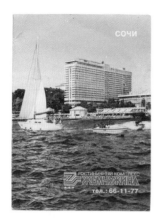

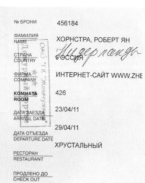

Hotel Zhemchuzhina

Our plan is to book a different hotel every time we visit Sochi. That will give us a good impression of prices and the quality of service. At the end of 2010, we reserve a room at Zhemchuzhina, the only hotel in Sochi that we stay at more than once. The complex is so big that it is easy to get lost. We do so regularly (and intentionally). Wandering aimlessly, we find ourselves in an old, unused auditorium or a banquet hall packed to the ceiling with junk one minute, only to stumble upon a wing of newly built meeting rooms the next. It is a sort of miniature version of Russia: every time you look around things have changed and you uncover new surprises.
[pp. 26–33, 342–43]

Sochi, 2010

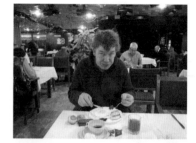

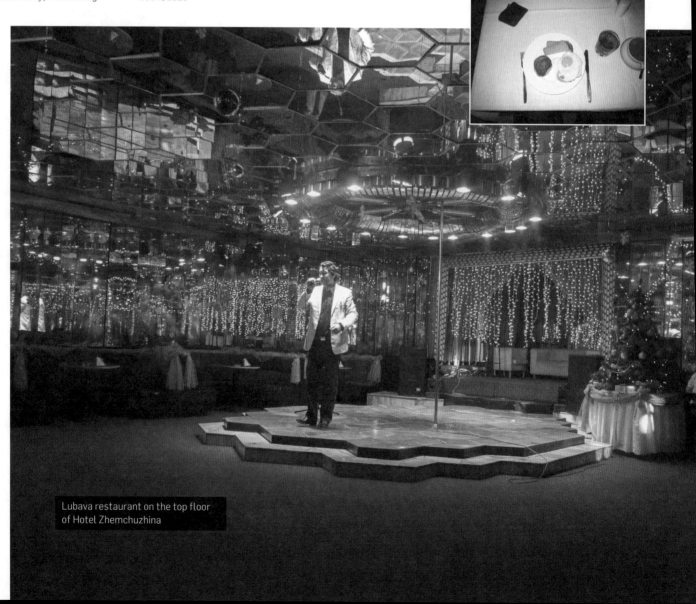

Lubava restaurant on the top floor of Hotel Zhemchuzhina

Olympic Object Tour

We realize soon after we start the Sochi Project that the construction of Olympic stadiums is never going to be our focus. It is the context in which the Games are taking place that interests us. Even so, we often go to look at the construction sites, just to see how things are organized and how the Sochi 2014 Organizing Committee deals with journalists. That is how we keep meeting Evgenia, head of media relations. In the early years she personally shows journalists and photographers around the construction sites for each Olympic "object" (a site or venue) in the mountains and on the coast, and enthusiastically points out the progress that has been made. As the Games approach, however, she is assigned more staff and the relationship becomes more professional. She now has a team of press officers—young men and women from Moscow—under her wing and we see her less often. [pp. 314–15, 326–27, 332–35]

Sochi, 2010

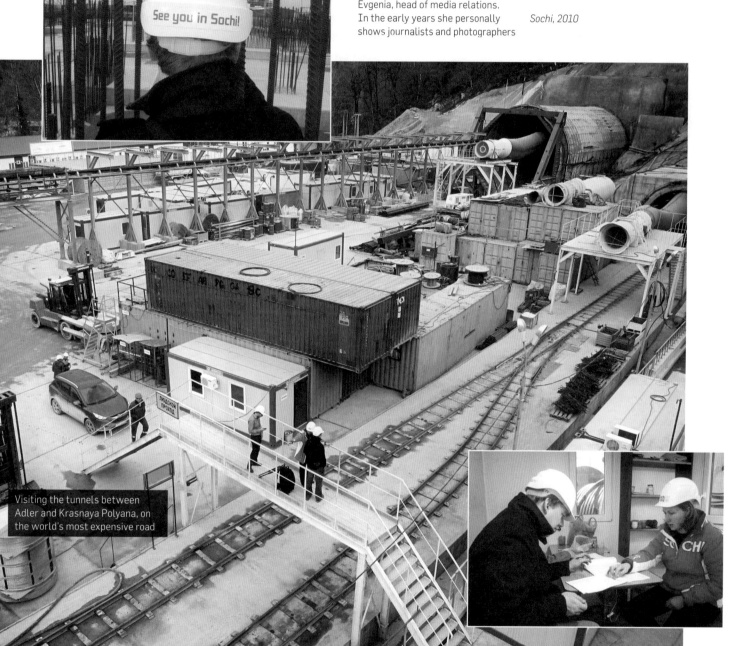

Visiting the tunnels between Adler and Krasnaya Polyana, on the world's most expensive road

Arnold with Evgenia, head of media relations of the Sochi 2014 Organizing Committee

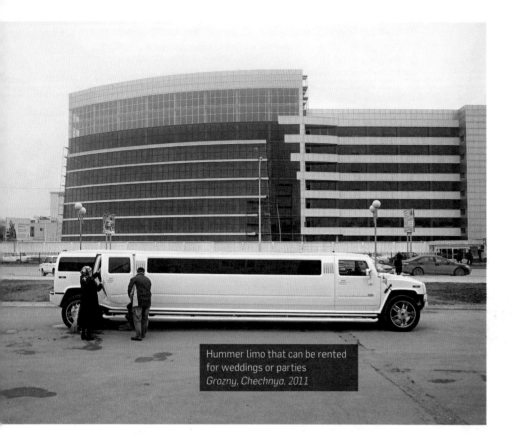

Hummer limo that can be rented for weddings or parties
Grozny, Chechnya, 2011

Arrested, Part II

Arnold has read an interview with the mayor of Shatoy, a village in the Chechen mountains. The mayor claims in the article that Shatoy will soon be a tourist destination, the "Switzerland of Chechnya."

We like the idea of visiting the mayor and finding out what has become of his plans. Just outside Shatoy we are stopped at a Russian army checkpoint. A dozen or so heavily armed soldiers are stationed there day in, day out, with little to do. A car of Dutch journalists is a wonderful diversion. A soldier tells us that 117 police officers were killed in Chechnya last year. He says that Shatoy is now quiet because there are ten soldiers to each inhabitant. We are not welcome. At the end of our conversation an FSB official arrives and commands us to follow him. We are arrested and taken for

Kidnapped by Adam

At the end of our second long day in Chechnya we decide to go for a beer—a seemingly simple undertaking in Russia, but not if you are in Muslim Chechnya. Our assistant Musa says he knows a place outside Grozny, but he prefers not to be seen there. "You can drop us off," we say courageously. In a gloomy upstairs room, we are served liter jugs of warm beer. Behind us a table of rowdy men have clearly been drinking for a while. Several younger men in dark leather jackets hang around them. The atmosphere is tense. One minute they dance exuberantly, the next someone dashes into the bar and a fight ensues, only to be broken up and the peace restored. When we ask the waitress for the check, she tells us that it has already been paid and puts a new jug of beer down in front of us. Our courage immediately evaporates. In the Caucasus, this means that you are at the mercy of your host. Not long after, a barely intelligible Chechen named Adam sits down at our table and informs us that we are his guests. He does not immediately strike us as the kind

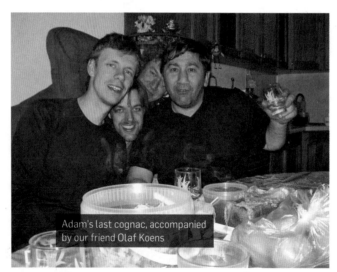

Adam's last cognac, accompanied by our friend Olaf Koens

of host we would want to spend the rest of the evening with.

Yet that is exactly what happens. Adam bundles us into his chauffeur-driven Mercedes, says he will drop us off at our hotel, but speeds past it at one hundred miles (160 kilometers) an hour toward his hometown, Gudermes, where he plies us with old cognac and fruit at the kitchen table. "I wouldn't normally do this, but my wife and children are on vacation and I'm making the most of it."

This photo shows him at the moment he is overwhelmed by alcohol. He collapses shortly afterward and drags himself to bed. The next morning his chauffeur drives us back to our hotel, again at breakneck speed. We never hear from Adam again.

Grozny, Chechnya, 2011

interrogation. We find out subsequently that Shatoy is a restricted area. The delay costs us at least an hour, but we are waved off by our interrogators with the announcement that we are free to look around Shatoy as long as we don't stay too long. We would do well to leave before it gets dark. We are given an FSB flag as a gift. So off we go to the local café, not only because we are hungry but also because it can be a good place to make contacts. Our meal is interrupted by two middle-aged men who conform to our stereotype of Chechen rebels. One of them is hunched over and walks directly to the TV, switches it to a local music channel, and turns up the volume. The other is missing an eye, but compensates with two guns, the largest of which (an Uzi-type weapon) he places ceremoniously on the table in front of him. We decide it is time to leave.

In the meantime our driver, Musa, has tracked down the local imam. Shawazhi turns out to be not only an imam but also the regional head and assistant to the parliamentary speaker. In Chechnya that makes you an important figure. As the sun sets and we shiver from the cold, Arnold subjects the man to an interview next to his car. A few minutes after Shawazhi has to "just" make a phone call, a black armored Lexus and another car carrying heavily armed soldiers pull up. It is Shatoy's chief of police, who has come to assess the situation. We conclude once again that it is high time to leave. In the twilight, we wave to the soldiers as we pass the Russian checkpoint. [pp. 258–59]

Shatoy, Chechnya, 2011

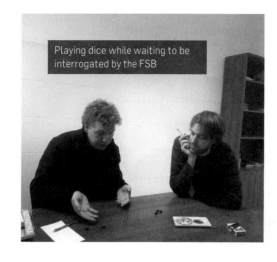

Playing dice while waiting to be interrogated by the FSB

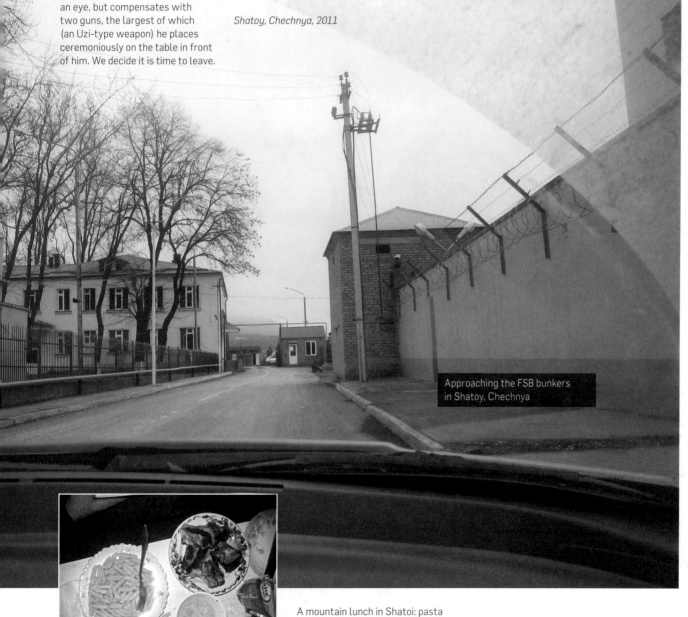

Approaching the FSB bunkers in Shatoy, Chechnya

A mountain lunch in Shatoi: pasta with wild garlic, wild garlic sauce, and garlic-grilled *shaslik*

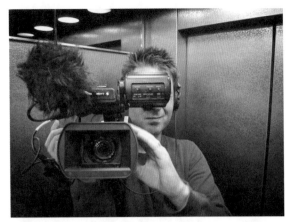

Followed by Cameras

In early 2011 Rob is approached by VICE, which wants to make a documentary about his work. The network offers to cover the cost of a short research trip for the Sochi Singers series, and in the spring of 2011 Rob is shadowed for a week by filmmaker Nick Ahlmark. When Rob takes a photo of a singer in a restaurant, Nick is standing next to him, filming. It is a rather unusual situation that is picked up via Facebook by Ivan Prozorov, Sochi correspondent for Russian television. It is common knowledge that television in Russia is a state medium. Anything goes, as long as it is not critical of the government. The fact that a Dutch photographer in Sochi is being followed by a British filmmaker is reason enough for Ivan to shoot a segment about it for Russian TV. And so Rob is followed by cameraman Nick, who in turn is followed by Ivan and his camera crew. [pp. 200–205, 338–39]

Sochi, 2011

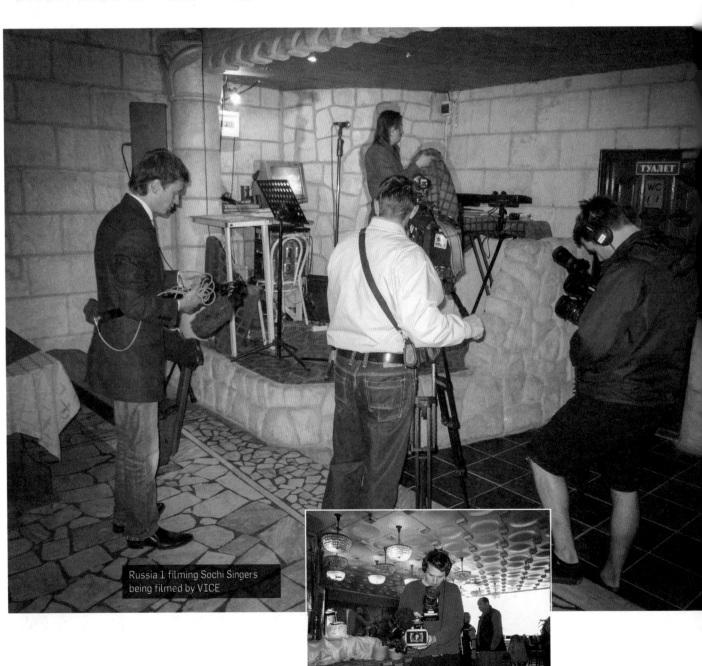

Russia 1 filming Sochi Singers being filmed by VICE

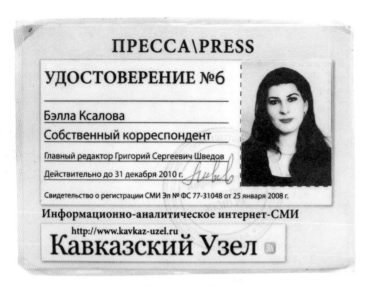

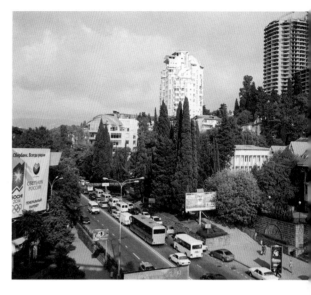

RIP Bella, 1984–2010

In 2011 we find out that Bella, with whom we had worked in 2009, has died. On the unlit streets of Cherkessk, she was hit by a car carrying four drunken passengers and an allegedly sober driver. We hadn't heard from Bella for a while, but that was not uncommon. She was sometimes unable to answer her phone for several months and she rarely checked her e-mail. The first time we worked with her, we tried for weeks to reach her to let her know when we would be arriving. Only when we had checked in to the hotel in Cherkessk and—in mild desperation—tried her again, did she pick up and less than an hour later was sitting in the trendy red leather bar downstairs. She was a passionate proponent of her republic and an opponent of social and political injustice. Her life was cut tragically short.

Cherkessk, Karachay Cherkessia, 2011

Permanent Traffic Jam

Over the course of the Sochi Project's five years, we must have spent the equivalent of at least a month in Sochi's traffic jams. The narrow coastal road is totally unsuitable for the volume of cars and Olympic construction vehicles that use it.

Sochi, 2011

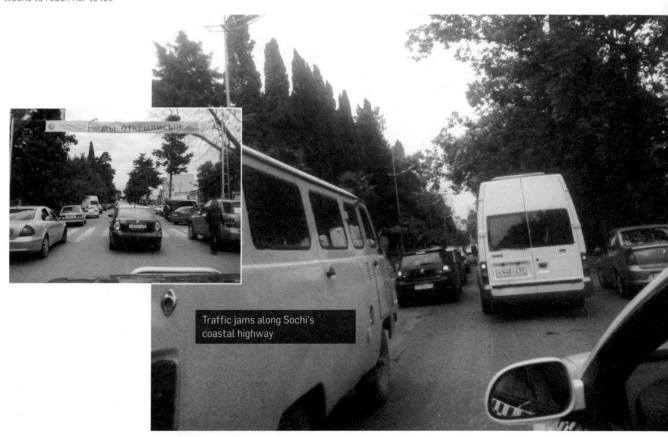

Traffic jams along Sochi's coastal highway

Soviet Camera

On a sweltering afternoon at the beach in Sochi, Rob receives a call from our friend Pavel: "My father-in-law has an old camera. Do you want it? It's been lying unused in the attic for at least twenty years." He arrives soon after with a dusty brown leather box containing a robust Kiev medium-format SLR camera. "I wanted to try it out," he says, "but I couldn't find a single photo shop in the area that still sells medium-format film." Rob happily borrows the camera and spends the next few days photographing in Sochi, until he suddenly remembers that old Soviet cameras often have defects. Sure enough, it turns out that the camera's film transport system does not work properly. The negatives are partially overlapping, which produces unexpectedly beautiful results. We decide to make a small sketchbook publication, *KIEV*, from the pictures, as an ode to old-fashioned analog photography.

Sochi, 2011

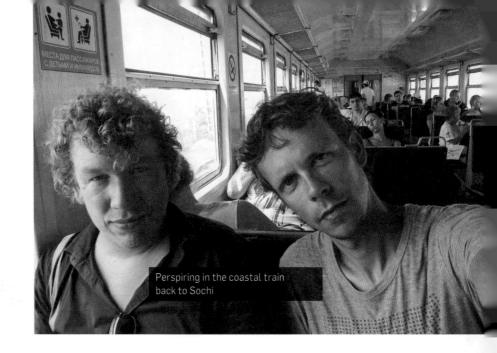

Perspiring in the coastal train back to Sochi

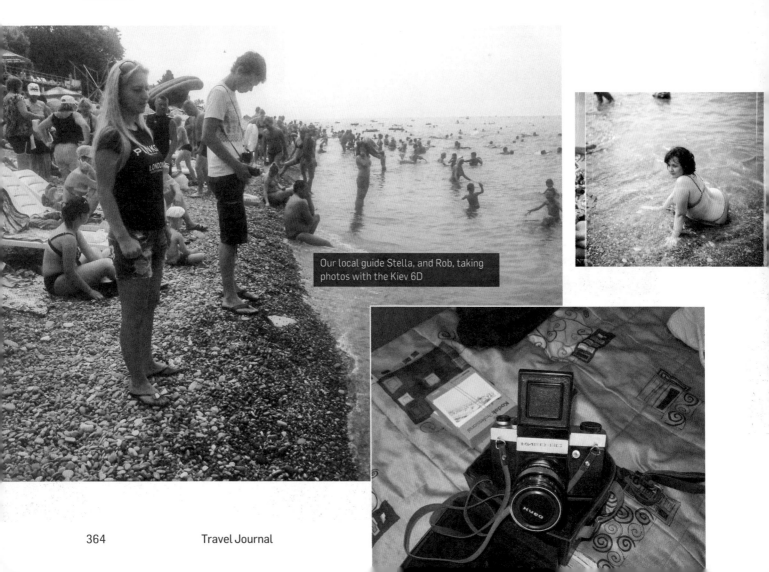

Our local guide Stella, and Rob, taking photos with the Kiev 6D

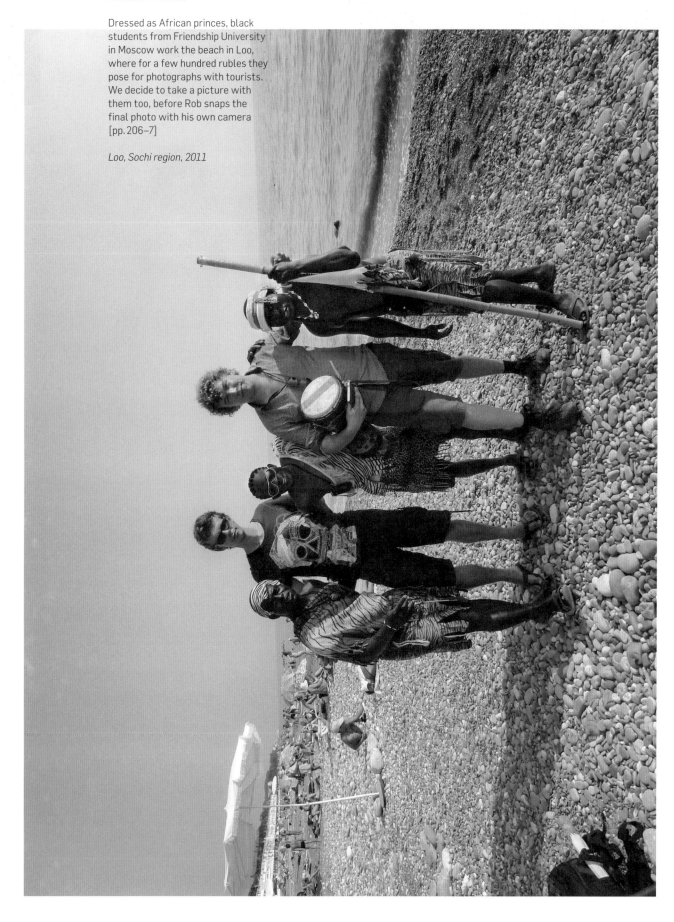

African Princes

Dressed as African princes, black students from Friendship University in Moscow work the beach in Loo, where for a few hundred rubles they pose for photographs with tourists. We decide to take a picture with them too, before Rob snaps the final photo with his own camera [pp. 206–7]

Loo, Sochi region, 2011

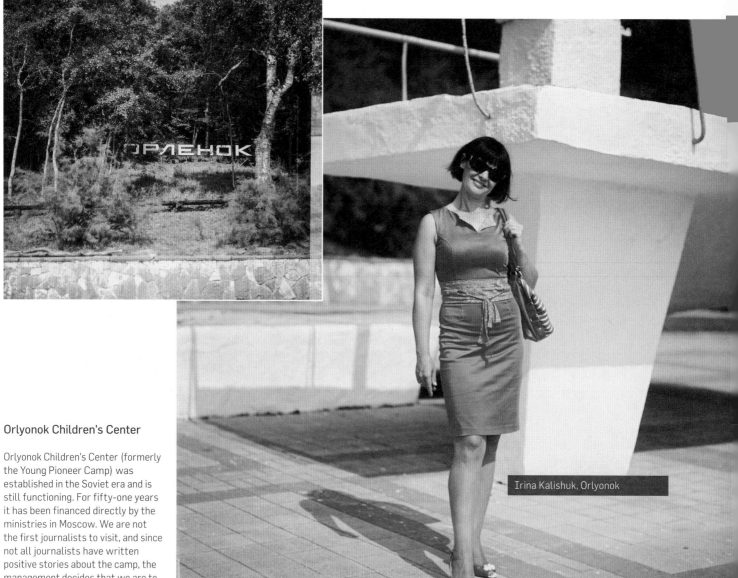

Irina Kalishuk, Orlyonok

Orlyonok Children's Center

Orlyonok Children's Center (formerly the Young Pioneer Camp) was established in the Soviet era and is still functioning. For fifty-one years it has been financed directly by the ministries in Moscow. We are not the first journalists to visit, and since not all journalists have written positive stories about the camp, the management decides that we are to be accompanied by a public relations representative at all times. We are assigned the ever-cheerful Irina Kalishuk. Over the following days we are not allowed to set foot in the camp without her, and additional assistants are frequently at our side.

We are shown the grounds on a tight schedule. We are certainly not allowed to wander as we please. The mess hall and sleeping quarters are off limits. "To visit those areas, the head doctor would have to examine you thoroughly and only with a medical certificate would you be able to gain access," Irina explains. She claims she herself has never visited them.

When we approach the groups of children who are playing sports, relaxing, or preparing presentations, the PR ladies swarm around Rob.

While he sets up his camera, they gesture to the boys and girls: "Smile, happy faces!" The PR madness soon infuriates us. "Just let us do our job the way we want to, otherwise we'll leave," we snap. "We know how to tell a good story." But it makes no difference. They have had bad experiences with foreign journalists, the women say, and they do not understand why a boy or girl with a neutral expression can look better than a child with a forced smile. [pp. 24–25, 52–55, 58–59]

Orlyonok, Sochi region, 2011

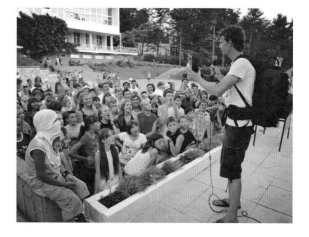

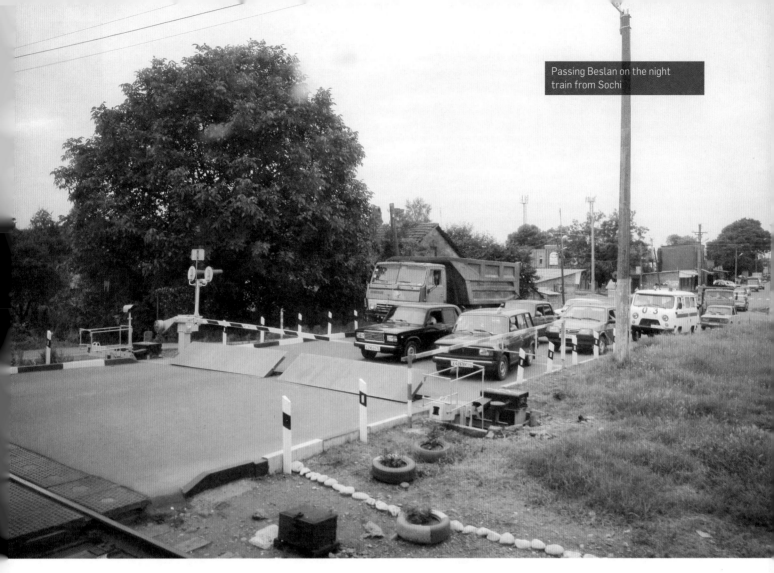

Passing Beslan on the night train from Sochi

Reaching the North Caucasus

It is not easy to reach the North Caucasus from Sochi. In principle, you could extend the road leading from Sochi to the Olympic ski resorts. But with the threat of attacks from the North Caucasus, the Russian government has decided it would be better not to have a direct link between the two. The distance from Sochi to Vladikavkaz is more than two hundred miles (350 kilometers) as the crow flies. There are two ways of getting there. The fastest is to fly to Moscow and then back to Vladikavkaz, a detour of about 1,300 miles (2,200 kilometers). The slow option is the train, which with a slight detour takes about eighteen hours to crawl over the mountains. For an extra one hundred rubles, you are treated en route to prepackaged mashed potatoes and sausages by a charming conductress.

Adler / Vladikavkaz, 2011

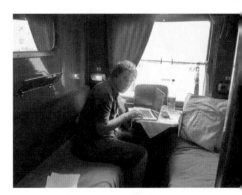

Sausage and mash breakfast, personally delivered by the carriage attendant on the night train to Vladikavkaz

Khava and Taimuraz

It is hot on the day that we go to the Prigorodny District for the first time. Our Ossetian assistant, Dina, has warned us repeatedly about what she regards as a dangerous area. Ingush live there and they are not to be trusted. This sentiment is wholeheartedly endorsed by our Ossetian driver, who does not let his Audi 80 out of his sight for a second. "They come with weapons, attack our markets, and kill our children. And what have we done in return? We live in peace. They are a dangerous people."

An Ingush woman is selling bottles of water at the side of the road and we decide to buy a few. We get to talking. Her name is Khava and she talks openly about the conflict between Ossetians and Ingush that broke out near her house in the early nineties and further back to her family's deportation and her birth in Kazakhstan. After an hour and a half she mentions in passing that her husband disappeared a few years ago when he went to buy groceries at the market in Vladikavkaz. He was probably kidnapped by the police, Ossetian men. Dina and the driver stare silently at the ground.

A little further along the road, three Ossetian men are passing time on a bench. As we try to strike up a conversation, the police arrive to check our papers. There is nothing to worry about. The men tell us that they fought against the Ingush in the early nineties, and Taimuraz, the most talkative of the three, makes no secret of the fact that he would do it again. We join them for slices of sausage and a glass of vodka, but Dina and the driver urge us to hurry up. They do not dare drive around here after dark.

Our day in the Prigorodny District turns out to be pivotal to our work in the North Caucasus. The tension, hate, prejudices, and simmering conflicts present in a few square kilometers, and the strong woman who embodies all the history of the North Caucasus, are captured in our book *The Secret History of Khava Gaisanova.* [pp. 212–20]

Chermen, North Ossetia, 2011

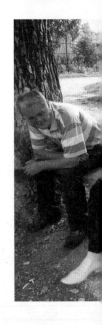

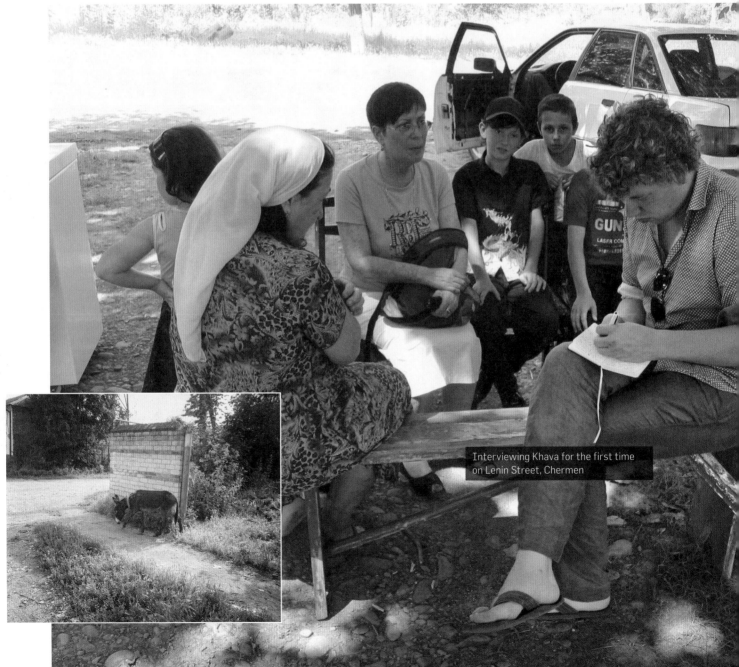

Interviewing Khava for the first time on Lenin Street, Chermen

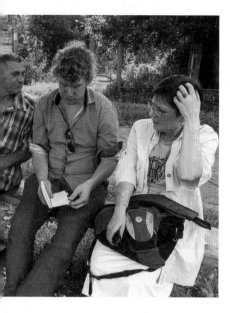

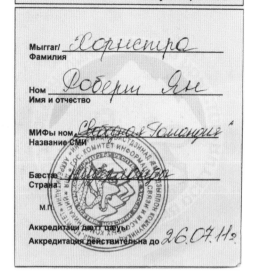

Torrent of Abuse

We want to go to South Ossetia. Well before our departure, the South Ossetian ambassador in Moscow had assured us that we did not need to apply for any special accreditation to enter South Ossetia as journalists. "As soon as you arrive, go to the central government building and report to the press department. Just like in Abkhazia. That's all," he told us.

At the border, it quickly becomes apparent that we do in fact need press accreditation and we risk being barred from the small country. An hour and a half and dozens of phone calls later we are allowed over the border, as long as we drive directly to the central government building in the capital, Tskhinvali.

"From now on I am your press accreditation," the head of the South Ossetian press department informs us with a triumphant look in his eyes. It turns out to be a canny trick. The former Soviet press officer only wants us to see Russia's reconstruction projects and he can only guarantee that if he is standing next to us. A press pass allowing us to travel freely is now out of our reach.

In order to placate him, we spend the first day visiting prestige projects, but we slip away on days two and three to photograph the rest of the country. We are subjected to a torrent of abuse on the last day as a result, which we resignedly accept. We finally get South Ossetian press accreditation, but only because we cannot leave the country without it. [pp.144–53]

Tskhinvali, South Ossetia, 2011

Interview with Eduard Kokoity, president of South Ossetia

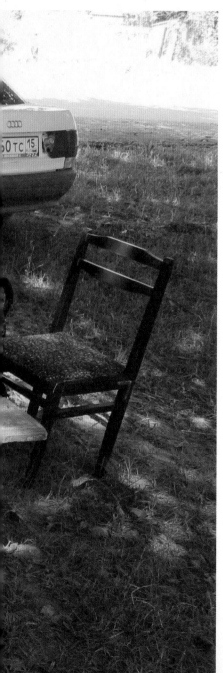

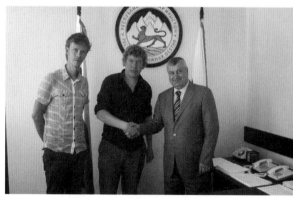

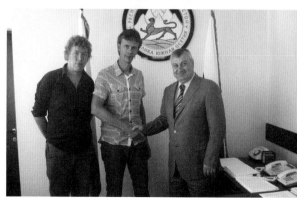

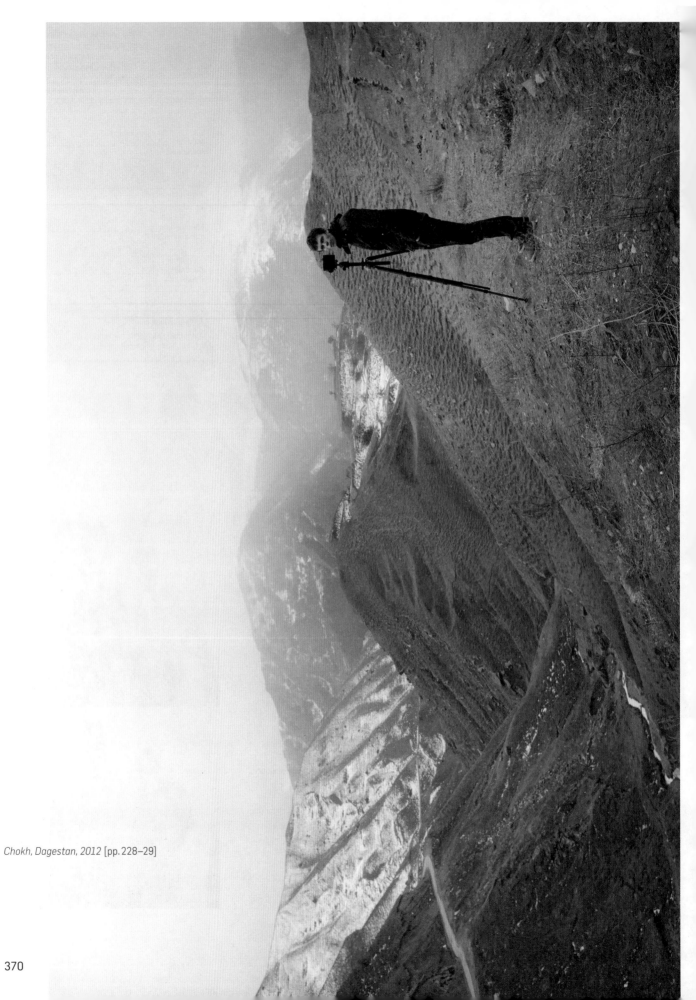

Chokh, Dagestan, 2012 [pp. 228–29]

Arrested, Part III

On legs trembling from the long, cramped journey through Dagestan's dramatic mountainous landscape, we take our first steps outside the car. We light cigarettes and look out over a long, slender valley. On the other side of it is our destination: Gimry, birthplace of the legendary Imam Shamil and several of his predecessors, and for two centuries the center of the uprising against Russian domination. We should have stayed out of sight in the car. Two unmarked armored vehicles hem us in, men in long leather jackets jump out, identify themselves, and order us to follow them to the nearby police station in Shamilkala. We are under arrest for trespassing in an area where a KTO (counter-terrorist operation) is currently in force. We understand why that would be illegal, but how could we have known about the KTO? We ask the local police and then the FSB: How is it that we asked masked soldiers and police officers at numerous checkpoints for directions and no one told us that Gimry was off limits? "That's not our problem," the officials say. "We're just following the law."

After the police and FSB have left the room, a short, gray immigration official enters and closes the door behind him. He inhales deeply and gives us a stern look. "Have you ever been imprisoned?" he asks viciously. We sigh. Here comes the intimidation. "Deportation would be such a shame," he adds melodramatically. He tries to extort money from us. We refuse to give him any. He decides instead to press charges.

After the immigration officer is finished with us, we are left at the mercy of men with leather jackets, fur collars, and greasy hair. We later learn that they are from the local antiterror department, responsible for disappearances and torture. They summon us to their lair in the basement. The wall is covered with dozens of mug shots. The gang leader does not talk to us, but hisses and huffs us to our seats. We are photographed with an iPhone and our names are written down. With pounding hearts we walk back to the police officers. We are subjected to our fifth interrogation of the day, this time by the police chief, a rotund man who tries to extract wax buried deep in his ear with a pencil, and subjects the result to an equally in-depth inspection.

We are eventually released, although the officer from immigration maintains that he will press charges and keeps hold of our passports. "Deportation, a lawsuit, or a hefty fine," he sniggers. He is angry that we refused to give him money. We could have made things much easier for ourselves. The next day we reluctantly make our way to the immigration office. We can only hope that the fine is not too substantial, that we do not have to appear in court. The man in charge turns out to be a friend of our interpreter. He puts us in the care of a sweet girl who practices her English on us, gives us cookies, and makes tea. He winks at us and pulls a bottle of cognac from his desk. "For the wasted time," he says. He has to settle the case correctly, but will try to get us off lightly. The two-day delay costs us a fine of fifty euros. [pp. 142–43, 260–61]

Shamilkala, Dagestan, 2012

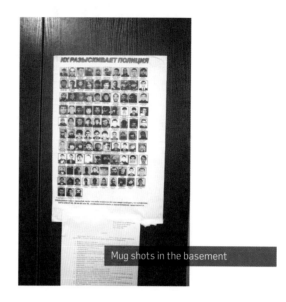

Mug shots in the basement

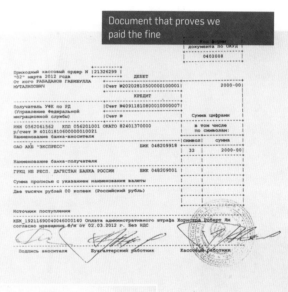

Document that proves we paid the fine

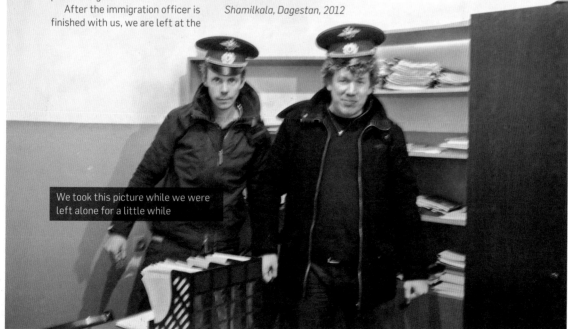

We took this picture while we were left alone for a little while

Visiting Nasibov

When we first travel to the North Caucasian republic of Dagestan in 2012, wrestling—the national sport—is one of our main subjects. It also proves to be the perfect cover for engaging with the local inhabitants. Wrestling is so deep-rooted that the sport automatically brings us into contact with all layers of society, from the elite to the working class to opponents of the current regime.

A lawyer from Khasavyurt tells us about a Sambo wrestler who was gunned down outside his parents' house. The shooters were never identified, although rumors circulated that the crime must have been committed by the security forces, given the unnumbered jeeps and the caliber of automatic weapons used. The next day we visit the victim's strictly religious father, Saidachmed Nasibov. In his house, women are not allowed into a room full of strangers. Female hands and arms extend toward us proffering cups of tea and bowls of dates until we reach the living room where they are replaced by one of the men. The conversation initially revolves around Nasibov's son, a talented athlete who had won a trophy at the national championships shortly before his death. His father shows us newspaper articles that claim another young man was the target and that his son was shot by mistake.

While we eat the delicious dates, the conversation slowly shifts toward Nasibov's views of Islam. He adheres to Salafism, a widespread, orthodox interpretation of the religion that the security forces and authorities associate with the armed revolt against the regime. Nasibov is a vocal man who seems disinclined to keep his views and beliefs to himself. Less than six months later, his outspokenness proves fatal. [pp. 268–69]

Kirovaul, Dagestan, 2012

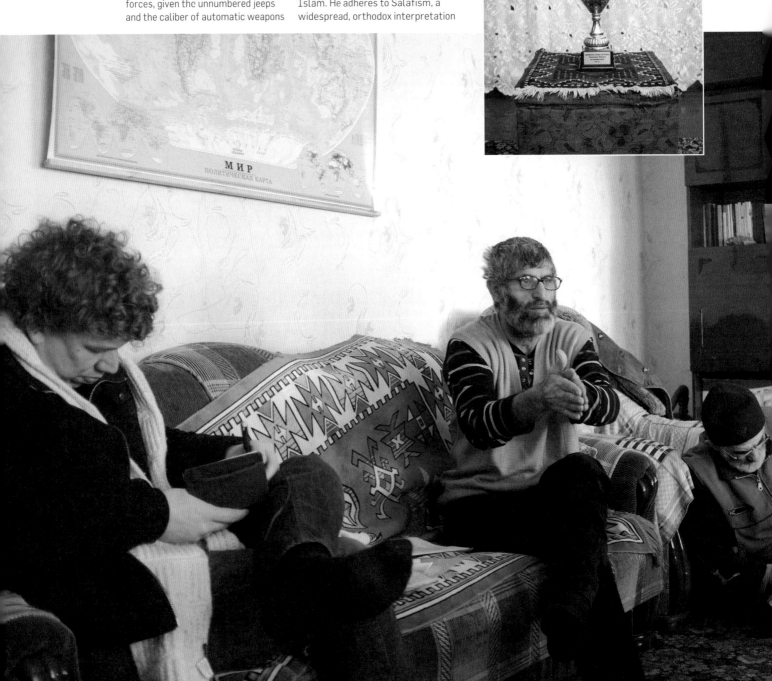

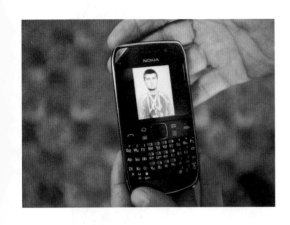

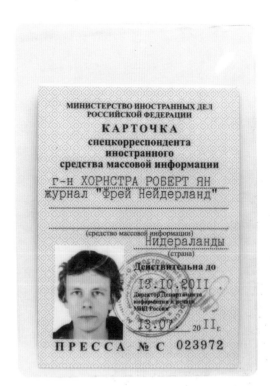

Essential Documents

During the first years we traveled with a press visa but without official press accreditation from the Russian Ministry of Internal Affairs. You can work unhindered in most places in Russia, something that is impossible in the North Caucasus. Your papers are checked at the border of every republic and police or security forces frequently appear out of nowhere to vet you. If any documents are missing, you are forbidden from working. Even if all your documents are in order, there is always a chance that an old law or rule will be dug up to prohibit you from working.

North Caucasus, 2012

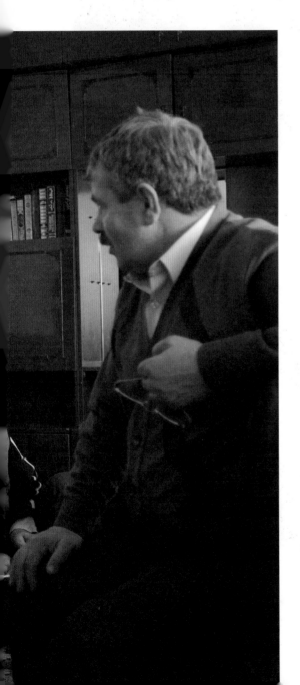

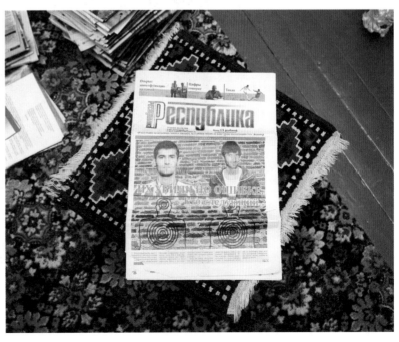

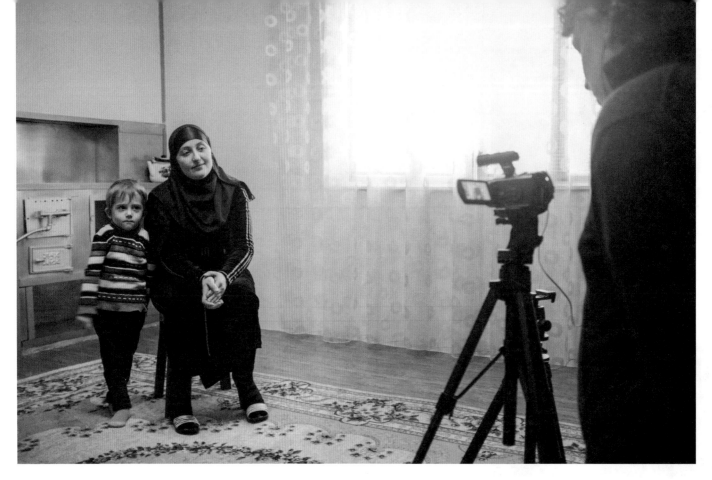

Arnold films Isita [pp. 272–75]
Yareksu, Dagestan, 2012

Drinking in Derbent

For our driver, interpreter, and fixer Habib, our trips through Dagestan are a nonstop party. He is an English professor at the university in Makhachkala, but away from his family and daily obligations, his boyish side appears. Every day, as evening approaches, his mustache begins to twitch and his eyes to twinkle. "Where shall we stop for a drink?" he asks. "And will there be women?" We are able to keep him in check with difficulty, until our last evening in the ancient city of Derbent. That warrants a drink.

Derbent, Dagestan, 2012

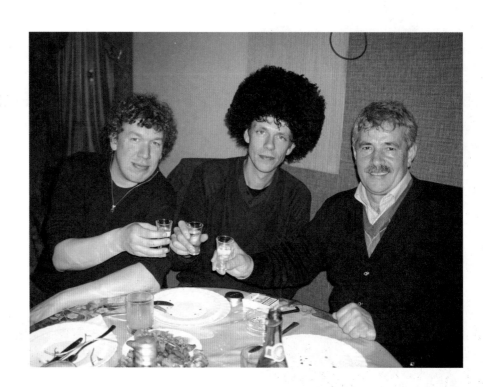

A Bottle of Cognac

A day after our arrest near Gimry, we go to Sogratl, another remote mountain village. We are in need of a relaxing evening. The president of the Dagestani journalists union has arranged for us to stay with friends of his. Since he had talked so enthusiastically about his village and during our interview had proved he enjoyed a good drink, we assume that it is not a religious place. Before we leave, Arnold puts a bottle of Dagestani cognac, which the president had previously given us as a gift, into his bag for our host. Our driver, Habib, also seems eager to reach the nearest kebab joint and pour a glass of the fiery liquid down his throat. After a five-hour drive,

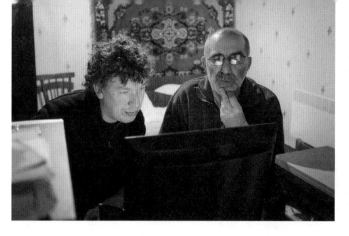

Checking out Islamic websites with Magomed Akhdukhanov

we hobble into the village, where a serious-looking bearded gentleman is awaiting us.

In his house, he shows us our accommodation and his veiled wife serves us pancakes. We could kick ourselves for having brought a bottle of cognac as a gift and decide that it is better not to give anything at all.

Habib, meanwhile, has snuck off to smoke a cigarette. The disappointment on his face is obvious. The rest of the evening is spent in labored conversation about religion. Everyone is relieved when we retire to bed early. [pp. 226–27]

Sogratl, Dagestan, 2012

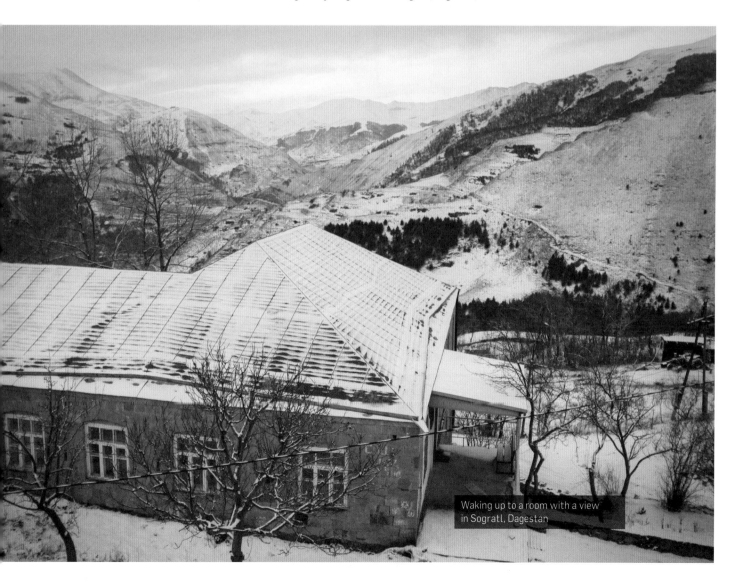

Waking up to a room with a view in Sogratl, Dagestan

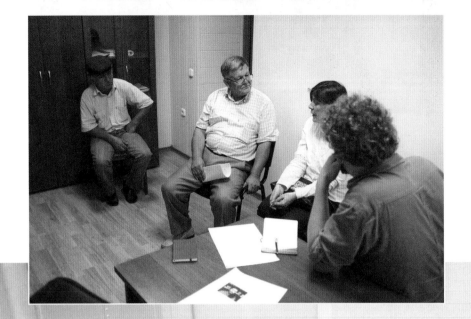

Nalchik Fathers

In a cramped office we hear the terrifying stories of fathers who found their decapitated sons on the side of the road. The old men are still in shock. Through the NGO that they founded, they try to make sense of the tragedy and prevent future violence. [pp. 256–57]

Nalchik, Kabardino-Balkaria, 2012

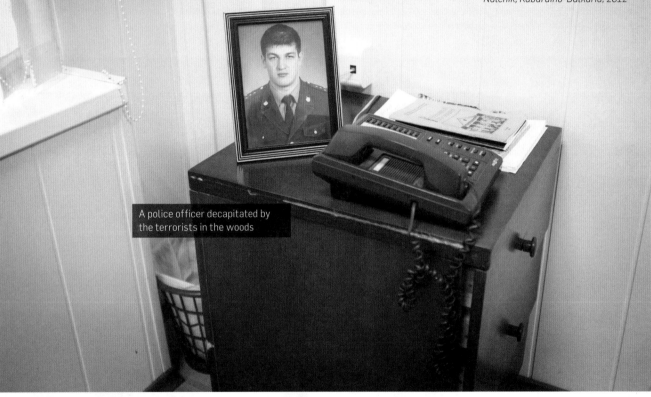

A police officer decapitated by the terrorists in the woods

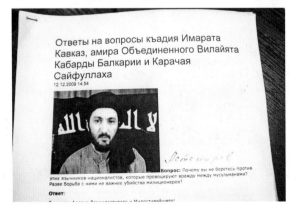

Notes on an Internet print-out depicting the local leader of the Islamic separatists

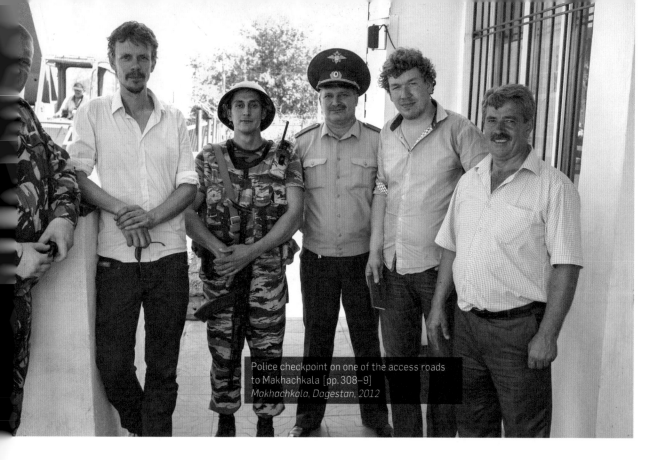

Police checkpoint on one of the access roads
to Makhachkala [pp. 308–9]
Makhachkala, Dagestan, 2012

Back to Visit Khava

After our return from Dagestan we decide to base our annual publication about the North Caucasus around a single protagonist. That protagonist is Khava, the woman whom we had met by chance at the side of the road in Chermen nearly a year earlier. Her life combines so many characteristic elements from the region. Her history reads like the history of the North Caucasus.

Although we are highly enthusiastic about the potential of the concept, there is one catch: Khava doesn't know. We first have to ask her if she even wants to be the subject of our book. A year after our first meeting we knock nervously on her iron gate. She seems happy to see us again. We have brought tulip bulbs and other Dutch gifts. We cautiously tell her that we have traveled throughout the North Caucasus and spoken to dozens of people. We explain that we want to describe the North Caucasus on the basis of one family's story. "And that's your family, Khava," we conclude.

She is quiet for several moments, expressing neither surprise nor joy. Maybe it will help to bring back her missing husband. She accepts our choice of her family's story as a given. [pp. 212–17]

Chermen, North Ossetia, 2012

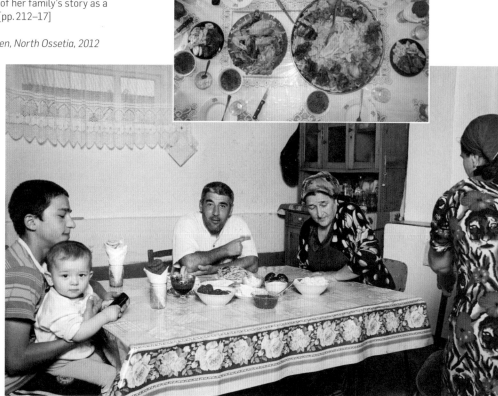

Arrested, Part IV

When Khava unexpectedly has to visit a sick aunt in Grozny, we decide to explore Chermen, the village in which she lives. Where better to start than the small, pretty village hall? The mayor receives us with open arms while at the same time instructing her assistant to call the FSB. Minutes into the interview, an oafish policeman arrives and asks us to accompany him to the FSB office in the district capital, Oktyabrskaya. He promises that it will only take five minutes. We refuse. "We have everything: accreditation, visas, registration. We're not going," we say. We know those Russian five minutes; they always end up taking far longer for a ridiculous conversation.

Half an hour later a senior officer appears. He remains cordial. Could we please come with him to clear a few things up? It really will only take five minutes, they'll drive us and bring us back. We don't believe a word of it, but understand that we have no choice. We get into the waiting jeep. It is the start of a six-hour bureaucratic marathon.

Russia is a bizarre country. This can't be said often enough. Applying for a visa and receiving press accreditation is only the start of it. Wherever you stay, you have to register at the local immigration office. Then you have the KTO areas

that appear spontaneously for a day, month, or indefinite period of time. You enter them unwittingly because no one can tell you in advance where they will be—it is a secret, after all. However, being arrested in one of those areas can result in a hefty fine and even deportation from Russia.

To top it all off is an arcane law from 1992 that specifies where foreigners can and cannot travel. According to a 2006 addition to the law, foreigners in North Ossetia are restricted to the larger cities and the main roads between them. We are doubly screwed. The director of the immigration service decides not to fine us on this occasion but to bring us before a judge. That can only mean one thing: deportation. The only additional power that judges have over immigration officers in these cases is that they can deport foreigners.

We appear in court the next morning. Two deputies from the immigration service are seated opposite us. Rob has prepared an impassioned plea in our defense. When he has finished, the judge admonishes the immigration service for our appearance in his courtroom. "Do you really want to deport them for this?" he asks. We are both fined fifty euros and allowed to leave. We never see Chermen, our protagonist's village, again.

Chermen, North Ossetia, 2012

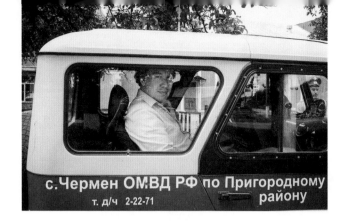

"We are Dutch journalists with accreditation from the Ministry of Foreign Affairs permitting us to work in the Russian Federation. We always strive to work according to the law and would like to apologize for breaking law 155.

"We have been to Chermen several times. In the past week officials in Chermen have checked our papers twice. None of them told us that we needed a special permit to be there.

"Although law 155 is intended for foreigners, it is only available in Russian. The law is accompanied by a request that Ministries of Foreign Affairs bring the law to the attention of embassies and consulates in Russia. However, no information to this effect was published on the website of the Dutch embassy in Moscow.

"We sincerely try to avoid situations like this. To this end, we always send a letter to the relevant authorities informing them in advance that we will be working in their region. We did this as a matter of course before our arrival in North Ossetia. A press secretary usually warns foreign journalists of any special rules or restrictions that apply to them. We received no response to our letter.

"We realize now that we were in violation of law 155, but believe it is important to ask to what extent we were responsible for breaking it. Law 155 restricts foreigners from moving freely in public spaces. Visiting a village is not something we expected to be illegal. We are thus of the opinion that local authorities have a responsibility to better inform foreign visitors.

"The fact that law 155 is only available in Russian, that no information about it is available on the websites of foreign embassies, that the North Ossetian press secretary did not tell us of any specific areas restricted to us, that local law enforcement and even the mayor of Chermen were unaware of the law, and that there are no signs in public spaces regarding restricted access make it almost impossible for us to know about and adhere to law 155.

"Although we broke law 155, we kindly ask the court to take all of the above into consideration before pronouncing its verdict."

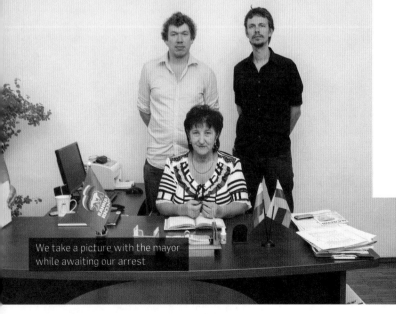

We take a picture with the mayor while awaiting our arrest

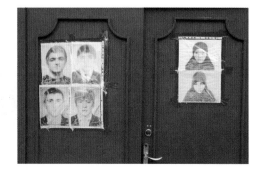

Daydreaming in Paradise

We are wandering along the main road in Ekazhevo, Ingushetia, when a middle-aged man waves us over. He opens the high iron gate of his property to reveal a small paradise. We see frolicking children and young animals and homemade swings. The sun streams through the fruit trees and the garden is full of vegetables. The house is admittedly small and ramshackle, but we hear laughter, and delicious home-baked bread and honey appear on the table. In a box under the table, kittens lap hungrily at a saucer of milk. It must be a wonderful place to grow up, far nicer than an apartment in Amsterdam, we muse.

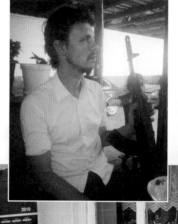

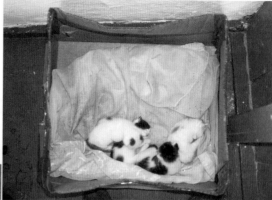

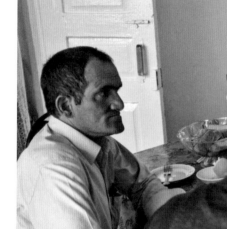

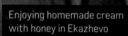
Enjoying homemade cream with honey in Ekazhevo

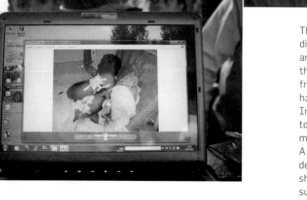

The man of the house, Amir, quickly dispels that dream. He shows us his armored car with its ten-centimeter-thick doors, bought secondhand from an official. "Without it I would have been dead long ago," he says. In the middle of the window next to the driver's seat we see a hole made by a ricocheting bullet. A former policeman, Amir was declared unfit to work after being shot by militants. His neighbor suffered a similar fate, although he is in a worse condition. On a laptop, the two men show us pictures of the neighbor in hospital. He is riddled with gunshot wounds. Aunt Lis pokes her head around the corner. She moved in with the family after she lost her home in Grozny during the war in 2004. She now languishes in a small room in the already crowded house. "Actually, we have it pretty good," says Amir and shows us a YouTube video in which a house across the street is crushed by an armored tank. Our feet are firmly back on the ground and we conclude that an apartment in Amsterdam is not so bad after all. [pp. 190–93]

Ekazhevo, Ingushetia, 2012

Car Trouble

There are few people in the world who would recommend breaking down in a village in the middle of Chechnya. Yet that's where one of the stabilizer bars of the old Volga in which we are traveling snaps. The driver, a man from Kabardino-Balkaria, is already piqued about being in Chechnya in the first place. We decide to leave the grumbling man with his vehicle and to seek shelter from the rain in a nearby store. The owner is initially non-plussed, eventually decides to help us find a taxi, offers us tea, and before we know it we are sitting at a table loaded with homegrown delicacies. That's the North Caucasus, too. [pp. 180–81]

Ishchersky, Chechnya, 2012

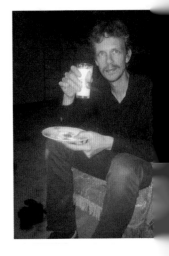

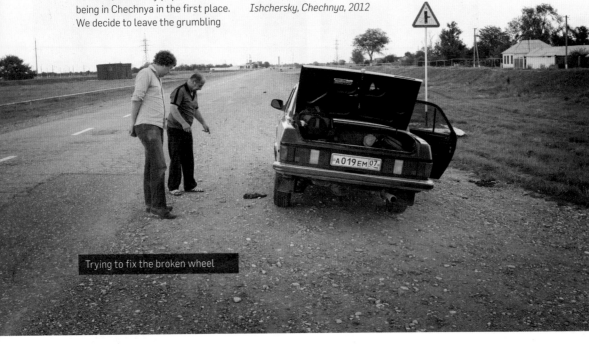

Trying to fix the broken wheel

New Cover for Empty Land, 2013

The Sochi Project's final production year is dominated by revisiting prominent people and places from our interim publications. One of the nicest things about slow journalism is that you can see with your own eyes the changes that have taken place over the years. Our last visit to Abkhazia was back in 2010. We are curious to see how the small country has evolved. At the same time we want to find out whether the story from our publication *Empty Land, Promised Land, Forbidden Land* is still current. We are considering a second edition, but only if the book is not outdated.

On our arrival in Abkhazia, we drive along a new highway that takes us north of Gagra and is equipped with the most modern LED streetlights we have ever seen. One of the first places we visit the next day is Tkuarchal, the former mining town where we shot the book's cover photo. Nothing has changed. Tkuarchal is illustrative of the rest of Abkhazia: empty and broken. Aside from renovations to schools and orphanages, little progress seems to have been made in the three years since our last visit.

The second, revised edition of *Empty Land, Promised Land, Forbidden Land* was published six months after our trip, with an updated photo on the cover.

Tkuarchal, Abkhazia, 2013

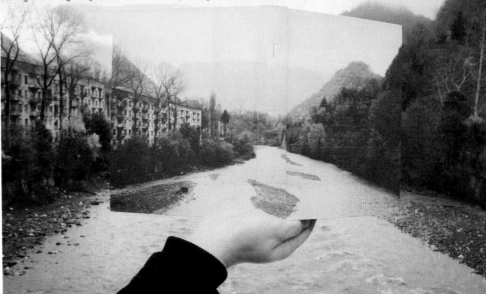

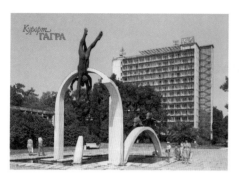

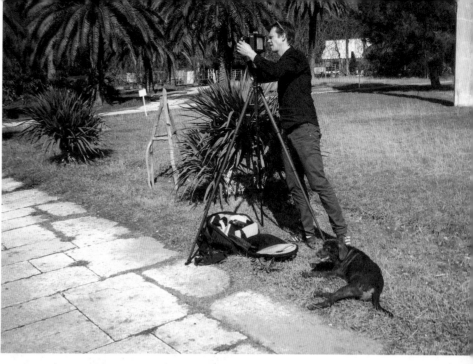

Rob remaking an old postcard
[pp. 60–61, 64–65]
Pitsunda, Abkhazia, 2013

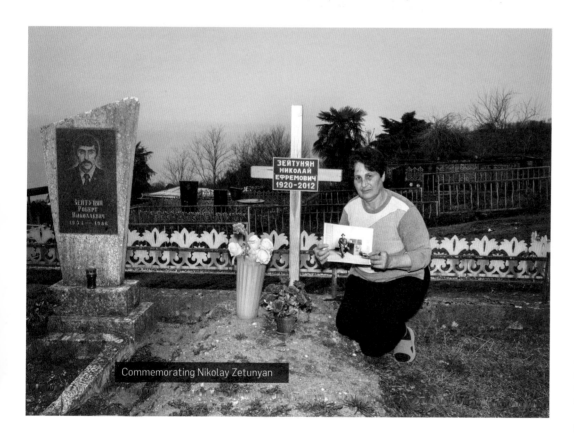

Commemorating Nikolay Zetunyan

Nikolay Yefremovich Zetunyan

For the third time, our taxi bumps toward Nizhny Eshera. The road is just as bad as it was on our first visit in 2009. As we drive under the railroad bridge, the car is almost submerged in muddy water. During that first visit, we met Nikolay Yefremovich Zetunyan on our quest to find World War II veterans. They are fascinating to photograph and are often a great source of information about their villages or towns. Moreover, they can be found everywhere: from rundown apartments and luxury condominiums in the cities to the remotest villages. Like wrestlers in the North Caucasus, they are a wonderful alibi for our activities and for making new links to other stories.

Zetunyan's house has a beautiful view of the Black Sea, and the garden is crowded with tangerine and walnut trees. It is idyllic. We return in 2010. We are really just curious to find out how he is and to give him the portrait we took a year earlier. We stay for a few hours, and Zetunyan is considerably more at ease than during our first meeting. Sitting on his porch, he tells us daring tales about the war and the sweetheart he met then: her name is still tattooed on his arm, to the displeasure of his current wife.

In 2013 Zetunyan's house appears deserted. The garden and porch look immaculate, but the door is locked. His neighbor informs us that Zetunyan died last year. His wife now lives with their daughter near Gagra. She last visited in the fall, to pick the tangerines. The neighbor shows us Zetunyan's grave. [pp. 80–83]

Eshera, Abkhazia, 2013

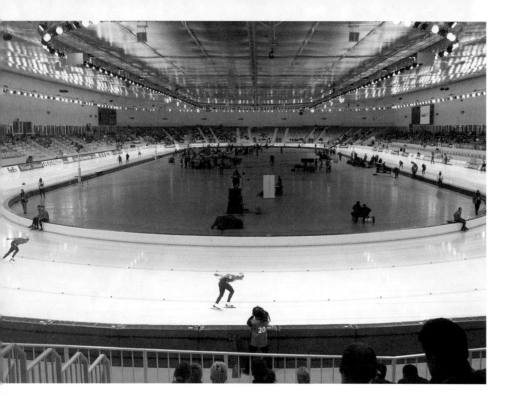

Speed Skating World Championship

In March 2013 we attend the World Single Distance Speed Skating Championships in Sochi, one of the last in a long series of tests to ensure that all the Olympic facilities meet international standards. It is our first encounter with the international sports press. Although our endeavor is hung on the largest sports event in the world, the Sochi Project is more about the context of the Games than the sports themselves. Former skating fan Rob can still dredge up some facts and figures from past championships, but among his fellow journalists, Arnold struggles to remember the names of even a handful of famous skaters.

It is striking that we still have every confidence in the upcoming Games while our sports colleagues trudge through the mud and stumble over building materials. This is not what they are used to a year before the Games. Russia seems to hold little interest for them. Conversation every morning revolves around the bizarre service in restaurants, cafés, and taxis. We learn to see the city as outsiders again.

At the same time, athletes, sponsors, and journalists invite us to talk about Sochi and the surrounding region. The Caucasus—so self-evident to us—is a mystery to them. [pp. 340–41]

Adler, Sochi region, 2013

An Appointment at the Ministry

If we want press accreditation, we have to pick it up ourselves at the Russian Foreign Ministry in Moscow, we are told. This was normally a formality that we could outsource to one of our contacts. Without accreditation, however, you are fair game in the Russian Caucasus. We visit the ministry. Two pleasant but formal officials give us a dressing down. We have been arrested too often and there are too many notes in our report. They show us the rules of working in Russia and threaten implicitly that a subsequent accreditation is not guaranteed. We are happy to be given this one. After filing away the cards, we bring up the Caucasus's peculiar, unpredictable laws and the near impossibility of

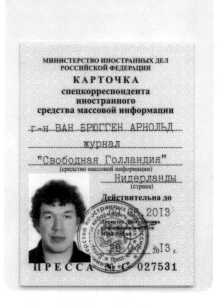

being able to do our jobs with rules and laws that we are unable to confirm in advance. The men have little to say. Moscow and the North Caucasus are worlds apart, even for these bureaucrats.

Moscow, Russia, 2013

Meeting former Dutch speed skater and gold medalist Marianne Timmer

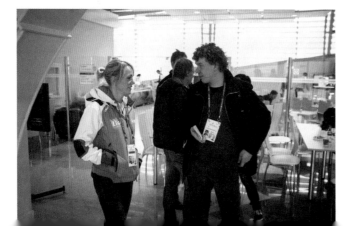

Refrigerators for Khava

On the day we launch our fourth annual publication, documenting Khava Gaisanova and the North Caucasus, our fixer, Dina, tells us that Khava's husband has officially been declared dead—standard procedure when someone has been missing for more than five years.

We had been thinking for some time of doing something for Khava. We had borrowed her life story for our history of the North Caucasus and were aware of her precarious situation. Dina tells us that Khava wants to open a roadside store. With the income, she hopes to be able to provide for her family and send her granddaughters to college.

We decide to raise money to buy equipment for her future store. A quick calculation indicates that three thousand euros (about four thousand dollars) should cover the costs. We make an appeal through our website, newsletter, Facebook, and Twitter. The response is heartwarming. Within two weeks we have reached our target, thanks to dozens of donations.

Strange laws and paranoid security forces mean that we are no longer allowed to visit Chermen, Khava's village. We arrange to meet in the Ossetian capital, Vladikavkaz, which is unfamiliar territory for Khava. This is where her husband was kidnapped and where Ossetians— the enemy in the last war she lived through—reside. For the first time we see Khava's gray hairs; she is afraid to wear a headscarf. Madina, her daughter-in-law, is with her and has already done a lot of legwork. She knows all the prices of refrigerators and counters. We look bashfully at our envelope of money. We hadn't expected things to be this expensive. But things look up at the wholesaler.

When Khava hears that she can select not only a refrigerator and two freezers but also a counter and scales, she is almost overwhelmed. "This is truly a miracle," she stammers over and over again.

We help Khava come up with a name for her new store (Orange Tulip, after the archetypal Dutch flowers we had given her a year earlier and which have become the hit of the village). We wish her luck in setting up the business and promise that on our next visit we will bring a board with the names of everyone who contributed to the store. [pp. 212–17]

Vladikavkaz, North Ossetia, 2013

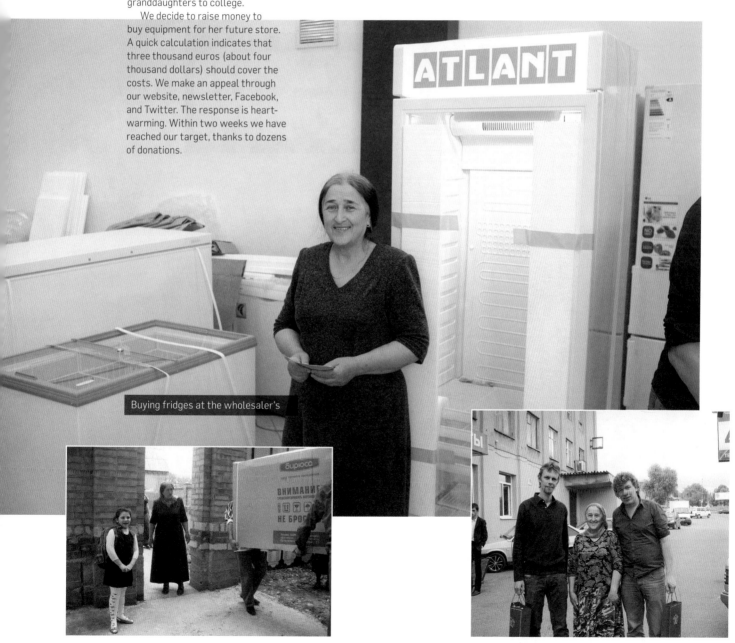

Buying fridges at the wholesaler's

Bella's Parents

We are unclear about the true cause of death of Bella, a journalist and friend who had shown us around Karachay-Cherkessia in 2009. She was hit by a car near her house, that much was clear. It was suggested in the media that she had received several threats shortly before her death, following articles on government fraud and corruption that she had written for the weblog *Caucasian Knot*. We decide to visit her parents.

It is an emotional afternoon. We meet her mother, Sofia, in Cherkessk. She recognizes us immediately from photographs Bella had shown her. Through her tears she tells us proudly about her courageous daughter who had never been able to sit still and was always looking for new experiences. She shows us piles of certificates, diplomas, and photo albums.

She is brief about the cause of death: it was an accident. Nothing

more, nothing less. Bella had gone to buy credit for her cell phone at a nearby store. She called her mother and, with the phone to her ear, she crossed the street. She was hit by a car carrying five people on their way back from a picnic. The crash could be heard hundreds of meters away. According to the police report, the driver, a local man, was sober, although he was speeding. He later rang to express his remorse. Bella's mother had recently found a photo in one of Bella's albums showing the two of them together. We are then taken to meet Bella's father. He receives us with a lavish picnic at the country home that he and his wife had been building for Bella and her brother in the family's village. It's all pointless now, her father says in the unfinished house. A year after Bella's death, her brother was killed, too. He was speeding on the Caucasus's winding roads.

Cherkessk, Karachay-Cherkessia, 2013

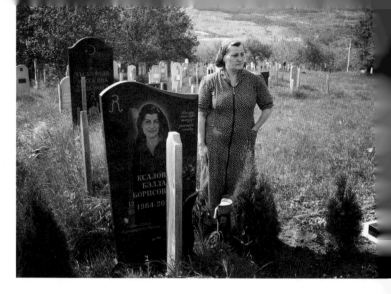

Visiting Bella's grave with her mother

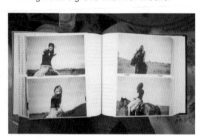

Bella's photo album

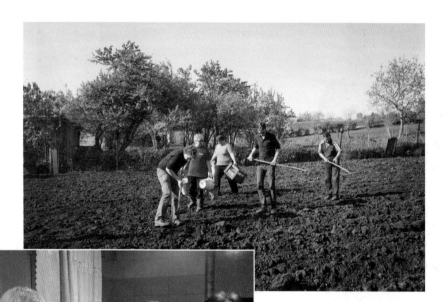

Revisiting Krasny Vostok

In 2010 we made the newspaper-cum-exhibition *On the Other Side of the Mountains* about the village of Krasny Vostok, where we had spent several days in 2009 and 2010. The newspaper was distributed around the world and exhibited on the walls of countless cultural institutions, schools, universities, and museums. Krasny Vostok was high on our list of places we wanted to revisit before the end of the project. Not only because we had fallen in love with the village and the family who had accommodated us so generously, but also because we had heard that the mayor, Taisya, had been replaced by the village imam.

Once again it is an exceptional experience. Our hostess, Stella, exploits every spare minute to stuff us with homemade delicacies while our host, Giorgi, plies us with alcoholic refreshment. We hear hilarious stories about our friend Aibasov, who allegedly does little else but chase "Uzbeekski," which evidently stands for every woman who crosses his path. We help plant potatoes on the land and picnic in the rugged countryside. In the meantime, we work on a story about the rise of Islam in the village. [pp. 160–77]

Krasny Vostok, Karachay-Cherkessia, 2013

Return to Georgia

Georgia is possibly our favorite destination in the Caucasus. Tbilisi, the capital, has a cultural and culinary climate that far exceeds the other cities in Southern Russia and the North Caucasus. We revisit refugees we had met on previous trips and take a dip in the ancient sulfur baths. One day we go to Pankisi Gorge, a former hotbed of North Caucasian activity in Georgia. This is where refugees who fled the war in Chechnya but still wanted to be close to their motherland set up camp. It is also the home base of international Islamic terrorist groups, claim the FSB, the pro-Russian Chechen regime, and, after 9/11, the United States. Today, peace has been restored. The

military and police checkpoints have been dismantled and in every house we visit we are treated to homegrown grapes, cheese, and sometimes even wine. Only the faithful at the mosque and the few remaining refugees are less pleased to see us. Every busybody is bad news, they know from experience. Georgia is our last stop and the Sochi Project is finished. We could go on for years, gathering interviews and images. Simultaneously, our archives of notebooks and negative binders suggest we have enough. It is time to tell the story.

Pankisi Gorge, Georgia, 2013

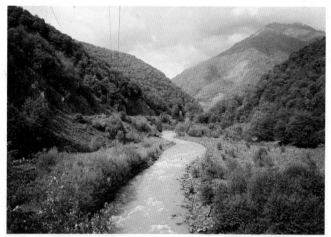

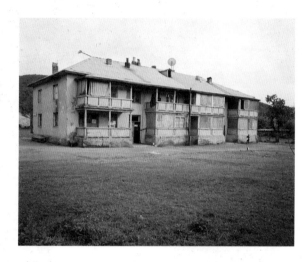

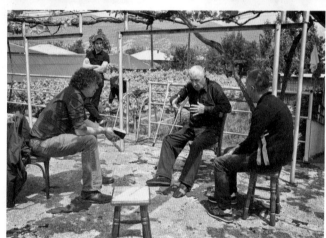

A Letter from the FSB

As this book is about to go to print we receive a letter from the FSB security service. It is a response to our request to visit Ingushetia's ski slopes. The republic sees a future in winter sports and is heavily promoting the area. We had expected permission to visit would be readily granted, but the answer is clear. No. We may not work or stay there, herd livestock over the border, or establish cultural activities.

Amsterdam, The Netherlands, 2013

Пограничное управление ФСБ России
по Республике Ингушетия
(наименование пограничного органа)

УВЕДОМЛЕНИЕ
об отказе в выдаче пропусков, разрешений

(дата выдачи уведомления: число, месяц прописью, год)

Настоящим уведомляется, что ____Хорнстр Роберт Ян____
(фамилия, инициалы)

Подавший ____7 марта 2013 года____ заявление (ходатайство)
(дата приема заявления)

о выдаче пропуска или разрешения (зарегистрировано под № 7/566)

с целью ____служебной деятельности____

____

Отказано в выдаче пропуска, разрешения.
(ненужное зачеркнуть)

Основание отказа: Закон Российской Федерации от 1 апреля 1993 г. №4730-1 «О Государственной границе Российской Федерации», Федеральный закон от 2 мая 2006 г. №59-ФЗ «О порядке рассмотрения обращений граждан Российской Федерации», на основании п. «в» статьи 25 «Административного регламента Федеральной службы безопасности Российской Федерации по предоставлению государственной услуги по выдаче пропусков для въезда (прохода) лиц и транспортных средств в пограничную зону, разрешений на хозяйственную, промысловую и иную деятельность, проведение массовых общественно-политических, культурных и других мероприятий, содержание и выпас скота в пограничной зоне, промысловую, исследовательскую, изыскательскую и иную деятельность в российской части вод пограничных рек, озер и иных водных объектов, где установлен пограничный режим», утвержденного приказом ФСБ России от 13 ноября 2012 г. № 572 (зарегистрирован в Минюсте РФ 19 марта 2013 года № 27754).

Начальник Управления _____ И.Цветков
(подпись) (инициалы, фамилия)

Исполнитель ____техник____ _____ О. Ляпунова
(должность) (подпись) (инициалы, фамилия)

Телефон ____55-16-97____
номер служебного (рабочего) телефона

Fuji X100 camera for quick digital snapshots

White umbrella (worn out after some days)

Mamiya 7II medium-format rangefinder camera plus 65 or 80 mm lens. Did not survive the Sochi Project.

Gossen Sixtomat flash light meter. Always comes back in a miraculous way after being lost.

Spare cables and batteries

wireless flash trigger

Polaroid 405 instant film holder for large format

Lumedyne flash head. The not-fancy-looking plastic one with straight cord.

"Anti-static" cloth, magnifier, and 135 mm lens for Large Format

Five film holders for ten large-format Kodak Portra negatives. Full of dust.

Horseman 45 HD large-format camera. Favorite camera. Never refuses.

Not visible: Gitzo tripod with a dangling leg

Lumedyne power pack with small battery. Problems ensured during security check at airports.

The Caucasus is comprised of more than just regional conflict and refugees, terrorism, and billion-dollar Games.

Bibliography

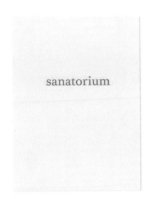

Sanatorium

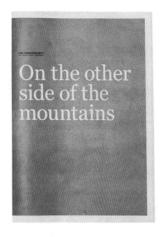

On the other side of the mountains

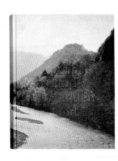

Empty land, Promised land, Forbidden land

Sochi Singers

Sochi is an elusive city. Strung along eighty-seven miles (140 kilometers) of coastline, it incites love and hate in equal measure. It is characterized by deserted beaches and rugged nature, but above all, noise, exhaust fumes, and the smoke of countless grills. *Sanatorium* was our first attempt to capture the city, by focusing on what had made it famous: the fresh air, healing waters, and medical facilities in Lenin's palaces for the proletariat. The book is an account of our stay in Sanatorium Metallurg, written as a fictionalized diary of a spa guest. Quotes from earlier articles about Sochi appear in the margins alongside the photos.

After our stay, Metallurg closed its doors for extensive renovations. In the run-up to the Winter Olympics in 2014, almost all the sanatoria would be converted into luxury hotels. There is no place for sentimentality when it comes to the past.

Utrecht, The Netherlands: self-published, 2009. 9 3/8 x 12 5/8 in. (24 x 32 cm), 40 pages, 20 color photographs, white folio with stitched binding, print run of 350 copies.

Our first encounter with the North Caucasus was of the region's most relaxed republic: Karachay-Cherkessia, on the side of the mountains from Sochi. There we discovered the village of Krasny Vostok, whose name means the Red East. We wanted to portray the village precisely because it is so ordinary: the defunct factory, the unemployment as well as the rural feeling that the place conveyed to us. It is barely 120 miles (200 kilometers) from Sochi, but a world away. The Caucasus is more than just conflict and refugees, fundamentalist Islam, or billion-dollar Games.

The publication came about because we wanted to design a flexible, portable exhibition for the European Month of Photography, a joint venture between European photography festivals in Rome, Berlin, Bratislava, Vienna, and Luxembourg. *On the other side of the mountains* is a sixty-four-page newspaper, which if you combine two newspapers, also functions as an exhibition measuring about 4 x 20 feet (1.2 x 6 meters).

Utrecht, The Netherlands: self-published, 2010. 11 3/4 x 16 1/4 in. (30 x 41 cm), 64 pages, 32 color photographs, 1/2 broadsheet, print run of 12,000 copies.

Empty land, Promised land, Forbidden land is the result of four trips to the tiny country of Abkhazia since 2007. A stone's throw away from the Olympic stadiums, Abkhazia is isolated, ruined, and seemingly without ambition. The country's story is particularly tragic for the thousands of refugees who fled in the early nineties and have little prospect of returning. The book became a journey of discovery, not only of the country itself but also of the places where the refugees live. One reviewer described the publication as a "boy's book" and a tribute to the indomitable Caucasian. In a region plagued by conflict, shifting borders, and absurd but brutal dictators, daily life is a feat of endurance. Nowhere was this more apparent than in Abkhazia, where every person's story could fill two history books.

Utrecht, The Netherlands: self-published, 2010. 7 5/8 x 9 7/8 in. (19.4 x 25.1 cm), 272 pages, 93 color photographs, hardbound with photo-illustrated boards, print run of 900 copies.

Reprint
Utrecht, The Netherlands: self-published, 2013. 6 4/5 x 8 5/8 (17.2 x 22 cm) 272 pages, 101 color photographs, hardbound with photo-illustrated boards, print run of 800 copies.

Sochi Singers is our second book about Sochi. While *Sanatorium* portrays the vanishing city of the past, *Sochi Singers* focuses on the modern metropolis where mass tourism holds sway. Sochi attracts mainly Russian tourists in the summer. On the one hand, they come looking for glitter and glamour and are prepared to pay for it; on the other, they attach great importance to Russian culture and traditions. This dichotomy is most obvious in Sochi's nightlife. Restaurants try to entice customers with flashing neon signs, semi-luxurious interiors, and an abundance of staff. At the same time, they uphold a long-established tradition of live musicians who belt out Russian chansons from behind an electric piano. *Sochi Singers* explores how a deeply rooted tradition goes hand in hand with the city's new capitalist allure.

Utrecht, The Netherlands: self-published, 2011. 11 5/8 x 15 in. (29.7 x 38 cm), 80 pages, 37 color photographs, softcover with dust jacket, print run of 1,000 copies.

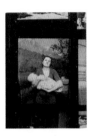

Safety First

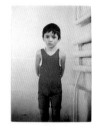

Life here is serious

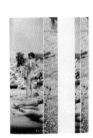

Kiev

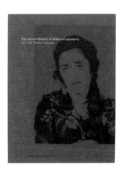

The Secret History of Khava Gaisanova

In 2011 we launched sketchbooks, a new series that provided an outlet for small, worthy stories that fell outside the scope of our other publications. We also hoped that the booklets, which all had the same format and print run, would generate additional revenue to cover the rising costs of the Sochi Project's final year. The first sketchbook, *Safety First*, is composed entirely of negatives that were damaged by X-ray scanners during our stay in Grozny. In the Chechen capital, these scanners are placed not only at the entrance to the airport and government buildings, but also in shops, gyms, restaurants, and outdoors on squares. In *Safety First*, Arnold explores the difference between security and a false sense of security in the North Caucasus, while Rob describes a day's work in the region with photos that initially appeared unusable.

Utrecht, The Netherlands: self-published, 2011. 5 7/8 x 8 3/8 in. (15 x 21 cm), 48 pages, 41 color photographs, hardbound with photo-Illustrated dust jacket, print run of 750 copies.

In our second sketchbook, *Life here is serious*, we describe the North Caucasus's most popular national sport: wrestling. Every town and village has a wrestling school, and North Caucasians consistently win medals at the Summer Olympics. In the Caucasus, wrestling is not just a sport, it is an integral part of the culture and history of a region paralyzed by war and violence. "Wrestling is serious," one coach told us, "because life here is serious." We initially used the sport as an alibi to travel around the region. However, it also resulted in wonderful stories and photo series, which give a unique sociocultural perspective of the North Caucasus.

Utrecht, The Netherlands: self-published, 2012. 5 7/8 x 8 3/8 in. (15 x 21 cm), 48 pages and 1 fold-out, 28 color photographs, hardback with photo-illustrated dust jacket, print run of 750 copies.

The third sketchbook, *Kiev*, is an ode to analog photography and depicts Sochi in the summer as shot from the hip. In 2011, Rob fell in love with a forty-year-old KIEV medium-format camera, which a friend gave him in Sochi. Over the following days, he roamed the city with his new acquisition and photographed things that he had never seen before through the lens of his Mamiya camera. When he got home and developed the film, he found that the KIEV's film transport system was defective. The photo-led booklet includes a short piece he wrote about analog photography and its wonderful unpredictability.

Utrecht, The Netherlands: self-published, 2012. 5 7/8 x 8 3/8 in. (15 x 21 cm), 16 color photographs, cardboard fold-out book in a photo-illustrated wrapper, print run of 750 copies.

After *On the other side of the mountains* and two sketchbooks, it was time for a comprehensive account of the North Caucasus. No other book took us so long to define. The region is so incredibly complex that we initially got lost in the details. A history of violence was to be the overarching theme, but then we met Khava Gaisanova and decided to focus on a single character. Khava lives in Chermen, a village in the heart of the North Caucasus. In 2007 her husband disappeared, like scores of men in the North Caucasus that disappear without a trace—kidnapped, arrested, or simply executed and buried in anonymous graves. So many elements of the region seemed to come together in Khava's story that we decided to use it as the basis for our book. In *The Secret History of Khava Gaisanova*, a grim picture unfolds of the region hosting the 2014 Winter Olympics.

Utrecht, The Netherlands: self-published, 2013. 7 7/8 x 10 5/8 in. (20 x 27 cm), 352 pages and 32-page insert, 107 color photographs, softcover, printed on newsprint, print run of 1,100 English copies and 1,100 Dutch copies.

This bibliography features the primary book publications created during the course of the Sochi Project; several of the featured publications were also issued as special, limited editions, including C-prints; additional published items include postcards and posters. A complete list of all items produced can be found on the Sochi Project website.

A Special Thanks to

Anoek Steketee, Jolien Steenman, Eefje Blankevoort, Hans Loos, Dina Djidjoeva, Stella Sorokina, Yulia Ochetova, Milana and Khibla Vozba, Angela Pataraya, Anna Nistratova, Svetlana Mikhailenko, Bella Ksalova, Musa Dexter, Habib Rabadanov, Tinatin Japaridze, Darejan Zatiashvili, Marika Asatiani, Revi Uznadze, Sergei Rasulov, and the many others who helped us on the road and at home.

Between 2009 and 2014, the following people generously donated their own funds to make the Sochi Project possible. We are very grateful to all of you.

Wim Aalbers
Wim Aardenburg
Ralph Aarnout
Johannes Abeling
Antoine Achten
David K. Adams
Liesbeth van Aerssen
Sander Agterhuis
Paul van Akkeren
Floris Akkerman
Jeroen Akkermans
Kirsten Algera
Yulan van Alphen
Johannes Amm
Roland Angst
Brechje Asselbergs
Jessica Auer
Neville Austin
Nico Baldauf
Inga Lára Baldvinsdottir
Harry Barkema
Peter Bartak
Saskia Barth
Eugenijus Barzdzius
Det Bazelmans
Stefan Becker
Nathalie Belayche
Valentino Bellini
Rainer Berg
Danielle van Berkel
Joost M. Beunderman
Mark Beunderman
Saskia van Beveren
Frederiek Biemans
Marc Bierings
Jes van der Bijl
Leontine Bijman
Michel Angelo Binsbergen
Eefje Blankevoort
Victor Blankevoort
Elgin Blankwater
Niels Blekemolen
Jelle Bloem
Jan Willem Bloemendaal
Kees Boef
Roos Boer
Maarten Boerma
Boudewijn Bollmann
Tjitske Boogmans
Flip Bool
Lex Boon
Kris Borgerink
Chloe Borkett
Willem van Borselen
Jack Bos
Maarten Boswijk
Nicolaas Bot
Gerwin Botterhuis
Els Bovenberg
Allan Bovill
Enda Bowe
Valentijn Brandt
Laura Bras
Patrick Bras
Karel de Bree
Jacco Brink
Corine van den Broek
Marca van den Broek
Gerard Broersen
Steve Brown
Guido Bruggeman
Anke van Bruggen
Erik van Bruggen
Janny & Popke van Bruggen
Roderick Buijs
Irma Bulkens
Lynton J. Bullen
Heleen Bulthuis
Tessa Bunney
Simon Burer
Melchior Bussink
Alfonso Calero

Romelia Calin
David Campbell
Stefan Canham
Theo Captein
Nelson Chan
Jasmin Chang
Francesco Chiericoni
David Christensen
Sally Clark
Chris Clement
Toon de Clerck
Luc Coffeng
Joerg Colberg
Rutger Colenbrander
Justin Collins
Giorgio Comai
Jeannette Cornelisse
Joelle Cornuz
Simon de la Court
L.J.A.D. Creyghton
Alexander van de Cruijs
Agnese Da Col
Benno van Daalen
Wiktor Dabkowski
Nelson Daires
Alessandro Dandini de Sylva
Dieter Danzer
Adrian Davies
Laura De Marco
Debras Debras
Maartje Degenaar
Dorothee Deiss
Peter M. Dekens
Els Dekker
Hans Dekker
Julie Del Piero
Helga Dichte
Andrea Diefenbach
Jaap Dijks
Emilio D'Itri
Martin Dixon
Stichting Doel Zonder Naam
Carola van Dongen de Boer
Thomas Donker
Ivan Donovan
Bryan Dooley
Albert Doorenbos
Louis S. Dowse
Carolyn Drake
Michiel Driebergen
Jochem Driest
Lodewijk Duijvesteijn
Derk Duit
Marc Duponcel
Thomas Dworzak
Tom Dziomba
Chris Ecclestone
Simen Edvardsen
Janus van den Eijnden
Simone van Eik
Anna Eikelboom
Jan Pieter Ekker
Simon Eliasson
Hanna Emmering
Frank van den Engel
Simone van Engelen
Michael Ensdorf
Leo Erken
Peter Evans
Nicole Ex Asselbergs
Sarah Eyre
Remi Faucheux
Federico Ferrari
Silva Ferretti
Olivier Fierens
Richard Fieten
Jonas Fischer
Judith Fischer
Eva Flendrie
Peter Flik
Regina Fluyt
Jan Willem Folkers

Joeri Folman
Markus Franke
Klaas Fris
McKenzie Funk
Esther Gaarlandt
Francoise Gaarlandt Kist
Thijs Gadiot
FreeLens Galerie
Isabel Garces
Dirk Gebhardt
Marijke Geelen Borker
Coen Geertsema
Jan van Gemert
Christo Geoghegan
Catharina Gerritsen
Bertus Gerssen
Carlo Gianferro
Heidi de Gier
Frits Gierstberg
Jasper Gilijamse
Roos Gils
Sebastien Girard
Mariette Glas Albers
Jan Glerum
Tino Glimmann
Lia Goldman
Otto Gooiker
John Gossage
Ingo Gotz
Annemarie Graft
Ian Graham
Emiliano Granado
Peter Granser
Stefanie Gratz
Simone de Greef
Hans Gremmen
Henk Greven
Jasper Groen
Johanna Groen
Martijn Groeneveld
Carla de Groot
Cocky de Groot
Inge de Groot
Sam de Groot
Feyoena Grovestins
Peter Guettler
Anke van Haarlem
Anne Haenni
Mieke Hageman
Arjan van Hal
Barbara Hanlo
Ingrid Harms
Gregory Harris
Neil Harrison
Egbert Hartman
Hans Ueli Hasler
Frans van Hasselt
Maarten van Heems
Mieke Heeringa
Michel Heesen
Maxim Heijndijk
Chantal Heijnen
Kysia Hekster
Wardie Hellendoorn
Mark Henderson
Hans Hendriks
Marlene Herkemij
Michael Hermse
Arthur Herrman
Paul Herrmann
Pauke van den Heuvel
Lorelei Heyligers
Marloes Hiethaar
Richard Higginbottom
Wieke Hoeke
Jorrit 't Hoen
Paul 't Hoen
Benjamin Hoewler
Eva Hofman
Jeroen Hofman
Emile Holba
Bert van Hoogenhuyze

Korrie Hopstaken
Joop Hopster
Jonas Hornstra
Joost en Joke Hornstra
Luc Hornstra
Maarten Hornstra
Tom Hornstra
Alexa ter Horst
Max Houghton
Laurien ten Houten
Marjan Hoving
Ewout Huibers
Elisabeth van 't Hull Vermaas
Eelco van Hulsen
Michiel Hulshof
Fred Icke
Tarek Issaoui
Mieke Jansen
Juliette Janssen
Lucia Janssen
Tom Janssen
Els Jekel
Michael Jellema
Fred Jelsma
Will Jenkins
Fanny Jol
Cornelie de Jong
Ralf de Jong
Mayke Jongsma
Stephan Jourdan
Antie en Jan Kaan
Tomas Kaan
Roy Kahmann
Karijn Kakebeeke
Felix Kalkman
Manja Kamman
Lizette van der Kamp
Hennie Kamphuis
Alke Kamstra
Emile Kelly
Dimiter Kenarov
Dolph Kessler
Vivian Keulards
Sophie Keurentjes
Robin Klaassen
Erik Klappe
Martijn Kleppe
Freya de Klerk
Anneke Kloostra
Jessica Knights
Kim Knoppers
Talmon Kochheim
Ria Kock
Olaf Koens
Helena de Kok
Stefan Kolgen
Dirk Kome
Suzanne Koopmans
Derin Korman
Christian Kosfeld
Meike Koster
Paul Kouwenberg
Ben Krewinkel
Erik Kroes
Lars Krueger
Jan Kruidhof
Annelies Kuiper
Sybren Kuiper
Jeroen Kummer
Tom Lagerberg
Martijn Lambarts
Raoul de Lange
Margaret Lansink
Pierre Le Gallo
Rindert W. Leegsma
Theo Willem van Leeuwen
Aernout Leezenberg
Alexandre Lefevre
Percy B. Lehning
Oscar Leker
Matthew Lemon
Beate Lendt

Dick van Lente
Andra Leurdijk
Carolyn Levisson
Natascha Libbert
Jann Liebert
Baptiste Lignel
Geisje van der Linden
Christine Lindo
Johan Linssen
Sjoerd Litjens
Dunja Logozar
Emmy Lokin Piscaer
Alma Loos
Hans Loos
Marijke Louppen
Ron Louwerse
Allard Luchsinger
Menno Luitjes
Celina Lunsford
Femke M. Lutgerink
Michael van Maanen
Gordon MacDonald
Igor Malashenko
Henrik M. Malmstrom
Paul Malschaert
Rense Mandema
Michael Marten
Jack Martin
Lesley Martin
Uwe H. Martin
Francesca Masarie
Anton Maurer
Russ McClintock
Michael Mccraw
Carol McKay
Harminke Medendorp
Andre van der Meer
Kristin J. Metho
Andrea Meuzelaar
Gustavo Miotti
William Mitchell
Jo Mockers
C.F. van der Molen
Henny Molenaar
Davide Monteleone
Giovanni Monti
Vittorio Mortarotti
Fotolab MPP
Gerda Mulder
Andreas Nader
Joachim Naudts
Patricia Nauta
Ben & Carien Neggers
Simon Neggers
Herbert Nelissen
Esther van Nes
Dieter Neubert
Jose Luis Neves
Floor Nicolas
Pepijn Nicolas
Pipo Nicolas
Leonie van Nierop
Marieke Nijhof
Bart Nijkamp
Alette Nijland
Michiel Nijland
Bram Nijssen
Corinne Noordenbos
Job Noordhof
Koni Nordmann
Daniel J. Norwood
Kenneth o Halloran
Laura Obdeijn
Giuseppe Olivieri
Hilje Oosterbaan Martinius
Jan Oosterman
Mieke Oostwoud
Henk Otte
Katrien Otten
Jetteke Ottevanger
Floris van Overveld
Ilker Ozdemir

Johannes Paar
Lodewijk van Paddenburgh
Emiliano Paoletti
Martin Parr
Nell Pastors
Lisette van de Pavoordt
Douglas Penn
Vanessa Penn
Henk Penseel
Sanne Peper
Steve Pepper
Marcus Peters
Anna Pfautsch
Andrew Phelps
Joao Pico
Cock Pleijsier
Rik Plomp
David Plummer
Astrid Pollers
Jan Postma
Corey Presha
Tom Price
Max Prooy
Jeppe van Pruissen
Mireille de Putter
Martin Pyper
Pierre Yves Racine
Ingvar Hogni Ragnarsson
Rianne Randeraad
Marco Rapaccini
Benjamin Rasmussen
Monique van Ravenstein
Katrien Raymaekers
Elsje van Ree
Eduard Rekker
Jukka Reverberi
Ramon Reverte Masco
Liza de Rijk
Wilfred Roelink
Mike Roelofs
Laura van Roessel
Loek van Roessel
Martin Rogers
Heidi Romano
Peter Rommens
Johannes Romppanen
Jacqueline de Rooij
Hans Roos
Sascha Roosdorp
Tijmen Rooseboom
Lex van Rootselaar
Pieter Roozenboom
Jewgeni Roppel
Jeanette van Rotterdam
Carsten and Sophie Rouault
and Rummel
Frank de Ruiter
Rixt Runia
Jacobien Rutgers
Erik Ruts
Dominique Sanchez
Alexander S. Sauer
Famke Schaap
David Schalliol
Jaap Scheeren
Pieter van Scherpenberg
Hannah Schildt
Patrizia Schiozzi
Addie Schiphorst Preuper
Mariko Schipper
Samuel Schliske
Nils Schmeling
Ralph Schmitz
Oliver Schneider
Andreas Schoening
Meindert Scholma
Soeren Schuhmacher
Gerrit Schurer
Hendrik Schwantes
Terri Schwartz
Hannah Schwarzbach
Roel Segerink

Dion Setyotomo
Fabio Severo
Geert Job Sevink
Jeroen Seydel
Patrick Sijben
Iris Sikking
Teresa Silva
Katja Sinnema
Fransje Sjenitzer
Anna Skladmann
Johan Slager
Bart Sleegers
Geert Slot
Robin Sluijs
Rob en Eva Sluys
Merlijn Smeele
Monique Smeets
Monique Smit
Joshua Joshua Smith
Lui Smyth
Hans Snellen
Frans Soeterbroek
Baato Soort
Peter Sorantin
Milena Spaan
Frieda Spanjersberg
Robert Specken
Sander Spek
Guido van Spellen
Sven Speybrouck
Marijn Staal
Michiel Stadhouders
Hans Stakelbeek
Petra Stavast
Bonnie Steenman
Conny Steenman
Jolien Steenman
Joop Steenman
Lorette Steenman
Jana Steffen
Roeland Stekelenburg
Anoek Steketee
Kitty Steketee
Truus Stevens
Alain Stoeckli
Glen Stoker
David Strettel
Margreet Strijbosch
Philip Stroomberg
Rik Suermondt
Evgenia Sveshinsky
Ton Sweep
Marlies Swinkels
Victor Taylor
Anne Tegelaar
Florens Tegelaar
Margriet Teunissen
Bjoern Theye
Mirelle Thijsen
Mandy Thomas
Marianne Timmer
Bas Timmers
Giovanni Toccafondi
Chiara Tocci
Jeroen Toirkens
Reinier Treur
Piero Turk
Robert van Ancum
Serge Van Cauwenbergh
Nele Van den Berghe
Pieter van der Straaten
Jerry van der Weert
Pieter Bas van Wiechen
Jan Vandemoortele
Anneke van Veen
Christiaan van Veen
Evelien Vehof
Hanneke van Velzen
Maaike Vergouwe
Mia Verhagen
Lucas Verheij
Ralf Verhoef

Kirsten Verpaalen
C.M.E. Versteeg
Henny Verstege
Danny Veys
Marieke Viergever
Giedre Virbalaite
Jon Vismans
Dirk-Jan Visser
Ellen Visser
Geert Vlastuin
Khio van der Vleuten
Henkjan van Vliet
Elise Volker
Jurryt van de Vooren
Tom Voorma
Zelda de Vries
Tanya Vriesman
Bas Vroege
David Vroom
Martijn de Waal
Theo de Waal
Gijsbert van der Wal
Jan van Walsem
Brendan Walsh
Rob Wandelee
Rolf Weijburg
Theijs van Welij
Hans van de Wetering
Rob Wetzer
Oliver Whitehead
Michael Wichita
Thomas Wiegand
Mick van de Wiel
Thomas Wieland
Friso Wiersum
Kitty Wigleven
Guido de Wildt
Andrea Wilkinson
Yannik Willing
Lars Willumeit
Goof van de Winkel
Marijke Winnubst
Jan Willem Wirtz
Peter van de Witte
Marieke ten Wolde
Stephen Wooldridge
Valentin Wormbs
Raimond Wouda
Marco Woyczikowski
Steffi Wurster
Natalie Wynants
Peter Yankowski Walker
Lap Ming Yeung
Maud van der Zant
Iris van der Zee
Antonia Zennaro
Elza Zijlstra
Damian Zimmermann
Isabell Zipfel
Wytze v.d. Zweep

The Sochi Project
An Atlas of War and Tourism in the Caucasus
Photographs by Rob Hornstra
Texts by Arnold van Bruggen

Front cover: Dmitry Chernyshenko, CEO of
the Sochi organizing committee, 2014
Back cover: At Orlyonok Children's Center,
restored under the inspired leadership of
Presidents Putin and Medvedev, Dimitri is
guarding a flag. Today, the camp's fifty-first
anniversary will be celebrated with a flag
parade, a flourish of trumpets, and a touching
speech given by a cheeky kid in the style of a
Soviet propaganda movie. Orlyonok, Sochi
region, Russia, 2011

Designer: Kummer & Herrman
Publisher: Lesley A. Martin
Production: Matthew Harvey
Senior Text Editor: Susan Ciccotti
Assistant Editor: Samantha Marlow
Copy Editor: Betsy Stepina Zinn
Proofreaders: Madeline Coleman,
Brian J. Sholis
Work Scholars: Luke Chase, Alison Karasyk
Translation: Cecily Layzell

The staff of the Aperture Foundation book
program includes Chris Boot, *executive
director*; Kellie McLaughlin, *sales and
marketing manager*; Amelia Lang, *managing
editor*; Barbara Escobar, *publicist*.

This publication was made possible, in part,
with generous support from Mondriaan
Foundation.

This publication has been published to
coincide with exhibitions at the following
venues:
— FotoMuseum, Antwerp:
October 25, 2013-March 2, 2014
— Winzavod, Moscow:
October 17-November 18, 2013 (cancelled)
— DePaul University Art Museum, Chicago:
January 16-March 30, 2014
— Fotohof, Salzburg, Germany:
January 30-March 22, 2014
— Noorderlicht FotoGalerie, Groningen,
the Netherlands: April 19-June 22, 2014
— Scotiabank CONTACT Photography
Festival, Toronto: May 1-31, 2014
— Aperture Gallery, New York:
May 30-July 10, 2014
— Photo Ireland, Dublin:
July 4-July 31, 2014
— Cortona On The Move Festival, Italy:
July 17-September 28, 2014
— Stedelijk Museum, Amsterdam (exhibition:
On the Move): August 29, 2013-January 18,
2014
— FotoFocus Cincinnati:
August 31-October 19, 2014
— FotoDC, Washington, D.C.:
November 7-December 7, 2014
— Center for Contemporary Art Ujazdowski
Castle, Warsaw: December 6–February 8, 2014
— CFD Barcelona:
February 20-April 16, 2015

Copublished with the Sochi Project
www.thesochiproject.org

Second edition
Printed in China
10 9 8 7 6 5 4 3 2 1

The Sochi Project was cofounded by Rob
Hornstra (born in Borne, The Netherlands,
1975) and Arnold van Bruggen (born in Texel,
The Netherlands, 1979), in association with
the design team Kummer & Herrman.
     Rob Hornstra (photographs) is a photog-
rapher and self-publisher of slow-form documentary work. He is head of photography at
the Royal Academy of Art, The Hague, and
also founder and former artistic director of
FOTODOK—Space for Documentary Photography. Hornstra is represented by Flatland
Gallery, Utrecht, The Netherlands.
     Arnold van Bruggen (texts) is a writer
and filmmaker, and founder of the journalistic
production agency Prospektor.
     Various elements of the Sochi Project have
garnered awards, including the Canon Prize
for innovative photojournalism in 2010; the
Magnum Expression Award in 2011; the Sony
World Photography Award (Arts and Culture
category) in 2012; and the World Press Photo
award for Arts and Entertainment Stories
in 2012. *The Sochi Project: An Atlas of War
and Tourism in the Caucasus*, first published
in 2013, is the recipient of the Dutch Doc
Photo Award, 2014; Dutch Design Award—
Communication, 2014; and Canon Prize for
Innovative Photojournalism, 2014.

Library of Congress
Cataloging-in-Publication Data

Hornstra, Rob.
   The Sochi project : an atlas of war and
tourism in the Caucasus / Rob Hornstra and
Arnold van Bruggen. -- Second edition.
      pages cm
   Published in conjunction with the exhibitions:
FoMu, Antwerp, October 25, 2013-March
2, 2014; Winzavod, Moscow, October 17-
November 18, 2013 (cancelled); DePaul
University Art Museum, Chicago, January
16-March 30, 2014; Fotohof, Salzburg,
January 30-March 22, 2014; Noorderlicht
FotoGalerie, Groningen, April 19-June 22,
2014; Scotiabank CONTACT Photography
Festival, Toronto, May 1-31, 2014; Aperture
Gallery, New York, May 30-July 10, 2014;
Photo Ireland, Dublin, July 4-July 31, 2014;
Cortona On The Move Festival, Cortona, July
17-September 28, 2014; Stedelijk Museum,
Amsterdam (exhibition 'On the Move'), August
29-January 18, 2014; FotoFocus Cincinnati,
Cincinnati, August 31-October 19, 2014;
FotoDC, Washington, November 7-December
7, 2014; Center for Contemporary Art
Ujazdowski Castle, Warsaw, December 6-
February 8, 2014 and CFD Barcelona,
Barcelona, February 20-April 16, 2015.
   Includes bibliographical references.
   ISBN 978-1-59711-334-2 (hardback :
alkaline paper)
   1. Sochi Region (Russia)--Pictorial works--
Exhibitions. 2. Sochi Region (Russia)--
Description and travel--Exhibitions. 3. Sochi
Region (Russia)--Social conditions--Exhibitions.
4. Social change--Russia (Federation)--
Sochi Region--Exhibitions. 5. Tourism--Social
aspects--Russia (Federation)--Sochi Region--
Exhibitions. 6. War and society--Russia
(Federation)--Sochi Region--Exhibitions. 7.
Hornstra, Rob--Travel--Russia (Federation)--
Sochi Region--Exhibitions. 8. Bruggen, Arnold
van--Travel--Russia (Federation)--Sochi
Region--Exhibitions. I. Bruggen, Arnold van.
II. Title.
   DK651.S66H67 2013
   947.5'2--dc23

2013025494

Aperture Foundation books are distributed
in the U.S. and Canada by:
ARTBOOK/D.A.P.
155 Sixth Avenue, 2nd Floor
New York, N.Y. 10013
Phone: (212) 627-1999
Fax: (212) 627-9484
E-mail: orders@dapinc.com
www.artbook.com

Aperture Foundation books are distributed
worldwide, excluding the U.S. and Canada, by:
Thames & Hudson Ltd.
181A High Holborn
London WC1V 7QX
United Kingdom
Phone: + 44 20 7845 5000
Fax: + 44 20 7845 5055
E-mail: sales@thamesandhudson.co.uk
www.thamesandhudson.com

aperture

Aperture Foundation
547 West 27th Street, 4th Floor
New York, N.Y. 10001
www.aperture.org

Aperture, a not-for-profit foundation, connects
the photo community and its audiences
with the most inspiring work, the sharpest
ideas, and with each other—in print, in person,
and online.